KU-481-586

Making Sense of the
TROUBLES

DAVID McKITTRICK
DAVID McVEA

PENGUIN BOOKS

PENGUIN BOOKS

Published by the Penguin Group
Penguin Books Ltd, 80 Strand, London WC2R 0RL, England
Penguin Putnam Inc., 375 Hudson Street, New York, New York 10014, USA
Penguin Books Australia Ltd, Ringwood, Victoria, Australia
Penguin Books Canada Ltd, 10 Alcorn Avenue, Toronto, Ontario, Canada M4V 3B2
Penguin Books India (P) Ltd, 11 Community Centre, Panchsheel Park,
New Delhi – 110 017, India
Penguin Books (NZ) Ltd, Cnr Rosedale and Airborne Roads,
Albany, Auckland, New Zealand
Penguin Books (South Africa) (Pty) Ltd, 24 Sturdee Avenue,
Rosebank 2196, South Africa

Penguin Books Ltd, Registered Offices: 80 Strand, London WC2R 0RL, England

www.penguin.com

First published by The Blackstaff Press 2000
This revised edition published in Penguin Books 2001
1

To our wives
and families

Contents

Introduction   ix

1   The static society   1
     1921–63

2   The O'Neill years   26
     1963–69

3   Descent into violence   53
     1969–71

4   The end of Stormont   76
     1972–73

5   Sunningdale, strike & stalemate   98
     1974–76

6   From Castlereagh to Warrenpoint   118
     1977–79

7   The hungerstrikes   134
     1980–81

8   Anglo–Irish accord   149
     1982–85

9   Enniskillen, Libya & bombs in England   167
     1986–93

10   Peace process   184
     1993–94

11   Decommissioning, Docklands & Drumcree   200
     1994–96

12   Breakthrough   214
     1997–2000

     Perspectives   230

     Chronology   243

     Tables   323

     Glossary   329

     Bibliographical notes   336

     Index   338

Introduction

The observation that nothing is more remote than the recent past is particularly applicable to the Northern Ireland troubles, since the understandable instinct of many people has been to shy away from them. For very many people it was a terrible period, in which a generation grew up not knowing peace or stability.

The troubles represent a lethal but fascinating time in Northern Ireland's history, bringing as they did not only death, injury and destruction but also huge political and social change. While some may argue that it may be too early for a full account of these years, there is so much material available, and so many memories are so fresh, that we believe a proper attempt can be made to make some sense of the troubles.

As the belief grows that the worst is past, we feel there is a need now for a review of what happened so that the mistakes of the past can be examined and learnt from. Many secrets doubtless remain to be revealed, and there is important information which may not emerge for many years, if ever. Some events and interpretations are probably destined to be disputed for decades, yet much of the course of the troubles, if not every detail, is reasonably clear even at this early stage.

The main political events are there for all to see, as are the main characters. So too, tragically, are the more than 3,600 deaths of the troubles, deaths whose consequences are all too evident to the relatives and friends affected. Both of the authors are acutely aware of this last, since we helped write *Lost Lives*, the 1999 book which gives an account of each troubles death. In writing this book it was always at the forefront of our minds that the troubles should not be regarded simply as a period of political upheaval but also as the time when so many lives were lost and so many people injured or bereaved. For this reason the reader will find here a greater than usual emphasis on the deaths as well as the major political events.

The idea for a concise history of the troubles came from Anne Tannahill of Blackstaff, who like us was aware of the absence of a succinct account. The original request from Anne was for 'a clear, concise, authoritative history' and we have adhered as closely as possible to that brief. We wish in particular to thank her colleague Carina Rourke for applying her editing expertise to our manuscript. We are also especially grateful to John Young, who read an early draft of the text and provided a great many valuable suggestions.

Hundreds of books and millions of words have been written on the troubles: *Lost Lives* alone, for example, contains almost a million of them. The aim of this book is to provide an overview, excising a great many details. When the choice was one of giving intricate detail or an accurate broad-brush overview, we almost always opted for the latter. There were many points where we were tempted to pause and indulge in lengthier analysis but for the most part we aimed instead for maintaining narrative pace and momentum. To complement this approach, we have provided a substantial chronology which gives greater detail on many events.

Our research involved consulting many of the hundreds of books on various aspects of this period, as well as going through primary source material in newspaper libraries and at the Public Record Office of Northern Ireland. In addition, David McKittrick has in three decades as a daily newspaper reporter on the troubles accumulated much material. This includes not just a vast collection of clippings and notes but also access to many of the participants, ranging through those responsible for governing in London, Belfast and Dublin to those involved in politics and violence, and in some cases both, covering the spectrum from politicians and officials to republicans and loyalists and all points between.

Given its history, both ancient and modern, Northern Ireland is unlikely ever to know perfect peace, for the troubles have added fresh grievances to ancient differences and there are many fresh and painful scars. The Good Friday Agreement and its institutions may take root and provide the basis for stability and a lasting settlement; or they may be brought down. Many hard-fought political battles lie ahead. In the meantime republican organisations and loyalist paramilitary groups, which have been a prominent part of the landscape, are not going to vanish overnight. Nonetheless, it seems timely to appraise what happened and why, and to try to make the recent past less remote.

1

The static society
1921–63

Protestants and Catholics

The troubles which broke out in the late 1960s had roots going back
many decades, for Northern Ireland never resembled a place at peace
with itself. In what are today assumed to be quiet and uneventful
periods, even a cursory glance at the records of the time reveals a most
unsettled society. A stream of incidents, large and small, testified to deep
and dangerous fault lines in the society. Viewed from this perspective, the
troubles can be seen as a more violent expression of existing animosities
and unresolved issues of nationality, religion, power and territorial
rivalry. They can be viewed in fact simply as a new phase in a continuum
of division. With hindsight the seeds of the later violence can be seen with
some clarity.

In the 1960s, as in later decades, four basic elements were present in the
Northern Ireland equation. First there were the Protestants, who made up

roughly two-thirds of the population of a million and a half. The vast majority of Protestants were Unionists, favouring the existing link with Britain. Although they always had criticisms of London governments, they emphatically regarded themselves as British and not Irish. They not only treasured the link with Britain but dreaded the alternative, which they envisaged as a united Ireland in which Irish nationalists would attack their political, religious and economic interests.

Almost all Protestants voted Unionist but scarcely any Catholics did. Catholics, the second major element of the equation, made up the other one-third of the population and in the main viewed themselves not as British but as Irish. Most of them regarded Northern Ireland as an un-satisfactory and even illegitimate state, believing that an independent united Ireland was the natural political unit for the island. The heart of the Northern Ireland problem lies in this clash between two competing na-tional aspirations. This basic competition is complicated by issues of power, territory and justice.

The third and fourth elements involved were the British and Irish governments. The word 'involved' is largely a misnomer, since until the late 1960s both attempted, generally successfully, to keep the Northern Ireland issue at arm's length. With the onset of the troubles, however, both were drawn ever more deeply into the problem.

The roots of that problem lay deep in history. As the twentieth century began the population of Ireland, which was a part of the United Kingdom of Great Britain and Ireland, was four and a quarter million, made up of three and a quarter million Catholics and just over one million Protestants. Most of the Protestants were descendants of settlers who emigrated from England and Scotland to various parts of Ireland with the encouragement of English governments, mainly in the sixteenth and seventeenth cen-turies. A major aim of the settlements was to plant a loyal British garrison community to establish control in the face of periodic Irish uprisings which at times threatened English security by linking up with England's traditional Catholic enemies, France and Spain.

At times some Protestants identified with Irish causes against the English, but these were the exceptions. Although there was some inter-marriage between the Catholic natives and Protestant settlers, the two communities, especially in the north-east, continued down through the years to regard themselves as largely separate entities. The Protestant settler community enjoyed political and economic ascendancy. The communities were differentiated primarily on the basis of conflicting national identities, but the various other important points of difference kept communal divisions fresh and potent.

As the nineteenth century ended there was increasing pressure in Ireland for what was known as Home Rule, whose supporters advocated a new Dublin parliament under Westminster's authority. At this stage the demand for complete Irish independence did not have significant support, but Home Rule seemed a real possibility. Unionists were strongly opposed to Home Rule, organising themselves to fight against the attempts of Liberal governments to bring it into being in the last two decades of the nineteenth century. Unionists feared Home Rule as a threat to the Union with Britain, and as a prelude to complete Irish independence and the ending of Protestant and British domination of Irish affairs.

Unionist resistance was strongest in the north-eastern counties where the largest concentration of Protestants lived. In the nineteenth century, especially around Belfast, a prosperous economy had been developed based on industries such as linen, shipbuilding and engineering. This north-eastern region was very much part of the British industrial economy, Belfast having closer ties and economic similarities with Glasgow and Liverpool than with Dublin.

Protestants mobilised formidable bodies such as the Ulster Unionist Council and the Orange Order, a long-established Protestant grouping, to oppose any weakening of the link with Britain and to safeguard Protestant interests. (There is much continuity here: the UUC was the forerunner of the Ulster Unionist party, which together with the Orange Order remains a powerful force to this day.)

Between 1912 and 1914 the British government again introduced a Home Rule Bill which this time seemed certain to become law. The response of Unionists was to pledge their determination to oppose Home Rule by 'all means which may be found necessary'. In the spring of 1914 Unionist leaders organised the smuggling in of 25,000 rifles and 3 million rounds of ammunition from Germany. These were used to arm an unofficial Protestant militia, the Ulster Volunteer Force. With vast rallies and drilling exercises, Unionism openly proclaimed its readiness to act outside the law. But just as a major military confrontation seemed inevitable, the outbreak of World War One intervened and the issue was put on ice for its duration.

1916 saw the Easter Rising in Dublin, with a small number of republicans staging an armed rebellion against British rule. The rising itself was quickly put down, but the action of the British government of the day in executing many of its leaders rebounded: London was deemed to have overreacted and a huge swell of sympathy for the republicans ensued. By the time World War One ended in 1918, the Irish desire for Home Rule had been swept away and replaced by the demand for an independent Irish republic. The newly formed Irish Republican Army, known as the IRA, began a violent campaign against Britain which is today referred to in the south as the War of Independence. After lengthy negotiations, Westminster in 1920 passed the Government of Ireland Act in an attempt to satisfy the conflicting demands of the two traditions.

In essence this act hoped to solve the problem by keeping all of Ireland in British hands while providing for a Home Rule parliament in the twenty-six southern counties, together with a separate devolved parliament for the six north-eastern counties. As well as having its own parliament Northern Ireland would continue to send MPs to Westminster. Aware of the rising nationalist tide, Ulster Unionists reluctantly accepted this and Northern Ireland came into existence. Irish nationalists rejected the plan and their war for independence continued until a treaty in 1921 created a twenty-six-county Irish Free State.

The new state

Northern Ireland was born in violence. From the first months of its existence there were occasional IRA raids from across the new border as well as major outbreaks of sectarian violence, especially in Belfast. In the two years from June 1920 until June 1922, 428 people were killed, two-thirds of them Catholic, fourteen people dying in one weekend. The communal violence in Belfast, which was on a scale and ferocity not equalled until August 1969, left a deep and bitter imprint on many in both communities.

The creation of Northern Ireland did not bring security for the Protestants despite their comfortable majority, for it was clear that London was never as committed to the Union as they were. They lived in a state of political nervousness, constantly fearing British policy might move to support a united Ireland. They also remained deeply suspicious of the half-million Catholics who found themselves within the boundaries of the new Northern Ireland.

Those Catholics considered themselves trapped in this new state, denied their Irish identity, cut off from their co-religionists in the Free State and politically powerless. To this was quickly added another complaint: that the Unionist establishment, which was to run the state on the basis of Protestant majority rule for the following half-century, actively discriminated against Catholics in the allocation of jobs and housing, over political rights and in other areas.

The boundaries of Northern Ireland which came into being in 1921 were essentially worked out between Westminster and the Ulster Unionist party. The six north-eastern counties of Ireland made up the new state, with Belfast as its capital. Unionists used the word 'Ulster' to describe the new entity, though nationalists objected to this. Catholics who use the term 'Ulster' generally mean one of the four ancient provinces into which Ireland was quartered, the others being Leinster, Munster and Connaught. This Ulster had nine counties, Antrim, Armagh, Down, Derry (only Unionists tended to call it Londonderry), Fermanagh, Tyrone, Cavan, Donegal and Monaghan. Although Northern Ireland consisted of only the first six of these, Unionists appropriated the word 'Ulster' and made extensive use of it. The defining feature of the new entity was its demographics: it was two-thirds Protestant and one-third Catholic, the guiding concept in deciding its borders having been that it should have a decisive Protestant majority.

In the early days many people, both Protestant and Catholic, were unsure whether the new state would survive. Some nationalists believed it to be too small to form the basis of a feasible state, and assumed it would prove unworkable. Some thought the promised review by a Boundary Commission would end its existence by reducing its size even further, although when the commission's report emerged in 1925 no changes to the border resulted. Many Protestants wondered whether Northern Ireland could hold out in the face of an apparently lukewarm British commitment, as well as hostility from nationalists both within its boundaries and from the new and almost entirely Catholic state to the south.

In the event, however, Britain attempted no withdrawal, the south attempted no invasion, and the northern Catholic minority proved politically impotent. Britain hoped the Irish question, as the issue had been known during the nineteenth century, had been settled by the partition of Ireland. The Free State was aggrieved by the loss of what it regarded as its rightful territory, but concentrated its attention on making a success of its own fledgling state.

Northern Ireland settled down, within a perhaps surprisingly few years, into what looked like stability. There was violence, but it was contained; there was a great deal of communal tension, but it too was contained; and after some troubled years a sullen form of peace descended. It was however a peace achieved at a high cost, for the new state had an imbalance at its heart. Most Unionist politicians had not wanted their own devolved parliament in Belfast, preferring to remain more closely integrated with Britain. But once the 1920 settlement had handed almost all political power into their hands, they realised they could make effective use of it to buttress and protect the new Northern Ireland.

This aim took precedence over all other considerations, including any thought of building bridges between Protestants and Catholics. Catholic representatives of the time tended to hope not for some new shared system, but for its collapse. They often resorted to boycotting the new institutions, both political leaders and Catholic bishops making no secret of their hope that Northern Ireland would not last.

The prevailing attitudes were aptly described decades later, in 1998, by Ulster Unionist party leader David Trimble, when he said in his speech accepting the Nobel peace prize: 'Ulster Unionists, fearful of being isolated on the island, built a solid house, but it was a cold house for Catholics. And northern nationalists, although they had a roof over their heads, seemed to us as if they meant to burn the house down.'

The Unionist party spoke for the overwhelming majority of Protestant voters, and since Protestants were in a majority it automatically became the new government. It was to hold this position for half a century, wielding virtually complete and certainly uninterrupted power. The Northern Ireland system was closely modelled on the House of Commons at Westminster, but crucially it lacked the element of alternation in government: the 1920 settlement had ensured that nationalists were forever excluded from power and that Unionists forever wielded it in unbroken one-party rule. The steps the Unionist party took in the 1920s to strengthen its own power, and to defend the existence of the state, created a system of extraordinary longevity which was to preserve and reinforce many of the attitudes of the 1920s.

The system survived for so long because of Unionism's monolithic strength, aided by divisions within nationalism and by Westminster indifference. It turned out not to be a fair arrangement, but in London's terms it worked, and a potentially vexatious state remained reasonably quiet.

The collective self-image of Unionists today is not far removed from that of their ancestors as they arrived in Ireland, or from that of the founding fathers of Northern Ireland. They saw themselves as a frontier community facing wily and violent enemies, and backed by only half-hearted friends. Unionists were for the most part an inward-looking people, conservative, cautious and suspicious of change. In this they followed the model of their forebears who, moving from England and Scotland and given territory in a hostile land, developed a defensive attitude evident in the later Unionist slogans of 'No Surrender' and 'What we have we hold' and 'Not an inch'. Socially Unionists could be warm-hearted and tremendously hospitable: politically they were fated to be eternally on the defensive.

The government system put in place in the 1920s is one of the keys to explaining the later troubles, since there was such extraordinary continuity in its workings over the decades, and since the outbreak of the troubles was so directly related to it. The Catholic civil rights movement would take to the streets in 1968 with complaints which related directly to the arrangements of the 1920s.

Consolidating control

From the start the Unionist party's leaders believed that the new state could only survive if the levers of power were firmly in reliable Protestant hands. The first instincts of Unionists, having been put in charge by Westminster, were to ensure that their power should be both undiluted and permanent. Thus one of the new government's earliest acts was to set about changing the voting system and local council boundaries inherited by the new Unionist government.

This was a key measure since the seventy-three local authorities were important as sources of power and patronage in areas such as housing and education. In the first council elections after partition, in 1920, the Unionist party had won control of around two-thirds of them, but some of those in nationalist hands were troublesome. A number of western councils had symbolically voted to secede from Northern Ireland and join the south, while others refused to acknowledge the authority of the new government. Northern Ireland's first prime minister, James Craig, responded quickly by revising the voting system and later altering boundaries so that Unionists could deal with such mutinous councils by simply assuming control of them.

In 1922 the voting system known as proportional representation (PR) was abolished. Its removal was by no means simply a technical adjustment, since it had been built in both as an actual safeguard for Catholic and Protestant minorities in the two parts of Ireland and also a symbol of respect for their views. The first-past-the-post system introduced in its place, together with the highly partisan redrawing of local government boundaries, was of huge benefit to the Unionist party. As a result of the changes nationalists lost their majorities in thirteen of twenty-four councils they had originally controlled. Surveying the electoral consequences decades later, Professor John Whyte concluded: 'Nationalists were manipulated out of control in a number of councils where they had a majority of electors. This is one of the clearest areas of discrimination in the whole field of controversy.'

Northern Ireland's second city, Londonderry, moved from nationalist to Unionist control even though it had a clear nationalist majority. Another adjustment was made there years later in 1936, when local Unionist party leaders feared they might lose control of the city. One of Craig's cabinet ministers wrote to him: 'Unless something is done now, it is only a matter of time until Derry passes into the hands of the Nationalist and Sinn Féin parties for all time. On the other hand, if proper steps are taken now, I believe Derry can be saved for years to come.'

The government did indeed take such steps, in the form of an ingenious new arrangement designed to ensure that around 7,500 Unionist voters returned twelve councillors while 10,000 nationalist voters returned only eight. Nationalists branded this boundary manipulation as 'gerrymandering', a term which was to have a prominent place in the political lexicon for many decades. In public Unionist party representatives denied gerrymandering in Londonderry and elsewhere, but in private some were more candid, one Unionist MP describing the new arrangements as a 'shameless and obvious gerrymander'. Another senior Unionist was to write to the Unionist cabinet in 1968, against the background of the civil rights campaign, saying:

> If ever a community had a right to demonstrate against a denial of civil rights, Derry is the finest example. A Roman Catholic and nationalist city has for three or four decades been administered (and none too fairly

which, taken together, amounted to a remarkable degree of control over most aspects of government and society. This control extended to the fields of justice and law and order. Judges and magistrates were almost all Protestants, many of them closely associated with the Unionist party. Between 1937 and 1968, for example, thirteen sitting Unionist MPs were appointed judges, moving effortlessly from making laws to administering them.

The Ulster Special Constabulary, the heavily armed auxiliary force later known more often as the B Specials, was exclusively Protestant. Although it seemed for a fleeting moment that the new police force, the Royal Ulster Constabulary (RUC), might become religiously integrated, it remained throughout its history more than 90 per cent Protestant. The police had no real operational independence, responding directly to directions from ministers, with senior police officers sometimes attending cabinet meetings. The political, legal and policing worlds were thus inextricably linked: one community governed, judged and policed the other.

RUC officers carried revolvers and sometimes heavier weaponry, while the armament of the B Specials included handguns, rifles and submachine guns. The police had at their disposal the Special Powers Act, a sweeping piece of legislation which allowed arrests without warrant, internment without trial, unlimited search powers and bans on meetings and publications, as well as providing far-reaching catch-all clauses. Most of these provisions were used sparingly but their existence, together with the large numbers of police and B Specials, brought Catholic complaints that policing had a military character and very often an intimidating effect. These security forces, once pointedly described as the armed wing of Unionism, not only maintained law and order but also provided jobs for Protestants.

This was one of many points of Protestant advantage in the field of employment. The civil service was predominantly Protestant, with perhaps 10 per cent Catholic representation in its lower reaches. A 1943 survey established that there were no Catholics in the 55 most senior jobs, with only 37 Catholics in the 600 middle-ranking posts. The picture was similar in most local authorities and other parts of the public sector, with only occasional exceptions. There were no Catholics among the cabinet, the senior staff in the Stormont Commons, the top ranks of the RUC, the Civil Service Commission and other important public bodies.

In the private sector many large firms, and indeed whole industries, commonly had workforces that were more than 90 per cent Protestant, while Catholics tended to predominate in some lower-status occupations such as the drinks trade. The jewels in Northern Ireland's industrial crown, such as its shipyards and heavy engineering concerns, employed few Catholics. Moreover there were, at times of high tension, periodic purges in which Catholic workers were forcibly expelled from some of the big companies. Unsurprisingly, Catholic unemployment was generally more than double Protestant unemployment, partly because of these patterns and partly because a higher proportion of Catholics lived in areas of high unemployment such as the west.

Part of this picture was the result of apparently innocuous practices such as recruitment of staff by word of mouth or on the recommendation of a friend or a relative. Usually this meant the hiring of another Protestant since most employers, particularly those with large concerns, were Protestant. Such habits, though seeming to be the natural run of things in the eyes of those who benefited from them, nonetheless played a part in perpetuating employment differentials.

Housing was another area that produced much Catholic complaint, especially after World War Two when a major building programme was introduced to improve the very poor housing standards. Housing was largely in the hands of local councils, and although many councils functioned in a non-controversial manner, in others policy was distorted for political ends. What made house building and allocation so sensitive was that voting in local government elections was limited to ratepayers and their spouses. A new house would thus often carry two votes, a matter that could be of great political significance in areas where the Unionist and nationalist votes were evenly balanced. The most frequent criticisms were of councils in western counties where battles for control were the hardest fought.

Votes had an extra significance in local government, where the electorate was a full one-quarter smaller than that for the Belfast parliament. Since only ratepayers and their spouses had the vote, others such as subtenants, lodgers and anyone living at home with their parents could not vote. This restriction, which most affected the poorer sections of the population, was later to provide one of the most potent slogans for the civil rights movement with its demand for 'one man – one vote'. Paradoxically, the acceleration in house building after 1945 heightened the potential for controversy by providing local councils with many more houses to assign. This was a heavily politicised activity: in some cases individual dwellings were allocated at council meetings, though more often allocations were decided by small groups of councillors on housing committees. In 1963 the Unionist chairman of Enniskillen housing committee made clear their approach: 'The council will decide what wards the houses are to be built in. We are not going to build houses in the South Ward and cut a rod to beat ourselves later on. We are going to see that the right people are put in these houses, and we are not going to apologise for it.'

The record of the Unionist government, particularly in its early decades, contains many instances of senior government ministers not only condoning similar practices but approving of them. The tone was set by Craig when, in response to criticism of the Orange Order, he told the Belfast parliament: 'I have always said I am an Orangeman first and a politician and member of this parliament afterwards. All I boast is that we are a Protestant parliament and a Protestant state.' Down the years this, slightly misquoted, entered political folklore as 'a Protestant parliament for a Protestant people'.

The Orange Order

The Orange Order, a Protestant organisation viewed by Catholics as bigoted and anti-Catholic but regarded by most Protestants as an important guardian of their heritage, held an important place in political life. The Unionist community contained in its ranks people who differed widely in terms of class, outlook and geography. While Catholics had only one church, Protestants were splintered into dozens of denominations, large and small, from high-church Anglicans to Presbyterians with a history of independence and dissent. The Orange Order played a key role in providing the political cement to hold them all together.

The Order was founded in 1795 following clashes between Protestant and Catholic factions in County Armagh. This mêlée, known now as the Battle of the Diamond, is one of the major events in Orange folk history, together with two incidents in the seventeenth century when Protestants prevailed over Catholics, the Siege of Derry in 1689 and the Battle of the Boyne in 1690. In later years the Orange Order established what came to be known as the marching season, holding hundreds of parades during the summer months. In the nineteenth century these gave rise to recurring riots, particularly in Belfast. One official report said: 'The celebration of that (Orange July) festival is plainly and unmistakably the originating cause of these riots.' It added that the occasion was used 'to remind one party of the triumph of their ancestors over those of the other, and to inculcate the feelings of Protestant superiority over their Roman Catholic neighbours'.

The Orange culture was separatist and anti-ecumenical. Although its regulations told its members to abstain from uncharitable words or deeds against Catholics, they were also pledged to 'resist the ascendancy of that church' by all lawful means. They were also warned not to attend 'any act or ceremony of Popish worship'. One observer summed it up: 'The Orange Order ensures that the majority of the majority maintain a rigid stance. It articulates their underlying fears in such a way as to suggest that there is only one way of guarding against the dangers: obstinate resistance rather than mutual accommodation.' Orange lodges provided the framework for the Ulster Volunteer Force, and from the start the new state took on a distinctly Orange complexion. An Orange lodge was established within the RUC, while Orangemen made up the bulk of the B Specials, who in some areas were based in Orange halls.

Politically too, Orangeism became an integral part of the state. Between 1921 and 1969 only three of fifty-four Unionist cabinet ministers were not members of the Order. Three others left the Order while in office: one was expelled for attending a Catholic service as part of his public duties, while another resigned when his daughter married a Catholic. Eighty-seven of the ninety-five Unionist backbenchers during the same period were members of the Order. The Order was institutionally linked to the Unionist party, occupying a substantial proportion of the seats on the Ulster Unionist Council, the party's ruling body. Many Unionist party meetings were held in Orange halls, with ministers using Orange platforms to deliver important speeches.

The power of the Orange Order during those years has been described by two senior Methodists: 'Membership was an indispensable condition of political advancement. It protected the employment of Protestants by its influence over employers, which is a polite way of saying that it contrived systematic discrimination against Catholics. Local authorities were dominated by members of the local lodges.' Orange marches became part of the fabric of Unionist government while at the same time nationalist parades were subject to severe restriction. The Twelfth of July celebrations, the climax of the Orange marching season, effectively became a ritual of state.

In essence Orange culture set the tone for Unionist rule at Stormont. One classic instance of the Orange Order's influence prevailing over other considerations was seen in 1934 when the Order complained that a Catholic was working as a gardener in the grounds of Stormont, the large east Belfast estate where a new parliament building had been built. The fact that the man had a distinguished war record and a personal reference from the Prince of Wales himself was not enough to overcome the Orange objection to his religion.

On numerous occasions over the decades complaints from hardliners within the Unionist party and the Orange Order galvanised the Stormont government into reassuring them. In 1933, for example, the Minister of Labour (and later prime minister) J.M. Andrews reacted quickly to rumours that the porters at Stormont included many Catholics. He told MPs: 'Another allegation made against the government, and which was untrue, was that, of 31 porters at Stormont, 28 were Roman Catholic. I have investigated the matter, and I find that there are 30 Protestants, and only one Roman Catholic there temporarily.'

This excess of populism was a familiar feature of the Unionist party leadership both before and during the troubles: again and again leaders were nervous of the Protestant grassroots and often reluctant to stand up to extremists. Their actions mirrored to an extraordinary extent, either through conviction or ambition, the views of their grassroots. Some ministers were personally frankly anti-Catholic; others did not necessarily hold extreme views, but regarded voicing them as a political necessity.

Ministers and MPs regularly made statements directed against Catholics. One minister, Basil Brooke, who was later to become prime minister, declared: 'Many in the audience employ Catholics, but I have not one about my place. Catholics are out to destroy Ulster with all their might and power. They want to nullify the Protestant vote and take all they can out of Ulster, and then see it go to hell.' When the then prime minister, James Craig, was asked to disown this statement he responded not with condemnation but endorsement, declaring in Stormont: 'He spoke entirely on his own when he made the speech, but there is not one of my colleagues who does not entirely agree with him, and I would not ask him to withdraw one word he said.' Other ministers transmitted the same unmistakable message. The Minister of Agriculture, Sir Edward Archdale, said: 'I have 109 officials, and so far as I know there are four Roman Catholics, three of whom were civil servants turned over to me, whom I had to take when we began.' Nationalist critics chronicled dozens of similar statements.

Craig and Brooke and many of their closest associates were from the upper strata of society. Craig was the son of a millionaire whiskey distiller, while Brooke came from a landowning family which had centuries earlier settled in rich Fermanagh farmland. The Unionist party was firmly in the hands of men from big business and the landed gentry, many of them well-educated and well-travelled. Yet very often they appeared to share the most basic sentiments of their grassroots. One cabinet minister would not use the telephone for sensitive conversations after he discovered 'with a great deal of surprise, that a Roman Catholic telephonist has been appointed to Stormont'. Craig's personal feelings were described by Dame Enid Lyons, wife of Joseph Lyons, who was prime minister of Australia in the 1930s. She recalled in her memoirs:

> Lord Craigavon, the fiercely anti-Catholic prime minister of Northern Ireland, asked Joe at a banquet: 'Lyons, have you got many Catholics in Australia?' 'Oh, about one in five,' Joe had replied. 'Well watch them, Lyons, watch them,' Craigavon had urged. 'They breed like bloody rabbits.'

Catholics were not actively persecuted by the authorities; they were not deported to the south; only a comparatively small number, nearly all active republicans, ever experienced internment without trial. The Catholic Church was free to go about its business, and to run its own schools and hospital facilities, though there was much wrangling about whether the Unionist government was adequately contributing to their upkeep. Nationalist newspapers, in particular the Belfast-based *Irish News*, were generally free to criticise the government and unceasingly did so. (That newspaper provided a daily reminder of Catholic disapproval of the state: for decades it refused to use the title 'Northern Ireland', referring instead to 'the Six County State'.)

But Catholics and nationalists were clearly regarded as second-class citizens, as intrinsically dangerous to the state, and as being less deserving of houses and jobs than their Protestant neighbours. A very few Catholics reached high office in the judiciary, the civil service and other spheres, but it was always clear these were to be exceptions to the general rule. The representatives of Catholics and nationalists were deliberately and efficiently excluded from political power or influence. This was not Nazi Germany or anything like it. But it was institutionalised partiality, and there was no means of redress for Catholic grievances, no avenue of appeal against either real or imagined discrimination. Freed from any effective oversight the Unionist machine was able to function without any checks or balances or mechanisms which might have curbed excesses.

The Catholic minority

In these circumstances most Catholic representatives resorted to the politics of bitter but ineffectual complaint, and indulgence in an often monotonous rehearsal of familiar grievances. Many stayed away from Stormont for long periods of time, maintaining that attendance was a humiliating travesty of parliamentary practice. The Catholic Church firmly hung on to its control of the education of its flock: this was a familiar stance of the Church in many countries, but in Northern Ireland there seemed an extra determination to keep young Catholics out of the clutches of Stormont. Some Unionists were to claim that Catholic children should take their places in the state-run schools attended by Protestants, but in truth neither side favoured religious integration in schools. Both were more comfortable with their 'own sort'.

The Catholic Church was not enthusiastic about integration, forbidding Catholics from attending Protestant church services. Many of the better-educated Catholics went on to the priesthood but overall the Catholic middle class was unusually small. Its members tended to service the Catholic community in areas such as the law, medicine, education, construction, shops and pubs. It was not until the introduction of UK-wide education reforms in the late 1940s that third-level education came within the grasp of working-class students, both Catholic and Protestant.

With Catholic unemployment at high levels and many of the better jobs regarded as the preserve of Protestants, the Catholic emigration rate was higher than that of Protestants. Many Catholic schools advised pupils not to apply to the civil service or local authorities for jobs, regarding such applications as pointless. Those few Catholics who did reach senior posts in areas such as the civil service tended to be viewed by their co-religionists as rare and faintly unpatriotic creatures. One of the most senior Catholic civil servants wrote in his memoirs that to other Catholics, people like him 'were lost souls'.

While there had always been a large measure of segregation between Protestants and Catholics, particularly in Belfast, the Stormont system helped ensure that such patterns would continue. The two communities mixed in some fields, but in their housing, education, and very often in their employment they kept apart. The situation was summed up in 1971 by a Catholic observer who said: 'If there is one thing which I have learned in my 30–40 odd years as a community social worker it is this: that, broadly speaking, two communities have lived side by side in Northern Ireland without really knowing each other, or without making any real honest, sincere and conscious effort to bridge the communications gap.'

Politics atrophied in both communities. Many Catholics simply did not vote or voted only rarely, succumbing to apathy brought on by the realisation that the Unionist voting machine was invincible. In contrast to the highly effective communication skills which it would develop during the troubles, the Catholic community was able to attract little attention or sympathy from outsiders. It often came across as negative, backward-looking and incessantly complaining.

When they did vote, a number of options were available to Catholics. The main Catholic voice in Stormont was provided by the Nationalist party, though the word 'party' is probably a misnomer for a body so disorganised and lacking in either central control or agreement on policy. The party's representatives frequently went their own individual ways, often resorting to boycotting Stormont. Its nominal leader in the 1960s, Londonderry accountant Eddie McAteer, was an early exponent of the ear-catching soundbite, but failed to develop a coherent philosophy or plan of action. He and his colleagues were often characterised as rural, old, staid, conservative and unimaginative. They tended not to be held in high esteem, even by their own voters. 'They were the boys who huffed in the corner,' a Catholic politician of a later age remarked. Another Catholic observer, who was a young teacher in the 1950s, recalled:

Unionists could despise the Nationalist MPs, as they did – almost as much as the nationalist population who voted for them despised them. It was because of the pointlessness of their political programme: they had none, except to say that in an ideal world this state wouldn't exist. But they had no programme to bring about this ideal world, no function other than to protest. There was nothing the Nationalists could do.

While Nationalists tended to dominate in country areas, Belfast was different. Here a number of canny representatives emerged from the backstreets to act as local champions. Some founded micro-parties whose titles included designations such as 'Republican', 'Socialist' or 'Labour'. The most successful of these was to be Gerry Fitt, a one-time merchant seaman and Belfast councillor who was elected to Westminster in 1966 on a Republican Labour party platform. In many Westminster elections, seats were contested by Sinn Féin on an abstentionist ticket, its candidates pledging not to take their seats if elected. The Sinn Féin of the 1950s bore little resemblance to the republican party that would emerge as an electoral force in the 1980s, its earlier approach being largely confined to the politics of the defiant gesture.

The IRA stayed in being throughout Northern Ireland's history, though it remained tiny and ineffectual before its rapid expansion in the early 1970s. Its sporadic campaigns were dealt with reasonably easily by the authorities: its most determined effort, in the 1950s, was crushed by the use of internment without trial on both sides of the border, and ignominiously petered out.

While internment and other security measures were the immediate causes of the IRA's periodic defeats, a much more telling factor lay in the judgement of the Catholic population as a whole that its violence was futile. Although most Catholics held the aspiration to one day see a united Ireland, this did not extend to enthusiasm for the bomb and the bullet. A major 1960s opinion poll found, in fact, that more Protestants than Catholics indicated they were ready to condone violence in support of political ends. The judgement of the *New York Times* following the fizzling out of the 1950s campaign seemed to be shared by most nationalists: 'The IRA belongs to history, and it belongs to better men in times that are gone. So does the Sinn Fein. Let us put a wreath of red roses on their grave and move on.'

Most Catholics looked to the south as, if not quite the promised land, at least an example of a society in which their national and civil rights would be recognised. The fact was, however, that while Catholic northerners looked fondly to Dublin, Dublin tended to regard them as an unwelcome nuisance. The south was absorbed with building its own structures and coping with the long-lasting after-effects of a bitter civil war.

Southern political leaders produced a fair amount of rhetoric concerning the north, generally denouncing partition as unnatural and unjust. Unionism was condemned for its discriminatory policies, and Britain was urged to solve the Northern Ireland problem. The suggested remedy was simplistic in the extreme: London, which had created partition and the border, was simply to announce plans to withdraw and thus bring about a united Ireland. This was clearly more of a slogan than a policy, in that it took no account of the likely Unionist reaction to such a move. The rights of Unionists, or the potential they had for resisting such a move, were barely contemplated. Irish nationalism became even fuzzier when the future of Unionists was concerned. It was sometimes suggested that many Protestants would withdraw with the British, returning to the English and Scottish homelands vacated centuries earlier by their ancestors. Alternatively, it was suggested that a British withdrawal would cause the scales to fall from Protestant eyes, allowing them to realise that they were not really British but Irish, at which point they would embrace a new future as part of the Irish nation.

Rhetoric was plentiful but in reality southern ministers had to accept there was little practical to be done. Northern Ireland and its Catholic minority were in a sense standing affronts to southern self-esteem, representing as they did constant reminders that the south's nation-building efforts were deeply imperfect. Politically, northern nationalist leaders were unwelcome ghosts at the feast in Dublin. Eddie McAteer recalled: 'I made many trips to Dublin for talks and consultations with Dublin ministers. I got hospitality but little real support. There was less than enthusiasm to get involved.' He was particularly disappointed in Seán Lemass, the Fianna Fáil leader who became Taoiseach (Irish prime minister) in 1959. McAteer wrote of meeting him:

> I got neither the encouragement nor understanding of our position that I expected. Lemass said that it appeared to him that the Catholics in the north were just as intractable as the Protestants. It was hardly the reaction that I expected from a Taoiseach with his republican background to the representative of the oppressed Irish minority in the Six Counties. I came away with the conviction that as far as Seán Lemass was concerned, the northern Irish were very much on their own.

Far from being acclaimed in Dublin, northern nationalist politicians were sidelined. They regularly pressed for invitations to state occasions in the south but were not particularly welcomed. They were invited to a presidential inauguration in Dublin in 1945 only after writing to complain that they had been excluded. In 1956, when McAteer asked for a chance to address the Dáil, as the Dublin parliament was known, he was refused. In Lemass's case the lack of sympathy went further and extended to active distaste for northern nationalists. After his retirement he said his impression of them was that 'for them the day partition ended would be the day that would get their foot on the throat of the Orangeman across the road'.

Such chilly receptions did not kill off northern dreams and the attraction of the south. One elderly Catholic woman recalled in the 1990s, 'I never thought of myself as being part of Northern Ireland. When you went across the border, you felt you were in a different atmosphere, relaxed, at home.' This was echoed by a Catholic teacher: 'Even in the fifties, when the southern state was a ramshackle affair, nothing to be admired, the state in Northern Ireland still lacked legitimacy. There was no emotional identification with it, and you ultimately didn't recognize its right to tell you what to do. You obeyed the law but that sort of commitment was not there in the mildest of nationalists.' An anecdote related by a Catholic woman helps explain why even an only theoretically welcoming south seemed preferable to northern realities. She recalled how, as a teenager in a small and predominantly Protestant County Armagh town, she was asked by a local Protestant doctor why she did not play table tennis with young Protestants in the local Orange hall. When she said she did not believe she would be welcome he persuaded her to go along, saying, 'Nonsense, you're being silly.' She recounted, 'I had a great evening, enjoyed myself very much, but the next day the doctor came to me, all embarrassed, and said: "I'm really sorry about this, but they've asked me to tell you not to come back. They were going to tell you this but I said I'd tell you." He was shocked and embarrassed. I never forgot that.'

Political stagnation

In both communities, social exclusion went hand in hand with political stagnation. The unchanging realities of politics can be illustrated by the electoral history of one constituency. Dehra Parker held the Londonderry City and County seat from 1921 until 1929 when she stood down to allow her relative Captain James Lenox-Conyngham Chichester-Clark, a member of the local gentry, to replace her in the new South Londonderry constituency. After his death in 1933 the seat returned, again uncontested, to Dehra Parker. She was returned uncontested in the elections of 1938 and 1945. Four years later she defeated a nationalist candidate and was subsequently returned uncontested in 1953 and 1958. In 1960 she resigned, handing over the seat to Major James Dawson Chichester-Clark, son of the earlier Chichester-Clark. He was elected unopposed and held the seat in uncontested elections in 1962 and 1965. He finally faced a nationalist challenge in 1969, and won. The seat was thus contested only twice in twelve elections over forty years. And the votes cast in the two contested elections, held twenty years apart, were uncannily alike: Dame Dehra won in 1949 by 9,193 votes to 5,909; Major Chichester-Clark won in 1969 by 9,195 votes to 5,812. The figures give some sense of the political stasis.

Unopposed elections were a feature of the Stormont system. Since elections were essentially decided on a religious headcount, the side which was in the minority in a constituency often simply gave up and stopped fielding a candidate there. In the South Antrim constituency, for example, the Unionist majority was so secure that for nine consecutive elections no nationalist went forward, a Unionist candidate being returned unopposed each time. This meant that no polling took place there in Stormont elections between 1929 and 1965.

The almost stultifying continuity was emphasised by the remarkable longevity of Unionist prime ministers. The first, Sir James Craig, held the post from 1921 until 1940. Although the second, J.M. Andrews, stayed only three years, the third, Sir Basil Brooke, lasted for twenty years. Those who served in their cabinets also tended to have a long political life span: by 1939 not only Craig but four of his seven ministers had been in the cabinet for eighteen years. Nor was this an era for young men: Craig was sixty-nine years old when he left office, Andrews seventy-two, Brooke seventy-four.

Although there were major economic changes over the decades, the basic elements of Unionist dominance, Catholic powerlessness and Westminster disregard survived relatively untouched even an event as cataclysmic as World War Two. The war years did produce one episode capable of shaking Northern Ireland to its political foundations, but the fact that it took place in private meant it had little effect on public opinion.

This occurred in 1940 when the Churchill government approached the Dublin Taoiseach, Eamon de Valera, with an offer to explore the option of declaring in favour of Irish unity in return for Irish wartime assistance. The Unionist government, on learning of this, was appalled and furious, but the initiative came to nothing. Wartime censorship kept the episode from the public, but it helped reinforce in Stormont ministers the awareness that Britain always meant more to Northern Ireland than Northern Ireland meant to Britain.

However, the fact that Northern Ireland was involved in the war effort while the south remained neutral meant that Unionism's stock rose in London while sympathy for the nationalist cause decreased. This was useful to the Unionist party when a post-war British Labour government was elected, and when in 1948 the Dublin government unexpectedly announced that Ireland, though effectively independent for many years, was formally declaring a republic and leaving the Commonwealth. This major constitutional change meant Labour needed new legislation to regularise Northern Ireland's position. Up to that point the Labour government had exhibited what one of its junior ministers, the pro-nationalist Lord Longford, described as 'a rather hazy benevolence' towards southern Ireland. This was very much a traditional Labour approach, for expatriate Irishmen and their descendants had played a significant role in the labour movement since its early days.

When it came to brass tacks, however, such sentiment went by the board. The government headed by Clement Attlee inserted a clause in the new Ireland Bill laying down that Northern Ireland would remain in the UK so long as a majority in the Stormont parliament in Belfast wanted it. Given Stormont's inbuilt Unionist majority, nationalists protested that the clause copper-fastened the partition of Ireland. But Attlee's cabinet tended to lean towards the Unionists, partly because his deputy Herbert Morrison was sympathetic to the Unionist cause, and partly because that cause had been much strengthened by Northern Ireland's war role.

Against this background the cabinet took a hard look at Northern Ireland and made some key political judgements. The first of these concerned the reality of Protestant power, with ministers delving back into the 1914 period and the Ulster Volunteer Force gunrunning. The 1949 cabinet minutes record Labour's conclusion: 'Unless the people of Northern Ireland felt reasonably assured of the support of the people of this country, there might be a revival of the Ulster Volunteers and of other bodies intending to meet any threat of force by force; and this would bring nearer the danger of an outbreak of violence in Ireland.'

A second issue was closer to home: that of the UK's wider strategic defence considerations. These were set out by the cabinet secretary, Lord Normanbrook, who wrote that the south's departure from the Commonwealth meant that keeping Northern Ireland within the United Kingdom had become 'a matter of first-class strategic importance to this country'. The issue was so vital, he argued, that even if Northern Ireland wanted to leave the UK it was unlikely that any British government could allow it to do so. The perpetual Protestant majority meant that Normanbrook's view was never put to the test.

What went by the board in 1949 was the issue which two decades later would give rise to the civil rights movement: the question of the fairness of the Stormont system. When Lord Longford protested that Catholics were being discriminated against he was allowed to address the cabinet which received him, he recalled, with 'chilly indifference'. The young Michael Foot supported the Ireland Act but at the same time called for a commission of inquiry into Stormont's 'monstrously undemocratic methods'. The minutes show, however, that the cabinet decided to keep its distance: 'It was the general view of ministers that the UK government would be ill-advised to appear to be interesting themselves in this matter.'

The remarks made by Foot and others in the Commons, together with the evidence of cabinet papers, show that the government was fully aware of the allegations that Stormont was being run in an unfair manner. It is clear that Attlee had few illusions about Stormont's record, for he turned down a request from the Unionist government to have the power to appoint Supreme Court judges transferred from London to Belfast. Attlee privately noted 'my impression that they would allow political considerations to influence their appointments'. Normanbrook agreed, writing to Attlee that the powers asked for 'certainly have the appearance of being directed to a much more sinister purpose'.

When in 1955 Conservative ministers turned their attentions to Northern Ireland, they took a view similar to that of Labour. One minister noted that the Union 'creates particularly tiresome problems' for the government and was 'apt to be a nuisance', in that it generated criticism from those of Irish descent abroad. But again defence considerations prevailed, the minister concluding: 'Nevertheless it must be recognised that the possession of Northern Ireland is of capital importance in the defence of Great Britain.' The advantages of retaining Northern Ireland, he wrote, 'are overwhelming'.

Thus the 1940s and 1950s came and went, with not even the war changing the basic grammar of Northern Ireland political life, and with the Unionist system as strong as ever. After World War One Churchill had written thus of the longevity of the Irish question, saying in an often-quoted purple passage:

> Then came the Great War. Every institution, almost, in the world was strained. Great empires have been overturned. The whole map of Europe has been changed. The position of countries has been violently altered. The modes of thought of men, the whole outlook on affairs, the grouping of parties, all have encountered violent and tremendous change in the deluge of the world. But as the deluge subsides and the waters fall short we see the dreary steeples of Fermanagh and Tyrone emerging once again. The integrity of their quarrel is one of the few institutions that have been unaltered in the cataclysm which has swept the world.

During World War Two Churchill's own offer on Irish unity could have changed the course of Irish history. It did not, however, and in 1945 he could have repeated every word of his earlier assessment. Not until the 1960s would the Northern Ireland system first begin to tremble, disintegrate, and then descend into violence.

2

The O'Neill years
1963–69

The years between 1963 and 1969 are often referred to as 'the O'Neill era'. This is entirely appropriate in that the personality and approach of the Stormont prime minister of the time, Captain Terence O'Neill, represented a striking departure from tradition. From the start there was a sense of generational change as he took over from the ageing Brooke, who had been in office for a full two decades. O'Neill's six-year term represented a turning point in Northern Ireland's history. The O'Neill years might be regarded as a tragic missed opportunity in that with hindsight they appear to have been the last chance to tackle, by political means and in a time of relative peace, Northern Ireland's structural problems. Opinions will differ on whether more skill and more luck could have averted the troubles. Terence O'Neill sought to change the entire tone of government, introducing the rhetoric of Protestant–Catholic reconciliation in place of the unapologetically Protestant stance of Craig and Brooke. In retrospect it was an inadequate attempt to brush away decades of division without tackling the underlying problems. These eventually produced a tidal wave of conflicting forces which swept O'Neill from office.

When O'Neill took charge of Northern Ireland it seemed, on the surface at least, reasonably tranquil. From the start of his premiership he asserted that he would be in the business of making changes and of producing 'bold and imaginative measures'. His proposition was that Northern Ireland could be reformed and modernised without endangering either the Union with Britain or his own party's unbroken run in government. The O'Neill government set about building new links with the trade union movement and attracting new investment from abroad to replace ailing existing industries. While such moves were initially generally uncontroversial, much debate was generated by his new emphasis on improving community relations. He became the first Unionist prime minister to pay regular visits to Catholic schools and to offer handshakes to nuns.

Northern Ireland was unused to all this, its first three prime ministers having been men of the laager who defined nationalists, and indeed Catholics in general, as hostile to the state. O'Neill, only the fourth prime minister in more than forty years, presented himself not just as open to change but as an enthusiastic advocate of reform. It was a time when the winds of change were sweeping through many parts of the western world. It was the decade when John F. Kennedy became US president, associated with the themes of youth, equality and new American frontiers. Closer to home, Harold Wilson and the Labour party came to power in Britain, again stressing modernisation. In the Irish Republic too change was the order of the day. There was even a reforming Pope, John XXIII, who instituted widespread reforms within Catholicism and encouraged ecumenical activity.

Terence O'Neill was far from being a dangerous radical. His background was Anglo-Irish, he was Eton-educated and he had served with the Irish Guards in World War Two, during which both his brothers were killed. Retaining his wartime rank as many Unionist politicians did, he was known throughout his political career as Captain O'Neill, entering Stormont in 1946 and spending seven years as finance minister before becoming prime minister. To the Unionist party he seemed a reasonably safe pair of hands, though he was sometimes prone to flights of fancy such as his 1958 whimsy of draining Lough Neagh and thus increasing Northern Ireland's six counties to seven. To the Unionist establishment which chose him as leader, after private consultations, he was above all else one of them, being a member of the gentry which dominated the party at its top levels.

In selecting O'Neill the party had passed over a more able and much more ambitious rival in the cabinet in the form of businessman Brian Faulkner. Faulkner's sense that he had lost because he was from the merchant class rather than the landed gentry would damage the relationship between the two men and undermine O'Neill's authority. Within months there was talk of moves to get rid of O'Neill, with Faulkner publicly denying involvement in any plot. But during O'Neill's time hardly a year went by without rumoured or actual attempts to unseat him, with Faulkner invariably suspected of complicity.

Economic pressures

O'Neill had practical reasons for pursuing modernisation, certainly in the economic sphere. Traditional industries such as shipbuilding and linen were in steep decline, shedding tens of thousands of jobs and forcing unemployment up to levels generally more than double the UK average. O'Neill set about planning a transformation of the economy, accepting ideas such as the creation of a new town, a second university and a new housing programme. His major drive to attract outside industry by improving the infrastructure and offering generous financial incentives worked to some extent, with the arrival of such big names as Grundig, Goodyear and Michelin. But unemployment remained high in a number of districts as the creation of new jobs barely kept pace with the loss of jobs from the older industries. It is scarcely a coincidence that some of the areas which were to feature prominently in the troubles, such as north and west Belfast and Londonderry city, were among those where poor housing and high unemployment persisted.

O'Neill's economic difficulties were accompanied by political problems. The sharp drop in economic activity towards the end of the 1950s coincided with the emergence of a new political challenge in the form of the Northern Ireland Labour party. This was a left-leaning party which, though it had both Catholics and Protestants in its ranks, supported the Union with Britain and attracted largely Protestant support. The NILP twice won four of Stormont's fifty-two seats, winning 26 per cent of the total vote in the 1962 election. For O'Neill it posed a double challenge. Just as Sir James Craig had feared in the early years of the state that the Unionist party might be faced by pro-Union rivals, so O'Neill was concerned that Protestant support might drain away to the NILP. Second, the surge in support for the NILP happened just before Labour came to power in Britain. Harold Wilson's 1964 arrival in Downing Street thus meant that the NILP had ready-made and very powerful friends across the Irish Sea. For Unionism, this dangerous conjunction meant it made even more political sense for O'Neill to stress industrial modernisation and religious bridge-building, since in doing so he was both stealing some of the NILP's clothes and in effect echoing the approach of the Wilson government.

All this had major implications since Wilson was instinctively anti-Unionist and was not well-disposed towards the Stormont regime. This meant that O'Neill was the first Unionist prime minister to be faced with a British counterpart unfriendly to his government. It was thus highly desirable, for a whole series of reasons, to project Northern Ireland as a modern state, at ease with itself and with its neighbours. The NILP was to be warded off; Wilson was to be persuaded that both Northern Ireland's economy and its politics were being updated in a progressive manner; and investors were to be presented with an attractive investment proposition. O'Neill was the first Unionist leader with a keen sense of public relations and the importance of image, grasping from the start that attracting new investment meant working to avoid any appearance of instability and of unresolved ancient quarrels. As part of his campaign he looked south, with an initiative aimed at ending the long cold war between Belfast and Dublin.

The Lemass visit

A similar economic evolution was already taking place across the border in Dublin, where Lemass was jettisoning the inward-looking, protectionist economics of his predecessor de Valera. North–south relations had been so glacial that prime ministers of the two states had not met since the 1920s, and there was virtually no co-ordination between the two governments. Years later a southern civil servant recalled that one of the few channels of communication was provided by rugby matches in Dublin, where Belfast and Dublin officials would meet discreetly to sort out shared problems.

By the mid-1960s the common aim of O'Neill and Lemass of attracting new investment led them to think of normalising relations. This brought O'Neill to take the initiative for which he is best remembered, inviting Lemass to Belfast in 1965. The visit was a political sensation since no Taoiseach had ever before made the journey to Stormont, and it was a gamble for both men. O'Neill later recounted that Lemass had remarked to him in a Stormont toilet, 'I shall get into terrible trouble for this.' O'Neill said he replied, 'No, Mr Lemass, it is I who will get into trouble for this.' O'Neill was correct, though at the time the visit was viewed as a great success for both men, many people north and south feeling that regularising relations should be added to the other 1960s innovations. For southerners the visit was a welcome move. O'Neill's standing remained high among sections of southern opinion through the years that followed and in 1969 he was voted Man of the Year by readers of a Dublin newspaper.

Most of Unionism voiced approval of the visit, though protests were staged by the Reverend Ian Paisley, a hardline young fundamentalist clergyman with a talent for self-publicity. Some Unionist ministers grumbled that the visit had taken place in strict secrecy, and that they had known of it only after Lemass was actually at Stormont, but overall the initiative was seen as a great success. O'Neill followed it up by twice visiting Dublin, and even the staid Nationalist party was stirred into uncharacteristic action, agreeing at Lemass's urging to assume the role of official Stormont opposition. This was seen as a significant political thaw. There was much talk of new dawns and new eras and bridge-building, especially in the Unionist *Belfast Telegraph*, which enthusiastically backed O'Neill's innovations. Its strong-minded editor, Jack Sayers, was influential with O'Neill and crusaded strongly on his behalf.

O'Neill's rhetorical tone was striking and even visionary: he appealed for 'a new pride in the province' and for 'all sections of the community to feel committed to the task'. He felt it essential 'to convince more and more people that the government is working for the good of all and not only those who vote Unionist'. This was stirring rhetoric, well in tune with the expansive modernising mood of the heady 1960s. The Unionist party did well in the 1965 election, with opinion polls of the time indicating a high degree of Protestant support for such initiatives.

Unionist opposition

Yet for a substantial minority of Protestants even these limited gestures seemed too much too soon, and too drastic a departure from Unionist tradition. The scornful Paisley verdict on O'Neill's bridge-building summed up what one end of the Unionist spectrum thought: 'A traitor and a bridge are very much alike, for they both go over to the other side.' The constant Unionist fear of the traitor within was to prove a fertile seam for Paisley to exploit in the years to come.

Unionists had been raised in a culture which defined the primary aim as preservation of the citadel. This, originally defined as defence of the Union, evolved into a defence of Stormont, with the Unionist party defined as the key instrument. The idea was ingrained in many in the Unionist community that Catholics *per se* were enemies of the state; indeed Craig and Brooke had defined them almost literally in those terms. Yet O'Neill was a Unionist prime minister with an outreach programme apparently designed to bring Catholics within the fold. Those who thought that Unionism was about preserving Protestant unity and control and keeping Catholics at arm's length were dismayed.

On one point these hardliners were certainly right, though whether it was a self-fulfilling prophecy remains open to argument. They viewed O'Neill's talk of winning Catholic support for Unionism as sheer fantasy, and indeed the decades that followed produced no real evidence of any appreciable Catholic support for Unionist parties. The fault line within Unionism between reformers and traditionalists was to remain visible throughout the troubles. One segment in effect would flatly refuse to contemplate striking a deal with Catholics and nationalists. At the other pole were Unionist party leaders and followers who hoped that such a deal could be done; and in between has been a volatile third segment, vacillating uncertainly between the two positions.

In the years which followed the Reverend Ian Paisley would grow from a semi-comical and apparently insignificant pantomime demon into a formidable figure in Unionist politics. He went on to build a vote which see-sawed between 10 per cent and a high point of more than 30 per cent of all votes cast. O'Neill's party in the decades ahead would remain the primary political voice of Ulster Protestants, but there would be many internal battles and defections, generally to groupings which viewed its policies as insufficiently hardline. The shadow of Paisleyism would forever hang over it, with the tactically astute cleric ever ready to poach its voters. The Unionist party itself would continue to encompass within its ranks dealers, non-dealers and the undecided, destined to remain in a permanent state of flux.

The recurring rumours of leadership challenges culminated in 1966 in a serious effort by some backbenchers to dislodge O'Neill in favour of Faulkner. Although the attempt was unsuccessful, it served to illustrate O'Neill's vulnerability inside even the parliamentary party. In essence he lacked not just standing in the party but also the personal and political skills necessary to see through even the modest changes he had embarked upon. Brooke had been a gruff old frontiersman who had helped create and run the B Specials in a perilous border area; O'Neill was a gentleman from a safe part of County Antrim.

O'Neill's brand of Unionism set him apart from many: he was an unconditional Unionist, identifying absolutely with Britain, while many of his critics were Ulster Unionists first and British second. His wife was English; he often seemed more comfortable in the English country-house world; and it came as little surprise when after his retirement he moved to Hampshire.

Although Unionists proclaimed the strength of their attachment to Britain, many of them instinctively found O'Neill to be too English. Anglican and English-educated, he possessed a nasal, aristocratic voice which made him sound as much an Englishman as an Ulsterman. This had considerable political significance, in that an important component of Unionism has been a distrust of the English and a suspicion of English motives. This derives in part from the fact that many Protestants come from Scottish Dissenting stock, a tradition which has its reservations about the English, and in part from the psychology of the settler who is forever nervous about sentiments back in the homeland. O'Neill, who projected complete faith in Britain, worried many Protestants in that he did not appear to share their almost genetic unease about London.

He also lacked the social and personal skills which were of much importance in a parliament of only fifty-two members: in this field, friend and foe agree, he was frankly terrible. One of his strongest cabinet supporters recalled: 'He lacked the common touch. He found it difficult to communicate warmth and friendliness. I found him distant and uninspiring: I would not, I confess, have felt like dying in a ditch for him.' A Unionist MP described him as 'the most egotistical man I have ever met, and altogether quite the most unpleasant personality I have ever encountered'. A Unionist political journalist commented: 'O'Neill was a disaster. Every time you met him you would have to be introduced to him all over again, whereas Faulkner might not have seen you for a year but would instantly know you.'

Rather than attempting to develop contacts with political colleagues, O'Neill fuelled widespread resentment by spending much time closeted with a small group of officials. The ablest of these was civil servant Ken Bloomfield, who was described by British prime minister James Callaghan as 'the brains of the outfit'. Bloomfield wrote later that O'Neill had no regular practice of talking things over with senior political colleagues, adding that 'his rather shy, lonely and not very communicative nature held him back from cultivating political intimates'. As early as 1965 the *Observer* newspaper reported:

> He is better liked outside his party than in it. Captain O'Neill brings his crises on himself by his brusque and ruthless handling of people. He has made enemies in politics and in the civil service, where his reshuffles and dismissals have been equally brutal. With a small coterie of advisers, his administration sometimes resembles a medieval court, and the roots of his personal power are perilously shallow.

Ian Paisley

In addition to internal party problems there were also dangerous splinters away from the mainstream, one of them the politically insatiable and highly divisive Reverend Ian Paisley. Paisley's has been an extraordinary career, encompassing politics, the pulpit, marches and rallies, and two spells in jail. It is a career packed with incident and drama, with a thousand demonstrations, diatribes, walkouts and incendiary rhetoric.

Paisley is not a politician with a sideline in religion; rather, he is a fundamentalist evangelical minister who is also in politics. O'Neill never could cope with him, and nor could any of the Unionist party leaders in the years that followed. Other figures might have been bought off by being brought inside the fold, but Paisley was not interested in joining any team. There was thus no real way for O'Neill or anyone else to silence his disruptive dissent.

Ordained a minister by his father, Paisley went on to become moderator for life of his own sect, the Free Presbyterian Church. In the 1960s he became a formidable street demagogue before turning to party politics: when O'Neill gave up his Stormont seat in 1970 it was Paisley who won it. Paisley did not create the fundamentalist and uncompromising strand in Unionism, but previously it had been contained within the Unionist party and the Orange Order. Paisley's flair for articulating and indeed amplifying the deepest fears of many Protestants meant he harvested votes in large numbers, and he went on to form first the Protestant Unionist party and later the Democratic Unionist party, which was to constitute a force in Unionist politics throughout the troubles. He was to be a permanent thorn in the flesh of both the Unionist party and the major Protestant churches, harrying those he denounced as too soft, too ecumenical or too accommodating. The Unionist party in particular always had to look over its shoulder at this vociferous rival.

Throughout the O'Neill years, Paisley staged an almost ceaseless series of demonstrations and stunts, among them a protest against the lowering of the flag on Belfast City Hall to mark the death of Pope John XXIII. With an estimated one thousand supporters he protested at 'the lying eulogies now being paid to the Roman anti-Christ'. In 1964 he was involved in a series of events that led to the worst Belfast street disturbances for thirty years. During the general election campaign of that year he protested at the display of an Irish tricolour in the window of the republican headquarters in the Catholic Falls Road district of Belfast. When the RUC removed the flag to forestall a Paisley threat to do so, the result was two days of serious rioting and many injuries.

In 1966 Paisley launched the *Protestant Telegraph* weekly newssheet and the Ulster Constitutional Defence Committee, a 'united society of Protestant patriots'. From this sprang the Ulster Protestant Volunteers, whose members featured at many Paisley demonstrations and counter-demonstrations. In the same year there were violent scenes during a Paisley demonstration at the Presbyterian General Assembly meeting in Belfast attended by the Governor of Northern Ireland, Lord Erskine.

Although it has often been asserted that the civil rights movement was the first body in Northern Ireland to exploit the new media age with skill, the fact is that Paisley was the first to make use of newspaper and television publicity. That the media were universally antagonistic towards both his beliefs and his methods was in the end of little moment to him: he realised at an early stage that any publicity was good publicity. Although the media in general portrayed him as an anachronistic crank, it gradually became obvious that he had substantial support within a section of rural and working-class Protestants. His mix of religious fundamentalism, political opportunism, personal charisma and talent for self-publicity was a potent one.

1966: loyalist violence

Just as this Protestant extremist was the first to exploit the opportunities of the media, other Protestant extremists were the first to take life. A rise in tension in 1966, as republicans celebrated the fiftieth anniversary of the 1916 rising, led to three killings carried out by a group styling itself the Ulster Volunteer Force. The UVF, though named after the organisation that had helped bring Northern Ireland into being, was a far cry from the original body of that name. It was instead made up of at most a couple of dozen men who met in backstreet pubs, many in the Shankill Road district, to discuss over drinks means of combating the practically non-existent IRA. A series of attacks carried out in a two-month period in 1966, many of which were drunken escapades, claimed three lives.

None of those killed was remotely connected with the IRA. The first victim was a 77-year-old Protestant widow who was fatally injured in a fire started by a petrol bomb aimed at a Catholic-owned bar. Their second was a Catholic man on his way home in the Falls Road district after a night's drinking: the gang shot him after hearing him shout 'Up the Republic, up the rebels'. Their third victim was a teenage Catholic barman who strayed into a bar in Malvern Street in the Shankill Road district. He was shot as he left the bar, the shooting becoming known as the Malvern Street murder.

Most people were aghast at such incidents, which were condemned from every quarter. The RUC quickly rounded up members of the gang, some of whom were given lengthy prison sentences. The events were an unwelcome reminder that for all the talk of modernisation, old enmities continued to simmer not far below the surface. The *Belfast Telegraph*, in a remarkably prescient editorial, gave this warning:

> Violence has been smouldering in Belfast and district for weeks past, and the point has been reached at which a united effort is called for to prevent crazy people leading the province on a path to self-destruction. No longer

may any Protestant wonder where his loyalties lie. They lie on the side of law and order and public decency. They can have nothing to do with those who have been sowing dragon's teeth, and can now see how terrible the harvest can be. Ulster is in danger of being thrown back into a dark past by sectarian forces which have too long been winked at by many who should know better.

But although most Unionists were against violence, a substantial number were also very much against Terence O'Neill. By 1967 sections of the Orange Order were in open revolt against him, critics at the main Twelfth of July demonstration passing out leaflets condemning his 'tottering leadership'. When a senior Orange official attempted to read out a resolution praising O'Neill his words were drowned by hecklers. An MP who was due to speak at a Fermanagh Orange demonstration withdrew when it became clear that the O'Neill resolution would not even be proposed. At another Orange demonstration a Westminster Unionist MP was dragged from the stage and beaten unconscious when he remonstrated with anti-O'Neill hecklers. Early the next year the prime minister himself was attacked with stones, flour and eggs by Paisleyite demonstrators while attending a Unionist party meeting in Belfast: his immediate sin had been to visit a convent school some days earlier. All of this meant that O'Neill was preaching a new accommodation against an increasingly unsettled background.

The civil rights campaign

Just as Unionism was showing signs of coming apart, Catholics and nationalists were breaking new ground in politics. They were finding novel means of making their political voice heard as British post-war educational reforms produced a Catholic middle class which was both larger and much more assertive than ever before. This new generation regarded the Nationalist party as outmoded and ineffectual, and viewed the IRA and Sinn Féin as belonging to a past age.

During the 1960s a number of Catholic voices emerged that not only criticised Unionism, as was traditional, but also argued for greater Catholic participation in the state. One of these was John Hume's. In 1964, as a 27-year-old teacher and credit union organiser, Hume urged Catholics in a newspaper article to be more outgoing, writing, 'There has been no attempt to be positive, to encourage the Catholic community to develop the resources which they have in plenty, to make a positive contribution in terms of community service.' His words were evidence of increasing Catholic restlessness with existing structures. A significant organisation emerged from Tyrone in the form of the Campaign for Social Justice. Consisting of thirteen Catholic professionals who included four doctors, it assembled and circulated detailed statistics in support of its allegations of discrimination.

A turning point came with the election of a Labour government in 1964. The Unionist party had not come into serious conflict with Conservative governments, and the post-war Attlee Labour government had offered no threat to the Unionist cause. But Harold Wilson as prime minister presented a very different figure since, instinctively anti-Union and representing a largely Irish Catholic constituency in Liverpool, he made no secret of his disdain for the Unionist party.

He was pressed into paying attention to Northern Ireland issues when in 1965 a Campaign for Democracy in Ulster (CDU) was formed at Westminster, attracting the support of around a hundred Labour backbenchers. With MP Paul Rose as its leading figure, the CDU took a lively and continuing interest in Northern Ireland affairs, campaigning against the long-standing convention which ruled out discussion of Northern Ireland affairs at Westminster.

An important figure arrived at Westminster in 1966 when Gerry Fitt, who was to have a long-running career in Northern Ireland politics, won the West Belfast seat for the Republican Labour party. An affable ex-seaman who enlivened every bar he visited, Fitt won many friends among Labour MPs with his endless flow of patter which effectively mixed anecdotes, jokes and shrewd political points. A cute backstreet politician with a power base in the rough Docks area of Belfast, he ran rings round the staid Unionists with his natural flair for publicity, his talent for impressing journalists, and his ready identification with many of Wilson's backbenchers. The *Belfast Telegraph* outlined the dangers Fitt posed to Unionism, noting a year after his election: 'He enjoys the friendly recognition of ministers and Labour backbenchers alike. He is an astute politician – one of the most effective non-Unionists who have been sent to Westminster by Northern Ireland – and his presence has materially helped to alter the climate of the Ulster Unionists.'

Wilson and his colleagues pressed O'Neill for reform. Minutes of 1966 and 1967 ministerial meetings reveal Home Secretary Roy Jenkins urging, ominously for Unionists, that 'a real effort should be made to meet some of the grievances which had been expressed: otherwise Westminster would be forced to act'. O'Neill told his cabinet that there was 'an underlying sense of pressure' coming from London. Many in Unionism, conditioned as they were to view criticism and opposition as conspiracy, were ill-equipped to respond to this new situation. O'Neill himself was clearly well aware that the game had changed and that pressure from London could not be dismissed, but many in his party were slow to grasp this.

It was against this background that Catholics and nationalists chanced upon a powerful new political instrument in the form of the civil rights movement. This was not a party but an umbrella group wide enough to embrace every anti-Unionist element in the land. It was amorphous in the sense that it had no coherent central leadership and no formal membership. In 1967 a committee emerged styling itself the Northern Ireland Civil Rights Association (NICRA), but from the start activists in many districts organised themselves with little or no reference to the supposed leadership. While NICRA was never more than the notional directing force, the theme of civil rights was to catch the imagination of the very many Catholics who were not members of any organised body. In 1968 it was to galvanise the Catholic community politically.

NICRA had a shopping list of demands which included one man – one vote, the redrawing of electoral boundaries, anti-discrimination legislation, a points system for housing allocation, the repeal of the Special Powers Act, and the disbanding of the B Specials. The most potent of these was the demand for one man – one vote, a reference to the different voting arrangements in Stormont and council elections. In council elections subtenants, lodgers and anyone living at home with their parents could not vote, so that around a quarter of Stormont voters had no say in local government elections. Opinions differ on the exact effect the introduction of one man – one vote might have had, though an unpublished Unionist government study concluded that nationalists would have benefited significantly in Tyrone, Fermanagh and Londonderry city. This might have led to a loss of Unionist party control over much of the west, which explains why Unionists were so strongly opposed to one man – one vote.

It was a touchstone issue but there were many other rallying points, and many reasons why even the more moderate civil rights figures were not inclined to give O'Neill the benefit of the doubt. By 1968 he had been in office for five years, yet his reform proposals still seemed largely confined to the realms of rhetoric. Nationalists debated whether he was a genuine reformer, a cunningly disguised unreconstructed Unionist of the old sort, or perhaps a well-intentioned man who was simply not in control of his own party. Many Catholics saw O'Neillism as a distinctly conditional advance in that at its heart lay an attempt to give the Unionist party a more accommodating aspect without affecting its hold on power. Complete success for O'Neill's project would have meant a continuation and in fact a consolidation of Unionist rule. Nationalists therefore wondered what they had to gain from the architect of a scheme designed to create a more intelligent form of Unionism rather than sponsor a genuine break-through on their behalf.

In any event, many of what O'Neill presented as reforms did little to better the lot of nationalists. Many of the new companies attracted to Northern Ireland wound up either in Belfast or in its satellite towns, often in mainly Protestant areas with mainly Protestant workforces. Catholics complained that the largely Catholic west lost out and was bypassed by the much-vaunted industrial modernisation. When a new city was planned, it was placed in a mostly Protestant area and pointedly named Craigavon in commemoration of the old Unionist prime minister. A second university was established but there was political uproar in the northwest when mainly Catholic Londonderry was passed over in favour of Protestant Coleraine. Londonderry's Catholics, and indeed many of its Protestants, claimed this was a perverse decision explicable only in sectarian terms.

Catholic politicians complained that while the Unionist rhetoric was new, the effect was the old discrimination under a new name. It was argued that in his five years in office O'Neill had hardly made a dent in the ingrained practices in fundamental areas such as schools, housing, jobs and local government. As late as 1967, for example, when three public boards were reconstituted, the seventy-nine members included only seven Catholics. It was also obvious enough that whether or not O'Neill was a genuine reformer there was a great deal of Protestant opposition to change, both inside and outside his party.

The civil rights movement encompassed supporters of the Nationalist party, members and supporters of the IRA, communists, liberals, trade unionists, assorted left-wingers and radicals, exuberant students, middle-class professionals and many more, united in a fluid coalition which was not to last for long before splitting back into its constituent components. Although Gerry Fitt and other prominent Catholic public figures were there too, it was a new breed of better educated representatives who came to the fore, including John Hume and psychology student Bernadette Devlin. The movement's principal activity was the staging of marches designed to generate media coverage and publicise the cause. The movement was much influenced by the model of Martin Luther King and the black civil rights movement in America, though it was also to draw inspiration from the street activities of students and others in Paris, Prague and elsewhere. This was to be the new politics which would break the old mould, and it was seized on with heady excitement.

1968: the mould breaks

The movement's first manifestation, in terms of generating publicity and highlighting an issue, came in 1968 when Austin Currie, a young Nationalist MP, staged a protest by squatting in a house in the County Tyrone village of Caledon near Dungannon. The episode has come to be regarded as a seminal moment in Northern Ireland's history, some even regarding it as the start of the troubles, or at least as the spark which ignited the bonfire.

County Tyrone had over the years generated many allegations of unfair housing allocation, and this particular case led to much local Catholic indignation. The facts were regarded by local Catholics as a clear example of politics and religion taking precedence over housing need. The house at the centre of the controversy was allocated, by a local Unionist party councillor, to a nineteen-year-old unmarried Protestant girl. She was secretary to the councillor's solicitor, who was also a Unionist parliamentary candidate. The girl was given the house in preference to two Catholic families, who had squatted for a time in the district, and who had complained that the same councillor had opposed the building of houses for Catholic tenants in the Dungannon area. A few days after the girl moved in, Catholic squatters in the house next door were evicted by police, with full television coverage.

Currie, an energetic MP who was to have a long political career, raised the matter unsuccessfully both with the local council and at Stormont.

Following a heated debate he was ordered to leave the Commons chamber. He then symbolically occupied the girl's house, remaining in it for some hours before being evicted by the RUC. One of the policemen who removed him was the girl's brother, who himself later moved into the same house.

The incident became a *cause célèbre*. Thousands attended a public rally addressed by Currie a few days after the squatting incident, and in August the civil rights movement staged its first protest march, from the village of Coalisland to the town of Dungannon. In a pattern which was to be repeated many times, a thousand members and supporters of Paisley's Ulster Protestant Volunteers gathered to confront them in Dungannon. The marchers, consciously emulating American civil rights protesters, sang 'We Shall Overcome'. Confrontation was avoided, but the pattern of demonstration and counter-demonstration was set.

It is no exaggeration to say that the next civil rights march made history, for the violence which accompanied it transformed Northern Ireland politics. The march, in the city of Londonderry on 5 October 1968, was organised by a left-wing group which was hopeful of provoking the authorities into confrontation. That strategy worked. First William Craig, O'Neill's particularly hardline Minister for Home Affairs, banned the march, a move which swelled the numbers attending it. Then the RUC spectacularly overreacted, using water cannon and batons on an obviously peaceful group of marchers.

Crucially, a Dublin television cameraman was on hand to capture the RUC actions on film. In particular he recorded the scene as a senior RUC officer uninhibitedly used a long blackthorn stick, the official symbol of his authority, to rain heavy blows indiscriminately on a number of marchers. The pictures of the officer fiercely laying about the demonstrators, then turning towards the camera, wild-eyed and almost out of control, were shown repeatedly at the time. In the years that followed the film clip was broadcast on television hundreds and perhaps thousands of times, making an appearance in almost all accounts of how the troubles broke out.

Local hospitals later reported treating seventy-seven civilian casualties, most of whom had bruises and lacerations to the head. The most important of those heads belonged to Gerry Fitt, who had taken three Labour MPs with him to Londonderry to witness the march, and had been in the front line when the police moved in. An official report later concluded that he had been struck 'wholly without justification or excuse' and that RUC men had used their batons indiscriminately. Fitt later recounted:

> A sergeant grabbed me and pulled my coat down over my shoulders to prevent me raising my arms. Two other policemen held me as I was batoned on the head. I could feel the blood coursing down my neck and on to my shirt. As I fell to my knees I was roughly grabbed and thrown into a police van. At the police station I was shown into a room with a filthy wash basin and told to clean up but I was not interested in that. I wanted the outside world to see the blood which was still flowing strongly down my face.

The images of Fitt's bloody head and shirt and of the incensed police officer flashed around the world and at a stroke rewrote the basic grammar of Northern Ireland politics. Disastrously for the RUC and the Unionist government, the film was to provide a worldwide audience with a vivid and endlessly repeated record of events which inflicted huge damage on O'Neill's government.

The events in Londonderry on 5 October caused an explosion of anger within the wider Catholic community. It guaranteed the civil rights movement a level of support in Northern Ireland and far beyond that was to prove irresistible. In the days and weeks afterwards, marches, sit-ins, demonstrations, protests and court appearances became almost daily occurrences. For its part the O'Neill government struggled to find ways to respond. O'Neill's instinct was that concessions had to be made quickly, but as he sought support for this many in the party demanded an old-style Unionist response to challenges by rebels. Even years later William Craig revealed a breathtaking ignorance of public relations considerations when he said: 'I thought the way the police acted on the day was fair enough. I would have intensified it. I wouldn't have given two hoots for the Labour MPs who were present, or the TV pictures.'

Comment in the British and world press and at Westminster was overwhelmingly critical, and the Westminster convention of not discussing Northern Ireland affairs evaporated. Wilson summoned O'Neill to Downing Street. The Stormont cabinet minutes for 14 October, nine days after the Londonderry march, record O'Neill as saying:

> Within the next month or so we must face Harold Wilson again. Now I ask

my colleagues to be realistic about the situation we are likely, indeed in my view certain, to face there. We shall be told that unless we can give a definite undertaking that we will introduce further reforms, Her Majesty's Government will no longer be able to stand aloof from the situation. Let's face the fact – HMG do not have to do something openly spectacular to make us feel the pinch: they merely have to be unwilling in the future to do any more exceptional things for us.

He told his ministers: 'Of course there are anti-partitionist agitators prominently at work, but can any of us truthfully say in the confines of this room that the minority has no grievance calling for remedy?' He added:

Believe me, I realise the appalling political difficulties we face. The first reaction of our own people to the antics of Fitt and Currie and the abuse of the world's press is to retreat into old hardline attitudes. But if this is all we can offer, we face a period when we govern Ulster by police power alone, against a background of mounting disorder. Are we ready, and would we be wise, to face up to this? We would have a very hard job to sell concessions to our people: but in this critical moment may this not be our duty?

William Craig was particularly opposed to concessions, warning of 'disastrous political repercussions' in the party if one man – one vote was conceded. According to the minutes, Craig 'could not agree that Mr Wilson should be allowed to tell them how to act. Although they should go to the meeting in a co-operative spirit, clearly they must be responsible to their own electorate, and Mr Wilson could be relied upon to appreciate this. Intervention would provoke a constitutional crisis and a massive uprising in the loyalist community.'

The cabinet discussed a number of reforms, but significantly could only agree on a few largely inconsequential measures and above all would not give the go-ahead for one man – one vote. A number of Unionists advocated reform, including backbencher Richard Ferguson who said, 'So long as this state of affairs continues it inhibits our progress and provides material for our opponents. Let us at least get the credit for putting our own house in order.' But such sentiments were unpopular messages to many in the Unionist community. One reason for this was the fact that to some Unionists the civil rights movement was simply the IRA and other anti-partitionists in a different guise, ostensibly asking for civil rights but actually intent on attacking the British connection. This analysis led many Unionists to oppose any concessions to the movement.

William Craig and others frequently alleged that the IRA was intimately involved in the civil rights movement, and in this they were correct. It was certainly the case that prominent IRA figures and other republicans had been present at the birth of the movement, but this was by no means the whole story. The IRA itself had had a major rethink since the abject failure of its 1950s campaign, and in the process had swung sharply to the left with prominent Marxists taking control. It moved away from the idea of using violence as its only tactic and became a left-wing pressure group agitating on issues such as housing, particularly in the south.

The civil rights banner gave the new-style IRA the chance to operate on another front and it enthusiastically backed the new phenomenon. Unionists like Craig were right when they said there were many republicans in the ranks of the civil rights movement, but wrong in thinking that the IRA was using the movement to foment trouble as a prelude to a new campaign of violence. They were also wrong in assuming that the IRA was a dominant force in the movement, since it was simply one component among many others, and never came close to taking charge of it. As an official report later put it, 'While there is evidence that members of the IRA are active in the civil rights organisation, there is no sign that they are in any sense dominant or in a position to control or direct policy.'

In a final memo to his cabinet before going to Downing Street O'Neill again unsuccessfully pushed for an agreed plan of significant reform, writing, 'It is not weakness but commonsense to go into the conference chamber with some weapons in our own hands, rather than be placed entirely on the defensive.' He was unsuccessful, however, in getting agreement for anything other than modest moves and promises to consider other reforms at some future stage.

Westminster pressure

O'Neill knew this was never going to be enough, and so it proved. The reception which he, Craig and Faulkner received at Downing Street on 4 November can only be described as a mauling at the hands of Harold Wilson and Home Secretary James Callaghan. The minutes show that in the wake of the 5 October march London–Belfast relations had changed utterly. Wilson pitched straight in, opening the meeting with a reminder that Stormont was subordinate to Westminster and following up with a direct threat to cut off some of Northern Ireland's money: some of London's subsidies, he said, 'would clearly be at risk in any situation in which the United Kingdom government needed to bring pressure to bear'. He went on to complain about the lack of one man – one vote and about Stormont emergency legislation.

Then Callaghan stepped in to warn that 'if there was any thought of just stringing the UK government along it had better be forgotten'. Agitation at Westminster for change was 'clearly about to grow on a massive scale', he said, pressing for early movement on voting reform and housing. Wilson returned to the attack with an even more overt financial threat, saying that if reform was not accelerated 'they would feel compelled to propose a radical course involving the complete liquidation of all financial agreements with Northern Ireland'.

It fell to O'Neill to reply to this onslaught, which was of a type none of his predecessors had ever had to face. Previous UK governments might have grumbled at the size of the subsidies required by Northern Ireland, but never had a prime minister directly threatened to take such drastic action. And while Wilson had previously pressed O'Neill to move faster on reform, such demands had never before been couched in terms of a financially menacing ultimatum. O'Neill responded by saying he had resolved to do everything he could to break down old animosities, adding he had been successful to the extent that the RUC had advised him that his personal safety was at risk, not from the IRA but from extreme loyalists. He argued that he had made considerable headway, with movement in terms of providing jobs for Catholics, housing, education and voting, pressing ahead in the face of opposition within his own party.

Craig added that local government reform was being energetically pursued even though this was, he said, a difficult and highly unpopular task. Disregarding Callaghan's strictures against any thought of delay, he said a review of local government which had started in 1966 would take another three years to complete. He went on at some length, saying many more houses for Catholics were planned, defending emergency legislation, and asserting that the IRA was behind the civil rights movement.

In the discussion which followed Callaghan and Wilson continued to push for speedy reforms, especially one man – one vote. Wilson illustrated the new influence of the media when he asserted: 'The television media could not be accused of falsifying their reportage of the occurrences. Opinion among moderate members, not by any means normally ill-disposed towards Northern Ireland, had been very critical of the police action at Londonderry.' Craig stoutly defended the RUC, saying that 'police action in the Londonderry riot had been examined exhaustively and minutely and there was no justification for the aspersions cast on the RUC'. His examination had completely vindicated the police, he said; Wilson's idea of holding an inquiry into the event would be 'quite disastrous' in undermining police morale.

Callaghan pointedly returned to the money issue, rehearsing in detail the financial benefits Northern Ireland received and again warning against delay in reform. Wilson summed up by saying that what the Stormont ministers had said 'could not be considered in any sense as satisfactory' and ordering them to draw up and send him a reform plan.

This very tense meeting ended with a final display of what can only be described as political obtuseness when Craig, in spite of the repeated threats to cut off money, asked for additional financial help for a large Belfast company. This caused Wilson to snap, in what may have been a loss of prime ministerial temper, that he was 'fed up with this firm which had become a kind of soup kitchen and was no good to anybody'.

With those angry words ringing in their ears the Unionists took the plane back to Stormont to consider the new realities of politics, and to ponder on whether Wilson was serious about his threat to cut off the money. O'Neill was convinced he meant it though Craig took the view that Wilson was bluffing, and that his bluff should be called. The Stormont cabinet as a whole concluded it was not a bluff and set about assembling a set of reforms which it hoped might satisfy London while proving acceptable to the Unionist party. In fact such a balancing act was never to be achieved. Ken Bloomfield summed up in his memoirs the pattern of events of the next four years as one of 'pressure for reform constantly increasing, agonising debate about further concession, and the announcement too late of compromises no longer acceptable to anyone. In a rising market, Unionism constantly tried, unsuccessfully, to buy reform at last year's prices.'

Within weeks the O'Neill government produced a five-point reform package which included establishment of a commission to run London-derry, changes in housing policy, limited voting reform, and a future review of emergency legislation. One week later, however, William Craig threw down the gauntlet both to O'Neill and to Wilson by questioning many of the proposed reforms and declaring at a rally: 'There is all this nonsense about civil rights, and behind it all there is our old traditional enemy exploiting the situation. The civil rights movement is bogus and is made up of ill-informed people who see in unrest a chance to renew the campaign of violence.' When O'Neill said in Stormont that he regretted the tone of these remarks Craig defiantly delivered the same speech again.

The temperature rose still further with a menacing confrontation between civil rights demonstrators and Paisley supporters in the city of Armagh. With an increasing sense that events were spinning out of control, O'Neill made a television appeal in December in an attempt to calm the situation. The Belfast Chamber of Trade called on shops to close early to enable people to watch the appeal, which was broadcast by both local television channels, with the *Belfast Telegraph* producing a special edition carrying what became known as 'the crossroads speech'.

Declaring that Northern Ireland was at a crossroads, O'Neill called for restraint from all citizens, saying a minority of agitators was responsible for starting the trouble in Londonderry 'but the tinder for that fire in the form of grievances, real or imaginary, had been building up for years'. To civil rights campaigners and the Catholic community he said, 'Your voice has been heard.' To Unionists he said: 'Unionism armed with justice will be a stronger cause than Unionism armed merely with strength.' Addressing both sides, he asked, 'What kind of Ulster do you want? A happy and respected province, in good standing with the rest of the UK, or a place continually torn apart by riots and demonstrations, and regarded as a political outcast?'

Within days, however, O'Neill's differences with Craig came to a head and the prime minister sacked his Home Affairs minister. This followed a speech in which Craig directly challenged Westminster's authority, declaring: 'I would resist any effort by any government in Great Britain, whatever its complexion might be, to exercise that power in any way to interfere with the proper power and jurisdiction of the parliament and government of Northern Ireland.' In the letter sacking him O'Neill referred to Craig's 'attraction to ideas of a UDI [unilateral declaration of independence] nature. Your idea of an Ulster which can go it alone is a delusion.' Craig joined the ranks of the disaffected on the backbenches, where important figures such as former minister Harry West were already calling for O'Neill's resignation.

After the speech, moderate elements in the civil rights campaign agreed to a pause in demonstrations to lower the temperature and test the government's reform promises. By this stage, however, O'Neill himself had become profoundly pessimistic. He wrote in a private letter on Christmas Eve, 'What a year! I fear 1969 will be worse. The one thing I cannot foresee in 1969 is peace. As I look in the glass darkly I see demonstrations, counter-demonstrations, meetings, rows, and general misery. In such an atmosphere of hatred would one in fact wish to continue this job – I doubt it.'

1969: end of the O'Neill era

O'Neill's pessimism was well-founded. Even as he spent Christmas in England, the People's Democracy (PD), a radical, mainly student civil rights group impatient with calls for restraint, set out on a march from Belfast to Londonderry which was to pass through a number of strongly loyalist areas. The PD regarded O'Neill's reforms as too little too late, particularly as they did not include one man – one vote. The march was challenged by groups of loyalists, many of them mobilised by eccentric Paisley ally Ronald Bunting, and there were a number of tense moments. Eventually, on 4 January 1969, it flared into open violence at Burntollet Bridge, in what would be regarded as one of the key events of the civil rights era. The march was ambushed by hundreds of loyalists at the bridge, a rural location in County Londonderry, with large numbers of attackers throwing stones and assaulting both male and female marchers with cudgels.

Once again the world's television screens were filled with images of demonstrators with blood flowing from head wounds; once again the episode was a public relations disaster for the Unionist government and the RUC. The police were accused of standing by as the ambush took place, and even of helping to engineer it, while a number of off-duty members of the B Specials were said to be among the attackers. The PD marchers themselves, who before the incident had been criticised by other civil rights campaigners as irresponsible and provocative, instantly won the sympathy of almost the entire Catholic community. The weeks which followed brought more and more demonstrations, with the RUC struggling to cope with so much unrest and street activity. The force, which had just over 3,000 members, was unused to dealing with so many marches and so much appalling publicity.

Desperately seeking to recapture the initiative, O'Neill announced the setting up of a commission to inquire into the causes of the events of 5 October in Londonderry. Such a move had been resisted by Unionists but now was seen as a way of buying time. Lord Cameron, the Scottish judge who headed the commission, would eventually produce a report highly critical of the Unionist government, but by the time he did so far worse disturbances had broken out. The decision to appoint Cameron was denounced by leading backbenchers Harry West and William Craig, but worse for O'Neill was the resignation of Brian Faulkner, which led to a bitter exchange of letters.

By the end of January Ian Paisley was in prison as a result of events during a demonstration in Armagh. In mid-February twelve hardline Unionist MPs met to demand O'Neill's resignation. It was becoming clear that the prime minister had few cards left to play, and in a final gamble he called an election in late February. It was a messy election campaign with a messy result. Most of the Ulster Unionist candidates were pro-O'Neill but a number made no secret of their opposition to him. Others were not official party nominees but nonetheless stood on a pro-O'Neill ticket. The result was a bitter and divisive campaign with much Unionist infighting.

When the votes were counted O'Neill had a bare majority in Stormont, but the Unionist vote had splintered in a way that was the stuff of Sir James Craig's nightmares. The party which had often been described as a monolith was a monolith no longer, and never would be one again. Far from delivering the decisive vote of confidence for which O'Neill had hoped, the election starkly illustrated the depth of divisions. It was a further blow to O'Neill's prestige and authority. The election was also highly significant on the Catholic side, where a number of Nationalist MPs were replaced by younger civil rights candidates, among them John Hume.

In the following weeks a number of bombings at electricity and water facilities increased the sense of instability. A thousand B Specials were mobilised to guard public utilities, together with a number of troops. The attacks were attributed by the RUC to the IRA, though much later it emerged that the bombs were the work of the loyalist UVF, which was successfully attempting to bring down O'Neill. He was later to write that he was 'blown out of office' by the bombings.

A by-election in March added to O'Neill's woes when the death of a

Unionist MP led to the arrival at Westminster of Bernadette Devlin, a student who was one of the most colourful and radical of the emerging civil rights figures. Her election and her particularly striking maiden speech in the Commons generated huge worldwide publicity, all of it adding to general Unionist frustration and to O'Neill's problems. In a final irony, just before he left office O'Neill managed to push one man – one vote through the cabinet, but the divisions in his party were too deep to allow him to continue. In the last days a relative, James Chichester-Clark, resigned from the cabinet. In a retirement address on television O'Neill referred to his gamble in calling an election, concluding that 'in many places, old fears, old prejudices and old loyalties were too strong'. In some areas loyalists celebrated his departure by lighting bonfires.

Opinions of his premiership differ. The nationalist *Irish News* said on his departure: 'The judgement of history will certainly be kinder to him than to his predecessors, who did nothing at all to bridge the chasm that divides our society and which Unionism of the anti-O'Neill variety still seems unwilling to attempt. At least Mr O'Neill tried.' Student leader Michael Farrell dismissed him however as 'a colourless figure who was largely a mouthpiece for technocrats in the civil service'. Maurice Hayes, a Catholic observer who later became a senior civil servant, praised O'Neill but listed his shortcomings as 'his lack of personal warmth, his difficulty with personal relationships, his inability to communicate, even with his friends, his defensiveness in the face of criticism and his inability to mend fences within the party'. The *Belfast Telegraph* concluded:

> Basically, his mistake was that as prime minister he never managed to establish a working relationship with his party. The leaders at grassroots level did not understand, or want to understand, his new brand of liberal Unionism, and in the end he probably had more friends outside the party than inside it. Not only had he to deal with a slumbering party, lulled by 40 years' unchallenged rule, but he had to try to modernise a province that was temperamentally unsuited and physically unprepared for change.

A Unionist journalist summed him up:

> He was essentially an Englishman. He was desperately out of touch with everything. I remember reporting on a speech he made at an Orange hall somewhere in County Down. First you had a speaker who got them all fired up with "no surrender" stuff. Then you had another who told a lot of

anti-Catholic jokes. Then you had Terence, stiffly reading out a 20-minute speech about the successes of a Belfast factory. Then you had another speaker and you were back to the good old Orange stuff again.

If O'Neill had difficulty in his relations with other Unionists, he also had little success in connecting with Catholics. A much-quoted remark he made after leaving office is cited as evidence of a supercilious and patronising attitude: 'It is frightfully hard to explain to Protestants that if you give Roman Catholics a good job and a good house they will live like Protestants, because they will see neighbours with cars and television sets. They will refuse to have eighteen children, but if a Roman Catholic is jobless and lives in the most ghastly hovel, he will rear eighteen children on National Assistance.'

Looking back on contemporary assessments, it is striking to note how much emphasis was placed on what was seen as O'Neill's unfortunate personality and his lack of personal and man-management skills. The clear implication is that a Unionist leader with greater talent might have enjoyed greater success. With hindsight it is fairly obvious that O'Neill's way of working made even more difficult what he described as a difficult and lonely office. By the time the crises of 1968 and 1969 arrived, the Stormont backbenches were stacked with disgruntled former ministers who felt unfairly treated, together with Unionist MPs who felt little personal loyalty to him. Many Unionists were prepared to go along with him, but many others simply said no, in the same way as, nearly three decades later, many would say no to the 1998 Good Friday Agreement. The Unionist machine was beginning to splinter into its constituent parts: O'Neill had not put the machine together, and did not know how to fix it.

The events of 1968 and 1969 tended to show O'Neill as a figurehead who was unable to bring Unionism into line with his own updated rhetoric. Although few now doubt that he genuinely wanted a fresh start, the gap between the rhetoric and the actual record is striking. Much of Unionism seemed impervious to the talk of change. Events such as the handling of the 5 October Londonderry march, which was first banned and then became the occasion for an intimidating display of police violence, seemed to show that the state could not cope with even peaceful protest.

O'Neill faced a nationalism reinvigorated by the civil rights movement and enlivened by a new generation of bright young leaders. From the Unionist side came not fresh thinking but Ian Paisley, a highly disruptive and destructive element, as well as opposition from within his own party. O'Neill also faced a demanding British prime minister in the person of Harold Wilson, who was not only generally unsympathetic to Unionism but also under pressure from Labour backbenchers. One of the great ironies of O'Neill's career was that he was in 1963 the first significant figure to start talking of change and reform, and in 1969 he was brought down when the debate over change spiralled out of control. He was the first Unionist leader to realise that Northern Ireland could not forever go on as it was, but he did not manage to convince Unionism as a whole of the need for change, or convince nationalists that he could deliver it. With hindsight, the notion that he might have persuaded Unionism to change its ways was as improbable as his scheme for draining Lough Neagh.

3

Descent into violence
1969–71

O'Neill's successor was his distant relative James Chichester-Clark, who was first and foremost a County Londonderry farmer and only secondarily a politician. A former Irish Guards officer, he was not only landed gentry but had an almost hereditary claim on his Stormont seat, members of his family having held it since partition. Most of the early assessments were that he was a basically decent man but not a natural politician. A Protestant official sympathetically described him as slow, phlegmatic, honest and sensible; a Catholic official called him, with less charity, 'a very limited and extremely wooden man who had been far out of his depth as a minister and was a cruel caricature as a prime minister'.

Such assessments were to be borne out, for he lasted less than two unhappy years before resigning and returning to political obscurity. He appeared to do so with a sense of relief rather than any sense of ambition thwarted. He never had much ambition to begin with, and in office soon concluded that like O'Neill he could not reconcile the competing pressures from Unionism, nationalism and London.

He had little in the way of a political honeymoon. He pressed ahead with one man – one vote and other reforms, but the focus was moving to the streets. The crunch came in August 1969, the crisis sparked off by controversy over a parade. The Apprentice Boys of Derry, an organisation similar to the Orange Order, wished to stage its traditional march in Londonderry. Both Stormont and the Wilson government debated for some time on whether the march should be allowed, concerned that there could be a major flare-up in the tinderbox atmosphere of the time. In the end permission was given and the feared flare-up duly took place, as early skirmishes between Catholics and Protestants escalated into what came to be known as the Battle of the Bogside. This amounted to something close to a full-scale uprising on the part of residents of the Bogside, a Catholic enclave close to Londonderry city centre.

It took the form of pitched battles between police and local men and youths using petrol bombs, bricks and any other missiles they could find to prevent the RUC from entering the district. Police replied with tear gas and by throwing stones back at the rioters. Fierce rioting went on for days, with many injuries on both sides: of one RUC unit of 59 men, 43 were treated for injuries.

When police vehicles at one stage breached barricades, Protestant mobs charged in after the RUC, smashing windows in Catholic houses. By all accounts the police had not planned this, but its effect was nonetheless galvanising. A local priest commented that this incursion 'brushed aside any hope of moderation or any hope of restoring calm. There was an apparent unanimity in opposition to the police force. Over the next few days the determination was so unanimous that I would only regard it as a community in revolt rather than just a street disturbance or a riot.'

In effect the authorities had, despite the deployment of a large proportion of the entire RUC, lost control of a substantial part of Londonderry¯ city. The running street battles meant that the police eventually became exhausted. Instead of abating, however, the trouble spread to other places including Belfast. This took place after a number of civil rights leaders called for diversionary activities outside Londonderry to 'take the heat' off the Bogsiders. Although most of those who made the call did not mean to stir up violence it broke out on a large scale, in particular in north and west Belfast. The city of Belfast had always had higher sectarian tensions than Londonderry, with large numbers of working-class Protestants and

Catholics living in close but uneasy proximity in places such as the Shankill and the Falls. A recurring history of violent clashes between such districts meant that outbreaks of trouble had an almost historical sanction.

The result was violence involving large numbers of Protestants and Catholics, centring on the Falls and in the Ardoyne–Crumlin Road area of north Belfast. Ancient guns came out of their attic hiding places, sending rifle and pistol shots ringing down the backstreets. Hundreds of houses were set on fire. Thousands of stones and other missiles were thrown, and barricades were erected across streets. The RUC staged baton charges, crowds surging back and forward between Protestant and Catholic areas.

Evidence given to the Scarman tribunal, the inquiry headed by a senior English judge to look into the disturbances, gives a flavour of the time. Describing the scene in Ardoyne its report said:

> The street lights in Hooker Street had been deliberately extinguished during earlier disturbances and the street was plunged in darkness, relieved only by fires burning in houses and other adjacent premises. In the Crumlin road and the side streets were to be found, and stumbled over, all the clutter of urban rioting – barricades, debris, flame, and liquid petrol. Normal traffic movement had stopped: the noise of hostile, jeering crowds, the crackle and explosions of burning buildings, and the shattering of glass had enveloped the area. But, save where the fighting was in progress, the streets were empty.

Amid all the chaos and destruction eight people lay dead, four of them killed by the RUC and another by B Specials. The police force, which was then only 3,000-strong, had reached its limits and with its men exhausted and in many cases injured Chichester-Clark asked London to send in troops to restore order. He did so with the greatest reluctance, since Wilson and Callaghan had already made it clear that they did not wish to deploy the military. They had also made it clear that if troops did go in, the political balance between Belfast and London would change fundamentally, since they would not place the army under Stormont control. When the first troops marched nervously on to the streets of Londonderry and Belfast, therefore, they did so with many political strings attached.

Soldiers on the streets

Callaghan was travelling in an RAF plane when the formal request for troops came through. He recorded in his memoirs that he was given a message on a signal pad: 'It tersely informed us that an official request for the use of troops had been made. I immediately scribbled "permission granted" on the pad and handed it back to the navigator. A few minutes later troops began to relieve the police in the Bogside amid loud jubilation from the inhabitants.' The arrival of the soldiers was welcomed by Catholics and brought a temporary respite from the violence, but as the smoke cleared the extent of the damage became all too clear. In addition to the eight deaths at least 750 people were injured, 150 of them having suffered gunshot wounds. 180 homes and other buildings were demolished, and 90 required major repair. Compensation was estimated to cost at least £2.25 million.

Around 1,800 families had fled their homes in the disturbances: the sight of their pathetic belongings being heaped on to lorries provided one of the abiding images of the troubles. Belfast had a long history of sectarian clashes; now it was permanently and physically scarred by ugly barricades across many of its mean streets. The original unofficial improvised barriers made of commandeered cars, corrugated iron and whatever else came to hand were replaced, as the years passed and violence continued, by larger and more substantial permanent brick and metal structures erected by the authorities. These 'peacelines' were to last into the twenty-first century.

The damage caused by the violence of August 1969 was not confined to the strictly physical. It deepened community divisions and increased bitterness, and it wrecked whatever relationship existed between a large proportion of the Catholic community and the RUC. Part of the Bogside became a 'no-go area', sealed off by barricades which remained in position until 1972.

Some of those who had been killed by the RUC died in controversial circumstances. In one incident an eight-year-old boy was killed in his Falls Road bedroom when a bullet from a heavy machine gun fired from an RUC armoured car ripped through walls and hit him in the head. In addition to the four Catholics killed on and around 14 August, three other men died following other brushes with the police in July and August. There were many stories of B Specials and on occasion RUC officers acting in concert with loyalist rioters during battles with Catholics. These reports sealed the fate of the B Specials, who were to be disbanded within months, and represented another grievous blow to the credibility of the RUC.

The relationship between the Westminster and Stormont governments also changed, Wilson and Callaghan taking a much more hands-on approach and the latter immersing himself in policy details. London officials were stationed in Belfast to act as London's eyes and ears, to pass on instructions to Stormont and, in Callaghan's words, to 'put some stiffening into the administration'. The most senior official sent over to Belfast reported back to London on the Stormont cabinet: 'In my view they were not evil men bent on maintaining power at all costs. They were decent but bewildered men, out of their depth in the face of the magnitude of their problem. I was convinced that not only did they want to do the right thing; they also wanted to be told what was the right thing to do.'

Senior Belfast civil servant Ken Bloomfield wrote that Stormont became 'a client regime, under constant supervision both at ministerial and official levels'. Faulkner wrote in his memoirs that Callaghan became 'Big Brother', adding, 'I increasingly felt that he was pressurizing and bullying Chichester-Clark into taking hasty decisions'. Faulkner was to write scornfully of Callaghan's trips to Belfast as 'superficial circuses and messianic visits'. Unionists objected both to Callaghan's close involvement and to the fact that in their eyes he took the nationalist side. When he visited the Bogside he was given a hero's welcome by Catholics who felt his presence signified an end to Unionist rule.

He and Wilson pressed Unionists hard for more and more movement on the reform front. Within a short time London had pushed through a reform package which included the end of the B Specials, an overhaul of policing and other measures. Less than two months after the mid-August violence the committee investigating policing, headed by Lord Hunt, recommended a thorough-going reform of the RUC, including its disarming, together with the abolition of the B Specials. A few months later an English policeman, Sir Arthur Young, was appointed head of the RUC with a brief to modernise the force.

Publication of the Hunt report was the occasion for not just political controversy but serious violence. Loyalists rioted on the Shankill Road in protest against the reforms, the irony being that when the Protestant guns came out they killed a member of the RUC. Constable Victor Arbuckle, the first member of the force to die in the troubles, was shot by loyalists protesting in defence of the RUC.

An important player arrived on the stage at this point in the form of the Irish Republic. Some in the south viewed the events of August 1969 as a valuable political opportunity, while others saw them as a grave danger to the stability of the southern state. When the explosion of violence took place the Taoiseach was Jack Lynch, a mild-mannered politician who had replaced Seán Lemass as leader of Fianna Fáil, the most republican-leaning of the southern parties. Lynch had met Terence O'Neill on several occasions but had not made a great priority of the Northern Ireland question. However, the violent upheaval and the first deaths posed the most fundamental of challenges to the south, which was suddenly confronted with the thorny unfinished business of partition. As one writer put it: 'The violence started and within a week set the ghosts of 50 years on the march.' A series of prominent northern nationalists streamed to Dublin asking for help. Many of them, including some leading political figures, asked for guns, arguing that force was the only way to prevent loyalists rampaging into the Falls and Ardoyne. The southern public had much sympathy with their northern co-religionists, though many would have drawn the line at sending them weaponry. Some of Lynch's ministers are believed to have favoured despatching not only guns but also Irish soldiers to the north.

Sending in troops would have been more of a token gesture than an actual invasion, since the Irish army was tiny in comparison to its British counterpart, with the capacity to hold perhaps a town or two for a very short time. Lynch opted for a less drastic line, though it was one which enraged Unionists. In a broadcast during the August 1969 crisis he declared: 'It is clear that the Irish government can no longer stand by and see innocent people injured and perhaps worse.' (This has gone down in popular folklore as the 'not stand idly by' speech, though Lynch did not use the adverb.) He also announced the setting up of field hospitals close to the border to treat injured northerners.

This hugely important intervention from a Taoiseach who could literally no longer stand by as the north exploded on his doorstep took Dublin policy further than it had ever gone before. But it also defined its limitations. There was support for northern nationalists but first and foremost the aim was to protect the southern state against becoming physically embroiled in the northern conflagration. Unionists condemned the broadcast, Faulkner accusing Lynch of 'pouring fuel on the northern flame in the hope that out of the chaos he would reap some benefits in terms of progress towards a united Ireland'. The broadcast caused Callaghan to wonder whether the field hospitals 'might conceivably be a blind for further troop movements'. Although Callaghan said in his memoirs that he did not really believe the south would invade, he added that officials discussed deploying British troops on the border, just in case.

Lynch made other moves. Some men from Londonderry were given arms training by Irish soldiers in Donegal, while at one point 500 rifles were moved up to the border. The government allocated £100,000 for 'the relief of distress', some of which would mysteriously vanish. Whether those in power in London, Belfast or Dublin liked it or not, and most did not, the violence of August 1969 brought the southern state into the northern political equation. In the years that followed, Dublin never again extricated itself from the Northern Ireland issue, though the south's private position was very different from its public position that Irish unity was the only solution. One of Harold Wilson's aides would later describe a lunch at which the British Labour leader floated a plan for a united Ireland: 'The fascinating moment at the Taoiseach's lunch came when Harold Wilson put forward the plan for turning the dream of unity into reality. I had thought they would jump for joy, but their reaction was more akin to falling through the floor.'

The northern violence also brought about hugely important changes within republicanism. Of the 1,800 families who fled their homes, the Catholic community had very much come off worst. 1,500 of those who moved were Catholic, which meant that more than 5 per cent of all Catholic households in Belfast were displaced. More than 80 per cent of the premises damaged were occupied by Catholics, and six of the eight people killed in mid-August were Catholics. Since one of the roles of the IRA was supposed to be the defence of such areas against incursions by the security forces or loyalists, much criticism was directed against the organisation for its evident ineffectiveness. The bitter phrase 'IRA – I ran away' is famously said to have appeared on a wall in the Falls Road area, reflecting the feelings of working-class nationalists in west and north Belfast that the IRA had failed them.

The first great hero of republicanism was Wolfe Tone, who was associated with the 1798 rebellion and the aspiration of bringing together Catholics and Protestants in the common name of Irishman. Although that was the high mythic theory of republicanism, the practical reality was that the majority of Catholics did not support the IRA, and looked to them only in times of high tension. In such times, and August 1969 was one of them, the IRA was supposed to protect areas such as the Falls and

Ardoyne against attack. The death toll, the pattern of destruction of property and the high number of Catholic refugees provided the starkest testimony that the IRA had not been organised or armed when the crisis came. The consensus in the Catholic ghetto backstreets was that an effective defence force was needed, and so a new IRA came into being. This new group may have emerged to defend the ghettos, but it would before long develop into an aggressive killing machine.

By 1969 the IRA was guided by left-wing theory and essentially led from the south of Ireland. It was so strongly wedded to the theory of forging working-class unity between Protestants and Catholics that even the August 1969 spasm of sectarian violence was not enough to shift its leadership from this quixotic notion. It was against this background that the fateful split occurred, late in 1969, which brought into being the Official and Provisional wings of the IRA. Broadly speaking the Officials were Marxists while the Provisionals were republican traditionalists, many of whom had been unhappy for some time with the IRA's direction. (They took their name from the proclamation used in the 1916 rising, which referred to a provisional government for a new Republic. The Officials technically retained leadership of the organisation, but the Provisionals were quickly to become the more numerous.)

The split took place following a series of tense and angry meetings of both the IRA and Sinn Féin. As the Officials continued to edge towards conventional politics the Provisionals cut their links, establishing the Provisional IRA and Provisional Sinn Féin. They dismissed what they viewed as the fanciful and unrealistic notions of the Officials and instead prepared for battle. Within months their approach was being described as 'combined defence and retaliation'.

On the Protestant side too men were forming vigilante groups and defence organisations, some of which would in time mutate into fully fledged paramilitary groups. More deaths followed those of August 1969 as tensions remained at a high level. In September a Protestant vigilante was shot dead following a dispute with Catholic counterparts in Belfast; some weeks later a Londonderry Protestant was kicked to death by Catholics during a confrontation between rival groups. On the night of the Arbuckle killing two Shankill Road Protestants were killed by army bullets. One, who was hit by a ricochet, was said 'to have been wandering about to see what was going on that night'. Then a UVF member blew himself up while attempting to set off a bomb in the Republic. Next came the first IRA fatality of the troubles, killed in a car crash while on active service: with him in the car at the time was the future president of Sinn Féin, Gerry Adams. On the surface, calm had been restored by the arrival of troops, but in the backstreets both republicans and loyalists were readying themselves for future bouts of confrontation.

1970–71: the violence increases

The year 1970 was to see continuing deterioration rather than any new stability. Callaghan kept up the pressure to maintain momentum in the reform programme. Chichester-Clark complied, though always against a background of grumbling and dissatisfaction from Unionist hardliners. This dissension in the grassroots was evident when votes drained away from the main Unionist party to Ian Paisley, who in this year was elected first to Stormont and then to Westminster. On the streets the situation degenerated as one deadly milestone after another was passed. Republicans and loyalists exchanged shots while the army came more and more into conflict with republicans and large sections of working-class Catholics, particularly in Belfast.

In June three Protestant men were shot dead by the IRA in north Belfast during large-scale rioting following an Orange march. Gerry Adams later noted: 'In this instance the IRA were ready and waiting and in the ensuing gun battle three loyalists were killed.' On the same day two more Protestants and a Catholic man died during clashes in and around the grounds of a Catholic church, St Matthew's, on the edge of the small Catholic enclave of Short Strand in east Belfast. A senior Belfast IRA leader of the time, Billy McKee, who was seriously injured in the St Matthew's church clashes, entered republican folklore by reputedly holding off Protestant gunmen almost single-handed and preventing a loyalist invasion of the Short Strand. His action did much to restore the ghetto credibility of the IRA as defenders of Catholic districts.

In early July came the Falls Road curfew, which can be seen as a final poisoning of the initially good relationship between Catholics and British troops. Following a confrontation between soldiers and locals, a large area of the Lower Falls district was sealed off by the army for several days while soldiers were sent in to conduct rigorous house-to-house searches. The exercise entailed ordering perhaps 20,000 people not to leave their homes. The searches uncovered more than one hundred weapons but in the process considerable damage was done to hundreds of households as soldiers prised up floorboards and ransacked rooms. In addition to such personal indignities there were four deaths, all caused by the army: three men were shot dead by troops while a fourth was crushed by a military vehicle. None of those killed had any IRA or other extreme connections. The sense that the army was being deployed against the general Catholic population was compounded when troops brought in two Unionist ministers to tour the area in armoured cars.

A senior civil servant recalled: 'It is hard to remember any other incident that so clearly began the politicisation and alienation of a community.' A moderate local councillor wrote: 'Overnight the population turned from neutral or even sympathetic support for the military to outright hatred of everything related to the security forces. I witnessed voters and workers turn against us to join the Provisionals. Even some of our most dedicated workers and supporters turned against us.'

Later in July came another violent landmark when the army shot dead a Catholic teenager in disputed circumstances during a riot in north Belfast. The army claim that he was a petrol-bomber was denied by local people. The tougher military line coincided with a change of government at Westminster. Labour lost the general election in June, with Wilson and Callaghan replaced by Conservative leader Edward Heath as prime minister and Reginald Maudling as Home Secretary.

Maudling, who had a reputation for being bright but lazy, provided a marked contrast to Callaghan, who had been a direct and powerful presence, pushing hard for reforms. Maudling was both less forceful and less absorbed by the conflict than Callaghan had been. He also assumed responsibility at a less promising time, at a point when violence, though by no means reaching the heights it would later touch, had become a background constant. A local civil servant later wrote: 'What you got from Maudling was the impression of a massive intelligence, only partly in gear, which moved sideways towards the problem, like a crab, and then scuttled back into its hole without actually coming to grips with it.'

The two quotations with which Maudling will forever be associated both speak to a Tory sense of pessimism and lack of firm ideas. First he created a political storm when he spoke of the concept of 'an acceptable level of violence', which was taken as a fatalistic acknowledgement that violence might never come to an end. And, second, he is said to have said to a stewardess, while flying back to London after a fruitless round of meetings in Belfast, 'What a bloody awful country. For God's sake bring me a large Scotch.' (Some versions render this as a gin and tonic, but the sentiment remains the same.)

With a less forceful sense of direction coming from the government, some of the initiative seeped across to the army who, with the enthusiastic backing of the Chichester-Clark administration, employed more aggressive tactics such as the curfew. But the tougher line did nothing to halt the general deterioration, and in August the first two RUC officers to be killed by the IRA died in south Armagh.

Politically Chichester-Clark found himself caught in the same permanently uncomfortable position as had O'Neill. On the one hand London continued to press for more and more political change; on the other Unionism, as Paisley's electoral successes showed, was becoming more hardline. And all this took place against a difficult background of continuing violence. Chichester-Clark's reforms included the introduction of one man – one vote and important changes in policing and housing. The Unionist grassroots were either unenthusiastic or downright hostile to this programme, but most of all they demanded tougher security. Since Unionists believed in a military solution, the demands were to 'Stop the army fighting with one hand behind its back', and to 'Go in there after them', meaning that the army should pursue the IRA into republican areas. Internment without trial, sealing the border, and flooding republican areas with troops were among the popular Unionist solutions. Chichester-Clark tried in vain to persuade the grassroots that the army should be subject to political restrictions, saying later, 'They were making it very difficult for me, at meeting after meeting. They could not grasp the fact that the army could not go in with enormous force.'

He also tried with equal lack of success to persuade the grassroots, as O'Neill had before him, that final authority rested with Westminster rather than Stormont. At one party gathering he opposed the motion 'That we will be masters in our own house', telling delegates that soon he would be in London seeking more money. He posed the question: 'Am I to go to London and say, "We want all this support and oh, by the way, my party ask you to keep your noses out of our business"?' He warned that unless the Unionist party could deliver 'reasonable policies of fairness and justice for everyone' then it might face direct rule from London. But he had neither the skills nor the opportunity to balance the competing forces or to seize the political initiative; the general feeling during his premiership was that he was out of his depth.

Important developments took place within nationalism, north and south, in the second half of 1970. The civil rights movement faded in importance, to be superseded by a new grouping, the Social Democratic and Labour party (SDLP), as the principal voice of nationalism in the north. The party consisted principally of anti-Unionist Stormont MPs, some from the labour tradition and some who had come to prominence in the civil rights movement. With Gerry Fitt as leader and John Hume as its chief strategist, the party would remain the largest northern nationalist grouping throughout the troubles.

In the south, meanwhile, politically sensational events took place. Following reports of an illegal attempt to import arms for the north, Taoiseach Jack Lynch had sacked two of his most senior ministers, Neil Blaney and the highly ambitious Charles Haughey. A third minister resigned in protest. Soon afterwards Haughey and Blaney were charged with conspiring to import arms and ammunition into Ireland. The case against Blaney was dropped at an early stage but Haughey went on trial, together with an Irish army intelligence officer, a senior republican from Belfast, and a Belgian businessman. All were acquitted by a Dublin jury following a trial in which Haughey and another cabinet minister flatly contradicted each other's testimony. When the verdicts came in, Haughey directly challenged Lynch, saying those responsible 'for this debacle should do the honourable thing'. Lynch, however, pointedly observed that he still believed there had been an attempt to bring in guns, and faced Haughey down. The episode remains a mysterious one, with few believing that the whole truth emerged. It did nothing to lessen Unionist suspicions of southern politicians, especially Haughey, who was later to become Taoiseach.

In Belfast the sense of crisis grew with an escalation of violence in early 1971. In February the deaths took place, on the same night in north Belfast, of the first soldier to be shot by the IRA, and the first IRA member to be shot by the army. Three days later an IRA bomb placed on a County Tyrone mountain for members of the security forces instead killed five civilians on their way to service a BBC transmitter. Later in the same month two policemen were shot dead, again in north Belfast.

In March came an incident which was regarded as a new low point. Three Scottish soldiers who had been drinking off-duty in a Belfast bar were lured to a lonely road on the outskirts of the city and shot dead by the IRA. The huge impact of their killings is still remembered by many as one of the key points in Northern Ireland's descent into full-scale violence. Three soldiers had already died in the troubles, but the Scottish soldiers were the first to be killed off-duty; two of them were brothers who were aged only seventeen and eighteen. A newspaper editorial commented, 'After all the horrors of recent weeks and months, Ulster people have almost lost the capacity for feeling shock. But the ruthless murder of three defenceless young soldiers has cut to the quick. These were cold-blooded executions for purely political reasons.'

As their funerals took place in Scotland, an estimated 30,000 people attended rallies in Belfast and elsewhere. Four thousand shipyard workers marched in Belfast demanding internment. A few days later Chichester-Clark flew to London to ask Heath for tougher security measures. When Heath offered only extra troops, Chichester-Clark returned to Belfast and resigned, stepping down from office with an almost visible sense of relief.

Faulkner becomes prime minister

Chichester-Clark was succeeded as Stormont prime minister by Brian Faulkner, who was easily the most talented Unionist politician of the time. Faulkner won the leadership election comfortably, defeating William Craig by twenty-six votes to four. It was widely said, correctly as it turned out, that he was probably Unionism's last chance to save the Stormont system. After O'Neill and Chichester-Clark, both of whom had the whiff of being amateurs in politics, Faulkner looked every inch the professional politician. He brought to the post of prime minister his obvious ability, both as an administrator and as a communicator and in both fields he was probably the finest Unionism had ever produced. He was credited with putting down the IRA's 1950s campaign, principally through the use of internment, and in the 1960s had been conspicuously successful in attracting new industry from abroad.

An ambitious man, Faulkner thought he should have had the premiership instead of O'Neill in 1963. He believed it was his again in 1969, only to be pipped by one vote by Chichester-Clark. Within the Unionist party he had moved tactically over the years from his early days as a stalwart traditionalist to a less distinct standpoint in the O'Neill years. But although his abilities were too obvious to be denied, he had also acquired a reputation for shiftiness and lack of loyalty. O'Neill and many others believed that during his premiership Faulkner had repeatedly tried to undermine him. During one leadership rumble against O'Neill, Faulkner had studiously and skilfully equivocated, causing one political journalist to accuse him of 'speaking in conundrums' and to comment: 'His attempts to keep out of trouble become more and more devious and unacceptable to those who above all respect a politician who talks straight from the shoulder.' This was the politician who now attempted to master the balancing act that had defeated both O'Neill and Chichester-Clark. London had a healthy respect for his talents and hoped he might succeed where his predecessors had failed, thus avoiding a resort to direct rule from Westminster.

From the start Faulkner attempted to strike a balance which would reassure both the Unionist grassroots and the British government through a combination of security and political measures. He first constructed a government which encompassed both wings of the Unionist party, the liberal and the hardline, as well as the first-ever non-Unionist cabinet minister in the form of an NILP politician. While it was true that the NILP man was neither a Catholic nor a nationalist and that the appointment was for only six months, this was nonetheless seen as an imaginative step.

Faulkner made his big political move in June 1971 by offering a shake-up of Stormont. Under his proposals three new committees would be introduced to review policy and advise on legislation, with opposition members chairing two of them. At first sight these appeared to be influential posts, and the SDLP gave the idea an initial welcome and entered talks on the proposals. Within weeks, however, politics was overtaken by events on the streets. To balance his political concessions, Faulkner had successfully pressed London for a tougher army approach, himself announcing in Stormont: 'Any soldier seeing any person with a weapon or acting suspiciously may, depending on the circumstances, fire to warn or with effect without waiting for orders.'

One result of this was seen in July when soldiers shot dead two Catholics, a man and a teenager, during disturbances in Londonderry. The authorities said the man had a gun and the teenager had a bomb, while local people insisted both were unarmed. The incident disrupted the political talks as the SDLP warned it would withdraw from Stormont unless an independent inquiry was established to investigate the deaths. When no inquiry was set up, the SDLP walked out of Stormont never to return, and Faulkner's committee offer became academic.

Internment

Faulkner was intent on balancing his Stormont committees offer with a radical security initiative in the form of internment without trial. Having helped build his own reputation with the use of internment in the 1950s, he saw it as a panacea which would halt the violence and in time provide a more peaceful atmosphere in which political progress would be easier. Others saw it as a measure of last resort and even desperation. Internment meant stepping outside the rule of law and abandoning legal procedures in favour of simply rounding up suspects and putting them behind bars without benefit of trial. It was bound to attract strong condemnation from nationalist and human rights bodies both at home and internationally.

The feeling which prevailed in both the Unionist and British governments was simply that the steady deterioration could not be allowed to continue. Maudling wrote later of internment: 'No one could be certain what would be the consequences, yet the question was simply this: what other measures could be taken?' He added, 'I think if we hadn't introduced internment there was the danger of the Protestant backlash. What we were always worried about was if people did not think the British government were doing all they could to deal with violence, they might take the law into their own hands.' As this indicates, the government had an eye not just to the rising tide of IRA activity but also to the possibility of an eruption of loyalist violence. The steadily rising graph of shootings and bombings, as well as the street rioting in republican districts, contributed to the sense that something had to be done.

It was for Faulkner something close to a last throw of the dice. Success would have meant he might go down in history as the man who ended the troubles and led Northern Ireland into a bright new future. And London fervently hoped he could pull it off, for he looked like the last best chance to stave off direct rule. A Northern Ireland official later wrote that all involved knew how high the stakes were, with London making it clear that if internment failed 'very fundamental questions could arise'.

So it was that in the early hours of 9 August 1971 a large-scale arrest operation, codenamed Operation Demetrius, was launched, with thousands of troops and police despatched to round up the IRA. The first swoops resulted in around 340 arrests, but almost immediately it became clear that little was going according to plan. It quickly emerged that the RUC Special Branch had not kept pace with the rapidly expanding

Provisional IRA and that its files were out of date and inaccurate. In any event many IRA men, suspecting that internment was on the way, had already gone on the run. The troops who were sent to make the arrests often found themselves at the wrong house, or finding not an IRA suspect but his father, or brother. Many of these were nonetheless arrested and taken in for 'screening'. Allegations that soldiers had in the process often used brutal methods were denied by the authorities but often substantiated by later inquiries and court proceedings. Many of those held were released within hours or days, often traumatised, radicalised and infuriated by the experience. It later emerged that more than a dozen suspects had been given special experimental interrogation treatment. They were subjected to sensory deprivation techniques which included the denial of sleep and food and being forced to stand spreadeagled against a wall for long periods. Taped electronic 'white noise' sounds were continuously played to complete the disorientation. Years later the European Court of Human Rights characterised this episode as 'inhuman and degrading' treatment.

Within two days more than a hundred of those detained were released, a pattern which was to be repeated in the months that followed: in the first six months of internment over 2,400 people were arrested, and most of them were freed after a short time in custody. The fact that this was clearly a highly inefficient operation was demonstrated both by the number of early releases and, most of all, by an eruption of violence on the streets. In the immediate aftermath of the first arrests widespread violence broke out in many areas, with major gun battles between the army and the IRA sometimes lasting for hours.

One author gave a flavour of the disruption in Belfast:

> The city was in turmoil, with confusion, distress and fear on all sides. Local people were erecting improvised barricades to seal off entry to Catholic areas, which were becoming increasingly isolated and cut off. Public transport had broken down, and there was increasingly a breakdown in services. There was ominous rattling of hundreds of bin-lids as communities sent out a call to arms and for defenders to man the ramparts. Buses were being hijacked on all sides, cars were dragged from burned-out showrooms, builders' skips, rubble, anything was being used to make barriers. Milk vans were being commandeered and the bottles used to make petrol bombs, pavements were being ripped up for missiles and to

build barricades. Smoke, fire, disorder, noise and impending disaster were everywhere.

A great deal of property was destroyed, while there was large-scale evacuation and flight by families. According to one official estimate at least 2,000 and possibly more than 2,500 families moved home around August 1971. Far from halting the violence, internment increased it tremendously. In 1971, before 9 August 31 people were killed; in the rest of August 35 died. Between 9 August and the end of the year around 150 people were killed. The dead included soldiers, members of the IRA and many civilians.

For Faulkner and for the rest of society this was not deliverance but something close to disaster, the opening of a new phase with a much higher level of violence. Confronted with this sharp deterioration Faulkner and Heath decided to press on in the hope of an eventual breakthrough against the IRA; but it was a breakthrough that never came. As the deaths continued Faulkner defiantly defended his policy, proclaiming: 'You can no more deal with such deep rooted terror without toughness and determination than you can excise a deep seated tumour without cutting the flesh. It is not a pleasant business. Sometimes innocent people will suffer.' He argued that internment was working: 'The army is fighting back, not only fighting back but taking the offensive, and now, loud and clear, we hear the squeal of the increasingly cornered rat.'

The use of internment was to continue for another four years, during which time it attracted much condemnation of Britain and never looked like defeating the IRA. It came to be almost universally regarded as a misjudgement of historic proportions which inflicted tremendous damage both politically and in terms of fatalities. It was also seen by nationalists as a cynical weapon, since they regarded Faulkner's primary motive not as a concern to reduce violence but as the partisan purpose of propping up his government and preserving Stormont. The internment process was an openly political one, Faulkner personally signing each individual internment order.

The ineptitude of the RUC Special Branch was compounded by the casual brutality used by troops during and after the arrest operations, often on people who were not members of the IRA. Internees were mostly held in poor conditions, some of them on an ageing ship in Belfast Lough and later at Long Kesh near Belfast. This was a former airfield whose rusty

Nissen huts and barbed wire, smacking as they did of a World War Two prison camp, constituted another long-running public relations setback for the authorities.

Faulkner was heavily criticised for the fact that not a single loyalist had been detained, leading to charges of blatant partiality. Faulkner recorded that Maudling had said to him, 'Lift some Protestants if you can', a remark which if accurately reported reveals much cynicism but also some grasp of public relations considerations. The failure to use internment against loyalists seemed to many to confirm that it was as much a political device as a security measure. Sir John Peck, then British ambassador to Dublin, wrote later: 'Internment attacked the Catholic community as a whole. What was worse, it was directed solely against the Catholics, although there were many Protestants who provided just as strong grounds for internment.'

The mood across the Catholic and nationalist community was thus one of communal outrage against a measure they viewed as the essence of injustice. In physical terms many Catholic working-class areas of Belfast were for months afterwards convulsed by gun battles and killings on the streets, while thousands of homes were searched by the army. In 1971 more than 170 people were killed; a further 2,600 were injured and 17,000 homes were searched. Unsurprisingly, there was massive alienation from authority. To the outside world internment might be seen as a response to IRA violence, but many Catholics in areas such as west Belfast regarded IRA activity as a response to violence from the authorities.

The upsurge in IRA violence demonstrated the underlying support the organisation could command among working-class Catholics. The Stormont and British rhetoric of the time commonly spoke of a handful of men of violence holding communities to ransom. The prevailing Unionist theory was that there was a military solution to the troubles and that the IRA could be isolated and defeated almost without reference to the wider political picture: hence Faulkner's image of 'excising a deep seated tumour'.

The fact that the IRA was able to escalate its violence in the wake of internment showed that in its strongholds it had a substantial and indeed rapidly expanding reservoir from which to draw recruits and other support. The official rhetoric had it that the time had come for ordinary Catholics to choose between terrorists and the men of peace, the security forces. The flaw in this projection was that, at ghetto street level, the security forces looked not so much like men of peace as agents of a state intent on attacking their neighbourhoods. The government had imperfect control over the squaddies on the street, who could often look on all Catholics as the enemy. There were innumerable cases of Catholic youths being kicked and punched, and sometimes arrested and ill-treated for no good reason; at the time these were airily dismissed as republican propaganda. The many thousands of house searches, often carried out as routine rather than as a result of information, similarly generated much bitterness. The authorities said they were a military necessity but the inevitable disruption and indignities generated great resentment among those inconvenienced, many of whom had no republican connections.

Another source of grievance was the considerable number of Catholics who died at the hands of troops. This is a largely disregarded phenomenon but it was especially evident in the second half of 1971. Of the 150 people who died in that period, almost half were Catholic civilians; and of these around 29 were killed by soldiers. In some cases the army acknowledged that its men were at fault and apologised for causing deaths. In other cases, including the deaths of teenagers as young as thirteen who were killed during riots, the army denied that disproportionate force had been used.

But in many other instances they said that men and youths they had shot dead had been armed when soldiers had shot them. In some cases this may have been true, but in most it was not. The non-involvement of many of those killed became evident later, at inquests or when the authorities quietly paid out substantial compensation to relatives of the dead. At the time, however, the army insisted that many of those shot were gunmen. Local claims that this was untrue were generally dismissed, the outside world tending to accept the word of officialdom rather than that of Falls Road residents. But locals had a fair idea of who was and who was not a gunman among their neighbours, and in some districts the feeling was universal that the army had not only shot without justification but had then denigrated those killed as gunmen when they were not. This sense was captured by John Hume in a case when a soldier shot dead in Londonderry a man said to be aiming a rifle at an army post. Saying that the army's statement was 'without the slightest shred of truth', Hume asked:

Can the army not in this case at least tell the full truth about what happened? He was not armed, nor had he any association with any sort of political body in this city. He was walking in the street with some friends at the time. He was shot down by an army bullet. Army statements about incidents in Derry have lost all credibility among people because they have been proved incorrect so often.

All of this meant that many non-republicans and their families became radicalised and often became republicans. But in the wake of internment Catholic alienation was almost complete, stretching well beyond republican districts. The SDLP, which had already withdrawn from Stormont over the two Londonderry killings, announced that it would not return until internment was ended. The party gave its support to a rent and rates strike which was so widely supported that the authorities estimated that 20 per cent of the entire population had joined it. In some areas more than 90 per cent of tenants were involved. Many Catholics withdrew from public life, while most nationalist representatives ceased to attend local councils. Some 200 Catholic members left the Ulster Defence Regiment (UDR), the force which had replaced the B Specials in 1970.

Anglo-Irish relations took a severe battering. Jack Lynch had cautioned strongly against internment, as Sir John Peck recorded in his memoirs. The Taoiseach had delivered to him, he wrote, 'the most serious and solemn warning that the consequences in the north would be catastrophic: for every man put behind the wire a hundred would volunteer'. Heath and Lynch took part in an extraordinarily angry public exchange of messages in the days after internment, momentarily flinging diplomatic convention to the wind. Lynch said that internment and military solutions had failed and that he supported 'the policy of passive resistance now being pursued by the non-Unionist population'. Heath in reply said his message was 'unjustifiable in its contents and unacceptable in its attempt to interfere in the affairs of the United Kingdom'. There was much more in this vein.

Within a few weeks, the two premiers had calmed down and Lynch flew to London to meet Heath. Personal contacts did not remove the difficulties, however, since Heath continued to put much store in a security solution while Lynch held that the problem was at root political. There was little or no personal affinity between them, Peck recording dryly that 'it would be an abuse of the English language to describe the talks as negotiations'. The ambassador noted in his memoirs: 'For the first half of my term of duty in Dublin I thought it very important that the prime minister and the Taoiseach should get together. For the second half

I rather hoped that they could be kept apart. It was not quite a dialogue of the deaf but I sometimes felt that a pair of powerful hearing aids would come in handy.'

There were many matters on which the two premiers were never to agree, in particular in the security field, with Lynch saying internment should be ended and Heath retorting that the Irish government should take much stronger action against the IRA south of the border. Many even worse Anglo-Irish spats lay ahead, yet in one area, the shape of future government in Northern Ireland, London and Dublin were gradually converging.

Although Faulkner, like Chichester-Clark before him, brought a raft of incremental reforms into effect, the policy of both London and Dublin was evolving. Crucially, they both moved away from the idea that a solution lay in the model of a Unionist government delivering a stream of concessions to nationalists. Both Chichester-Clark and Faulkner had produced reform after reform, to disapproving mutterings from the Protestant grassroots; but now the idea took hold that what was needed was not reforms but participation.

London and Dublin found common ground in the concept that Catholics had to be brought into government. They would never wholly identify with the state, the theory ran, if they remained in perpetual opposition, and so had to become part of the fabric of administration. This idea gained currency, giving rise to the emergence of terms such as 'community government'. The initials 'PAG' made an appearance, signifying what was defined as a 'permanent, active and guaranteed role for the majority and minority alike'.

Dublin wanted the abolition of Stormont and remained formally committed to the traditional goal of Irish unity. But Lynch was also thinking in terms of nationalist involvement in government, through SDLP participation in a new administration and through new north–south links. Heath did not want to abolish Stormont but he too was thinking of a power-sharing arrangement, as he later wrote: 'In order to give Catholics a real stake in society, it was not enough for them to be protected from discrimination. They also had to be given a positive role in governing the country in which they lived. I also believed that the Republic of Ireland had to be brought into the relationship once more.'

In September Heath took pride in staging a meeting involving himself, Lynch and Faulkner, which he described as one of the historic events of his premiership. Faulkner attracted criticism from hardliners for agreeing to take part in the meeting but felt he could not turn down Heath's invitation. Internment had delivered not peace but increased violence and in doing so had comprehensively wiped out the possibility of any new agreement on Faulkner's terms. The SDLP was adamant it would not return to Stormont while internment lasted. From Faulkner's point of view, however, his fate depended on persisting with internment until it began to produce positive results. Heath was impatiently casting around for new ideas, and was clearly thinking in terms of involving Dublin, an idea bound to stir strong Unionist opposition.

Even worse, from the point of view of Faulkner and other Unionists, was the fact that Harold Wilson, as leader of the opposition, was attempting to put a united Ireland on the British political agenda. In November he presented in the Commons a convoluted scheme which envisaged Irish unity in fifteen years, with the south rejoining the Commonwealth. This was to come to nothing, but it was unsettling to Unionists, showing as it did that major British political figures were beginning to think the previously unthinkable. In response Faulkner persisted with his ideas for new Stormont committees chaired by nationalist politicians, and took the unprecedented step of appointing to his cabinet G.B. Newe, a respected Catholic community worker who was active in public life but attached to no political party. He thus became the first ever Catholic Stormont minister. Nationalists criticised Newe for swimming against the abstentionist nationalist tide, denouncing the appointment as gimmickry.

In the wake of internment the problem had become one of battling simply to keep the administration functioning. The seriousness of the situation was evident in a meeting between Heath and Faulkner in October 1971, the minutes of which were released in 2000 in advance of the normal thirty-year rule as part of documentation for the Bloody Sunday inquiry. The meeting began with Heath saying that 'the situation was now grave socially, economically and politically, and the British public was losing patience'. Faulkner agreed, pointing out that a high-level British official had concluded that the economic situation was 'desperate'. He also revealed that senior Belfast civil servants had, 'in a review of the economic and social position, indicated that a breakdown in government might occur in a matter of weeks'. Such apocalyptic assessments give an indication of the overall sense of rapid deterioration. The option of closing down Stormont might have had more attraction at this point had London not been receiving the warnings from the army about the possible consequences of doing so. A Ministry of Defence document, released during the Bloody Sunday inquiry, revealed that the army had advised 'that in the event of direct rule the cooperation to be expected from the civil service, the public utility services etc would be less than has hitherto been assumed in London'. The memo added:

> This renders the direct rule option even less palatable than we have always suggested. Moreover it is at least possible that a situation in which the army was either fighting both sides in the middle of a civil war or (with whatever help was available from GB police, prison service etc) having virtually to run Northern Ireland, would, quite apart from its military implications, be very difficult to sustain in British political terms.

December brought an incident with one of the highest civilian death tolls in the troubles: a small Catholic bar in north Belfast, McGurk's, was blown up with the loss of fifteen lives. A powerful explosion caused the old building to collapse, reducing it to smouldering rubble. Local people, members of the security forces and emergency crews pulled away the debris with their bare hands.

The attack was the work of the UVF which, together with the UDA, was growing in strength in areas such as the Shankill as loyalists became more and more anxious about the army's evident inability to defeat or even contain the IRA. UVF involvement was confirmed years later when a member of the organisation confessed and was jailed for life. At the time, however, both Stormont government and army sources flatly denied that loyalists were responsible, claiming that both forensic and intelligence evidence showed that the IRA was to blame. They alleged the bombing was not an attack on the pub but the premature explosion of a device which was being stored inside it. These false claims, disputed at the time by the IRA and nationalist representatives, fuelled nationalist alienation from the authorities, who had of course argued that no loyalists were dangerous enough to be interned. Much more loyalist violence lay ahead.

4

The end of Stormont
1972–73

1972: the most violent year

The worst year of the troubles was 1972, its death toll of almost five hundred far exceeding that of any other year. Fourteen of those deaths occurred in Londonderry on 30 January, in what was to be remembered as one of the key events of the troubles, Bloody Sunday. What happened on that day was to drive even more men and youths into paramilitary groups. Thirteen people were killed and another thirteen were injured, one fatally, when soldiers of the Parachute Regiment and other units opened fire following a large illegal civil rights march in Londonderry city.

Both the Provisional and Official IRA denied that any of their units were involved. Soldiers claimed they came under intensive attack from gunmen and from nailbombers but local residents disputed their account, saying they had opened fire without justification. No soldiers were either killed or injured by gunfire or nailbombs, and no weapons were recovered by the army.

Catholic priest Father Edward Daly, who later became Bishop of Derry and will always be associated with Bloody Sunday, witnessed the death of a seventeen-year-old youth as both ran away from soldiers. He said he saw the youth laughing at the sight of a priest running: 'The next thing he suddenly gasped and threw his hands up in the air and fell on his face. He asked me: "Am I going to die?" and I said no, but I administered the last rites. I can remember him holding my hand and squeezing it. We all wept. We got him to the top of the street. I knelt beside him and told him, "Look son, we've got to get you out", but he was dead. He was very youthful looking, just in his seventeenth year but he only looked about twelve.' The shootings produced one of the lasting images of the troubles in photographs and television film of Father Daly waving a white handkerchief while helping carry a fatally wounded youth out of the killing zone.

Father Daly said later: 'A lot of the younger people in Derry who may have been more pacifist became quite militant as a result of it. People who were there on that day and who saw what happened were absolutely enraged by it and just wanted to seek some kind of revenge for it. In later years many young people I visited in prison told me quite explicitly that they would never have become involved in the IRA but for what they witnessed, and heard of happening, on Bloody Sunday.' In his memoirs Gerry Adams wrote: 'Money, guns and recruits flooded into the IRA.'

The incident had enormous ramifications, taking a place in Irish history as a formative moment which not only claimed fourteen lives but also hardened attitudes, increased paramilitary recruitment, helped generate more violence, and convulsed Anglo-Irish relations. In 1998 Tony Blair, as prime minister, announced the establishment of a full-scale judicial inquiry.

The effect at the time was a dramatic increase in nationalist alienation. In the aftermath of the shootings Irish nationalists, north and south, erupted in shock, the Irish government recalling its ambassador from London. Bernadette Devlin rushed across the floor of the Commons and scratched Maudling's face. Most of those Catholics who had not yet left public life now did so, while in the Republic a day of national mourning was held on the day of the funerals. After some days of protests a large crowd cheered as the British embassy in Dublin was set alight and destroyed. In his memoirs, ambassador Sir John Peck wrote:

Bloody Sunday had unleashed a wave of fury and exasperation the like of which I had never encountered in my life, in Egypt or Cyprus or anywhere else. Hatred of the British was intense. Someone had summed it up: 'We are all IRA now.' The already shaky position of Jack Lynch, the Irish Taoiseach, was now extremely precarious, and the threat posed by the IRA to democratic institutions in the Republic would now be far more serious.

More violence followed three weeks later when the Official IRA staged a revenge attack on the Parachute Regiment's headquarters in Aldershot. Their attempt to kill paratroopers instead killed a Catholic chaplain, a gardener and five women members of the domestic staff. A fresh wave of nationalist indignation followed publication of the report into Bloody Sunday carried out by the Lord Chief Justice, Lord Widgery. His conclusion that the firing of some paratroopers had 'bordered on the reckless' brought a deluge of criticism and allegations that it was a 'whitewash' and a cover-up rather than an honest attempt to find out how fourteen people came to be shot dead by soldiers.

Early March brought a particularly shocking IRA attack when a bomb went off in a popular Belfast city centre bar, the Abercorn, on a busy Saturday afternoon. Two young women were killed and seventy others were injured. Some of the horror was conveyed in a newspaper report: 'Two sisters have both been seriously maimed. One, who planned to marry, has lost both legs, an arm and an eye. Her sister has lost both legs. Last night their mother was under sedation. A male victim lost two legs, and a female lost one leg and one arm. Another female lost one limb and three of the injured have lost eyes.' The Royal Victoria Hospital used a disaster plan for the first time. A senior doctor recalled, 'We were seeing injuries we had never seen before. The victims were black from the dirt and dust that was thrown up by the bombing. There was also a powerful smell of burning. The high proportion of young people struck everybody.'

Two weeks later came another horrendous incident when seven people were killed by a 200lb IRA car bomb left in Donegall Street, close to Belfast city centre, following contradictory telephoned warnings. The explosion injured 150 people, including many who were fleeing from a bomb scare in an adjoining street. The *Belfast Telegraph* reported:

Donegall Street looked like a battlefield. When the smoke and dust from the blast cleared, injured people were seen lying in pools of blood on the roadway. Some of the casualties lay in agony with glass splinters embedded in their wounds. A body was blown to pieces by the force of the explosion, which rocked the entire city centre. An old man was comforted on the footpath. As he lay barely conscious, he was unaware that half his leg had been blown off in the explosion.

The final weeks of Stormont

All of this increased the sense of crisis and galvanised the British government. Heath noted in his memoirs: 'The atmosphere had now grown more poisoned than ever and I feared that we might, for the first time, be on the threshold of complete anarchy.' He, Maudling and other ministers had already considered a wide range of options, some of which would have greatly alarmed Unionists had they known of them. One idea was for a repartition which would divide Northern Ireland into Protestant and Catholic districts, with the latter being allowed to join the Republic. Another was to have Northern Ireland governed jointly by Britain and the Republic, its citizens having dual citizenship. Heath seems to have considered and rejected these options, though intriguingly the minutes of one meeting of ministers, released in the spring of 2000, mention the possibility of Irish unity. Recording the gist of ministerial discussions, this document said: 'If the object were to preserve the option of creating a united Ireland at some time in the future, it might be better to seek first for a political solution in which the minority were persuaded to participate in government.'

But many other ideas were in the air and when, five days after Bloody Sunday, Faulkner went to Downing Street he found, in his words, questions coming at him thick and fast. Discussion touched, among other things, on handing over some areas to the Republic; on a referendum on Northern Ireland's constitutional position; on what would happen if troops were removed from Catholic areas; on ways of involving Catholics in government, and on transferring control of security to London.

Faulkner urged Heath to persevere with internment, arguing that if violence could be ended then he 'would be in a strong position to urge magnanimity upon the majority'. He spoke against most of Heath's ideas, making clear his two main sticking points. The first was opposition to guaranteeing Catholics a place in government. He argued strongly against a new coalition involving Unionists and nationalists, saying it was unworkable and would result in 'a bedlam cabinet, a kind of fragmentation bomb virtually certain to fly apart at the first meeting'. He also refused to contemplate a Westminster takeover of security powers, saying this would 'reduce our government to a mere sham'.

Heath and his ministers were unconvinced by Faulkner and had lost confidence in the ability of the Stormont regime to restore order, though Faulkner did not appear to realise this. He wrote later that he had several times asked if direct rule was in prospect and was assured that it was not.

Within the Unionist community, however, many did not believe that Stormont was secure or that the IRA was on the road to defeat. This was put most forcibly by William Craig, who had been roundly beaten by Faulkner for leadership of the Unionist party. He formed an organisation called the Ulster Vanguard movement, and, while remaining a member of the Unionist party, used Vanguard as his own power base, designing it as an umbrella group to enlist as many supporters as possible from the various loyalist groupings which were springing up in response to the mounting tension.

He associated with some loyalist paramilitary organisations such as the UDA. Advocating a semi-independent Northern Ireland he staged a series of Oswald Mosley-style 'monster rallies', arriving complete with motor-cycle outriders to inspect thousands, and sometimes tens of thousands, of men drawn up in military-style formation. What Craig said at the rallies and elsewhere was even more alarming. In a series of what became known as the 'shoot-to-kill' speeches he openly threatened the use of force, declaring: 'We must build up dossiers on those men and women in this country who are a menace to this country because one of these days, if and when the politicians fail us, it may be our job to liquidate the enemy.'

Part of the message here was a warning to Britain not to bring down Stormont, but Heath was undeterred. When Faulkner received another summons to go to London on 22 March, it was for a meeting which would spell the end of Unionist government. He appears to have been totally surprised when Heath announced that he wanted to begin phasing out internment, to take over control of security, and to move towards power-sharing with Catholics. Faulkner was to write: 'We were more puzzled than angry. We decided that Heath was bluffing.' Heath in turn was to write of Faulkner: 'Initially he seemed to think that we were bluffing.' But nine hours of argument failed to shake Heath, and when Faulkner returned to Belfast to talk it over with his cabinet they unanimously voted to resign. Heath had apparently expected this.

One of the few points of substance on which the memoirs of Heath and Faulkner differ is on the prospect of direct rule. Faulkner accused the British prime minister of misleading him, writing: 'The rug was pulled out from under my feet, and it came to me personally as a bitter blow. I was shaken and horrified and felt completely betrayed.' Heath by contrast wrote that he had specifically made it clear to Faulkner when he became Stormont prime minister 'that if significant progress was not made in the next year or so, we would have to introduce direct rule. He did not like the prospect and later claimed he had been duped by us. This is not so. He was aware, from the day he took office, that his premiership was Stormont's last chance.'

A two-day protest strike which was called by Craig and Vanguard brought Northern Ireland to a virtual standstill in late March with up to 200,000 workers downing tools, most motivated by indignation, some by intimidation. Industry, commerce and most public services ground to a halt as electricity production was cut to one-third of its usual level. Around 100,000 people made their way to Stormont for a rally at which Ulster flags outnumbered Union Jacks, a sign of Protestant anger with London. Faulkner and Craig both addressed the crowd, though those who thought this an indication of a new Unionist unity were to be proved wrong. Stormont adjourned for the last time at 4.15 p.m. on 28 March, ending an existence of just over half a century.

The ending of Stormont rule was an emotional and traumatic time for Protestants and Unionists, involving as it did the demise of the institution which they regarded as their chief bulwark against nationalists and republicans. Brian Faulkner had been prime minister for just a year, the sixth and last person to hold that office. His premiership had indeed been Stormont's last chance. The irony was that the man regarded as Unionism's most professional politician had in the space of a year made two major miscalculations. First he thought internment would significantly improve the security situation, and second he thought Heath would not abolish Stormont. He was not just wrong but spectacularly wrong in each case. He further overestimated the RUC and underestimated the IRA.

For his part, Edward Heath had travelled a considerable political distance in a short time. To begin with he regarded Northern Ireland as more of a security problem than a political problem, and was prepared to give Faulkner the chance to proceed with heavy emphasis on security. By

March 1972 Heath still believed in strong security measures, but he had come to place much greater importance on political initiatives, which included the involvement of Dublin and moves towards powersharing. In the process he came to conclude that Stormont as then constituted was irreformable, that a cross-community government had to be fashioned and that, in his words, 'only direct rule could offer us the breathing-space necessary for building it'.

Stormont fell because, with Northern Ireland locked in serious crisis, Heath came to conclude that Faulkner could deliver neither security success nor political progress. Internment, as well as being disastrously counterproductive on the streets, had also destroyed all hope of early political advance. Faulkner had made it clear that he would not relinquish certain areas of Unionist power to London, especially responsibility for security, and would not agree to powersharing with nationalist parties. Although he had invited two non-Unionists into his cabinet, both were there at his personal invitation: he drew the line at having representatives of nationalist parties in it.

It is certainly true that violence increased greatly in August 1971, though it is also probably true that it would have gone up in any case, given that both the IRA and loyalist groups were becoming bigger and more organised, as the increase in IRA violence and the bombing of McGurk's bar testified. Nonetheless, three events taken together – the introduction of internment, Bloody Sunday and the fall of Stormont – served to trigger the worst violence ever seen in Northern Ireland. Faulkner portrayed Stormont's end as primarily the achievement of the IRA, declaring: 'Chief amongst those who have sought the emasculation and ultimately the downfall of Stormont have been the IRA terrorists themselves.' Heath also admitted that he was shaken by the violence, and that he feared complete anarchy.

It seems unlikely, however, that violence alone would have brought Stormont down. The pressure came not just from IRA violence, but from rejection of Stormont by the entire Catholic community. The writing may have been on the wall as early as the summer of 1971, for Heath was to write that the SDLP walkout had 'deprived Stormont of any remaining legitimacy'. The rent-and-rates strike, the withdrawal of many nationalists from public life, and the poor state of Anglo-Irish relations were all signs of complete and apparently irreversible nationalist alienation from the old Stormont system. IRA bombs were the most dramatic manifestation of this, but the sense was strong that the Catholic community, whose expectations had been raised so much, had rejected the old system once and for all. And Heath, having concluded that Stormont was part of the problem rather than part of the solution, thus consigned it to history.

The 1972 figure of almost 500 killings stands as a vivid illustration of the lethal depths to which the troubles descended. There were almost 2,000 explosions and over 10,000 shooting incidents, an average of around 30 shootings per day. Almost 5,000 people were injured. Almost 2,000 armed robberies netted £800,000, most of it going into paramilitary coffers. In the worst month of the entire troubles, July 1972, almost a hundred people died as both republican and loyalist groups went on an uninhibited rampage. As the year opened, 17,000 soldiers were available for duty; when it ended a series of hasty reinforcements had brought the figure to 29,000.

The car bomb, a terrifying and often entirely indiscriminate weapon, was introduced by the IRA, causing many deaths, terrible injuries and enormous damage. Violence from loyalists increased significantly from the spring of 1972 when working-class Protestants turned in their thousands to paramilitarism as insecurity and uncertainty soared. Furtive meetings between the IRA and British politicians, first Harold Wilson and later the Tories, reinforced Unionist fears that Britain was attempting to negotiate with republicanism behind Unionist backs. Any hopes that the closure of Stormont and the end of Unionist rule would lead to a reduction of violence were soon dashed. In the twelve months up to direct rule, 250 died; in the twelve months which followed, the killing rate doubled.

It is also worth remarking however on what did not happen. Despite being fearful and insecure about their future, the Protestant community did not attempt to oppose the imposition of direct rule. Although there was deep resentment at the removal of Stormont, there were no serious signs of mutiny among the Protestants who predominated in the civil service and the RUC. The acceptance of direct rule may have been surly, but it was nonetheless acceptance.

Talks and violence

Direct rule was intended as very much a temporary system while a cross-community successor to the Stormont system was devised. In London, responsibility was transferred from the Home Office to a new department, the Northern Ireland Office (NIO). Its first head, who was known as the Northern Ireland Secretary, or more often in Belfast as the Secretary of State, was William Whitelaw. Whitelaw, who in later years would go on to become deputy leader of the Conservative party, was a wealthy landowner whose political skills lay in the field of conciliation. A natural consensus politician in the high Tory mould, he was adept at personal relations and maintained contact with a wide range of opinion.

His task was to kick-start politics and open negotiations with the parties. In the early months of direct rule he attempted to placate both Unionists and nationalists against the background of steadily worsening violence and continual security crises. Many of the main parties and other elements were not speaking to each other, while the SDLP had for many months refused to meet British ministers. Whitelaw moved quickly to improve his relations with nationalists and republicans by releasing a number of internees and making other conciliatory moves. One of the most important of these, which was to have significant long-term consequences, was to defuse a republican hungerstrike by conceding 'special category status' to prisoners associated with paramilitary groups. This amounted to an acceptance of the IRA argument that its prisoners were different from other inmates jailed for criminal as opposed to paramilitary offences. It was a later attempt to withdraw this concession which led to the republican hungerstrikes and political upheavals of 1980 and 1981.

Anxious to explore the minds of IRA leaders, Whitelaw arranged for senior republicans to be flown, in the strictest of secrecy, to a government minister's home in Chelsea in July. The republicans included veterans and younger elements such as Gerry Adams and Martin McGuinness. The importance of Adams was emphasised by the fact that he was released from prison to make the trip. McGuinness later recalled: 'I was 22 years of age, and I couldn't be anything but impressed by the paraphernalia surrounding that whole business, and the cloak and dagger stuff of how we were transported from Derry to London. I was on the run at the time. There were contacts with the British government and we insisted on a written note from them which would guarantee our safety in the event of us agreeing to go to London. That we were given, and it was held by a lawyer acting on our behalf.

'We assembled in Derry, six of us, and we were taken in a blacked-out van to a field in which a helicopter landed. We were put in the helicopter and brought to the military end of Aldergrove airport near Belfast. We were brought then on by RAF plane to a military airfield in England, where we were met by a fleet of limousines. They were the fanciest cars I had ever seen in my life: it was a most unreal experience. We were escorted by the Special Branch through London to Cheyne Walk and there we met Willie Whitelaw. We were offered drinks at the meeting and we all refused.' McGuinness added: 'The only purpose of the meeting with Whitelaw was to demand a British declaration of intent to withdraw. All of us left the meeting quite clear in our minds that the British government were not yet at a position whereby we could do serious business.'

Whitelaw was as unimpressed with the republicans as they were with him. He recorded in his memoirs: 'The meeting was a non-event. The IRA leaders simply made impossible demands which I told them the British government would never concede. They were in fact still in a mood of defiance and determination to carry on until their absurd ultimatums were met.' The very fact that the meeting took place, however, was of great psychological importance in both political and paramilitary circles, being regularly cited in support of the argument that Britain might someday not rule out doing a deal with violent groupings.

Unionists were appalled when news of the exercise broke, stirring as it did their traditional fear that Britain might betray them. Others too disapproved, such as Garret FitzGerald, later Fine Gael Taoiseach and for years a major influence in Anglo-Irish relations. He wrote: 'The contacts that had taken place had the effect merely of prolonging the violence by deluding the IRA into believing that a British government would eventually negotiate a settlement with them.' As the troubles developed, a sporadic channel of communication was to remain open between the British and the IRA, even as the republican campaign of violence went on. In the 1990s this channel would play an important role in the developing peace process, but Whitelaw concluded after the Chelsea encounter that the new political structures he hoped to construct had no place in them for republicans.

He sounded out loyalist paramilitaries too, on one occasion meeting loyalists wearing masks and sunglasses in his Stormont Castle office. But a few days after his encounter with republicans a brief IRA ceasefire broke down. The IRA and the British government had met face to face, each concluding that the other was unreasonable and in effect beyond political reach. The IRA stepped up its violence with a vengeance, while loyalist groups also began killing on a large scale.

By this stage it was clear that working-class Protestants were flocking to unofficial defence organisations in their tens of thousands. The huge rise in violence following internment meant many Protestants lost confidence in the security forces, with the result that vigilante organisations sprang into being in Protestant areas. They felt politically insecure, wondering who would prevail in the fierce battles between the army and the IRA, while many of those who lived close to republican areas also felt physically insecure.

At first the authorities did not display serious concern about the groups of men who barricaded districts and patrolled them, sometimes carrying sticks and clubs. According to official minutes Faulkner had told Heath in late 1971: 'Their purpose was to identify and exclude terrorists in places where the security forces could not guarantee protection. It was worth considering whether they could be employed as an "eyes and ears" force on a regular basis.' Heath turned down the idea.

It soon became obvious that this was more than simple vigilantism. The majority of those who joined such groupings were not necessarily extremists, but within their ranks were some hundreds prepared to resort to open violence. The bombing of McGurk's bar was one example of this, but as 1972 went on there were more and more killings of Catholics, carried out in particular by militant pockets within the UDA. By the end of the year loyalists had killed 120 people.

The UDA also made its point in a more public way by staging large marches in Belfast with thousands of men parading in semi-military uniforms including combat jackets, bush hats, sunglasses and sometimes masks. These were not openly violent occasions, although there were occasional confrontations with the army; but the message that Protestants were if necessary prepared to fight for their cause was unmistakable.

Horror piled on horror in July 1972. The restlessness of the mid-1960s had first degenerated into the violent clashes of August 1969 and now descended further into killings at a rate of three a day. That month had many of the features which were to become all too familiar as the troubles went on. Republicans killed Protestants while loyalists claimed Catholic lives, often with particular savagery. On 11 July a number of drunken loyalists broke into the home of a Catholic family, killing a mentally handicapped youth and raping his mother. At the resulting murder trial a lawyer told the court: 'The restraints of civilisation on evil human passions are in this case totally non-existent. You may well think that in this case we have reached the lowest level of human depravity.'

Republicans meanwhile set off bombs which killed large numbers of people. Nine died in Belfast on what came to be known as Bloody Friday, as the IRA detonated twenty devices in just over an hour, injuring 130 others and producing widespread confusion and fear in many parts of the city. According to one account: 'In many places there was panic and pandemonium as shoppers and others heard bombs going off all over the city. The carnage, with some people blown to pieces, was such that the number of dead was unclear for some time, newspapers at first reporting that eleven people had been killed.' A police officer who went to a bomb scene in Oxford Street said: 'You could hear people screaming and crying and moaning. The first thing that caught my eye was a torso of a human being lying in the middle of the street. It was recognisable as a torso because the clothes had been blown off and you could actually see parts of the human anatomy.' In his memoirs Brian Faulkner wrote: 'Few Ulster people will forget seeing on television young policemen shovelling human remains into plastic bags in Oxford Street.'

Yet still the horror continued. On the last day of the month nine people, including a child and old people, were killed by IRA car bombs left in the previously peaceful County Londonderry village of Claudy. Apart from the human tragedy involved, both Bloody Friday and Claudy were seen at the time as major political setbacks for the IRA. The security forces were able to capitalise by moving into Londonderry, in a massive exercise known as Operation Motorman, to remove the 'no-go areas' which had been controlled by the IRA. But although this was a short-term setback for the republicans their campaign of violence went on regardless. At the beginning of 1972 the IRA had predicted imminent victory: by the middle of the year, both they and the authorities were geared up for a conflict that both rightly suspected could be long and bloody.

New proposals

It was against a background of such unremitting violence that Whitelaw turned to the task of finding a new political settlement. The SDLP was at that point recommending that sovereignty over Northern Ireland should be shared by London and Dublin. Brian Faulkner meanwhile called for a return of Stormont though with nationalist influence on some committees and some new links with the south, approaches that were viewed as modest concessions to Catholics.

In November 1972 Whitelaw published a discussion document, *The Future of Northern Ireland*, which set out the government's approach in general terms. It was important in that it laid out many ideas which were to form the basis of the approach of both this government and future administrations. The discussion document stressed Northern Ireland's financial dependence on Britain, pointedly adding that membership of the United Kingdom 'carries with it the obligations of membership including acceptance of the sovereignty of parliament as representing the people as a whole'. But in a major departure the document formally conceded that Dublin had a legitimate interest in Northern Ireland affairs, declaring: 'A settlement must recognise Northern Ireland's position within Ireland as a whole. It is therefore clearly desirable that any new arrangements should, whilst meeting the wishes of Northern Ireland and Great Britain, be so far as possible acceptable to and accepted by the Republic of Ireland.' The document introduced to the political lexicon the phrase 'Irish dimension' in acknowledgement of the south's interest.

In his memoirs Heath explained the rationale for this: 'It was no good just pretending that nationalist aspirations did not exist and that Irish nationalism in Northern Ireland would either be contained or burn itself out. The strength of feeling in the Catholic community had to be addressed, and that meant finding some way of involving the government of the Republic directly in the affairs of the province.' The document continued the gradual redrafting of London's approach to Northern Ireland and the possibility of a united Ireland. It said: 'No UK government for many years has had any wish to impede the realisation of Irish unity, if it were to come about by genuine and freely given mutual agreement and on conditions acceptable to the distinctive communities.'

The discussion document laid down that unfettered majority rule was a thing of the past and that future devolution would be on a basis of partnership. New institutions, it stipulated, must 'seek a much wider consensus than has hitherto existed. As a minimum it would mean assuring minority groups of an effective voice and a real influence; but there are strong arguments that the objective of real participation should be achieved by giving minority interests a share in the exercise of executive power.' In putting the concepts of powersharing and an Irish dimension on the table as the pillars of a future settlement, London had defined what were to be the main constitutional battlegrounds for the next three decades.

These ideas held no attraction for the IRA, which saw them as desperate attempts to shore up crumbling British rule. It remained intent on fighting on in the hope of wearing down the British will and bringing about a British withdrawal. But the new concepts were much welcomed by the SDLP and the Irish government, both of which had been lobbying for such an approach.

The proposals were much more problematic for Unionists, representing as they did a radical departure from the old system of majority rule. Faulkner did not consort with paramilitary groups, but others on the Unionist side were less fastidious. The most outspoken Unionist politician was William Craig, whose Vanguard movement continued to hold rallies and threatened a range of protests which included a Protestant rent-and-rates strike, a boycott of council elections and a refusal to pay gas and electricity bills. These generally came to nothing, but what really raised the temperature were Craig's fiery speeches. Addressing a meeting of the Monday Club group of far-right Conservatives in London he said, 'I am prepared to come out and shoot and kill. Let us put the bluff aside. I am prepared to kill and those behind me will have my full support. When we say force we mean force. We will only assassinate our enemies as a last desperate resort when we are denied our democratic rights.' There were calls for Craig's prosecution: some argued he was giving voice to legitimate Protestant anger, while others accused him of recklessly fanning the flames of violence.

But if the authorities were alarmed by Craig they were relieved by an unexpected new tack taken by Paisley, who during 1972 temporarily switched from incendiary demagoguery to an uncharacteristically moderate note. Instead of stirring Protestant anxieties he suddenly sought to soothe them, taking the line that the loss of Stormont was not the end of the world. 'Stormont is a thing of the past and there is no good use for Unionists to think that, by some way or other, Stormont shall return,' he declared. Denouncing Craig's threats, he told supporters, 'The voice of Mr Craig and the advice of Mr Craig are the voice and advice of folly. Do not be misled. Do not wreck your country and bring it to an end by self-inflicted wounds. Do not copy the deplorable tactics your enemies have adopted.'

Paisley's approach at this stage was to advocate stern security policies, including twenty-four-hour curfews in republican areas, but instead of calling for the return of Stormont he become an integrationist, one of those rare Unionists who believed a new Stormont would tend to separate Northern Ireland from the rest of the UK. It was an interesting theory but at the time there were few Unionist takers for it, and eventually Paisley would quietly abandon it and return to more familiar ground.

By this point Unionism had splintered, with Faulkner prepared to negotiate, Paisley pressing for integration, and Craig apparently bent on confrontation. Prominent Unionist former ministers such as Harry West and John Taylor demanded a return to the old Stormont system, while many other politicians added to the general confusion by changing their minds and their political lines, sometimes several times. Faulkner found it difficult to hold his party together, particularly since he was advancing the problematic policy of negotiating with a British government which had, in the eyes of most Unionists, been guilty of a betrayal in removing the Stormont system. Some liberal Unionists drifted away from politics entirely, depriving Faulkner of potentially useful support.

1973

At the beginning of 1973 the United Kingdom and the Irish Republic became members of the European Economic Community (EEC), a development which over time had a major effect on Anglo-Irish relations. Disparity in the wealth of the two countries had added to the historical distance between coloniser and colonised, with Irish dependence on British trade reinforcing this. Their simultaneous entry to the EEC, however, helped alter some of the fundamentals of the relationship and increased the south's international standing. Joining Europe also markedly increased the Republic's sense of national self-esteem as Irish ministers, and some talented Dublin civil servants, were seen to perform well on the international stage. British and Irish officials also formed useful working relationships which would later be important in developing greater understanding and mutual respect.

But meanwhile the violence continued. Security force arguments that loyalist violence was too unplanned to be susceptible to internment became steadily less tenable, and in February the first loyalists were interned. The move was followed by a one-day strike, backed by a range of loyalist paramilitary and political groupings, which was marked by considerable loyalist violence and five deaths. On the republican side the IRA gradually changed the emphasis from open confrontations and car bombings to more carefully planned sniping attacks, together with bombing attacks in England. Bombs planted in London in March 1973 led to one death and almost two hundred injuries, the first of many sporadic but often spectacular IRA attacks in England which in the course of the troubles would take more than a hundred lives. This figure was low in relation to the overall death toll, but the political impact of attacks in Britain was often great.

On the political front, 1973 saw Whitelaw continuing to draw the parties into talks on a settlement. A referendum or border poll was held in March, with voters asked whether they wanted Northern Ireland to remain part of the United Kingdom or join a united Ireland. The exercise was supposed to reassure Unionists that, whatever other changes might be on the way, their place in the UK was secure. In the event all shades of nationalist opinion boycotted the exercise, resulting in an almost entirely Unionist turnout. On a 59 per cent poll, 99 per cent voted to stay in the UK, only 1 per cent favouring a united Ireland. Unionists drew some fleeting cheer from the result, though there was no sign that it gave them any lasting reassurance.

By the spring of 1973 London's thinking had crystallised and was laid out in a government white paper entitled *Northern Ireland Constitutional Proposals*. This proposed the introduction of proportional representation, the same system James Craig had abolished in the 1920s, to elect a new assembly to replace Stormont. A new devolved government or executive would be made up from the major parties, including both Unionists and nationalists. The white paper reaffirmed Northern Ireland's constitutional status within the UK but envisaged new north–south links. It also made it clear that London intended keeping control over sensitive matters such as security, the legal system, emergency powers and elections.

The white paper reaffirmed that the concepts of powersharing and an Irish dimension were to be the mainstays of a new settlement. It said that government 'can no longer be solely based upon any single party, if that party draws its support and its elected representatives virtually entirely from only one section of a divided community'. The white paper advocated the creation of a Council of Ireland for consultations and co-operation with the south.

Faulkner accepted the white paper as a basis for negotiation, though his party's council endorsed his line without enthusiasm. William Craig meanwhile broke with the Unionist party, converting his movement into the Vanguard party. Others within Unionism, including Ian Paisley and the Orange Order, flatly denounced the white paper as unacceptable. There was much confusion in Unionist ranks as prominent figures toyed with alternatives such as forcing a return to Stormont, integration with Britain, independence from Britain, and even the idea of negotiating a new federal Ireland with nationalists. But none of these notions took root, partly because they seemed unrealistic or undesirable to mainstream Unionists, and partly because there were so many personality differences between leading Unionist figures. In the end the central divide within Unionism came down to those headed by Faulkner who found the white paper an acceptable basis for talks, and those, such as Craig and Paisley, who did not.

Although the rejectionist Unionists were against Faulkner and against Whitelaw, personality and political differences meant they were clearly not united in leadership, aims, methods or alternatives. Political groupings, and sometimes loyalist paramilitary groups, from time to time formed umbrella groups but these tended to be shifting, unstable and suspicious coalitions which knew what they stood against but disagreed on what they stood for.

All parties had difficulties with Whitelaw's proposals. For many Unionists, powersharing with nationalists and a Council of Ireland were objectionable, for all Whitelaw's stress on Northern Ireland's guaranteed status within the UK. For the SDLP the initiative was in most aspects a huge advance, even though it fell well short of the London–Dublin joint authority the party had advocated. The continuing use of internment also posed a major problem for the SDLP.

Elections to the new assembly were held in June 1973. During the campaign the wily Faulkner repeated that his party would not share power with any party 'whose primary objective was to break the link with Great Britain'. Some Unionists appear to have voted for him on the assumption that this meant he would not share power with the SDLP. Afterwards, when it emerged he was indeed prepared to sit in government with the SDLP, opponents accused him of misleading voters. His reasoning was that ending the Union, while perhaps the ultimate ambition of the SDLP, was not its primary objective.

The election result was yet another illustration of Unionist divisions. Thirty-nine of the Unionist party candidates gave their allegiance to the Faulkner approach but, in an echo of O'Neill's 1969 crossroads election, ten others refused to do so. Unionist rejectionists won 27 of the 78 assembly seats with 235,000 votes, while Unionists supporting the initiative won 22 seats with 211,000 votes. Faulkner thus emerged from the election leading a bitterly divided party and without a majority among Unionist voters. His best hope was that, if a working system of government could be set up, its successful functioning would gradually attract more Unionist popular support.

The powersharing project that was to follow was based on the idea of combining the more moderate parties in a new coalition which would run Northern Ireland on a partnership basis. Both republican and Unionist extremes were to be excluded from this centrist idea – in fact they excluded themselves by refusing to take part in it – but as time went by, the theory ran, support for the extremes would dwindle.

While this scheme was politically coherent, two sets of statistics, concerning electoral support and the level of violence, help show just how formidable were the forces ranged against it. A majority of Unionist voters were against the proposition, while perhaps 30,000 or more of them were so opposed to accommodation that they joined loyalist paramilitary groups prepared to use force to resist what they saw as any further erosion of Protestant rights. There was a certain overlap of the political and paramilitary within the assembly itself, where half a dozen or more anti-deal Unionists had connections with shadowy loyalist groups. In the political centre only a small number of voters supported cross-community parties, the non-sectarian Alliance party being the most prominent, with 9 per cent of the vote.

On the nationalist side the SDLP dominated, having taken 22 per cent of the overall vote and representing in one party virtually all of constitutional nationalism. Nationalism had by this stage regrouped into two very distinct and opposing positions, most Catholics voting for the SDLP. Republicans were not, however, represented, having boycotted the elections: in the 1980s they would build a significant vote but during the 1970s they did not contest elections. Most of those who opted for a violent path came together in the IRA, known in those days as the Provisional IRA, which believed in an eventual republican victory achieved through force. Only a few individuals and organisations, such as Bernadette Devlin, the rump of the Civil Rights Association, and the Official IRA, did not align themselves with either of the two large nationalist groupings.

Republicans made their presence felt not in the assembly but by means

of the continuing IRA campaign of violence. The death toll fell sub-
stantially in 1973, almost halving from the previous year's figure of 497.
The number of victims in almost every category roughly halved. In round
figures during the year 130 civilians were killed as well as 80 members of
the security forces. Republicans were responsible for 140 deaths, loyalists
for 90 and the security forces for 30. The year also had fewer horrors than
1972, though there were some multiple death tolls, as in Coleraine in
County Londonderry where an IRA bomb killed six people. There were
also fewer loyalist torture killings, though UDA members killed an SDLP
politician and a woman friend by stabbing them dozens of times.
Although taken overall the year was a clear improvement on 1972, the
continuing violence provided an unhelpful backdrop to attempts to build
a new politics based on harmony and partnership. The total figure of 263
killings meant that hardly a newspaper or evening television programme
did not bring news of either a killing or a funeral.

When the assembly met it turned into a forum for division rather than
for a new start. Its first meeting in July set a pattern of repeated unruly
gatherings, with hours of rowdy and rancorous debate, many obstructive
points of order and a great deal of personal abuse. Yet even as the assembly chamber became a byword for acrimony, real negotiation was
going on behind the scenes as Whitelaw, the Unionist party, the SDLP and
Alliance argued out the details of a new settlement. In October Faulkner
won the support of his party's standing committee for powersharing with
the SDLP, though only by the narrow majority of 132 votes to 105.

A new element of inter-party trust appeared as the negotiations went
on, helped by the SDLP's position on one touchstone issue, when the
party indicated it would call for an end to the rent-and-rates strike which
it had previously endorsed as a protest against internment. But such
thorny subjects as the composition and powers of the new executive and
the Council of Ireland, together with issues such as policing and internment, were difficult areas which required many months of negotiation.

Faulkner was forced to fight major battles within his own party as
senior figures such as John Taylor fought a strong rearguard action
against the emerging new settlement. Faulkner eventually won the
backing of his party's ruling council, though by the ominously small
majority of 379 votes to 369.

By November the talks had achieved agreement on most of the major
issues but were stalled on the composition of the eleven-man executive

(no women were in line for office) and had yet to settle the form of the Irish dimension. Faulkner insisted that his party should have a majority in the executive while the SDLP and Alliance pointed out that he did not command a majority within Unionism and certainly not within the assembly. Whitelaw told Edward Heath that he expected the talks to fail and made plans to return to London to make a statement in the Commons on 22 November. On the day before, however, he piled the pressure on the parties to reach agreement by having his helicopter land, visibly and very noisily, on the lawn outside Stormont Castle where the talks were taking place.

A last-minute breakthrough was achieved with the aid of the ingenious device of creating a new category of extra ministers. Faulkner would have a majority within the eleven-strong executive, which was to be made up of six Unionists, four SDLP and one Alliance. But four extra non-voting ministers were to be appointed, so that the full executive would consist of seven Unionists, six SDLP and two Alliance members. This piece of sleight-of-hand meant that Faulkner could claim he had a Unionist majority while non-Unionists could simultaneously claim he had not.

Sunningdale

The next step was to assemble the three parties which would form the executive, together with the London and Dublin governments. They met at a civil service training centre at Sunningdale in Berkshire in late 1973, the deal which emerged from it becoming known thereafter as the Sunningdale Agreement. Whitelaw, the principal architect of the new settlement, was promoted to a senior post in London, Heath believing that he needed his talents for his government's confrontation with trade unions in Britain. He was replaced by the less experienced Francis Pym only four days before the Sunningdale conference took place.

The principal tasks of the gathering were to agree on the Council of Ireland's composition and functions, to deal with the subject of greater north–south security co-operation, and to attempt to settle the constitutional status of Northern Ireland. After high-pressure late-night sessions, with Heath personally taking a leading role, the shape of the Council of Ireland was eventually hammered out. It would consist of seven northern and seven southern ministers, a consultative tier with thirty members of the Irish parliament and thirty members of the assembly, and a permanent secretariat. It was to have 'executive and harmonising functions'.

All of this was alarming to Unionism, smacking as it did of a dangerous and potentially growing Dublin foothold in Northern Ireland affairs. Faulkner thus tried hard to water down the powers of the Council of Ireland but in the end had to accept much more than he had bargained for. He later defended his concessions on the council's functions and powers on the basis that they were 'nonsense' that 'meant nothing in practice' because executive ministers and the assembly would have to agree to anything proposed by the new body.

Although London and Dublin were able to reach agreement on most issues, they had to agree to differ on a number of points and especially on one hugely important issue. In the absence of an agreed single statement on the status of Northern Ireland, the governments agreed that separate statements should be printed side by side in the final conference communiqué. This was seen both as an oddity and as a sign of continuing British–Irish differences. The Irish government statement 'fully accepted and solemnly declared that there could be no change in the status of Northern Ireland until a majority of the people of Northern Ireland desired a change in their status'. Dublin did not, however, propose to delete or change Articles 2 and 3 of the Irish constitution, which Unionists regarded as an offensive claim to jurisdiction over Northern Ireland. Some in Dublin favoured such a move, but the problem was that the constitution could only be changed by a referendum. If a referendum had been held and lost, the entire initiative would have been undermined.

On the issue of cross-border security co-operation there was also much division. Faulkner's main demand was for the extradition of suspects to Northern Ireland, but Dublin resisted this, proposing instead the creation of a single all-Ireland court and a common law enforcement area, allowing terrorist offenders to be tried in whichever jurisdiction they were arrested. The fact that the issue was referred to a London–Dublin commission was a significant blow to Faulkner. He had hoped to return from Sunningdale with a southern guarantee of Northern Ireland's status and a new extradition deal which he could present as political and security gains.

The Sunningdale conference dealt also with the issue of policing. John Hume held that it would be difficult for SDLP members to take their places in a Northern Ireland executive if they were not able to give support to the police force. He argued however that this support would be almost impossible to sell to nationalists unless the police force was tied in some way to the Council of Ireland, a link which could offer the nationalist community some guarantees on policing. Although the SDLP had reluctantly conceded that there would be no change to the name of the RUC, at Sunningdale they were insistent that the Council of Ireland must have some policing oversight role. In his memoirs the Irish Foreign Minister, Garret FitzGerald, recalled that the Dublin delegation privately concluded that the Unionists had fared badly on most of the major issues, and thus it decided that on policing Faulkner should be allowed to prevail. The result was that the council's role in policing was largely cosmetic. Faulkner would later insist that this role was 'tenuous and totally meaningless', but for many Unionists the mere existence of a council was objectionable.

The Sunningdale conference was something of a cultural clash: the Unionist delegation decided not to use the drinks cabinet provided in their room in case their judgement should be affected. Other delegations laboured under no such inhibitions, first exhausting their own supplies and then gladly accepting the Unionist supplies. Faulkner's team instead sent out for Polo mints. However, the hours of intense negotiations engendered growing understanding and respect. Faulkner would later write: 'There was a feeling of comradeship and trust between those of us who had been through hundreds of hours of negotiations, and a sense almost of moral purpose.'

As the parties returned to Northern Ireland, Unionists could point to a reassuring Irish declaration on Northern Ireland's status, a law commission to tackle cross-border security problems and a Council of Ireland which they argued was largely toothless. The SDLP could claim victories in securing a role at the highest level of government, together with new all-Ireland institutions with the potential to evolve. Both the SDLP and the Faulkner Unionists claimed success, but as one historian pointed out: 'They were contradictory arguments. The success of the agreement depended on neither side listening to what their allies were saying about it.'

5

Sunningdale, strike & stalemate 1974–76

Powersharing

The first day of January 1974 was intended to be a historic day for Northern Ireland as the powersharing executive took office. With Brian Faulkner as chief minister and SDLP leader Gerry Fitt as his deputy, the administration brought together ministers from the Unionist party, the SDLP and Alliance. Billed as a chance for a fresh start, the powersharing executive was hailed as a momentous new departure. Politically it was certainly light years away from the Stormont majority rule system, for instead of the traditional all-Unionist cabinet the executive included prominent nationalists. John Hume was minister for commerce while Austin Currie, who had led the well-remembered Caledon squat, became housing minister. This new arrangement had the goodwill of almost the whole world; certainly the fervent good wishes of Britain and the Republic went with it.

But right from the start it was beleaguered, facing as it did opposition both from the IRA and from a majority of the Protestant population. The IRA sought outright victory, while many Unionists simply would not accept the new deal. Some Unionists feared the new arrangements were the start of a slippery slope towards a united Ireland; others simply could not abide the thought of having Catholics in government. All this meant that while the new arrangements had majority support within the assembly, and indeed within Northern Ireland as a whole, they had the support of fewer than half of Unionist voters and politicians.

The Unionist party itself was the scene of internal running battles. Three days after the executive came into being, a meeting of the Ulster Unionist Council was called to discuss a motion condemning the Council of Ireland. The Ulster Unionist Council's eccentric structure meant it included delegates from affiliated organisations such as the Orange Order; some delegates were not even members of the party, and some were actually members of rival parties such as Vanguard. When Faulkner's opponents won the vote by 427 votes to 374 he resigned as party leader, to be replaced by the uncompromising Harry West. Faulkner would eventually establish a new grouping to be known as the Unionist Party of Northern Ireland, with the backing of around twenty members of the assembly.

Thus after only one week of the new Northern Ireland executive's existence its head had effectively lost his party, which meant that all three major Unionist parties – the UUP, DUP and Vanguard – were opposed to the entire initiative. Paisley and the other anti-Sunningdale Unionists, who had already formed an umbrella United Ulster Unionist Council (UUUC), were now joined by West and the main Unionist party.

A further problem for the executive was that the Sunningdale Agreement was in reality an agreement to reach an agreement, with much remaining to be finalised. With the details of the Council of Ireland still to be worked out, Faulkner found it difficult to answer the wilder allegations of Unionist opponents. He was unable to gain political cover by pointing to significant gains in cross-border security, while the whole Sunningdale project was not helped by the fact that during the executive's existence violence rose. The increase on the republican side was fairly modest, but loyalist killings trebled.

Issues which Sunningdale was supposed to settle refused to go away. In a newspaper interview within days of the conference the Taoiseach, Liam

Cosgrave, said, 'There is no question of changing our constitution with regard to our claim of sovereignty over all of Ireland.' This was damaging to Faulkner's claim to have won a significant concession from the Republic in recognising Northern Ireland's status. He suffered a further blow when in January a legal challenge was mounted in the Dublin courts, charging that the Irish government's Sunningdale declaration on the status of Northern Ireland was unconstitutional. To win the case the Irish government was obliged to argue that nothing they had agreed affected the south's claim of jurisdiction over Northern Ireland contained in Articles 2 and 3. This was seen as confirming the accusation of the anti-Faulkner Unionists that he had not managed to dilute the south's claim.

Later in January the first meeting of the assembly since Sunningdale reached a new peak of unpleasantness as scenes of open violence broke out. Rejectionist Unionists attacked Faulkner supporters, with five RUC officers injured in the disturbances. One newspaper described the scene:

> The loyalists entered at 2:30 in the afternoon, prayed, and rushed forward to seize the seats designated for the executive. There were shouts and howls. Some climbed up and danced on desks. Other loyalists leaped upon the table beside the dispatch box, removed the mace, and began a parade about the chamber. One danced upon the speaker's table and shouted, 'We have driven the money-changers from the temple.' He then chained and padlocked himself to a bench.

Despite such histrionics members of the executive attempted to get on with running their new departments, quickly developing a perhaps surprising spirit of co-operation among traditional opponents. But although in administrative terms the executive made a promising start, political events in Britain were to undermine its standing. Heath, who was locked in a struggle with the miners and other trade unions which resulted in strikes and widespread disruption, called a general election for the end of February. The outcome of the contest was a major blow for the executive since the rejectionist Unionists, organised together in the UUUC, co-operated to nominate agreed candidates on a single straightforward anti-Sunningdale ticket. One of their more potent slogans was 'Dublin is just a Sunningdale away.'

Every circumstance seemed to conspire against Faulkner. He was attempting to have Unionists actively endorse a system radically different from anything that had gone before, and one that was susceptible to charges that it might weaken the link with Britain. The UUUC representatives by contrast had the reassuring tone of being unity candidates intent on maximising the Unionist vote. In some constituencies UUUC candidates looked such obvious winners that Faulkner did not even field candidates against them. Instead, the executive parties found themselves standing against each other in many constituencies. The tribal imperative worked in favour of the UUUC since in most constituencies they seemed the men most likely to avert a nationalist victory. Just when Faulkner was trying to sell the proposition of a new partnership across the divide, the venerable Unionist duty of preventing nationalists from winning seats reasserted itself.

When the votes were counted, the anti-Sunningdale Unionists had won eleven of the twelve Northern Ireland seats. Gerry Fitt was now the sole pro-Sunningdale MP. The leaders of the three main Unionist rejectionist parties, Paisley, Craig and West, were all elected in a harmful blow to the executive's credibility and authority. Nowhere in the statistics was there any comfort for the pro-Sunningdale camp. UUUC candidates amassed over 300,000 votes while Faulkner's supporters managed only 94,000. The charge that Faulkner spoke for less than half of Unionists had received irrefutable electoral proof.

In Britain Heath lost the election, Harold Wilson returned to power with a minority Labour government, and Merlyn Rees arrived in Belfast as a new and inexperienced Northern Ireland Secretary. Labour inherited an initiative which was not of their making, and which had been badly wounded by the rejectionist Unionists. Perhaps it was not surprising that the new government would later be accused of not giving its all in defence of the new deal.

Following the disastrous election result, Faulkner insisted on a secret renegotiation of the Council of Ireland, arguing that the election had shown that the council as it stood was unacceptable to Unionists. He said of the general election vote: 'It represents the fears of the Unionists, fears about the unknown and the unknowns expressed in that term Sunningdale. People don't know what Sunningdale is and they fear a sell-out on the constitutional position.'

The April announcement that there was not to be extradition of IRA suspects from the south to the north handed the UUUC another weapon to use against Faulkner, the common loyalist charge being that the south was soft on the IRA. Relations within the assembly remained acrimonious, with the UUUC members making it clear they did not accept the legitimacy of the new executive. Sometimes they boycotted the proceedings, sometimes they attempted to snarl them up with obstructive tactics, and sometimes a roughhouse developed. Some UUUC members were courteous individuals but many were not. One assembly official recalled in his memoirs: 'Ministers, especially Faulkner, were abused verbally on every occasion and sometimes even physically. Faulkner was spat upon, jostled, reviled and shouted down. It was sad to see him spat upon by lesser men, political pygmies and procedural bullies and wild men of the woods and the bogs.'

The disruption and occasional fisticuffs poisoned the atmosphere but showed no sign of bringing down the fledgling institutions. That was soon to be achieved however by a loose coalition of loyalist politicians, groups of workers and, above all, paramilitary groups. They did it not through political means but by a Protestant general strike which saw aggressive picketing, threats and intimidation, and widespread power cuts.

The UWC strike

Although loyalist one-day strikes had been staged on a number of occasions in 1972 and 1973, the fact that they almost invariably degenerated into violence meant the tactic was generally looked on as discredited. The strike of May 1974 was different in that it had an obvious and vulnerable target to attack in the form of the Sunningdale Agreement and the executive, featuring as it did such Unionist hate-figures as Fitt and Currie.

A number of elements were involved in the organisation of the strike. The nucleus was a group styling itself the Ulster Workers Council (UWC), consisting of trade unionists and others, some based in key industries with predominantly Protestant workforces. These included shipbuilding, heavy engineering and, above all, electric power generation. In May 1974 hardly anyone had heard of the UWC, and hardly anyone took them seriously when, in response to an assembly vote endorsing the Sunningdale Agreement, the organisation announced a general strike. The UWC had approached a number of loyalist politicians for support, but most of these were unenthusiastic, doubting the organisation's capacity to deliver. Some of the paramilitary groups, in particular the Ulster Defence Association, were much more interested in the idea.

On the first day of the strike, 15 May, the vast majority of workers travelled to work as usual. UDA leader Andy Tyrie later recalled arriving at the almost deserted strike headquarters: 'I suddenly realised that the UWC did not really exist as an organisation. And there was no strike in existence either.' Tyrie and the UDA took the initiative and by the middle of the day UDA members were, as Tyrie put it, 'persuading' workers that they should not be working. It was not long before the strike ceased to be merely a concept and became an organised campaign.

This meant blocked roads, hijacked cars, and visits by masked men to factories. In many areas barricades became a familiar sight, with cars, lorries and other obstacles slung across roads in makeshift obstructions. Bands of men and youths, sometimes carrying clubs and staves, were often in attendance. There was relatively little overt violence but then there did not have to be: motorists were not about to tackle groups of loyalists, risking perhaps a beating and the loss of their vehicle. It was intimidation on a huge scale. Another highly effective strike weapon arose from loyalist control over the power stations: within a short time electricity output was reduced to 60 per cent and power cuts forced workplaces to close. This pattern continued for the course of the two-week strike, so that for many workers it was a lockout rather than a strike.

The lack of electricity was one vital point; another was that the army and RUC did not set about keeping the roads open in a determined fashion. In a few instances blockades were dismantled and the pickets were dispersed, but very often if a road was blocked it stayed blocked. Security force patrols continued, but soldiers and pickets generally kept their distance from each other.

The army took the straightforward position that their job was to combat terrorism and not to curb street protests, an approach outlined years later in an interview by the late General Sir Frank King, who was then General Officer Commanding of troops in Northern Ireland. He related:

> When the strike started I remember having a conference and deciding not to get mixed up in it. What amazed us at the time was that we never had any aggro at all with the strikers. They never once stopped an army vehicle – as far as we were concerned it was almost as if the strike was not on at all. Dealing with intimidation was a police job. The fact that the RUC didn't do too much about it was no concern of ours. We were angry at the time but it wasn't our job. If Rees had ordered us to move against the barricades we

would have said, 'With great respect, this is a job for the police. We will assist them if you wish, but it's not terrorism.'

During the strike there was, in fact, a bombing attack which claimed more lives than almost any other single incident in the troubles, but it took place not in the north but south of the border. This was what came to be known as the Dublin and Monaghan bombings, which on the third day of the strike killed twenty-five people in Dublin and a further seven in the border town of Monaghan. Three separate car bombs went off without warning in Dublin, causing carnage during the evening rush hour. One newspaper report described the scene: 'Dozens of people lay on the pavements and in the road and in front of broken shops, dead, dying or screaming with pain and shock. A newspaper photographer was sick when he saw a gutter literally running with blood. A few feet away was a human leg and next to it a head.' A report on the inquest said: 'Horrifying head wounds, loss of limbs, enormous lacerations and the presence of debris and shrapnel in the victims' bodies were described to the court. Most of the victims died from multiple injuries, shock and haemorrhage.' Loyalist sources said the UVF was responsible for the attacks, but some years later it was alleged that British intelligence had played a part, a claim which led to a long-running campaign by relatives for an inquiry into the episode.

Back in Belfast the strike revealed daily the impotence of both the British government and the fledgling executive. Since the executive had no power over security and law and order its members could only complain bitterly to Rees that control of the streets had been conceded to the UWC and their paramilitary allies. UDA leader Tyrie would admit later that a major show of force by the RUC and the army at the start might have destroyed the momentum of the strike, but it is clear that Rees and the army had serious doubts about the possibility of defeating the strike through open confrontation. On one day it was said that 2,000 soldiers and police were required simply to keep five main roads into Belfast open. By the second week of the strike, power seemed to have shifted from Rees and the executive to the loyalist strikers.

General King was influenced in his stance by his judgement that the executive was already dead in the water. He said in the interview: 'Although armies are non-political, we were a fairly sensitive barometer of feeling. Every time a patrol went out they were debriefed by an intelligence officer or intelligence sergeant, and they repeated every little bit of gossip they heard along the way. It was clear even before the strike that the executive was already dead as a doornail. For months it had been losing support and power. One could feel them losing power.'

The army was insistent that its engineers could not move into the power stations and crank up electricity generation to a level which would end the daily power cuts. It said they could generate only a small amount of power but could not distribute it. The army also warned that other workers would walk out if they moved in, and that loyalists might sabotage generators with, as the general portrayed it, disastrous results – 'sewage bubbling in the streets, perhaps cholera, no bread, no milk, no power for the hospitals'.

Whatever the initial reactions of the Protestant middle class to an exercise so clearly enforced by paramilitaries, many of its members came to endorse the strike. In his memoirs Rees recalled returning late one evening to the Culloden hotel in affluent north Down. Describing walking through the plush lounge largely occupied by Protestant customers, he remembered: 'The cry of "traitor" came in unison, a spontaneous response of anger. We the Brits were the outsiders.'

Throughout the strike the executive continued to function. It eventually announced the postponement of much of the implementation of the Council of Ireland until after the next assembly election: some weeks earlier this might have had a major impact, but with virtually all attention now focused on the streets the move seemed barely relevant. A reluctant decision by the Wilson government to use the army to break the loyalist control of petrol and oil supplies, largely at the insistence of executive members, made things worse. In a petulant television broadcast known thereafter as the 'spongers speech', Wilson referred to loyalists as 'people who spend their lives sponging on Westminster and British democracy and then systematically assault democratic methods'. He asked contemptuously: 'Who do they think they are?' The description infuriated almost all Unionists, one senior assembly official describing it as 'catastrophically unhelpful'. In the days that followed many loyalists proudly and defiantly sported pieces of sponge in their lapels.

After two weeks of the strike, and after Rees had refused Faulkner's call to him to open talks with the strike leaders, Faulkner concluded that there was no help for the executive and resigned. It was the end of a unique constitutional experiment which had taken almost two years of hard work to construct, but which survived for only five months. Following Faulkner's resignation, Rees announced the winding-up of the executive, and the two governments and the powersharing parties trudged dispiritedly back to square one.

In the years since then, debates have continued about whether the authorities could have handled the strike better and prevented the rejectionist Unionists from winning such a victory. As usual, there have been allegations of both conspiracy and cock-up. There have been allegations that military or intelligence elements opposed to the Sunningdale Agreement, or disinclined to make efforts to support it, helped ensure its downfall. It is certainly the case, on General King's own admission, that he could hardly have done less in support of the executive.

The argument is that more vigorous action by the authorities, in terms of propaganda and publicity, in terms of giving the army stronger direction, in terms of keeping the roads open and in terms of preserving power supplies, might have preserved Sunningdale. Rees was certainly an inexperienced minister whom a number of commentators have criticised as too indecisive a man for a post which, at that moment of emergency, called for swift and resolute action. A newspaper quoted one of his officials as saying, 'I don't mind Merlyn wrestling with his conscience for ages over every issue. What I mind is that the result always seems to be a draw.'

Rees himself would later argue in a television documentary: 'I didn't let them win. They were going to win anyway. It could not be done, that's the short answer. The police were on the brink of not carrying out their duties and the middle class were on the strikers' side. This wasn't just an industrial dispute. This was the Protestant people of Northern Ireland rising up against Sunningdale and it could not be shot down.'

It was certainly the case that the Sunningdale initiative had already run into severe problems, and that the strength of loyalist opposition to it might well eventually have brought it down. On the other hand, no one can know whether a defeat for the strikers might have provided a boost for the new government which might have seen it through to eventual success. Robert Fisk's book on the strike, *The Point of No Return*, is highly critical of the inactivity of the NIO and the security forces but significantly concludes: 'Even if the police had chosen to act against the men who wanted to overthrow the state was this option open to them? The evidence is that it was not.'

The agreement's basic unpopularity in the Unionist community was made worse by Faulkner's loss of the leadership of the Unionist party, the Dublin constitutional court case, the damaging February elections, and the continuing violence. Rees wrote of Faulkner: 'British governments had expected too much of him. He had been obliged to go into no-man's-land with his troops left far behind.' Senior official Maurice Hayes agreed:

> There is now plenty of evidence that he was pushed farther than he should have been, and beyond his power to deliver. The general consensus now is that the nationalist side overbid their hands, and won. It is clear that Faulkner was saddled with a load which he could not carry and which eventually brought him down, and with him the whole power-sharing experiment.

Another continuing debate concerned whether the sharpest loyalist opposition to Sunningdale had been generated by the Irish dimension or by powersharing. Most commentators held that the Dublin connection had been the more potent, though others disagreed. One Catholic official concluded: 'I believe that the fundamental, gut objection all along was to sharing power with Catholics, and that opposition to the Council of Ireland was a smokescreen to conceal a much deeper and atavistic historic antagonism which had not been put to rest.'

Strike aftermath

While loyalists celebrated their victory with a huge rally at Stormont, much of the rest of the world viewed the downfall of Sunningdale as politically catastrophic and profoundly depressing. The new system had appeared to offer the possibility of eventually settling the troubles by giving moderate Unionists and nationalists a chance to work together. The theory had been that the old Stormont Unionism had failed to preserve order through its insistence on excluding Catholics from power. It seemed obvious that the way to stabilise the state was to reassemble Stormont with a Catholic component. Thus a coalition of the two religions would isolate the extremists on both sides and Catholics could be brought to identify with the state as they never had before.

But a great many Protestants had never subscribed to this proposition, and scepticism in their community rose steadily as the months passed with no let-up in violence. The sense grew that Sunningdale offered not a new beginning but a dangerous threat to their interests. Furthermore the partnership concept was shattered by the harsh reality of the strike, which demonstrated that Protestants collectively had both the determination and the ability to bring down a system they opposed. They had a clear numerical majority in Northern Ireland; they held the key jobs in the key industries; and they had shown they could bring Northern Ireland to a standstill. Although some argued that Rees had been at fault, the general moral drawn was that Unionists had demonstrated their power of veto.

This was accepted, however reluctantly, in the Republic as well as in Britain. Until May 1974 many in the south had airily assumed that northern Protestants would come to see that they had been simply wrongheaded in opposing partnership and eventual Irish unity. But the strike, coupled with the carnage of the Dublin and Monaghan bombings, brought home the extent of loyalist determination to oppose what they regarded as dangerous.

The theory that only some form of partnership government would work continued to hold sway in London and Dublin and within the SDLP, but the success of the strike was taken as demonstrating that it was impossible to put that theory into practice. A collective nationalist rejection of the old Stormont had eventually brought that institution down; now Unionists had managed to destroy its successor. The analysis that there appeared to be a double veto, with Unionists and nationalists able to deny the other what they wanted, caused a great many to conclude that this was a problem without a solution. That element of Unionism which had been prepared to share power virtually disappeared overnight. Rees went back to the drawing board in search of some new avenue of progress. He found none, since Unionists and loyalists, suffused with the glow of their victory, were in no mood to accept anything other than a return to majority rule.

The schizophrenic Unionist attitude towards law and order and legitimate protests had rarely been seen in a more illuminating light than in the strike's aftermath. The part of the Unionist psychology which held that protest was legitimate and sometimes essential meant that there was widespread Protestant support for the stoppage, despite the obvious use of violence and intimidation. During the strike senior politicians, who would later express horror at any idea of contacts with 'IRA terrorists', routinely sat in meetings with representatives of paramilitary groups which had many members serving prison sentences for murder. Yet once the collapse of the executive had been achieved, the law-and-order strand of the Unionist psyche reasserted itself.

Everyone went quietly back to work and waited to see what the government would do next. Politically Rees felt he could do little. His best effort, after much tortured thought, was to decide to establish a 'constitutional convention' to bring local politicians together in the hope that they might find a new agreement among themselves. Rees was criticised for allegedly abdicating governmental responsibility and putting the onus on local parties to find a solution. He refused however to take any more serious political initiative though he did make a move in another direction, which was towards the paramilitary groups and in particular the IRA.

The IRA's killing rate had halved, from 280 in 1972 to 280 in the following two years, but it remained the major taker of life. Although Whitelaw had concluded in 1972 that his meeting with the IRA had been useless, Rees again put out feelers towards the republicans. In this he appears to have been encouraged by the NIO's most senior civil servant, Sir Frank Cooper, who had a reputation for being both forceful and devious. In 1974 Rees legalised both Sinn Féin, the IRA's political wing, and the UVF, partly to facilitate the business of talking to them. Republicans and loyalists were regularly invited to Laneside, a large government-owned house in a plush area of County Down, for informal chats with officials.

The talks which ensued, there and elsewhere, helped lead to IRA ceasefires in 1974 and 1975. There are many conflicting accounts about what was conveyed and why, with allegations that the officials involved in the discussions led republicans to believe that their goal of British withdrawal was a distinct possibility. It was certainly an era of furtive contacts and murmured assurances: many mysteries persist about what was said and what was meant. There is no real evidence however that a British withdrawal was ever intended, whatever was discussed at Laneside.

The contacts did not at first result in a reduction of IRA violence. In the autumn of 1974 the IRA maintained a concerted campaign not just in Northern Ireland but also in England with a number of bombings which were to have lengthy legal sequels. Explosions at bars in Birmingham killed 21 people and injured almost 200 more, while 7 people died in the bombings of pubs in Guildford and Woolwich. While the IRA inflicted much damage on people and property it also suffered numerous casualties. By the beginning of 1974, almost 150 of its members had been killed, and hundreds more were behind bars.

In 1974, as contacts between the IRA and the government developed, there was no shortage of official and unofficial go-betweens. In one unprecedented move a group of senior northern Protestant churchmen travelled south to meet IRA leaders at Feakle in County Clare, reporting back to NIO officials on their talks. IRA demands which included a British declaration of intent to withdraw were conveyed to Rees, the IRA promising a cessation of violence in return. The organisation next delivered a brief ceasefire over the 1974 Christmas period. Rees responded by signing no new internment orders and giving an assurance that security force activity would be scaled down. He also sanctioned official contacts with the republicans to supplement the many unofficial contacts.

The IRA ceasefire survived into 1975 and, despite IRA complaints that the British were not responding to their proposals, it was extended and in February declared indefinite. Rees responded by continuing to release detainees, by scaling down army operations in nationalist areas, and by setting up 'incident centres' from which republicans could report on events in particular districts. In a formulation which would be important in later years, Rees also signalled that the British government had no territorial or political interests in Ireland beyond its obligations to the citizens of Northern Ireland. The SDLP and the Irish government strenuously objected to all of this, complaining that such moves enhanced the credibility of the IRA and Sinn Féin at their expense. While Rees insisted that there were no secret deals with the IRA, rumours were rife that the continuing contact between the government and republicans might lead to a British withdrawal.

The formal ceasefire lasted for much of 1975 but was often breached. A number of members of the security forces were killed in attacks which the IRA characterised as retaliations for official breaches of the ceasefire. Overall in 1975, 33 security force personnel died, exactly half the toll of the previous year.

Loyalist violence remained at a high level with both the UDA and UVF highly active. The IRA responded by becoming embroiled in what was described as sectarian 'tit-for-tat' exchanges, with more than forty Protestants killed in 1975 and January 1976. A few of them had loyalist connections but most were chosen at random. The attacks included an attack on an Orange Order meeting in south Armagh in which five were killed, a bombing and shooting attack on a Shankill Road pub which also killed five, and the killings of ten Protestant workmen, again in south Armagh, in retaliation for loyalist killings. Republican theorists, who say that loyalist groups are sectarian but insist that the IRA is not, look back on this particular period with some embarrassment. A violent Provisional IRA feud with the Official IRA in the autumn of 1975 added to the death toll.

By early November the ceasefire existed only in name and the incident centres were closed. In December Rees released the final internees and declared internment to be over, but was able to tell the Commons that in 1975 more than 1,100 people had been charged with paramilitary offences, and that the prison population had risen by 40 per cent. Meanwhile, of course, no steps towards British withdrawal had been taken. In fact, during the ceasefire period the authorities had been carefully planning a new security phase.

The mid-1970s ceasefire period is remembered in republican folklore as a disaster which brought the IRA close to defeat. It was said to have reduced morale and recruiting, and in republican terms it diverted the IRA's energies away from the security forces and into overtly sectarian killing and internecine feuding. Most republicans came to believe that the episode was essentially an exercise in deception, with officials promising the earth to a gullible republican leadership, which was headed at that time by southern veterans Ruairí Ó Brádaigh and Dáithí Ó Conaill. Northern republicans such as Gerry Adams and Martin McGuinness would later take control of the republican movement, arguing that the mid-1970s leaders had been duped. Years later McGuinness declared: 'The former leadership of this movement has never been able to come to terms with this leadership's criticism of the disgraceful attitude adopted by them during the disastrous ceasefire in the mid-1970s.'

The Rees convention

On the party political front, the constitutional convention produced only one moment of real interest. The whole exercise looked unpromising from the start, since in the wake of the UWC strike neither Unionists nor nationalists were in any mood to make concessions. Nationalists tended to feel that the British government had abdicated its fundamental governmental responsibilities and had caved in to intimidation. The general Unionist sense was that Sunningdale-style powersharing and the

Irish dimension had been banished and that majority rule should now be re-established. This majoritarian sentiment was reinforced in the Westminster election of October 1974, when the UUUC MPs held ten of their eleven seats.

The elections to the convention in May 1975 produced a result which practically ensured that the new body would not produce agreement, since UUUC candidates won 47 of the 78 seats with 55 per cent of the vote. Support for Faulkner collapsed, with his UPNI taking less than 8 per cent of the vote. In the assembly in 1974 he had around twenty supporters but in 1975 he had only five. The man who had been close to the centre of power for so many years now cut a forlorn figure on the convention's backbenches, where his much-depleted band of supporters served as a daily reminder of the eclipse of moderate Unionism.

Before convention members got together at Stormont, Rees ordered workmen into the chamber to rearrange the furniture in the hope of encouraging them to think in terms of consensus rather than confrontation. Curved cross-benches were installed to make the point that Unionists and nationalists should aim to meet each other in the middle. The UUUC's overall majority ensured, however, that the creative carpentry was in vain.

It was true that there were many stresses and strains and personality differences within the UUUC, encompassing as it did West, Craig and Paisley and some independents. In the aftermath of the strike there had been a brief tussle between Unionist politicians and loyalist paramilitants who argued that their efforts during the stoppage entitled them to political representation. Although the politicians won these exchanges fairly easily, perhaps half a dozen of the 47 Unionist members had some form of paramilitary associations. Most of these were linked not to the UDA or UVF, groups actively engaged in assassination campaigns, but to what were called 'doomsday' or 'respectable' groups, who saw themselves as being in the business of preparing for a possible civil war.

The fact that they, and many others, thought in such apocalyptic terms illustrates that the first half of the 1970s was a highly uncertain time in which many believed the worst might happen. Northern Ireland, after its first four decades of sullen stability, had gone through the political unrest of the 1960s followed by large-scale violence and constitutional upheavals: nobody was really sure what might come next, and many feared the worst. A common observation in shops and pubs at the time was, 'It'll get worse before it gets better.'

There were many in both Unionism and nationalism who suspected that in the wake of the strike Britain, feeling even less loyalty to the Unionist community than previously, was tempted by the withdrawal option. The SDLP urged the Irish government to prepare contingency plans for a doomsday scenario, a prospect Dublin took seriously. Dublin minister Garret FitzGerald, worried that Wilson might opt for British withdrawal, lobbied Henry Kissinger who was then US Secretary of State. He told Kissinger that Dublin might seek American assistance 'in persuading Britain not to embark on a course of action that could be so fraught with dangers'. FitzGerald's fears, as he later acknowledged, were groundless.

In the convention meanwhile Unionist members, whatever their differences, came together for key votes, their combined strength meaning that they always won on the important issues. There was no repeat of the unruly scenes of the assembly, since Unionists now regarded themselves as being in control. Yet even as Unionists flexed their majoritarian muscles in the chamber, surreptitious talks went on behind the scenes with the SDLP. These talks produced one intriguing idea known as 'voluntary coalition'. The idea, advanced primarily by William Craig, who had undergone a remarkable change since his 'shoot-to-kill' days a few years earlier, suggested the establishment of a new Unionist-dominated administration, with a prime minister who would invite SDLP members into his cabinet. The model was primarily based on the type of emergency coalition which had governed Britain during World War Two. The concept appears to have been discussed by leading members of the major Unionist parties, but all of them except Craig hurriedly backed away from it.

He not only failed to carry the UUUC with him, but failed to convince his own Vanguard party. He and a few assembly members, including future Unionist party leader David Trimble, were banished from the UUUC, which even without them still had an overall majority in the convention. There was no agreement between the UUUC and the rest of the assembly's members. The UUUC drew up a report which was essentially a Unionist wish-list, seeking a return to majority rule and ruling out any new Council of Ireland. The report wanted a new Stormont with even greater powers, a doubling of Northern Ireland seats at Westminster, and the introduction of an oath of allegiance to the Queen for all major appointments. Nationalists were offered little more than the prospect of chairing some committees.

The other parties, complaining their views had been ignored, boycotted the final debates and submitted minority reports. Rees asked the Unionists to reconsider but they stuck to their original report and in March 1976 he wound up the convention. Realistically, there was no chance of the British government accepting the convention report. Its underlying philosophy was simple: the restoration of Unionist majority rule, with a coalition headed by West, Paisley and Craig's successor, Ernest Baird.

The government was in a double bind. The display of loyalist strength in the UWC strike had led the government to conclude that it could not impose powersharing and an Irish dimension on an unwilling Protestant population. But at the same time it was not about to agree to the UUUC's demands to turn the clock back and revert to majority rule. The idea of Catholics and nationalists accepting a rebirth of Stormont was equally out of the question. The problem was what political policy the government might pursue if both powersharing and majority rule were non-starters. Its answer was to move away from the idea of finding political agreement and to concentrate instead on the security and economic fields. This new approach was personified in a new Northern Ireland Secretary, Roy Mason, who replaced Rees in September 1976.

The violence continues

The years 1975 and 1976 were a time of major violence which claimed almost six hundred lives. The IRA was as ever the highest single taker of life though loyalist groups were highly active. The army suffered far fewer casualties in 1975–76, losing 30 men compared to 250 killed during the previous four years. Killings attributed to the army were also well down: 20 people died at the hands of troops in these two years compared to 170 in the years from 1971 to 1974. But the civilian casualty rate remained high as the IRA and loyalists, particularly the UVF, carried out many attacks that resulted in civilian casualties. These included many bombings and shootings which caused multiple deaths. The IRA attacked a number of Protestant bars, while the UVF and UDA targeted many Catholic pubs.

A few incidents stand out. One was the January 1976 IRA attack, at Kingsmills in south Armagh, on a coachload of Protestant workmen, following a wave of anti-Catholic attacks by the UVF. IRA gunmen lined up the workmen at the side of the road and opened fire with at least four weapons, killing ten men. Also well-remembered are the actions of the IRA unit which became known as the Balcombe Street gang in and around London. They carried out up to fifty bombings and shootings in the London area during 1974 and 1975, especially an intense burst of violent activity in late 1975 which included no-warning bomb attacks on pubs and other premises. Fifteen people were killed.

Loyalists were more unabashedly and consistently sectarian than the IRA. Republicans often denied the IRA was involved in sectarian killings and sometimes used a cover name to claim responsibility for attacks. The UVF and UDA, by contrast, made little secret of the fact that they regarded the Catholic population in general as legitimate targets, and made no bones about attacking Catholic bars and other targets with the aim of killing as many as possible. In one UVF killing spree on a single day in October 1975 twelve people died in an unprecedented wave of shootings and bombings. Most of those killed were Catholic, though the death toll included four UVF members killed when their own bomb exploded prematurely. Thirteen UVF bombs went off during the day.

One of the UVF members involved in the killings was Lenny Murphy, who was later to be killed by the IRA. He was leader of the Shankill Butchers gang, a collection of UVF members responsible for a large number of murders which together make up what are probably the most notorious sequence of killings in Northern Ireland. The deaths, which stretched over many years, included both sectarian killings and many loyalist feud deaths. They included shootings, bombings and in particular killings carried out with knives and by savage beatings. The most infamous were those of seven Catholics who between 1975 and 1977 were picked up at random during the hours of darkness. The victims were picked out solely for their religion. They were then killed with implements such as cleavers, axes and the butchers' knives which earned the gang their nickname. Some had their throats cut and others were tortured. In a statement to police about one victim a member of the gang said: 'When he was lying on the ground I cut his throat. It was a butcher's knife I had, sharp as a lance. I just slit his throat right open.'

While Murphy himself did not take part in all of the killings he was regarded as the gang's leader and driving force, even while in prison. During an inquest a detective said of him: 'He was a ruthless, dedicated terrorist with a sadistic streak, regarded by those who knew him well as a psychopath. He inflicted terror on those around him.' The ferocity of some of the killings meant that the gang's actions remained fresh in the public consciousness years after the actual events. Many of the gang were jailed in a large-scale trial in 1979. Eleven gang members were sentenced on more than a hundred charges which included nineteen murders, receiving a total of 42 life sentences, along with sentences of imprisonment amounting to almost 2,000 years. Passing sentence the judge said: 'Many of the murders you have pleaded guilty to were carried out in a manner so cruel and so ruthless as to be beyond the comprehension of any normal person.' Murphy was himself already in jail serving a sentence for lesser offences. He was not charged in the Shankill Butchers trial and was never convicted of murder.

One incident which sent shock waves through Anglo-Irish relations was the IRA assassination of the British ambassador to the Republic, Christopher Ewart-Biggs, in Dublin in July 1976. The attack took place just beyond the gates of his County Dublin official residence: his car was blown up by a landmine, killing him and his secretary. He had been ambassador for only twelve days before his death. It later emerged that Merlyn Rees had at the last minute been forced to cancel plans which would have meant that he too would have been travelling in the convoy. Garret FitzGerald, then Irish foreign minister and later Taoiseach, wrote of the ambassador: 'He was to pay his first official visit to me at 10 a.m. Just as I had finished clearing my desk to receive him, I was told there had been an explosion near his residence. I was filled with horror at the atrocity, with shame that Irishmen had murdered the envoy of a neighbouring country, and with shock at our failure to protect him.'

A month later, in August 1976, came another terrible incident which, at the same time as taking the lives of innocents, momentarily seemed to hold out the hope of helping bring an end to the violence. It would prove to be a false dawn. The incident began when a member of the IRA was shot dead by troops at the wheel of a car during a car chase in west Belfast. The vehicle careered out of control and mounted the pavement at a school where a Catholic woman, Anne Maguire, was walking with her three children. The car crushed them all against railings.

The crash killed eight-year-old Joanne Maguire and her brothers John, aged two, and Andrew who, only six weeks old, was being pushed in a pram. Anne Maguire was unconscious for two weeks before awakening to discover that three of her four children were dead. As one account put it,

'When the wrecked car, pram and bicycle were removed local residents set up a little shrine at the mangled railings. Flowers and candles marked the scene of a tragedy that cut through the emotional defences of a community inured to all manner of atrocity.'

The wave of anger and grief generated by the deaths gave rise to the Peace People movement, led by two Belfast women, Mairead Corrigan, the children's aunt, and local woman Betty Williams. The movement quickly snowballed, its early rallies attracting tens of thousands of people and huge international publicity. As the months passed, however, the movement suffered from outside criticism, internal bickering and personality clashes. The award of the Nobel Peace Prize to its two leaders did nothing to halt the arguments and the slide in its credibility and popularity, critics accusing them of mercenary motives. The movement eventually petered out, a transient phenomenon with powerful initial impetus but which in the end did not deliver peace.

In a tragic postscript Anne Maguire took her own life some years later, leaving a note for her surviving children which said, 'Forgive me – I love you.' Although she regained her health she never recovered psychologically from the loss of her children. Her sister Mairead Corrigan later wrote: 'Anne never saw her children buried. In her own mind she refused to accept their deaths. She would often talk about seeing them playing in the garden. Their deaths and the brain bruising she suffered resulted in psychotic depression. Anne became a troubled soul, knowing no peace of mind. She seemed to lock herself in a private world with her dead babies.'

No one could know it at the time, but late 1976 and early 1977 were to mark the end of the most violent phase of the troubles. These months were followed by no new political agreement, but the killing rate dropped dramatically. The statistics tell the story. Of the approximately 3,600 troubles deaths, almost exactly half took place in the period of five years and four months which began when internment was introduced in August 1971. In the final months of 1971 the total killed was 149; the total deaths for the five years which followed were, in rough terms, 500, 260, 300, 260 and 300. In the quarter-century which followed, deaths would never exceed 125 in a single year. But the deaths, though fewer, were to continue for a quarter of a century and more.

6

From Castlereagh to Warrenpoint
1977–79

The second strike

R oy Mason, who took over as Northern Ireland Secretary in September 1976, was very different from Merlyn Rees in both style and substance. Rees's two and a half years in Belfast had been a harrowing time for him, as Harold Wilson's press secretary Joe Haines observed: 'Northern Ireland wore out Merlyn Rees. He ached, and looked as if he ached, with tiredness after his first 15 months in office.' Haines saw him as 'a good, kind and able minister who had become trapped by his office and was too exhausted to realise he had little more to offer'.

Roy Mason was a very different character. A tough Barnsley ex-miner who was short in physical stature but long on self-confidence, he was as decisive as Rees had been tentative. He arrived in Belfast following a spell as defence minister, a job which encouraged him to think in terms of a military approach. Where Rees had rambled, Mason was blunt; where

Rees had anguished about the complexities of office, Mason tended to reduce policy to brass tacks.

Almost from the start he made a number of strategic choices. While Rees had maintained contact with republicans with the aim of gaining ceasefires, Mason quickly made it clear that he was in the more straightforward business of defeating the IRA. At his first press conference he described the IRA as 'reeling', and within months had closed down Laneside, the NIO residence associated with suspicions of underhand deals. This sent out a signal that the days of secret conversations were over. Many had not trusted Merlyn Rees when he declared that a British withdrawal was not in prospect. When Mason gave such assurances, which he did with regularity, he tended to be believed. This was largely because he was so clearly determined, in the language of the day, to 'take on the terrorists'.

He also made it clear that the days of political initiatives, on the scale of Sunningdale or even the constitutional convention, were over. He spoke of steering clear of 'dramatic initiatives that might lead to failure and leave people in deep despair again'. He remarked later in his autobiography: 'I thought it futile to barge in with great plans and programmes and proposals for constitutional change.' This approach dismayed many local politicians, who saw it as a declaration that they were redundant and were to be sidelined. Concluding that a search for political agreement among the parties was pointless, Mason instead concentrated on security and the economy in the hope that militant republicanism could be defeated by a mixture of security force activity and job creation.

Unionists meanwhile approached the late 1970s with a mixture of satisfaction and frustration: satisfaction that they had comprehensively defeated the Sunningdale powersharing initiative, but frustration at Westminster's flat refusal to bring back majority rule. The 1974 UWC strike had shown muscle, while the Unionist strength in numbers was also evident in the convention and Westminster elections which had established beyond doubt that anti-deal Unionist parties were very much dominant. But while they were clearly in the ascendant they could not deliver a new Protestant ascendancy. While Unionism had the negative power of being able to prevent powersharing, it conspicuously lacked the power of persuasion. No significant body of opinion in the Commons supported the convention report's demand for a return to majority rule; in fact in all the years that followed, Unionism failed to persuade any significant section of opinion of the merits of simple majority rule.

May 1977 brought an attempt by some sections of Unionism to extract by coercion what could not be achieved by persuasion, via an attempt to stage a rerun of the 1974 UWC strike. Although the UUUC was still in existence at this stage as a political co-ordinating body, it divided and fell apart on the issue of a second strike. Ian Paisley and Ernest Baird were enthusiastic, but major elements such as Harry West's Ulster Unionist party and the Orange Order disapproved. Paisley and Baird became involved, together with the UWC and paramilitary groups including the UDA, in a new organisation styling itself the United Unionist Action Council (UUAC).

In April this body announced that an indefinite strike would be launched the following month, with the aims of pressurising Westminster into a stronger security policy and the return of majority rule. From the start the odds seemed to be against the success of the strike, with little real appetite for it within the general Protestant community. There was a clear division in Unionist ranks on the tactic; Mason was more to the liking of most Unionists than Rees, and the early months of the year had seen a reduction of violence. There were also no unpopular targets around, as there had been in 1974 in the form of the Sunningdale Agreement. The move was opposed by almost the entire business community, trade unions and the main Protestant churches. Paisley and Baird did their best to stir up feelings with over-the-top rhetoric, Baird accusing Westminster politicians of losing their sense of British identity and having 'maybe more in common with Communist Russia or anarchy than they have with the British way of life'. Paisley too condemned British politicians: 'When I consider the drunkenness, lewdness, immorality and filthy language of many MPs, I care absolutely nothing for their opinions. Ulster Protestants are not interested in gaining the goodwill of such reprobates.'

When the strike was launched on 2 May, widespread intimidation was evident from the outset, the RUC receiving 400 complaints on its first day. Although many workplaces opened normally there was a steady stream of closures during the day. Gangs of up to a hundred UDA men appeared on main roads in loyalist areas of Belfast, vehicles were hijacked and roads strewn with broken glass, and many businesses reported threatening telephone calls.

Within days, however, a drift back to work was reported. A crucial factor was that the authorities performed very differently in 1977 than they had in 1974. They had clearly absorbed many lessons from the previous stoppage and had made contingency plans. Mason also proved to be a much more determined figure than Rees. When loyalists blocked a main road in east Belfast, police and troops in riot gear were sent in to move them on, and after a brief skirmish the loyalists took to their heels. Thus while intimidation and roadblocks had some effect, the security forces were seen to be working to keep roads open.

Another vital factor was that there were virtually no power cuts. Some power workers co-operated with the strike leaders, but a majority resented being dragooned into the front line of a strike which lacked widespread support. Some of them stopped work but most stayed at their posts, supplying enough electricity to avoid widespread cuts. The only interruptions to supply came in a few areas where loyalists set off explosive devices.

Behind the scenes Mason and Paisley were locked in intense efforts to lobby the power workers, oil tanker drivers and other key workers. The turning point came when workers at the principal power station, Ballylumford, voted by 286 to 171 in a secret ballot not to support the stoppage. By this stage, leaders of the three main Protestant churches were protesting against what they described as 'extensive intimidation and brutality'.

Increasingly desperate, the loyalist paramilitary groups escalated their violence, and there were three deaths in one day as loyalists blew up a filling station and shot dead a bus driver. None of this helped the strikers' cause and the stoppage was ignominiously called off soon afterwards, Paisley declining to stand by a pledge to retire from political life if the strike failed. Although the strike collapsed, Mason acknowledged in his memoirs that it was a close-run thing, writing: 'At any moment during the ten days of crisis, the balance could so easily have tilted against the government. Intimidation might have worked; Paisley might have succeeded in rallying the great mass of Protestants.'

It seemed a humiliating defeat for Paisley, yet within a week of the strike's end came local council elections which offered a telling insight into the Protestant attitude towards protests in general and Paisley in particular. In the poll, Paisley's party vote dropped only slightly. It was a demonstration of his own extraordinary resilience and a demonstration too that the Unionist electorate did not punish those representatives whom it felt had protested too much. Those such as Brian

Faulkner who were considered too accommodating could be heavily penalised at the polls, but those whose line was thought too hard were not.

Because it petered out, the second strike has received little attention in accounts of the troubles. The fact is that the stoppage took place exactly as one phase of the troubles was ending and another was beginning. How much this watershed was due to the strike and its outcome, and how much may have been sheer coincidence are matters for debate. What is not in question is that the level of violence plummeted so dramatically around this time that 1977 can only be regarded as an important turning point in the troubles.

Violence and changing security policy

The 308 deaths of 1976 were followed by only 116 in 1977. The troubles would drag on for a further quarter of a century, but the early months of 1977 mark the halfway point in terms of lives lost. The most dramatic change in the casualty figures was the decline in the number of civilians killed, from 220 in 1976 to 55 the following year.

Violence by loyalists decreased from 127 killings in 1976 to just 28 in 1977. In the five years prior to 1977 the loyalist toll was 590; in the five years from 1977 on it was only 84. Most immediately this was attributed to the defeat suffered by the UDA, the largest of the Protestant paramilitary organisations, in the UUAC strike. In the years that followed membership of such groups as the UDA dropped sharply, while many other less active paramilitary organisations, such as the Orange Volunteers, virtually disappeared from the scene.

There were deeper reasons for this than simply the failure of the strike. For one thing, Mason's approach caused many loyalists to conclude that it was simply no longer necessary for them to involve themselves in paramilitarism. Mason's political line, which he pursued with ever-greater confidence following the strike, was to go after the IRA and loyalist paramilitants with tougher security policies. As this policy became clear and the overall level of violence fell, many working-class Protestants concluded that the IRA was being tackled with determination, that the Union looked safe, and that their presence in the paramilitary ranks was not needed.

The Rees administration had made various plans aimed at putting security policy on a more logical and rational basis, and Mason and the new Chief Constable of the RUC, a shrewd Englishman called Kenneth Newman, built on these to produce a coherent if often controversial strategy. Among important strategic changes to security and political policy were the concepts of 'criminalisation' and 'Ulsterisation'. The first meant that the IRA and other paramilitary groups were to be denied any acknowledgement of political motivation, and were to be treated in exactly the same way as those the authorities sarcastically called 'ordinary decent criminals'. Mason and others spoke regularly of the IRA as a mafia-style organisation headed by 'godfathers' who were said to care more for money than for patriotism. The policy was partly motivated by a desire to change perceptions of the conflict from the colonial war of republican propaganda to that of a campaign against criminal gangs. The battle over criminalisation would later come to a head in the prisons. Ulsterisation was a play on the word 'Vietnamisation', the process by which the US army in Vietnam had recruited and trained locals to take the place of US troops in the front line. In a Belfast context this involved planning a gradual decrease in the number of regular troops and their replacement by an expanded RUC and UDR. It also meant what was known as 'police primacy', giving the RUC the lead in security matters and placing the army largely under its direction.

The policy brought about striking changes in casualty patterns. In 1972, 110 regular soldiers and 40 locally recruited personnel were killed. For 1976 the corresponding figures were 14 and 40, with local deaths outnumbering the deaths of regular troops in almost every year of the decade that followed. In spite of the high casualty rates, large numbers of local men, almost all of them Protestants, were ready to join the RUC and UDR, both of which consistently had more applications than vacancies. Ulsterisation also made broad political sense in that the drop in regular army casualties helped prevent any build-up of sentiment in Britain for a withdrawal from Northern Ireland.

Internment had been ended at the end of 1975, and an alternative approach was developed to put paramilitants and especially IRA members behind bars using the criminal courts. Since the early 1970s the trials of defendants charged with troubles-related offences had taken place not before a jury but before a single judge. Juries had been abolished following the 1972 Diplock report which had highlighted the fear of paramilitary intimidation of jurors. For the same reason witnesses were in short supply and very often refused to testify. Forensic evidence was of some use, but the authorities realised that the most effective way of securing convictions was to extract confessions from the accused.

This simple fact became the new central plank of the RUC's battle with the IRA and loyalist groups. Its detective ranks were reorganised, with specialist collators appointed, in the largely pre-computer age, to amass and analyse every scrap of evidence. Trained teams of interrogators were then put to work in new specially designed interrogation centres, most notably at Castlereagh in east Belfast. IRA and loyalist suspects were rounded up by the score and subjected to intense interrogations, with many of them subsequently charged with serious offences. As this system, which functioned with the regularity of a conveyor belt, got under way, it was found that although violence was decreasing, the number of people being charged stayed at more than a thousand a year. Lengthy remand periods meant that even those eventually acquitted were often taken off the streets for more than a year.

Before long, most cases heard by the non-jury courts consisted of the prosecution producing an incriminating statement or statements which the defendant was said to have made voluntarily while in Castlereagh or one of the other interrogation centres. The classic defence in such cases was for the defendant to say that the statement was not admissible in evidence because it had been extracted through either physical or psychological ill-treatment. The outcome of the trial would then turn on whether the judge ruled that the statement had been extracted by fair and legal means or whether detectives had extracted it through threats or by beatings. Both republicans and loyalists claimed brutality had become routine within Castlereagh and that convictions were being secured 'through the systematic application of torture techniques'. There were also stirrings of concern among civil liberties groups and other bodies. Garret FitzGerald records that leaders of the Presbyterian Church privately asked him to use his influence on the British government because they believed a number of loyalist suspects had been beaten during interrogation.

Other aspects of security policy also became decidedly tougher, with increased use of the army's undercover SAS regiment to stage ambushes in which IRA members were shot. During 1978 four members of the IRA were killed in this way, the SAS also accidentally killing three uninvolved civilians in the same year.

Party differences

Dublin and the SDLP quietly applauded Mason's performance in the UUAC strike, lamenting only that he had not been in office during the 1974 strike instead of Rees. Nevertheless, the constitutional nationalists were much against Mason's approach of downplaying politics and concentrating on security, since to them it was an article of faith that there was no military solution and that the troubles could only be ended by political means.

The SDLP came out of the experiences of Sunningdale, the UWC strike and the constitutional convention a greatly disillusioned party. Until the 1974 strike, things had seemed to be going well for constitutional nationalism: first Wilson and Callaghan had pushed for reforms, and then Heath had gone further and decided that nationalists needed to be in government. Heath had also come to support the existence of a strong Irish dimension, and Dublin had become established as a major element in the Northern Ireland question. Things had fallen apart, however, with the UWC strike, the resurgence of hardline Protestant power, and Labour's subsequent unwillingness to consider taking on the loyalists again. Brian Faulkner's untimely death in a horse-riding accident in 1977 seemed to epitomise the demise of moderate Unionism. From this viewpoint the convention had achieved little beyond confirming that with West, Paisley and Baird in control of Unionism there was no prospect of accommodation. One newspaper columnist wrote of the SDLP: 'Since the convention's failure the party has clung to a position which more and more of its members see as entirely honourable and yet completely nonsensical – offering partnership to parties who don't want it. The Unionists don't want to know them.'

The SDLP and in particular John Hume, its chief strategist, reacted to these unwelcome but unmistakable facts of life by moving to internationalise the question. Hume gradually shifted the focus away from the search for powersharing in Belfast and into an Anglo-Irish context, pressing London and Dublin to work together on a new approach. He also went further afield, cultivating the American political and media establishment to great effect. As early as 1977 he played a major part in persuading the most significant Irish-American politicians, who included Senator Edward Kennedy and the Speaker of the House of Representatives, Tip O'Neill, to unite as an Irish-American political force.

One motive for this was to wrest Irish-American influence away from the republican movement, for many Irish-Americans simplistically viewed the conflict in Northern Ireland as a classic colonial struggle between British occupying forces and the gallant freedom-fighters of the IRA. In this romantic version of events many complicating factors, including the very existence of the Unionist population, simply did not exist when viewed from across the Atlantic. This enabled the IRA to obtain both money and guns from Irish-Americans. Hume and the Irish government, which was represented in Washington by some exceptionally able Irish diplomats, sought to deny Irish-American influence to the republicans and instead harness it as a resource for constitutional nationalism.

Nationalist disenchantment with London increased as the belief grew that the Unionist party was gaining fresh influence at Westminster, not through force of argument but because James Callaghan's government had a dwindling majority and was anxious to persuade Unionists not to help bring it down. Callaghan supplied Unionists with a number of modest concessions including an increase in the number of Northern Ireland seats in the Commons. Nationalists accused Callaghan, who had been seen as being pro-nationalist in the late 1960s, of involvement in a sordid deal with Unionists.

Although there was never any question of Callaghan agreeing to the return of majority rule, by this stage some Unionists were themselves questioning whether this would be a good idea. Harry West as party leader and indeed the vast bulk of Unionist voters were still wedded to traditional devolution, but the alternative idea of integration with Britain was quietly gaining ground. The concept, which had been espoused briefly by Paisley around 1972, never found widespread support among the Unionist grassroots but it did take root in some important sections of the party. Among its devotees were MP James Molyneaux, who in 1979 was to succeed West as party leader, and his close associate Enoch Powell, the one-time Tory minister who had become a Unionist MP after splitting with the Conservative party on the race issue. Part of the attraction of integration was that, since majority rule seemed unattainable, it might be the next best thing and would be easier to achieve. It received philosophical underpinning from Powell, who had constructed intricate theories on why it, rather than devolution, was the best way of securing the Union. The notion grew that direct rule, which was not strictly integration but was leaning in that direction, was not a regrettable necessity but a system which could itself have beneficial effects and might be built upon.

Mason meanwhile strove as far as possible to present a normal face to the world, paying close attention to measures to strengthen the local economy. He staked a great deal of credibility, and a very great deal of public money, on a flagship project designed to provide a dramatic kick-start. In an attempt which was simultaneously imaginative, desperate and foolish, Mason announced a £56 million government subsidy to glamorous American car maker John De Lorean to establish a new plant to produce futuristic luxury sports cars on the outskirts of west Belfast. Years later the venture was to end in a costly fiasco, the plant eventually closing with much of the money unaccounted for, no cars being produced for sale and no lasting jobs.

Republican evolution

Meanwhile significant changes were taking place within the republican movement with a younger northern element, most importantly Gerry Adams and Martin McGuinness, taking power from the older southerners Ruairí Ó Brádaigh and Dáithí Ó Conaill in a bloodless coup. Adams emerged from behind bars in the spring of 1977 following a spell in prison where he had built a reputation as a formidable theorist. Once back on the outside he deftly eased the old guard aside. The northerners argued that the ceasefire of the mid-1970s had been disastrous for the IRA and that not enough was being done to counteract the Castlereagh interrogation system. Once in charge, the new leaders made many significant changes in terms of both republican politics and of the structure of the IRA.

They set out to dispel among republicans the belief that an IRA victory was just around the corner, a belief that had lingered since the 1975 ceasefire. The new orthodoxy was set out in a speech, largely drafted by Adams, which was delivered in 1977 by respected republican veteran Jimmy Drumm. This declared: 'The British government is not withdrawing from the Six Counties. It is committed to stabilising the Six Counties and is pouring in vast amounts of money to assure loyalists and secure from loyalists support for a long haul against the IRA.' Adams later explained in his autobiography: 'We had not yet developed an integrated or strategic overview, but our entire struggle was at a crucial juncture, a defining moment, and we were convinced that the struggle needed to sort itself out and to go on.'

To cope with the British long haul the IRA would develop what came to be known as the 'long war', a war of attrition which it accepted would have to go on for years. The IRA fell back on hoping that political stalemate, continued violence, occasional attacks in Britain, international pressure, the enormous cost and the apparent insolubility of the problem would ultimately sap Britain's will to stay in Northern Ireland. To the republican mind, Unionists were not a major problem, being merely puppets of British imperialism. In republican theory the real enemy was Britain; and once Britain had been defeated Unionist resistance would simply collapse.

There was increasing internal republican debate on future tactics. Adams in particular argued the need for the IRA campaign to be augmented by political action, a notion in which can be seen the germ of his later emphasis on building up Sinn Féin into an organisation in its own right. Adams, who in this deeply militaristic movement always thought in conspicuously political terms, was to write: 'There is now a realisation in republican circles that armed struggle on its own is inadequate and that non-armed forms of political struggle are at least as important.' More than a few republicans noted the similarities with the road taken into politics by the old IRA in the 1960s. The difference this time was that entry into the political arena was being advocated by republicans whose continued commitment to the armed struggle was beyond doubt, and who saw the politics as part of the war.

The same northern leadership that was urging more emphasis on politics was simultaneously reshaping the IRA into a more effective killing machine. The IRA was partly reorganised into a cell structure in order to guard against the effects of informers and interrogation. It also widened its range of targets, killing a number of senior business figures and explaining in statements that such individuals were attempting to stabilise the economy and were therefore 'part of the British war machine'. Prison staff also became what the IRA termed 'legitimate targets', with many killings of off-duty officers. A new threat to the security forces emerged with the appearance of what was known as 'the M60 gang', a group of IRA members armed with heavy M60 machine guns smuggled in from America where they had been stolen from US armed forces. The weapon, which was capable of firing 600 shots a minute, proved devastating in urban ambushes, claiming the lives of eight members of the security forces. The IRA also kept up its attacks on the locally recruited security forces, causing the deaths of many RUC and UDR members.

February 1978 brought another of those events which recurred peri-odically during the republican campaign, in which the IRA both inflicted great human tragedy and damaged its own interests. This was the bombing of La Mon House, a small hotel on the outskirts of east Belfast. IRA members attached a bomb to a grille on a window, as they had done at several other business premises, and made off. But unlike other occa-sions the warning given was inadequate and the premises had not been evacuated when the device went off. The result was devastating.

The device produced an effect similar to napalm, sending a fireball rushing through the window and through a room containing dozens of people attending the annual dinner-dance of the Irish Collie Club. A waitress said later: 'People were on fire, actually burning alive. I watched men pulling long curtains off the rails and wrapping people up in them to try to put out the flames. I could smell the burning flesh. I didn't realise at the time what I was smelling but I realised later what that dreadful stench was.'

The explosion killed twelve people, seven of them women, and injured more than thirty others. Those who died included three married couples; all the victims were Protestants. A local paper reported: 'For those who were there to see this holocaust it was sickening. Sickening to see pieces of a human body, limbs and other parts of the body being lifted. Many of them were just pure red flesh so indistinguishable that even forensic science experts found difficulty in sifting out their identification.' Thou-sands of posters showing a charred and incinerated body, so burnt as to be unrecognisable, were distributed by the RUC.

In his memoirs Adams claimed the incident left him despondent, de-pressed and deeply affected by the deaths and injuries, adding: 'I could also feel two years of work go down the drain.' Up until the La Mon bomb the IRA had been causing fewer civilian casualties, partly because the drop in loyalist violence had brought a sharp decrease in tit-for-tat kill-ings, and partly because it knew how counterproductive civilian deaths were.

For the IRA the almost unimaginable horror of the La Mon attack was a disastrous setback, since although it regarded itself as an army, almost the entire world regarded La Mon as sheer terrorism, indefensible on any basis. In IRA terms this was one the lowest points of the troubles, giving the authorities great scope to move against them. The security forces duly took the initiative, making twenty-five arrests in west Belfast in the aftermath of the explosion. Among those arrested was Adams, who was not charged in connection with the attack but was accused of IRA membership. He was acquitted, though only after spending months back behind bars.

It soon became apparent, however, that although the world at large had recoiled from the horror of La Mon the republican core support had remained loyal. But it was clear that the IRA was at a low ebb, the La Mon attack demoralising its members and the Castlereagh system sending a steady stream of them behind bars, either for lengthy periods on remand or for even lengthier sentences following conviction.

There were rumours that the IRA, which was undoubtedly much weakened, might be forced into declaring a ceasefire. The difference between this ceasefire and the 1975 one, it was said, was that this would be unilateral rather than as a result of an agreement with the government. It would, in other words, signal a defeat rather than a deal. Emboldened by intelligence reports to this effect Mason made several highly optimistic statements forecasting that the IRA was on its last legs, saying at one point: 'My view is that their strength has waned to the point where they cannot sustain a campaign.'

The anticipated ceasefire never arrived, and things began to go wrong for the authorities in terms of the Castlereagh system. This was producing results in putting republicans behind bars, but in the process it was attracting more and more criticism. The government issued blanket denials of any wrongdoing, Mason describing criticisms as 'wild allegations'. In his autobiography he listed a series of killings and summed up: 'Words cannot express the disgust I felt when the people responsible for such evils bleated about the alleged erosion of their human rights.'

Interrogation was not a gentle business. Questioning, by rotating teams of detectives, could go on for six to eight hours a day with few breaks, and even long into the night. The courts threw out some cases, but for the most part allowed detectives a great degree of latitude, one senior judge ruling that a blow to the face which left the nose 'swollen and caused it to bleed' did not necessarily mean a subsequent confession was inadmissible as evidence. The assumption was widespread that fists were being freely used in Castlereagh and elsewhere. As one newspaper columnist summed up: 'Hardly anyone believes that members of the RUC do not rough up suspects. The only things in question, in the minds of most, are how frequently such treatment occurs, whether it is sanctioned at top level, and whether it is justified.'

Mason was to recall in his memoirs: 'I had been harassing the IRA with as much vigour as was legally acceptable in a liberal democracy. I was being as tough as I could be; and though my policy was undeniably a ruthless business, it at least meant that the level of violence was beginning to come down.' The government found itself locked in a propaganda firestorm with republicans, one denying ill-treatment in Castlereagh while the other claimed it was routine and rife. The problem for the authorities was that the republican claims were at least partly backed by non-republican sources.

A 1978 Amnesty International report concluded that 'maltreatment of suspected terrorists by the RUC has taken place with sufficient frequency to warrant the establishment of a public inquiry to investigate it'. Under pressure from this and numerous other allegations the government established a judicial committee to investigate. In the meantime a leading police doctor caused a major stir when he said he had seen a large number of people who had been physically ill-treated while in custody. When it appeared in 1979 the official report judiciously steered away from making direct accusations against the police, but made dozens of recommendations which taken together amounted to a programme for a complete overhaul of interrogation safeguards and complaints procedures. Once these were enacted the level of complaints dropped dramatically.

Hopes for an IRA ceasefire faded as Mason's assessments were shown up as unrealistic. While he had talked enthusiastically of rolling the IRA up 'like a tube of toothpaste', a leaked 1979 army document written by a senior army officer painted a very different picture of the organisation. He wrote:

> There is a stratum of intelligent, astute and experienced terrorists who provide the backbone of the organization. Our evidence of the calibre of rank-and-file terrorists does not support the view that they are merely mindless hooligans drawn from the unemployed and unemployable. The IRA will probably continue to recruit the men it needs. They will still be able to attract enough people with leadership talent, good education and manual skills to continue to enhance their all-around professionalism. By reorganizing on cellular lines, PIRA has become much less dependent on public support than in the past and is less vulnerable to penetration by

informers. The campaign is likely to continue while the British remain in Northern Ireland.

The IRA was not the only danger on the republican side, for the much smaller Irish National Liberation Army (INLA) claimed an increasing number of lives from the late 1970s on. This group began life in the mid-1970s as a Marxist grouping to the left of the IRA, but as the years went by it became much more republican than socialist. It carried out a high-profile attack during the Westminster general election campaign in the spring of 1979. Airey Neave, who was the shadow Northern Ireland Secretary and one of Conservative party leader Margaret Thatcher's closest aides, died when members of the INLA planted a booby-trap bomb which exploded underneath his car as he drove out of the House of Commons. He had been in charge of Thatcher's successful campaign for the Tory leadership against Heath in 1975, and was expected to become Northern Ireland Secretary after the general election.

The election of the Thatcher government in May brought a new Northern Ireland Secretary in the shape of Humphrey Atkins, who is remembered as a less forthright and less forceful minister than Mason. The Thatcher government had only been in office a few months when two events on a single day, 27 August, created a major security crisis. These were the assassination of the Queen's cousin, Lord Mountbatten, and the deaths of eighteen soldiers at Warrenpoint in County Down.

Mountbatten died in the Irish Republic, together with three other people, when an IRA device exploded on board his pleasure craft in the sea off County Sligo, where he regularly holidayed. A great-grandson of Queen Victoria, he had served in the Royal Navy in both world wars, subsequently acting as the last British viceroy in India, overseeing the ending of British rule.

Within hours of his death came the Warrenpoint bombing, a two-stage IRA attack which inflicted on the army its worst casualty toll during the troubles by killing eighteen soldiers, sixteen of them members of the Parachute Regiment. The attack began as a convoy of two army trucks led by a Land Rover made its way along a road running parallel to Carlingford Lough, which at that point marks the boundary between Northern Ireland and the Republic. At this spot the Republic is only a few hundred yards away across the inlet.

An 800lb IRA bomb hidden in a trailer by the side of the road, concealed among bales of straw, was set off, killing six soldiers. When other troops arrived at the scene there was gunfire across the lough from IRA members in the Republic. The surviving paratroopers and the other soldiers who had gone to the scene established a defensive position behind nearby gates and a wall, not realising that the IRA, guessing that they would do so, had concealed a second device there. This large bomb was detonated half an hour after the first explosion, killing a dozen more soldiers. The incident was described as the Parachute Regiment's worst setback since Arnhem in World War Two. The deaths of the soldiers and Mountbatten had a huge impact, sparking a major Anglo-Irish political crisis and marking out that day as one of the most dramatic of the troubles.

The Mason era was a true turning-point in that violence fell dramatically, and would never again rise to the scale experienced in the 1971–76 period. But the highest hopes of the Mason era were dashed: the theories that the De Lorean project could help turn round the economy, that Castlereagh would crush the IRA, that a military solution was possible without the need for political action. August 1979 cruelly shattered hopes that the troubles might be tailing off, leaving Northern Ireland to face the unpalatable fact that violent conflict looked set to continue indefinitely, and that the long war still had a long way to run.

7

The hungerstrikes

1980-81

1980

This was a year of comparative calm before the storm which was to break in 1981. It was a year when violence continued at a fairly low level while a half-hearted attempt at making political progress petered out within months. On the political front, in late 1979, Humphrey Atkins had announced plans for a conference of the major parties on devolution. The fact that the government made little attempt to apply serious pressure to the participants meant that from the start expectations were low. *The Economist*, for example, in an article entitled 'An initiative born to fail', declared, 'Even before the launch it was clear that the move stood little or no chance of success. Not a single Northern Ireland politician expects any real gains to come from the exercise.'

The conference precipitated an important personnel change at the highest level of Northern Ireland politics. Gerry Fitt, leader of the SDLP since its formation in 1970, believed his party was wrong in its decision to boycott the conference and resigned from it. More generally he complained that the SDLP was becoming less socialist and too nationalist. The party's other most prominent socialist, Paddy Devlin, had already gone, citing similar reasons.

Fitt and Devlin had been among Northern Ireland's best-known political personalities since the 1960s, providing much of the SDLP's early socialist character. Devlin had once declared, in a statement which also reflected Fitt's approach: 'I am basically a trade unionist and a socialist. I am not a Catholic or an Irish nationalist.' Both disapproved of the SDLP's increasing commitment to a stronger Irish dimension and its move away from the idea of powersharing.

As the years went by, however, the SDLP became greener and less left-wing, a process which was mirrored within the republican movement and within northern nationalism in general. The move away from the left was also in line with the trend in Britain, where Thatcherism was becoming the order of the day. Fitt and Devlin had thus tended to become isolated as nationalism shifted in a direction they disliked. When they eventually left, the fact that no one of note followed their lead illustrated the sense that they were figures who had not evolved in line with the rest of the party.

Fitt's natural successor as leader was John Hume, who as deputy leader had always been seen as the party's dominant theorist and strategist. The unique feature of Hume, who was already a well-known figure in both Europe and the US, was seen as his ability to combine theory with practical politics. He was among those who challenged the traditional nationalist assertion that the root of the problem was the British presence in Northern Ireland. He argued that the heart of the Irish question was not the British but the Protestants, that the problem was the divisions between Unionist and nationalist, and that partition was not the cause of division but a symptom of it. The mission of nationalism, he contended, was not to drive out the British but to convince Unionism that its concerns could be accommodated in an agreed Ireland.

The agenda for the Atkins conference illustrated that significant changes had taken place in London's thinking in ways which struck out in the opposite direction to the SDLP's progressively greener line. An official working paper set out a number of models, most of which were variations on the theme of powersharing. Some of its models envisaged having nationalists in government; others did not. The working paper specifically ruled out any return to either the old Stormont system or any revival of the Sunningdale Agreement, saying there was no prospect of agreement on either scheme. In a major change of policy, it flatly ruled out any Irish dimension, Atkins saying that, if the Irish dimension was raised at the conference, 'I shall rule it out of order, I shall say that it is out of order'.

This was clearly a major retreat from the approach of the last Conservative government which had insisted on the Irish dimension and whose preferred solution had been Sunningdale. At the same time the fact that a return to majority rule was firmly ruled out meant the conference held little attraction for Unionist politicians. While the SDLP eventually agreed to attend, to the surprise of many the conference was boycotted by the Ulster Unionist party, which had also acquired a new leader in the person of James Molyneaux.

Molyneaux took over in 1979 from Harry West, who had been trounced by Paisley in a European election. The party's official policy remained that of devolution, but it was an open secret that Molyneaux's personal preference was for integration. Seen in this light, his decision to stay away from the Atkins conference on devolution was perhaps predictable.

Although he was to serve as leader of the Unionist party for more than a decade and a half, until 1995, Molyneaux was such a quiet, reserved figure that he hardly became known to the British public. While his long-time rival Ian Paisley was noisy and obstreperous, Molyneaux was unfailingly courteous, the most low-key of politicians. What he had in common with Paisley was that he was simply not in the business of making a deal with nationalists. His belief, unshaken during his long years as Unionist leader, was that Unionism was best served by adopting a defensive posture to fend off all new initiatives and attempts at finding inter-party agreement. He once compared his role to that of 'a general with an army that isn't making anything much in terms of territorial gains but has the satisfaction of repulsing all attacks on the citadel'.

The models put forward by Atkins had included one which had evidently been designed to attract Molyneaux's interest, but the Unionist leader decided to steer well clear of the whole exercise in the hope that it would fizzle out and pave the way for a new integrationist approach. The government never would come round to an integrationist approach, but the Atkins conference certainly did rapidly peter out.

Violence and the prisons

The death toll for 1980 was 86, a considerable drop from the previous year's toll of 125. The year brought a new tack in loyalist violence, as the UDA expanded its activities from the random killing of Catholics to attacks on a number of prominent nationalist and republican figures. These included Protestant nationalist politician John Turnly, university lecturer Miriam Daly, and INLA activist Ronnie Bunting. In another attack in January 1981, Bernadette McAliskey, who as Bernadette Devlin had been MP for Mid-Ulster, had a near-miraculous escape from death when she and her husband were repeatedly shot by UDA gunmen.

What all these targets had in common was their prominence in what was known as 'the H-blocks campaign', which was waged in support of the continuing protests by republicans inside the Maze, the new name for Long Kesh prison. This dispute had been going on since 1976, though attracting little attention from the outside world. In late 1980 and in 1981, however, it developed into a fierce battle which is seen as one of the most important watersheds of the troubles.

In 1972 William Whitelaw had granted what was known as 'special category status' to prisoners associated with paramilitary groups. He had done so to defuse a hungerstrike by republican prisoners, at a time when he was anxious to open exploratory links to the IRA. The prisoners demanded to be treated differently from inmates jailed for criminal as opposed to paramilitary offences. Whitelaw would in later years admit that he had made a mistake in introducing special category status, or 'political status' as it was called by republicans, and subsequent Labour administrations worked on ways of bringing it to an end.

In the absence of adequate cell accommodation, internment and the special category system had given rise at Long Kesh to what in many respects resembled a World War Two prisoner-of-war camp. The internees and convicted prisoners lived in wartime Nissen huts within barbed-wire compounds. The continuation of special category status was a logical affront to the approach of criminalisation developed by Rees and later put into effect by Roy Mason, in that it was taken as an affirmation that jailed paramilitary inmates were in a sense political prisoners.

Republican and loyalist internees and 'special cats', as they were nick-named, served their time in compounds inside Long Kesh, where they responded to orders not from warders but from their paramilitary 'OC', or

Officer Commanding. To a large extent they controlled their own compounds. They wore their own clothes, were not forced to work, and were allowed additional visits and parcels. Prisoners and prison officers went their parallel but largely separate ways, with soldiers guarding the perimeter. The prisoners, divided into compounds by organisation, basically ran their own lives. It was this semblance of prisoner-of-war status which Rees had decided should end.

The authorities shied away from the idea of removing special category status from those inmates who already had it, correctly surmising that any such attempt would result in major disturbances. In late 1975 Rees announced that from early 1976 special category status would be phased out, with newly convicted prisoners expected to wear prison uniform, carry out prison work and have only limited association with other prisoners. These prisoners would be held not in the compounds but in newly built cell blocks in another part of the prison. These became known, because of their shape, as the H-blocks. Furthermore, there was to be an end to the segregation of paramilitary and non-paramilitary inmates. The H-blocks, as the authorities would repeatedly insist, provided some of the most modern prison conditions in western Europe. Loyalist prisoners initially objected to the changes and briefly staged protests but reluctantly accepted the new circumstances.

Many republican prisoners by contrast determinedly resisted the changes, seeing prison uniform in particular as a badge of criminality they refused to acknowledge. A republican song became the unofficial anthem of the protest, summing up their attitude:

> I'll wear no convict's uniform,
> Nor meekly serve my time,
> That England might
> Brand Ireland's fight
> Eight hundred years of crime.

From the autumn of 1976 on, republican prisoners refused to put on prison clothes, and were punished by being kept in their cells wrapped only in a blanket. A refusal to wear prison uniform left prisoners naked, confined almost permanently to cells and regularly punished for non-conforming by three days 'on the boards' when all cell furniture was removed. Without uniform there were no family visits and remission was lost, which in practice could double the time spent in prison.

By mid-1977 almost 150 prisoners were refusing to co-operate with the authorities. Mason had approached the issue with characteristic grit, declaring in his memoirs: 'Whatever happened I was determined not to budge. The prisoners were criminals and as far as I was concerned would always be treated as criminals.' Relations between prisoners and prison officers, which in the compounds were largely remote, rapidly became bitter. Prisoners complained of beatings by groups of warders, while outside the prison the IRA went on a systematic offensive against prison officers. Nineteen were killed between 1976 and 1980, with ten dying in 1979, one of whom was deputy governor of the Maze with particular responsibility for the H-blocks.

Adams wrote in his biography: 'Bitterness between prisoners and screws was extreme. The screws were implementing a criminalisation regime, which included the violence and indignity of forced washing. The IRA meanwhile were carrying out a policy on the outside of shooting members of prison staffs.' After prisoners stepped up the protest by smashing cell furniture they were each left with only a mattress and blankets. By 1978 there were already 300 'on the blanket'. As early as 1977 senior IRA members inside and outside the prison were suggesting to them that the protest was going nowhere, but the advice to drop it was rejected.

A frequent Unionist, and sometimes government, misconception throughout the years of protest was that these prisoners were unfortunate victims who were being sacrificed by a ruthless IRA leadership. In fact all the evidence points to an IRA leadership opposed to and frustrated by the tactics of the prisoners. These formed the one group within republicanism which was in a position to act against the wishes of the leadership in that they were accorded a freedom of action not normally permitted to others. They also had strength of numbers, for at any given time there were probably more IRA members in prison than outside: in 1980 for example there were over 800 republican prisoners.

The problem for the 'blanket men' was that by 1978 the protest was in its third year, the prison system appeared to be containing it, and outside the prison they had little support apart from the rest of the republican movement. A newspaper reported in early 1978: 'The current campaign has been going on for 18 months, with no sign of abating but equally no sign of success. Public support is minimal.' With their morale low, the prisoners stepped up the protest by resorting to a tactic which was simultaneously repulsive and, in Mason's later words, 'a brilliant stroke'. They launched what was initially a 'no wash' protest. As one prisoner wrote later: 'The pressure was on for movement. So we decided to escalate the protest and embark on the no wash protest. On hearing this, morale rose again. The lads were on a high.'

Up to that point they had left their cells to wash, empty their chamber pots, have showers and attend mass. Now they refused to leave the cells at all, leaving prison officers to empty the chamber pots. The clashes this led to meant that excrement and urine literally became weapons in the war between prisoners and prison officers. The no wash protest quickly became the 'dirty protest' with the remains of food and the overflowing chamber pots left in cells. Soon the protest was again escalated, prisoners spreading their excrement on the cell walls. As conditions reached dangerous levels with maggot infestations and the threat of disease, the prison authorities forcibly removed prisoners to allow cells to be steam-cleaned with special equipment. The prison authorities also responded with forcible baths, shaves and haircuts of protesting prisoners.

The dirty protest succeeded in its aim of winning publicity for the prisoners. The leader of the Catholic Church in Ireland, Cardinal Tomás Ó Fiaich, brought the issue to the fore when he paid a much-publicised visit to the jail and emerged to say he had found conditions similar 'to the plight of people living in sewer-pipes in the slums of Calcutta'. While he stopped short of calling for the reintroduction of special category status, he said republican prisoners must be looked upon as different from ordinary prisoners. He declared: 'No one could look on them as criminals. These boys are determined not to have criminal status imposed on them.'

Mason, like Unionist politicians, was outraged by what he later described as the cardinal's 'emotive and grossly biased' words. The Northern Ireland Secretary had until that point regarded the protest as embarrassing but containable, but the cardinal's visit received worldwide coverage. Mason later wrote: 'The image of prisoners naked in their cells with nothing for company but their own filth is undeniably potent, and it was being trumpeted round the world. But despite the adverse publicity I couldn't give in. To do so would give the IRA its biggest victory in years. It would mean the abandonment of the policy of police primacy and the rule of law.'

Although a major propaganda war raged between the republicans and the government from then on, there was still only minimal sympathy for the protesters. By 1980 even this extraordinary protest had become part of the prison routine, republican veteran Joe Cahill reluctantly concluding that 'the main demonstrations on the H-block issue have remained within the nationalist ghetto areas'.

The first hungerstrike

In 1980 the prisoners decided to employ what was seen as their ultimate weapon: a hungerstrike. It was a tactic with a chequered but revered place in republican history, being regarded as close to the ultimate in self-sacrifice and possible martyrdom. Although special category status had first been won in 1972 with a hungerstrike, other uses of the tactic had not proved effective. In the light of this record the overall republican leadership was very much against the idea, Adams recording that he wrote to the prisoners: 'We are tactically, strategically, physically and morally opposed to a hungerstrike.' One prisoner who was to spend seventy days on hungerstrike later wrote that if the IRA had forbidden the move 'it would have been an absolute disaster because people would have gone on hungerstrike anyway, and it would have caused a major split within the IRA'.

Seven prisoners, who included one member of the INLA, went on hungerstrike in October 1980. Republicans abandoned their other protests, ending the killing of prison officers and winding down the dirty protest. There were five demands: the right to wear their own clothes; no prison-dictated work; free association; weekly letters, visits and parcels, and the restoration of all remission lost as a result of the protests.

Their adversary in chief was Margaret Thatcher, whose reputation as the Iron Lady was partly to stem from her stance during this period. At the time however she was a relatively untested prime minister who had not yet established her full authority. She saw the prison confrontation as one between good and evil, democracy and terrorism. She had lost a close friend and associate, in Airey Neave, to republican violence, and as prime minister had been shaken by the Mountbatten assassination and the deaths of eighteen soldiers at Warrenpoint. As the hungerstrike began she stated: 'I want this to be utterly clear – the government will never concede political status to the hungerstrikers or to any others convicted of criminal offences.'

Through intermediaries the Northern Ireland Office indicated to republicans that concessions on matters such as clothes and the nature of work would be possible, but only once the hungerstrike was ended and prisoners conformed to the prison regime. Previous clandestine IRA links with MI6 were reactivated and a government document making some proposals was circulated. In December 1980, when one of the hunger-strikers lost his sight and was removed to a Belfast hospital, by all ac-counts on the point of death, the prisoners called off the hungerstrike amid much confusion. Although Sinn Féin initially claimed victory, it soon emerged that the prisoners had not triumphed. Exactly what con-cessions had been promised, how they were supposed to be implemented, and whose fault the breakdown was has been the subject of much debate. What was clear, however, was that prisoners had not won their demands, and as this became clear plans were laid for a second hungerstrike.

The second hungerstrike

The second hungerstrike began on 1 March 1981: this was to be a phased exercise, with the first republican to go on hungerstrike being joined at intervals by other inmates from both the IRA and INLA. The first to refuse food was the IRA OC in the Maze, Bobby Sands, whose name was to become known all over the world. Sands was to be joined on hungerstrike after two weeks by another inmate and then another each week thereafter, with the purpose of creating ever-increasing pressure on the government. In launching the second hungerstrike Sands and the others again rejected the advice of the outside IRA leadership. The IRA felt the hungerstrikes represented a serious diversion of resources of all kinds from their main campaign of violence, and feared another dama-ging and divisive failure.

From the beginning of the second hungerstrike it was judged highly likely that this time there would be deaths, for Sands and the others believed the fiasco of the first strike had to be avenged. His own re-putation for determination was evident in his nickname Geronimo. He grew up in the mainly Protestant Rathcoole estate on the outskirts of north Belfast, but his family were among a large number of Catholics forced to leave the area by a systematic campaign of loyalist intimidation. The family moved to west Belfast where he became an active member of the IRA, serving a short prison sentence in the early 1970s before being sen-tenced in 1977 to fourteen years' imprisonment after being arrested in possession of a gun in a car while on an IRA operation.

Tensions mounted to an extraordinary degree as the strike went on amid a major propaganda battle, with polarisation between ordinary Protestants and Catholics reaching new levels. For many nationalists the brutal clarity of the issue left no room for ambiguity, and many who did not support the IRA nonetheless reacted against what they saw as British inflexibility.

In propaganda terms Sands benefited from the fact that he developed an aura of victimhood and self-sacrifice. He was a convicted member of the IRA yet his personal image was highly media friendly. He had been jailed for having a gun rather than for murder, and the photograph of him which appeared thousands of times in newspapers and on television projected a good-looking young man with long hair, sporting a fetching grin. The fact that he looked more like a drummer in a rock band than a ruthless terrorist was important in the propaganda battle that raged all around the world.

As the days passed, numerous groups and individuals sought to mediate in the dispute, but they made little progress with either the prisoners or the authorities. The IRA suspected such groups were likely to confuse the issues, bypass the IRA itself or be manipulated by the authorities. The fact that IRA violence continued, including the killing of a young mother in Londonderry, merely hardened the characteristic Thatcher resolve. She observed that 'if Mr Sands persisted in his wish to commit suicide, that was his choice'.

Although Adams and the republican leadership had been against the hungerstrike, sheer chance delivered them a golden political opportunity. Five days after Sands began refusing food, independent nationalist MP Frank Maguire died suddenly, creating a by-election in the Fermanagh–South Tyrone Westminster constituency. Maguire's brother was dissuaded by republicans from going forward, and Sands became the sole nationalist candidate. In the election he beat Harry West, the former Unionist party leader who was attempting a comeback, to win the seat by 30,492 votes to 29,046 on an 87 per cent poll. It was a propaganda victory of huge proportions for the IRA, made possible by the widespread nationalist sense that Thatcher was adopting altogether too rigid a stance. Since Sands's victory was one of the key events in the development of Sinn Féin as an electoral force, some observers regard it as the genesis of what would eventually become the peace process. At the time, however, it made no difference to the government's attitude, and the stalemate continued.

Sands died at 1.17 a.m. on 5 May, instantly becoming one of republicanism's most revered martyrs. Thatcher coldly informed the Commons that 'Mr Sands was a convicted criminal. He chose to take his own life. It was a choice his organisation did not allow to many of its victims.' But although there was little sympathy in Britain, his death generated a huge wave of emotion and anger among republicans and nationalists, an estimated 100,000 people attending his funeral. From the wider world came much international criticism of Britain and of Thatcher, who was widely condemned for inflexibility. World attention was focused on Belfast, Adams later recalling that the death of Sands 'had a greater international impact than any other event in Ireland in my lifetime'.

The widespread street disturbances arising from the hungerstrike helped drive the death toll for 1981 up to 117 from the previous year's total of 86. Deaths caused by the security forces increased as troops and police used large numbers of plastic bullets in response to street disturbances. As a result seven Catholics were killed, two of them young girls. Although the security forces usually maintained that those killed had been active rioters, it often emerged afterwards that this was not so. In five of the seven cases, inquests later specifically found that those who died had been innocents, and more than £75,000 was paid out in compensation cases.

James Prior, who replaced Humphrey Atkins as Northern Ireland Secretary in the autumn of 1981, recalled in his memoirs: 'The police and army were firing prodigious numbers of plastic bullets. A number of innocent people, including children, were killed or maimed, their deaths adding to all the bitterness.' One example of this was the death of an innocent fourteen-year-old girl, Julie Livingstone, who was killed when she was struck by a plastic bullet. She had not been involved in rioting and her family later received compensation. Her mother recalled: 'She was a lively wee girl, into everything, keeping the wee lads going. The despair would hurt you now and again. Most days you get it some part of the day. I'll never get rid of her name – she wrote it anywhere, inside the airing cupboard and on books. I was changing a pillow and she had written her name on the inside of it. In the kitchen, just under the cooker under the wallpaper, she must have lifted a brush and written her name on the bare wall.'

Such tragedies were not confined to the nationalist side. In the same month as the Julie Livingstone killing, during rioting which followed the death of Sands, a crowd in north Belfast stoned a milk lorry. The vehicle went out of control in a hail of missiles and crashed into a lamppost, killing Protestant milkman Eric Guiney and his fourteen-year-old son Desmond who was helping on the milk round. After the deaths Mrs Guiney said: 'Everyone loved Desmond – he was always such a jolly wee boy and would have given you the coat off his back. Once when they changed part of the milk round, the customers phoned the dairy to ask them to put Desmond back.'

The months that followed are remembered as being particularly grim and destabilising as the confrontation continued, with neither the government nor the hungerstrikers prepared to give way. With hindsight, it is clear that each deeply misunderstood the other: Thatcher never came close to grasping the IRA's psychology, while some republicans persisted in believing that she was bound to give in eventually. Even after six hungerstrike deaths Brendan McFarlane, who had taken over from Sands as the IRA OC in the Maze, wrote in a smuggled message to Adams, 'I do feel we can break the Brits.'

The unyielding attitude of both sides resulted, between May and August 1981, in the deaths of a total of ten hungerstrikers, seven from the IRA and three from the INLA. As the summer progressed and prisoners died, numerous mediators tried to resolve the problem with no success: the Red Cross, a European Court of Human Rights delegation, the Catholic Church in Ireland, a Vatican representative, John Hume, Irish government representatives, the IRA–MI6 secret link.

Prior visited the Maze and had a glimpse through a window of a prisoner on the forty-sixth day of his hungerstrike. Prior recalled later: 'He was just sitting there, staring into space. There was no great sense of agony, of emaciation, nor any sign of pain. I was struck by how much this man looked at peace with himself.' Prior said he began to realise that there were on both sides 'a number of people of utter determination and conviction, prepared to commit acts of violence and in a stubborn, yet courageous, way to accept the inevitable and to die'.

The ending of the hungerstrike came soon afterwards, largely through the intervention of the families of prisoners, encouraged by prison chaplain Father Denis Faul. The families began to realise that the government would not concede, and to conclude that the deaths of their husbands and sons were both inevitable and futile. An increasing number of families took action once their sons had lapsed into the coma which normally preceded death, asking the authorities to medically revive them. In October the hungerstrikers called off the protest, thwarted by their families rather than by the government or the prison authorities. Within days Prior eased regulations to allow prisoners to wear their own clothes at all times and made limited concessions on the other demands.

The original feeling among republicans was that they had suffered a huge defeat in the hungerstrike. One prisoner wrote: 'Despite my relief that no one else would die, I still felt gutted because ten men had died and we had not won our demands. My morale was never as low.' Thatcher had taken on the IRA head-on and in the end their willpower cracked while hers did not. She said at one point, 'Faced with the failure of their discredited cause the men of violence have chosen in recent months to play what might be their last card.'

Yet hers was a Pyrrhic victory. One newspaper recorded:

> This has been one of the best times the IRA has ever had. The Northern Ireland problem is seen worldwide as the IRA has always wanted it to be: the hammer and the anvil, the Brits versus the Provos, nothing in between and nobody else relevant. The paradox at the centre of all this success for the Provisionals is that their gains have come through an election won by the very opposite of a Provo campaign, a campaign based on an appeal to save life, and through the self-sacrifice of their men. Somebody somewhere among the Provos has finally come to accept the truth of the old saying that it is not those who inflict the most who ultimately win, but those who endure the most.

The hungerstrikes had lasting effects, most of which were bad for the authorities and for almost everyone apart from the republican movement. For one thing, the extended trauma of the months of confrontation seared deep into the psyches of large numbers of people, stirring many deep and troubling emotions. Community divisions had always been deep, but now they had a new rawness. Prior said he arrived in Belfast to find 'an embittered and totally polarised society'.

Aftermath

In November 1981, IRA gunmen assassinated the Reverend Robert

Bradford, a Unionist MP and Methodist minister who had advocated a tougher security line against the IRA. At the funeral James Prior was jostled and verbally abused by angry loyalists, several hundred surging forward to bang on the roof of his car. He was hissed as he walked into the church, and as he left he was again surrounded, some members of the crowd calling, 'Kill him, kill him'. The day of the funeral was marked by a widespread work stoppage by Protestants as memorial services were held in many towns. Paisley threatened to organise tax and rent strikes as part of a protest campaign to make Northern Ireland 'ungovernable', and loyalists staged a day of action at which members of a 'third force' were paraded.

Those who had already viewed Northern Ireland as a dysfunctional society whose people could never be brought to live amicably together seemed confirmed in their view, while many others sadly concluded that they were probably correct. Certainly the fact that an apparently modern society had been so convulsed for so long left the lasting impression of structural political instability.

As far as IRA prisoners were concerned the 1981 hungerstrike had ended in defeat. Although they were subsequently allowed to wear their own clothes, this was granted as a concession from a government which appeared to have won the exchange. As the IRA prisoners saw it, ten colleagues had given their lives, apparently in vain. Describing the hungerstrike as 'an Everest amongst the mountains of traumatic events which the Irish people have experienced', Gerry Adams would write a decade and a half later, 'I cannot yet think with any intensity of the death of Bobby Sands and the circumstances of his passing without crying.'

Yet the hungerstrike was to bring republicans many gains. The ten deaths effectively put an end to the criminalisation argument. The hungerstrike had not technically achieved special category status but in effect it had achieved something much more potent: political status. There could have been no more definitive display of political motivation than the spectacle of ten men giving their lives in an awesome display of self-sacrifice and dedication. It was possible to view this as outlandish fanaticism, and many did; but it was not possible to claim that these were indistinguishable from ordinary criminals. The hungerstrikers thus won political status in the eyes of the world.

Radicalised recruits flocked to the IRA and Sinn Féin, swelling the ranks of both and laying the foundations for both further violence and an infiltration of the political system. The republican electoral advances pointed to a new potential in the north and possibly south. Ahead lay more violence and a regular vote for Sinn Féin.

This fired sweeping new ambitions among the republican leadership. Three weeks after the end of the hungerstrike, Adams aide Danny Morrison outlined to the Sinn Féin ard fheis (annual conference) a grandiose new vision, declaring: 'Who here really believes we can win the war through the ballot box? But will anyone here object if, with a ballot box in one hand and the Armalite in the other, we take power in Ireland?' Adams would later sum up the paradoxical outcome of the hungerstrike which he had never wanted: 'Physically, emotionally and spiritually, the hungerstrike was intensely draining; yet we derived immense new energy, commitment and direction from the extraordinary period during which our ten comrades slowly and painfully sacrificed their lives.'

8

Anglo–Irish accord
1982–85

Men of violence

The years after 1981 saw a variety of political and security initiatives as London and Dublin sought to cope with the aftermath of the traumatic hungerstrike period. The IRA once again returned to bombing targets in England, while the security forces attempted to counter them with new military and legal measures. Loyalist killings went on at a relatively low level, while 1982 saw the violent end to the violent career of one of the most notorious loyalist killers. This was Lenny Murphy, who as leader of the UVF Shankill Butchers gang had been involved in at least eighteen killings over a full two decades. Murphy met his own death at the hands of IRA gunmen who shot him twenty-two times as he drew up in his car outside his girlfriend's home.

Although attention has tended to be concentrated on such well-remembered incidents, the sobering fact is that over the years of the troubles tens of thousands of men became involved with violent republican and loyalist groups. 600 or more men were convicted of murder, while many times that number were jailed for lesser offences. Republican groups estimate that there are 15,000 republican ex-prisoners while at a rough guess around the same number of loyalists also served sentences. In other words, more than 30,000 men were involved with groups that have carried out killings and a great deal of other violence, a statistic which illustrates how deeply society was permeated by paramilitarism.

Although the number of IRA killings fell slightly, the organisation carried out major attacks in Britain. Two attacks on a single day in July 1982 killed a total of eleven soldiers in two London parks, one of the highest military casualty tolls of the troubles. The first device was detonated as a troop of soldiers in full regalia made their way on horseback through Hyde Park on their way from their Knightsbridge barracks to Whitehall. Four soldiers died. In Britain an extra dimension of condemnation arose from the fact that a number of horses were also killed in the Hyde Park explosion. One horse which survived numerous injuries, Sefton, become an equine symbol of British defiance of the IRA and something close to a national hero. A newspaper reported: 'The horror of the incident was brought home to the public through gruesome pictures broadcast on lunchtime television, showing a scene of carnage and devastation. Eye-witnesses gave graphic accounts of charred bodies and people and horses with terrible injuries.' A few hours later a bomb went off in Regent's Park as military bandsmen performed a lunchtime concert at an open-air bandstand. The device, which had been placed under the bandstand, killed seven soldiers.

Another IRA attack in London came in December 1983, when a bomb left in a car outside Harrods department store exploded seven days before Christmas while the area was thronged with shoppers. The explosion, which killed six people, was generally regarded as a setback for the IRA because of its civilian death toll.

The IRA was not the only dangerous republican group in these years, since the smaller INLA was also intermittently active. This group, which had come into being in the mid-1970s, showed over the years an extraordinary capacity to revive itself after setbacks and once again flare into violent life. Many of the setbacks were self-inflicted: time and again internal feuds broke out, claiming the lives of many of its members. The years 1981 to 1983 were its most lethal with fifty-three people dying at its hands. Although it had initially had a left-wing ideology it degenerated over the years into a collection of local gangs often dominated by personalities who had parted company from the IRA, usually because they were considered too erratic.

Two of the best-known of these were Dessie 'Border Fox' O'Hare and Dominic 'Mad Dog' McGlinchey, who were both active in these years. O'Hare revelled in his reputation as a fearsome killer, claiming in a newspaper interview that he had killed approximately twenty-six people, an estimate security sources did not contest. His victims included many members of the security forces as well as a number of INLA members killed in the spasms of feuding which periodically racked the organisation. In his interview he said of one INLA member he had killed: 'I would have burned him alive if I had the chance.' In the case of another INLA man, O'Hare and his associates used bolt cutters to sever an earlobe and a finger. O'Hare commented chillingly, 'We just wanted to kill him, to give him a hard death. They were a bad crowd. I had a deep hate for him and all those guys. I did not want him to die lightly.' O'Hare was regarded as such a menace to society that he was eventually jailed for forty years, the longest jail sentence ever handed down by a court in the Republic, even though he was convicted of lesser offences than murder.

Dominic McGlinchey was one of the most feared gunmen to emerge in the troubles, first as a member of the IRA before being expelled for 'indiscipline', and then as leader of the INLA. In a newspaper interview he boasted of killing around thirty people, saying: 'I like to get in close to minimise the risk for myself. We were involved mainly in the killing of UDR men and policemen, and we did a fair few bombings of police barracks and towns.' McGlinchey and his wife were both to die in feud shootings.

The highest death toll inflicted by the INLA came in December 1982, when seventeen people were killed in an attack on a bar at Ballykelly in County Londonderry. Eleven of the dead were soldiers based in the garrison town. The others were civilians, four of them women, who were attending a disco in the bar. The bomb used in the incident was a comparatively small device but it was placed near a support pillar in a function room. Over 150 people were in the room when the bomb exploded, bringing down the roof. An army officer who rushed to the scene spoke of finding bodies 'like dominos, one on top of the other'. The majority of the dead were not killed by the blast but were crushed by fallen masonry.

In his memoirs James Prior wrote: 'As we flew in, the white ribbons cordoning off the area marked a scene of total devastation. The bar and dance hall had been reduced to smouldering remains, completely flattened by the bomb. The whole roof collapsed on to the crowded dance floor. It is a miracle that more were not killed.' An INLA spokesman declared: 'We believe that it is only attacks of such a nature that bring it home to the people in Britain and the British establishment. The shooting of an individual soldier, for the people of Britain, has very little effect in terms of the media or in terms of the British administration.' In his newspaper interview McGlinchey admitted he was involved in the incident.

The INLA argued that the disco constituted a military target, but another of its attacks in this period, in November 1983, was capable of no such interpretation. This took place at a small Pentecostal church at Darkley close to the border in County Armagh. Members of the sixty-strong congregation, made up mainly of farming families, were singing 'Are you washed in the blood of the lamb?' when gunmen arrived and sprayed the building with bullets, killing three of the church elders. At least three gunmen stood outside the hall and strafed it, wounding seven more people as up to forty bullets passed through the thin wooden walls.

Accounts of the troubles inevitably concentrate on major incidents such as these, partly because of the death tolls, partly because such attacks often had political significance and in part because many of them are among the best-remembered incidents of the troubles. Over the years, however, the majority of those who were killed died singly, in individual incidents. The following are representative or at least illustrative of the vast majority of troubles victims.

Francis McCluskey, aged forty-six, was among the many Catholics killed by loyalists, in particular in the north Belfast area. In August 1982 he was walking to work when two masked men chased him and shot him six times. His wife, who was pregnant at the time of his death, later gave birth to their ninth child, whom she named Francine in memory of her husband. Detectives told the inquest he was the victim of a loyalist sectarian attack; a relative said he was murdered for no other reason than his religion.

Some months after his death his wife said: 'He was so happy that morning. When he was up and about the whole house joined in. He was a terrible one for playing jokes, an innocent man whose life revolved around me and the children. I remember him asking me for another kiss but I laughed that he had already had his share of two that morning. Those were the last words he said. Francis went out full of fun. That night he came home in a coffin. Francine will know that her daddy loved us all very much. I hold no bitterness towards my husband's murderers. I can just feel sorry for them and their parents. The baby will grow up without any hatred or malice, but love for the father she never knew.' In the course of the troubles loyalists were responsible for the deaths of just over one thousand people, most of them civilians.

Hugh Cummings, thirty-nine, was one of two hundred UDR members who died, many of them while off-duty, meeting his death like Francis McCluskey in August 1982. A part-time member of the UDR, he was shot by the IRA in the town of Strabane as he got into his car, the fourth member of the local UDR company to be killed in a seven-month period. His family refused to accept a letter of sympathy from James Prior which was delivered to them on the day of the funeral, sending it back with a message that 'the hands of the security forces should be freed'. A spokesman for the family said: 'Nothing is being done. Feelings are running very high on this issue here. Innocent, defenceless people are being mown down and no action is being taken against the godfathers who are walking the streets. They are getting away with murder.'

Security reactions

The security forces reacted to the continuing violence in a number of ways. The RUC created its own SAS-style unit, training its men for violent encounters with the IRA and INLA. Known as E4A its approach was based, in the words of a senior police officer, on 'speed, firepower and aggression'. All these characteristics were on display when, in three separate incidents in a period of a month, E4A members shot and killed five men and a youth, all in County Armagh. Three were IRA members, two were in the INLA and one was a civilian. Some of these were clearly dangerous men, but all those killed were unarmed when shot.

In the first incident three IRA members were killed when police fired 109 shots at their car. In the second a teenager who was a civilian was shot dead and another was seriously injured. In the third incident two members of the INLA were shot dead in a car. These events, which came to be known as 'shoot-to-kill' incidents, were surrounded by controversy which persists to the present day. They also gave rise to long-running legal sequels. In the case of the three IRA men, three policemen were charged with murder. In acquitting them a senior judge generated further controversy when in congratulating them he added: 'I regard each of the accused as absolutely blameless in this matter. That finding should be put in their record along with my own commendation for their courage and determination in bringing the three deceased men to justice, in this case the final court of justice.'

The controversy which followed the killings led to the appointment of the Deputy Chief Constable of the Greater Manchester Police, John Stalker, to investigate the incidents. Stalker, who claimed his inquiries had been obstructed, was later removed from the inquiry in controversial circumstances when disciplinary charges were brought against him in Manchester. These were later dropped. A final report of the inquiries was not published but in 1988 it was announced in the Commons that although evidence had been found of attempts by police officers to pervert the course of justice, there would be no prosecutions on the grounds of national security. The inquest into the IRA deaths became a protracted affair, with five different coroners appointed to handle the hearing at various stages. Eventually in 1994 a coroner said he was abandoning the proceedings, which had become the longest-running inquest of its kind in British legal history. These circumstances gave rise to continuing nationalist and republican allegations of a cover-up.

Another significant development in the first half of the 1980s was the police use of supergrasses, which for several years inflicted considerable damage to both republican and loyalist groups. The supergrass system entailed persuading former members of such groups to testify against their alleged former associates, in exchange for a new life outside Northern Ireland. Immunity from prosecution was sometimes granted, along with payment of substantial sums of money.

Although the system gave rise to human rights concerns, on a practical level it took large numbers of active republicans and loyalists off the streets. In some cases thirty or more defendants were charged on the word of one supergrass. Some were sentenced to long terms of imprisonment, and even those who were eventually acquitted generally spent many months behind bars while awaiting trial. The remand record was held by an INLA member who was held on the evidence of five separate supergrasses. All the cases against him eventually collapsed, but in the meantime he spent four years and four months on remand. (The irony in his case was that shortly after his release he was shot dead in an INLA feud.)

Campaigns against the practice were waged by republicans, loyalists and human rights groups. One of the main criticisms was that large numbers of people were being convicted sometimes on the word of a single person, who admitted he had himself been involved in paramilitary activity and sometimes pleaded guilty to murder. In most cases there was no corroborating evidence. The practice caused much disruption to both republican and loyalist organisations, and may have been one of the causes of the comparatively low level of loyalist violence around this time.

At least twenty-five supergrasses emerged during this period, providing information which led to the arrests of nearly 600 suspects. At one stage around 230 men were held in prison on their evidence. The courts were initially enthusiastic about the supergrass phenomenon. In one case a judge described aspects of a supergrass's testimony as 'unreliable, false, bizarre and incredible' but then went on to convict defendants on the basis of other parts of his evidence.

The classic security force problem throughout the troubles was that they believed that through their intelligence agencies they knew a great deal about who the leaders of paramilitary groups were, and who had ordered or carried out many killings and other offences. As in other countries, however, their difficulty lay in converting intelligence into evidence which would stand up in a court of law. The supergrass tactic seemed to offer a mechanism for achieving this. As time passed, however, the legal and political controversy grew and judges became more cautious about convicting. In a key IRA case a senior judge cleared thirty-five defendants. He said that while there was more than a trace of probability that many of the defendants were members of an illegal organisation, the supergrass was 'a selfish and self-regarding man to whose lips a lie invariably came more naturally than the truth'.

One of those taken out of circulation by the supergrass system was Gerard Steenson, a highly active INLA gunman with the nickname Doctor Death, who was convicted of sixty-seven offences and given six life sentences for murder. The judge in the case was clearly correct in saying of him: 'Of all those who have appeared before me he is undoubtedly the most dangerous and sinister terrorist – a ruthless and highly dedicated, resourceful and indefatigable planner of criminal exploits who did not hesitate to take a leading part in assassinations and other crimes.'

Yet the system began to fall apart as judges signalled their dissatisfaction with it, and most of those charged, including Steenson, eventually walked free. Appeal courts overturned a number of verdicts, and as more and more cases collapsed the system was eventually abandoned.

It is hardly surprising, given her reputation for combativeness, that approaches such as the creation of E4A and the use of the supergrass tactic should have been deployed during Margaret Thatcher's years as prime minister. Described by James Prior as 'a natural sympathiser with the Unionists', she had briefly toyed with the idea of a majority-rule government with strong guarantees for the minority. In her own words, however, 'it was not long before it became clear to me that this model was not going to work, at least for the present'. She explained: 'There was no getting away from the fact that, with some justice, the long years of Unionist rule were associated with discrimination against Catholics.'

Her first stab at a political approach had taken the form of the abortive Atkins conference. The next came in 1980, when she made an effort to form a working relationship with Charles Haughey, Jack Lynch's successor as Taoiseach. Despite their very different nationalist instincts, she was prepared to do business with him and, to the surprise of most, this unlikely couple at first got on well. A Thatcher biographer attributed this to 'a certain roguish mutual admiration', while Prior described it as 'apparently a great love match'.

Two summit meetings went exceptionally well, in particular one which came to be known as 'the teapot summit' because of Haughey's gift to Thatcher of an elegant Georgian teapot. An eye-witness said: 'She was charmed by the teapot. He was an extraordinarily charming man when he wanted to be and he exercised all his charm on her. The relationship just grew from there.' But disillusion set in very quickly. Haughey suggested their meetings had led to a constitutional breakthrough and did not set 'any limits on the arrangements that might be agreed'. His Foreign Minister made things worse by adding that 'all options are open' and that 'everything is on the table'. This was taken as implying that Thatcher had agreed radical solutions which might even include moves towards Irish unity. She was furious.

She wanted closer Anglo-Irish relations but a united Ireland was not on her horizon, and she felt betrayed by what she regarded as a gross distortion of her position. When she and Haughey next met she delivered what was described as 'a monologue, a diatribe' by one of those present. This source added, 'She couldn't speak coherently, she was in such a rage. She just said in no uncertain terms what she thought.' Haughey had overplayed his hand and his relations with Thatcher never recovered, and in fact deteriorated even further when differences developed during the 1981 hungerstrike and the Falklands war.

The next political initiative originated not with Thatcher but with James Prior whom she had despatched to Belfast as a form of exile after he proved too moderate and too 'wet' in handling industrial relations as Employment Secretary. The Belfast post was described by Prior in a disgruntled moment as 'the dustbin of British politics', a cabinet colleague saying Thatcher's motivation was 'to get him out of the prime minister's hair'. The initiative he designed took the form of an idea known as rolling devolution. He had modest ambitions for the scheme, seeing it as an attempt 'to narrow the differences, to try to bring the disagreement within proportions which are at least manageable'. His plan was for an elected assembly to which powers would be transferred as and when the parties reached a certain level of agreement in particular areas: the greater the agreement, the more power would be transferred. Prior described it as 'the same step-by-step approach that I had applied with some success to the changes in industrial relations legislation'.

But approaches useful in dealings with British trade unions turned out to be less effective in Belfast. Few were enthusiastic about his plan, and there was open opposition from many quarters. The critics included many in his own party, up to and including the prime minister herself. She allowed Prior to put legislation for the assembly through Westminster but, as he later testified, 'She made her views abundantly clear, saying that she thought it was a rotten Bill.' Several dozen Tory backbenchers agreed, harassing Prior with filibustering tactics in the Commons.

Nationalists were also against the scheme, Haughey condemning it as 'one of the most disastrous things that has ever happened in Anglo-Irish relations'. Prior was instructed by Thatcher to tone down the modest Irish dimension he had envisaged. In his memoirs he described this move as 'probably our great mistake' in that it led to the SDLP refusing to take its seats in his new assembly. Sinn Féin took a similar position, which meant that from the start the assembly was a nationalist-free zone, serving only as a platform for Unionist speeches and never offering any real hope of political progress.

The rise of Sinn Féin

The next initiative of the Thatcher years was much more far-reaching, more carefully thought out and in the end would come to be seen as a watershed, both in terms of Anglo-Irish relations and in changing the course of the troubles. It would produce the Anglo-Irish Agreement of 1985, which in many ways broke the mould of London–Dublin relations.

The new initiative had its roots largely in the reaction of first Dublin and later London to the rise of Sinn Féin as an electoral force in the wake of the 1981 hungerstrike. Within republicanism Adams and others had always been wary of what they pejoratively referred to as 'electoralism', suspecting that entering the political processes would blunt the IRA's revolutionary edge. But when they saw the many thousands who had voted for Bobby Sands they realised that they had stumbled on a basis for broadening their campaign.

As a result they transformed Sinn Féin from little more than a flag of convenience for the IRA into a political organisation with a life of its own. Many republican sympathisers who baulked at joining the IRA, or had been through its ranks and did not wish to return, were prepared to work for it politically. Republicans thus turned to contesting elections in earnest, with spectacular initial success which was enhanced to some extent by the ancient art of vote-stealing. In four elections between 1982 and 1985 Sinn Féin averaged around 12 per cent of the total vote and 40 per cent of the nationalist vote, establishing itself as the fourth largest party and a political force which could not be ignored. Its best performance came in 1983 when it took more than 100,000 votes and, in a victory of great symbolic significance, had Gerry Adams elected as Westminster MP for West Belfast. Adams's election victory won him new allies among the British Labour left and he made several trips to England, attracting saturation publicity as he met figures such as Ken Livingstone. The subsequent election of almost sixty Sinn Féin representatives to local councils brought widespread Unionist protests and often disruption at council meetings. Sinn Féin was the focus of all attention and there was much worried talk that its foray into politics was poisoning the wells of political processes.

Emboldened by their advances in the north, the republicans turned their eyes south. At the height of the hungerstrikes a number of republican prisoners put themselves forward in southern elections and two of them were elected to the Dáil. This was taken as a sign that a great potential for republican growth existed in the south, with Sinn Féin well placed to pick up votes in border counties and from the disaffected Dublin poor.

Party politics in the south was particularly fragmented at that stage, as a decline in the fortunes of the largest party, Fianna Fáil, prevented it from securing an overall majority. This created the possibility that a handful of Sinn Féin members could find themselves in a pivotal position in the Dáil. All of this was alarming for southern politicians, who feared their political system was about to be invaded by republican revolutionaries intent on overthrowing it from within. One Irish minister spoke fearfully of the prospect of 'IRA army council deputies (members of the Dáil) stalking the corridors of Dáil Eireann, holding the balance of power'. At that moment many republicans believed that the new strategy of combining IRA violence and political activity offered a route to victory, and enthusiastically set about building up Sinn Féin.

One of the southern figures most perturbed by the Sinn Féin advance was Fine Gael leader Dr Garret FitzGerald, who during the 1970s and much of the 1980s played a central role both in domestic southern politics and Anglo-Irish relations. He was significant both in terms of his actions during his two spells as Taoiseach, and intellectually as one of the key thinkers who helped redefine Irish nationalism. FitzGerald's nightmare was that Sinn Féin might actually overtake John Hume's SDLP as the principal voice of nationalism in the north. He viewed Sinn Féin as a malignant dry rot which threatened to spread south. He feared, as he later explained in his memoirs, that 'the situation there could get out of control and threaten the whole island, for in those circumstances the IRA might seek a violent confrontation with the Unionists and try to follow this by an attempt to destabilise the Republic'.

Some in the British government shared his concern, Prior warning a private Conservative meeting that the island of Ireland could become 'a Cuba off our western coast'. If that happened, he said, one could foresee the whole of Ireland being taken over by the Marxists of Sinn Féin. The main British aim at this time was to contain a dangerous situation and restore as much stability as possible. The lack of success of the Prior assembly put paid to the idea of making progress through the devolution of power to Northern Ireland politicians. Attempting to integrate Northern Ireland with Britain, as advocated by Molyneaux and some other Unionists, was rejected. Withdrawal was not favoured because it would inevitably be viewed as a defeat for Britain at the hands of terrorism, and because in any event it could result in a level of violence worse than anything yet experienced.

Constitutional nationalists, meanwhile, went back to basics. Acting on an idea put forward by Hume, FitzGerald convened a New Ireland Forum to act as a think-tank for all shades of constitutional nationalist opinion. Senior figures from all the major constitutional nationalist parties debated the way ahead for months. Its 1984 report reproached the British government for allegedly insensitive security policies and for concentrating on crisis management. Calling for a major reassessment by Britain, it warned: 'Constitutional politics are on trial. This requires priority attention and urgent action to halt and reverse the constant drift into more violence, anarchy and chaos.' The report put forward options such as a united Ireland, a federal Ireland and joint London–Dublin authority over Northern Ireland, also mentioning, in what looked like a throwaway line, that 'the parties in the forum also remain open to discuss other views which may contribute to political development'.

All shades of Unionist opinion summarily rejected the three main forum options. So too did Thatcher, and with such brusqueness that she caused a crisis in Anglo-Irish relations. A unitary state, she told the media, was out; a federal Ireland was out; and joint authority was out. Her response, which became known as 'Out, out, out', was taken as an affront by all sections of opinion in the Republic. A senior British minister would later describe this as 'a humiliating episode' for FitzGerald.

Thatcher had hoped to work with FitzGerald to improve London–Dublin relations and to increase cross-border security co-operation, but the 'Out, out, out' furore looked like jeopardising her hopes. Taken aback, she asked FitzGerald how she could made amends. With hindsight it can be seen that this was a crucial moment in Anglo-Irish relations. Over the years one of the specialities of Irish diplomacy has been to turn apparent reverses to Dublin's advantage, and this is what happened.

In fact the two governments had for some time been exploring the possibility of a far-reaching new agreement designed to bolster constitutional nationalism against the menace of Sinn Féin and the IRA. This now intensified. The initiative had the support not only of Hume but also, more unusually, of a number of key British civil servants. The move thus originated in Dublin but was endorsed and jointly crafted by senior British civil servants and diplomats. Chief among these was Sir Robert (now Lord) Armstrong, who was then cabinet secretary. He and other formidable mandarins, all of whom were convinced something needed to be done, were put to work on an Anglo-Irish committee with an equally formidable and experienced team of Irish diplomats including Seán Donlon and Dermot Nally. They had the support of Foreign Secretary Sir Geoffrey Howe, who described the officials as a 'galaxy of skill'. The approach of containment and crisis management was left behind as the team went to work in a determined attempt to seize the initiative from the republicans.

Thatcher's motivation in approving the new negotiation sprang primarily from security considerations and the desire to reduce violence. Howe later wrote: 'It was this point that always drove Margaret most strongly – security, success against the men of violence, was her main preoccupation.' FitzGerald argued primarily from a political point of view. He pressed the need to reduce nationalist 'alienation' so much that, according to Howe, Thatcher would cry, 'I do wish you would stop using that dreadful word, Garret.' One of the British negotiating team later said privately:

> Perhaps Mrs Thatcher had a less than comprehensive grasp of Irish history but she's an intensely pragmatic politician. She was conscious of the need to do something – not to solve the situation, but to move it forward from the impasse which it had reached. It was logical to explore the possibilities of the Anglo-Irish dimension.
>
> Those of us negotiating were under a clear political direction to reach an agreement. We were aware of history but we were not cowed by it. We met on equal terms. We were able to meet with a degree of personal commitment to achieving something, and in an atmosphere of trust and friendship. We were aware of national obligations but we shared a common commitment and a common sense that we were engaged in a very important and very exciting and rather new stage in the long history of relations between Britain and Ireland.

A complex negotiation followed, civil servants in all taking part in thirty-six meetings. British and Irish ministers, including Thatcher and FitzGerald, met regularly to review progress. Among the many ideas considered and rejected were joint authority, the placing of an Irish minister in Belfast, and a joint north–south policing zone on the border. This negotiation was ultimately successful, in the eyes of both governments, in that it produced the Anglo-Irish Agreement of November 1985. But the process of negotiation was itself important in that key figures in London and Dublin developed relationships of trust and friendship. Anglo-Irish relations had often been difficult and many more rocky periods lay ahead; but the mid-1980s represented an important turning point in that Dublin, and important figures in London, came to see the Northern Ireland question as a common problem which was best managed jointly. FitzGerald would later explain:

> In the 1970s London and Dublin were thought to be pursuing different policies with different attitudes, because the focus of attention in people's minds was on Irish unity versus Northern Ireland remaining part of the UK. It was therefore thought to be a conflict of interest. But the reality, because of the IRA, has been that that long term divergence of interest has been subordinated to the common concern, the restoration of peace. That change from a position of polarised attitudes to one of common purpose has been the fundamental change of Anglo-Irish relations in the last twenty years.

While constitutional nationalism was intent on making progress through peaceful negotiations, the IRA went on prosecuting its war. In one of many incidents nine RUC officers, two of them women, were killed when an IRA mortar made a direct hit on an RUC canteen in the grounds of the police station in Newry, County Down.

Then in October 1984 a bomb meant for Margaret Thatcher exploded at the Grand Hotel in Brighton during the Conservative party conference. The blast, which took place in the early hours of the morning, demolished much of the façade of the old building. It missed its primary target, the prime minister, but killed five other people including an MP and the wives of three more Conservatives. A chilling IRA statement addressed to Thatcher said: 'Today we were unlucky, but remember, we have only to be lucky once. You will have to be lucky always. Give Ireland peace and there will be no war.' It was the closest the IRA had come to striking at the heart of the British political establishment, and the shock waves reverberated throughout Britain and Ireland; but the long, careful Anglo-Irish negotiation kept inching painstakingly forward. Howe would write that the Brighton attack did not perceptibly alter Thatcher's approach 'save to reinforce the dominant importance which she already attached to closer security co-operation'.

Anglo–Irish Agreement

The document Thatcher and FitzGerald formally signed in Hillsborough, County Down, in November 1985 was by any standards a historic one, giving the Republic as it did a significant consultative role in the running of Northern Ireland. The agreement opened with a statement by the two governments that any change in Northern Ireland's status could only come about with the consent of a majority of its people. For the governments, this was clearly an advance on the separate statements printed side by side in the Sunningdale Agreement.

The agreement then unveiled intricately crafted new structures, at the heart of which was an intergovernmental conference to be jointly chaired by London and Dublin ministers. This was to be serviced by a small secretariat of British and Irish civil servants based at Maryfield, a closely guarded office building on the outskirts of east Belfast. At the intergovernmental conference the Irish government could put forward views and proposals on almost any subject. The Republic was given no executive power, but the agreement committed the two governments to making 'determined efforts' to resolve their differences within the conference.

Almost everyone was surprised that Thatcher was prepared to sign such a document. Howe wrote later that the personal chemistry between herself and FitzGerald was decisive, saying that the Taoiseach's 'manifest sincerity over meeting after meeting could not have been more effective'. Thatcher had a reputation of being one of the few British politicians to retain any personal commitment to the Union between Britain and Ireland; moreover, as European and other countries had ample cause to know, she was famously jealous and protective of British sovereignty. That sovereignty was technically untouched by the Anglo-Irish Agreement, yet its nationalist tone was obvious to everyone. It was certainly evident to Unionists, who were unanimously appalled by its contents, believing that it weakened the Union. It was a nightmare for Protestants in general in that they felt spurned and abandoned by a government whose leader was supposed to have strong Unionist instincts.

The Unionist party's approach had been to leave things to James Molyneaux, who was said to have the ear of the people who mattered at Westminster. He had early on opted out of any negotiations, believing that by doing so he was ensuring that no real deal would be possible: his theory was that Britain and Dublin could not formulate an agreement without the input and consent of Unionist politicians. It was a historic mistake, in that London examined Molyneaux's integrationist approach and found it wanting. His suggestions of modest local government reform and procedural changes at Westminster did not begin to address the central question of what was to be done to improve relations with Dublin and to tackle Catholic alienation and the joint menace of the IRA and Sinn Féin.

Since many Unionists had initially relaxed on being reassured by Molyneaux that their interests were safe, the trauma of the agreement was all the deeper for being unexpected. They saw it as striking at their own sense of Britishness, and saw it too as Britain entering a compact with their ancient opponents. They regarded it as a deal done in an underhand way, with the prime minister taking far-reaching steps without consulting Unionist leaders. Thatcher herself tended to regard the accord as a security initiative rather than a historic new beginning. Howe later reflected: 'It took a gigantic struggle by many far-sighted people to persuade her; but although her head was persuaded, her heart was not.'

Unionists saw the agreement as a victory for constitutional nationalism, and constitutional nationalism agreed with them. It represented in fact an unprecedented new partnership between London and Dublin: in the years which followed that partnership had tense and difficult moments during many political and security crises, but though battered it was not broken. The agreement greatly reduced the practice of megaphone diplomacy, Irish politicians no longer stomping the US censuring Britain. London, for its part, seemed glad to have the south as an active ally in running the north.

This was partly because important sections of the British establishment had come to appreciate that constitutional nationalism had essentially redefined itself. This process was first seen in the civil rights campaign, which represented a major departure from old-style nationalist politics, and from the traditional nationalist assumption that the heart of the problem was the British presence. The previous nationalist recipe for solving the problem had therefore been to persuade the British to leave – or, in the view of the IRA, to force them to do so. The assumption was that Unionists, faced with an imminent British withdrawal, would embrace a new destiny as a minority in a united Ireland.

The new nationalist theory, as evolved by Hume, FitzGerald and others, rejected many of the old assumptions. In this revised view the key to the problem was not Britain but the Protestant community. The import was that the British presence was not imperialist but neutral, that the border was maintained not because of British interests but at the insistence of the Unionists, and that Irish unity could only come about with Protestant consent. The real border, it was now said, was not geographical but in men's minds. Though very different from conventional Irish nationalism, this doctrine by no means jettisoned the idea that a united Ireland was the ultimate solution. Unity, the rhetoric had it, would come through reconciliation rather than coercion.

As the years of violence dragged on there was a steady convergence of London and Dublin opinions, and of interests. The Republic no longer saw itself as warring with the British over the fate of the north: instead, the two governments came to view it as a difficult and dangerous problem for both. The emphasis thus switched to joint management and containment. The agreement reflected the fact that constitutional nationalism had shifted its emphasis away from simple separatism and towards accommodation. Dublin accepted, if grudgingly, that a united Ireland was not on the horizon, but in the meantime the accord was to give Irish nationalists a say in the formulation of British policy.

As it became clear that Molyneaux had been wrong about an agreement, Unionists threatened large-scale protests for more than a month before its signing. In apocalyptic terms Paisley's deputy Peter Robinson predicted confrontations with the security forces, demanding, 'What is Mrs Thatcher going to do after she has shot the first thousand Unionists in the streets of Belfast?' Paisley himself said that the proposals would be 'resisted to the very death' and accused the prime minister of being prepared 'to wade knee-deep in the blood of loyalists for this document of treachery and deceit'.

In an emotional speech Unionist MP Harold McCusker told the Commons that he 'never knew what desolation felt like until he read the Agreement', adding that now his constituents would be 'Irish-British hybrids'. In the immediate aftermath of the signing of the agreement most attention was focused on Protestant attempts to bring it down. Unionists flocked to a huge rally at Belfast City Hall, some estimates putting the attendance at well over 100,000 people. Unionist-controlled councils adjourned their meetings in protest. The Northern Ireland Secretary, Tom King, who had taken over when James Prior's successor Douglas Hurd had been moved on after only a year, was physically attacked by loyalists when he visited Belfast City Hall.

Unionist opposition to the agreement was so deep that it lasted for years, with protests ranging from political boycotts to mass rallies, demonstrations, and an increase in loyalist killings. Unionists objected not just to the text of the agreement but also to what a Protestant clergyman described as 'all the stuff in there between the lines'. Many nationalists also believed, or at least hoped, that they detected a barely concealed agenda on the British side, with London signalling that it did not forever expect to be in charge of Northern Ireland.

There were violent clashes between protesters and police, in one of which a Portadown loyalist was killed by a plastic bullet fired by a police officer, the first and only Protestant plastic bullet death. Loyalist paramilitants launched a systematic campaign of intimidation against RUC personnel, petrol-bombing the homes of police officers: more than 500 police homes were attacked, and 150 officers were forced to move house. Unionist politicians boycotted government ministers, and there was much rhetoric threatening the use of force. The fifteen Unionist MPs resigned their seats to force by-elections, a move that backfired when one of the seats was lost to the SDLP. A loyalist 'day of action' brought much of Northern Ireland to a standstill, but many Protestants disapproved of the widespread intimidation and riots which accompanied it.

Unionist politicians tried a range of approaches. At one point Peter Robinson joined a gang of loyalists who staged a late-night incursion into County Monaghan to demonstrate, they claimed, inadequate border security. Security was however sufficient to effect the MP's arrest, a second humiliation coming when he pleaded guilty in a southern court and paid a £15,000 fine for unlawful assembly.

The agreement survived it all. Historian Alvin Jackson summed up: 'The Unionists had once again backed themselves into a tactical dead-end in order to demonstrate the intensity of their convictions. Unionist tardiness and negativism had led inexorably towards marginalisation and humiliation.' The Unionist trauma was obvious, but the agreement posed great challenges for republicans too. They recognised it as a major departure in British policy, but debated long and hard about its exact significance.

9

Enniskillen, Libya & bombs in England
1986–93

When republicans contemplated the Anglo-Irish Agreement they were in the first instance most worried about its security aspects. The agreement was accompanied by new moves such as the erection of a string of watchtowers aimed at curbing IRA activities along the border, particularly in south Armagh. Republicans worried too that friendlier London–Dublin relations would bring a new level of isolation for republicanism and perhaps an erosion in the Sinn Féin vote. Britain was clearly intent on forging a new deal with constitutional nationalism and in doing so was prepared to stand up to fierce Unionist opposition. The IRA had seen itself as engaged in an anti-colonial, anti-imperialist freedom struggle. Suddenly, however, the supposed imperialist power had made an important move which cast it in a new light. This raised the issue, in more thoughtful republican minds, of whether a continuation of violent action represented the best way ahead. A senior Sinn Féin source later said privately: 'We saw the coming together of Dublin and London, and this proved London could be shifted. The fact that Britain moved unilaterally was pivotal. They hit the Unionists a kick in the balls, saying to them, "We've tried to work with you but that failed." That didn't go unrecorded in republicanism.'

In November 1986, the desire to modernise republicanism to keep abreast of such developments brought Sinn Féin to drop its age-old policy of refusing to take seats in the Dáil. The old guard, led by Ruairí Ó Brádaigh, fiercely resisted this, warning that dropping abstentionism from Sinn Féin's constitution would spell the beginning of the end for republican militancy. At a highly charged special conference debate, Sinn Féin thrashed out an issue which would be critical in setting the future direction of republicanism. For more than six decades it had been an article of faith that Sinn Féin members should not actually take their seats in the Dáil. The more traditional republicans regarded themselves as the keepers of the sacred republican abstentionist flame, while the Adams faction argued that the time had come for a change.

This faction believed there was a substantial vein of support to be tapped in the south, Martin McGuinness predicting that Sinn Féin could win up to five Dáil seats if abstentionism were abandoned. He swung opinion at the conference with a decisive speech in which he declared: 'They tell you that it is inevitable certainty that the war against British rule will be run down. These suggestions deliberately infer that the present leadership of Sinn Féin and the IRA are intent on edging the republican movement on to a constitutional path. Shame – shame – shame. I reject the notion that entering the Dáil would mean an end to Sinn Féin's unapologetic support for the right of the Irish people to oppose in arms the British forces of occupation. Our position is clear and it will never, never, never change: the war against British rule must continue until freedom is achieved.'

It is interesting to wonder whether, as he spoke those words, the republican ever envisaged that he would one day take office as education minister in a Stormont administration. The vote in favour of dropping abstentionism was 429 to 161: the republicans had potentially entered a new era.

The late 1980s and early 1990s were not a good time for politics either within Northern Ireland or in terms of Anglo-Irish relations. Political Unionism remained in protest mode for years after the Anglo-Irish Agreement, for some time refusing to meet government ministers, who would venture out of their heavily fortified offices only furtively and under heavy escort. The Unionist goal was defined, if it was defined at all, as the negative aim of bringing down the agreement rather than producing a positive alternative.

Nationalists initially regarded the agreement as a major and possibly historic advance, but gradually disillusion and disappointment set in. Their general assumption that the accord would give rise to a series of significant reforms which would be to the nationalist advantage proved unfounded. Margaret Thatcher and Tom King, who were unnerved by the furious Unionist response to the agreement, and disappointed that greater security gains did not follow, decided that the priority was to soothe Protestant fears and opted for consolidation rather than any evolution of the agreement. As a result the accord did not prove to be an engine providing the sort of development which Unionists had feared and nationalists had anticipated.

London–Dublin relations, which had been so good at the time the Anglo-Irish Agreement was signed, deteriorated as the south became dismayed by the British decision to apply the brake to the reform process. They were also made more difficult by a series of sometimes heated disagreements between the governments on legal and human rights issues including the Stalker affair and the long-running cases of the Birmingham Six, Guildford Four and Maguire family. In these three cases Irish people had been jailed for lengthy terms, sometimes for life, in connection with bombings in England during the 1970s. In each case Britain resisted Dublin's arguments that miscarriages of justice had taken place. It was not until the 1990s that all the sentences were quashed, proving Dublin's point.

Britain was in turn highly critical of the Republic for the recurring complications in extradition cases which generally resulted in the failure of London's attempts to have republican suspects handed over from the south.

For a brief moment, at the time of the Anglo-Irish Agreement, nationalists had delightedly thought that Thatcher had been convinced that any solution would be political rather than military, the old issue over which Edward Heath and Jack Lynch had disagreed so strenuously. The standard British justification for heavier security measures was that the state had the duty to take exceptional measures to protect itself and its citizens. The standard Irish rejoinder was that injustices had counterproductive consequences for public confidence in the security forces, the courts and eventually the whole system of government. The bottom line for both governments was that the Anglo-Irish Agreement was worthwhile and should be maintained, but both felt it failed to deliver its full potential.

The Libyan connection

Republicans meanwhile pursued a double strategy, attempting to penetrate the political system while at the same time rearming themselves with an arsenal so large that it converted them into one of the world's best-equipped underground organisations. They did so with the help of the Libyan ruler, Colonel Gaddafi, who gave the IRA an unprecedented amount of weaponry.

Gaddafi had provided guns and money to the IRA in the early 1970s but his interest appeared to have cooled until 1984, when his relations with Britain sharply deteriorated. As a result he renewed the relationship, giving the IRA large stocks of modern military hardware. Four separate shipments of arms made their way from Libya to Ireland in the mid-1980s, bringing the IRA around a thousand rifles together with fearsome weapons such as Semtex plastic explosives, heavy machine guns firing armour-piercing rounds which could cut through even protected police vehicles, SAM-7 missiles and anti-aircraft guns capable of downing helicopters and planes, and even flame-throwers.

The authorities knew nothing of the Libyan link, which amounted to the worst British intelligence lapse for decades. Both the IRA and Libya itself were under surveillance from a battery of security agencies, yet all the resources of the RUC, military intelligence, MI5 and MI6 had failed to uncover the Libyan connection. In the meantime the authorities at first mistakenly believed that the fight against the IRA was going fairly well, for the death toll was down and republicans seemed if anything to be short of weapons. No one realised that the organisation was simply keeping its powder dry by not using any of the heavy weaponry in case its appearance should disclose its Libyan source and cut the supply route.

The new weapons meant the IRA was able to step up its violence, not just in Northern Ireland but also in England and Europe. The Libyan armament was brought into play only gradually, but as it came into greater use the IRA killing rate rose from thirty-seven in 1986 to fifty-eight in 1987 and sixty-six the following year. The IRA aim was to reverse the pattern of security force casualties, for more RUC and UDR personnel, sometimes called the 'Ulsterised' security forces, were being killed than were regular British troops. In the years 1985 to 1987, for example, nine regular soldiers were killed compared to seventy-one police and UDR members. The republicans coldly set out to kill more British troops, calculating that this was the way to increase the impact of their violence.

The IRA thus stepped up violence in England, attempting to move from the previous pattern, which was generally one of hit-and-run, and instead establish an ongoing presence in Britain, with IRA members and supporters waging a sustained and in effect continuous offensive. They attacked a wide range of targets including military personnel, who tended to be more relaxed in Britain than in Northern Ireland. This approach was further extended to mainland Europe, where British troops came under attack in Germany and neighbouring countries. This expanded IRA campaign was to prove such a danger that the Ministry of Defence was forced to spend £126 million on anti-terrorist security measures at military bases in Britain and West Germany.

In Northern Ireland the IRA staged a series of what they termed 'spectaculars', in which prominent people or large numbers of security force personnel were killed. These included the 1985 incident in which nine RUC officers were killed by a mortar bomb which landed inside the grounds of Newry police station in County Down, and the 1987 assassination of a senior judge and his wife in a border landmine attack.

At the same time the security forces hit back against the IRA with SAS ambushes. The most notable of many such incidents took place in May 1987 when eight IRA members were killed as they attacked a small RUC station in the County Armagh village of Loughgall. The heavily armed IRA unit was attempting to blow up the part-time station when waiting SAS soldiers opened fire on them, inflicting what was in terms of lives lost the worst single setback during the modern history of the IRA. Several of those killed were regarded as being among the IRA's most proficient and most dangerous members.

November 1987 brought an even more crushing shock to the republican cause. No IRA members died in the incident, but the eleven civilian fatalities represented a hammer blow to the IRA's support and Sinn Féin's prospects for political expansion. This was the Enniskillen bombing, which took place on the morning of Remembrance Day as large numbers of Protestants gathered in the Fermanagh town in readiness for the annual parade and service. A large IRA device hidden in a community hall just behind them exploded without warning, demolishing a wall and bringing down tons of masonry. A man who lived nearby said, 'The explosion itself seemed to last about fifteen seconds. Then there was a dead silence for ten seconds. Then there was sobbing and crying.' As the dust cleared the disbelieving survivors made frantic efforts to dig victims from the rubble.

A local man, Gordon Wilson, gave an account of how he lay trapped in the debris holding his daughter's hand, in a radio interview which is remembered as one of the most poignant and affecting moments of the troubles. They talked for a while but then Marie said, 'Daddy, I love you very much', and fell silent. Mr Wilson survived the ordeal but his daughter did not. After her death he summoned the strength of character to say, 'She was a great wee lassie. She was a pet, and she's dead. But I bear no ill will, I bear no grudge.' The final death toll was eleven but more than sixty other people, aged from 2 to 75, were injured. Five of the dead were women. The IRA had desecrated an occasion set aside for the remembrance of the dead, and the world condemned them for it. Two themes flashed round the world in the wake of the bombing: one was that the IRA had killed eleven Protestant civilians as they gathered on Remembrance Day; the second was the almost superhuman display of Christian charity and forgiveness shown by Gordon Wilson.

A few days after the bombing a senior IRA source acknowledged the damage it had inflicted on his movement, saying:

> Politically and internationally it is a major setback. Our central base can take a hell of a lot of jolting and crises with limited demoralisation, but the outer reaches are just totally devastated. It will hurt us really badly in the Republic more than anywhere else. We were trying to convince people there that what's happening in the north is a legitimate armed struggle. But the obloquy we've attracted cuts the ground from under us. It allows the Brits to slot us into the category of terrorists and that's bad. People in the IRA just feel sick. This is probably the worst year the IRA has had for five years.

Enniskillen was clearly a grave setback for the republican movement, but two other almost simultaneous events combined to make the month of November 1987 a watershed. First a French customs patrol intercepted a trawler off the coast of France, finally alerting the authorities to the Libyan arms connection. For the first time the authorities north and south of the border realised the scale of the threat posed by the IRA. The Dublin government was particularly alarmed by the revelation, realising that the IRA now possessed weapons which might even match those available to the Irish army itself.

This sense of alarm in the south was heightened even more by an extraordinary episode over which the IRA had no control. Dessie O'Hare, the renegade INLA member, and a small gang kidnapped a Dublin dentist. They held him for several weeks until, in an action that appalled the entire country, O'Hare hacked off two of his captive's fingers with a chisel. Shortly afterwards the dentist was rescued, but for the following three weeks O'Hare and other gang members were pursued by police over large stretches of Ireland, twice shooting their way out of roadblocks and injuring several gardaí before their eventual capture. The fact that he had been able to remain at large for weeks, and his ability to outgun gardaí in their clashes, sapped public confidence in the police.

The combination of the Enniskillen bomb, the Libyan guns and the O'Hare dragnet created widespread alarm that the northern conflict was spilling across the border and threatening the stability of the entire island. From that point on, Sinn Féin expansion was not a possibility in the south: the republican ambition of having up to five members holding the balance of power in the Dáil vanished in the month of November 1987.

Violence 1988–90

The year 1988 brought no statistical rise in violence, but it included some terrible incidents which have remained in the memory of many who lived through them. One sequence in particular, in March of that year, will always be associated with one of the darkest and most traumatic periods of the troubles, when for a time violence seemed to be spiralling completely out of control. The sequence began not in Northern Ireland but in the British possession of Gibraltar. In the first week of March three IRA members, one of them a woman, were shot dead in disputed circumstances by the SAS in what came to be regarded as one of the most controversial incidents of the troubles. Although the IRA unit was intent on staging a bomb attack against British soldiers, the fact that they were unarmed when killed led to widespread criticism of the authorities. Controversy stemmed from claims by witnesses that the IRA members may have been attempting to surrender, and that they were shot while lying on the ground. The SAS members involved said the three had been given a chance to surrender but had failed to freeze immediately and had made suspicious movements.

The three shot dead were elevated to instant republican martyrdom. Hundreds gathered at Dublin airport as their bodies were flown to Ireland, thousands lining the route as the coffins were driven to Belfast. The killings not only sparked off intense international controversy but also led on to an unprecedented cycle of death and brutality. Many thousands more attended the funerals in west Belfast, but in Milltown cemetery mayhem broke out when to general amazement a lone loyalist gunman, Michael Stone, launched an attack on mourners. After much initial confusion Stone, a stockily built man with long hair and a moustache, was to be seen firing a handgun and throwing hand grenades towards the gravesides.

He then jogged towards a motorway several hundred yards away, pursued by hundreds of men and youths. On his way he periodically stopped, firing shots and throwing grenades to hold back his pursuers, killing three of them. He eventually reached the motorway, but by that stage had apparently exhausted his supply of grenades and ammunition. An incensed crowd overpowered him and beat him unconscious before police arrived and saved his life. Most of this extraordinary scene was televised.

More was to follow. One of those killed by Stone was a member of the IRA, and as his subsequent funeral made its way to Milltown a car carrying two British army corporals unaccountably drove into the cortège. Mourners besieged the car, assuming that its occupants were loyalists intent on a repeat attack. Dozens of them rushed forward, kicking the car and attempting to open its doors. Both the soldiers inside the car were armed, and one climbed partly out of a window, firing a shot in the air which briefly scattered the crowd. The crowd surged back, however, again attacking the vehicle, and the corporals were eventually pulled from the car and punched and kicked to the ground. They were then dragged into a nearby sports ground where they were again beaten and partially stripped. Finally they were driven to a patch of waste ground and shot dead. The sequence of events is still remembered, often with a shudder, as an almost unreal period of instability and polarisation.

The violence was unremitting. For one thing the loyalist killing rate rose sharply, from only 5 deaths in 1985 to a total of 62 in the following three years, as both the UDA and UVF increased their activity in the wake of the Anglo-Irish Agreement. Their victims were mainly civilians, 40 of them Catholics and 8 Protestants. Although loyalists always harboured the ambition to kill active republicans, they rarely managed to do so, with only half a dozen Sinn Féin or IRA members or supporters among the dead in this three-year period. More republicans were to be targeted in subsequent years but at this stage Catholic civilians bore the brunt of the loyalist violence. As in previous bouts of loyalist violence the victims were often chosen at random or because they were convenient targets.

As always, however, republican violence attracted more attention than did loyalist killings. The IRA was active on many fronts, causing the deaths of a substantial number of Protestants whom it claimed were loyalist extremists involved in violence. Some were but some were not. The IRA also stepped up its killings of regular soldiers, particularly in 1988, causing the deaths of fourteen soldiers in two incidents by blowing up coaches in Lisburn in County Antrim and Ballygawley in Tyrone.

These attacks spurred Thatcher into a legal clampdown on republicans. A high-level review led to a series of measures which included banning Sinn Féin voices from the airwaves, a loss of remission for paramilitary prisoners, and a partial withdrawal of the right to silence of paramilitary suspects. The authorities were also clearly concerned by the new IRA campaign in Britain and mainland Europe. While the attempt to attack troops in Gibraltar had failed, in the following year an IRA bomb killed eleven army bandsmen at a military music school at Deal in Kent. There was also a series of lucky escapes for troops at barracks in England and Germany as the IRA attempted to inflict large-scale loss of life by placing bombs at army sleeping quarters during the night. A further major tightening of security was ordered following the IRA assassination in 1990 of Ian Gow, a Conservative MP who had been both a personal friend of Thatcher and a strong supporter of the Unionist cause. He died in a car booby-trap explosion at his home in Sussex.

But even as the IRA celebrated such deaths as successes, the organisation's members were also killing substantial numbers of civilians, generally by accident. So many were being killed that Adams as Sinn Féin president publicly appealed to IRA volunteers in 1989 to avoid such incidents, saying: 'At times the fate of this struggle is in your hands. You have to be careful and careful again. The morale of your comrades in jail, your own morale and of your comrades in the field, can be raised or dashed by your actions. You can advance or retard the struggle.' The lesson to be drawn from the pattern of deaths, however, was that the waging of high-level campaigns of violence made civilian deaths an inevitability. The pattern was different on the republican and loyalist sides, in that the latter's main target grouping was Catholic men.

Republicans during this period hotly denied any sectarian motivation to their actions, saying they wished to kill only those who were part of the 'British war machine'. In pursuit of this they targeted, among others, prison officers, legal figures, and civilian contractors who carried out building work and other jobs for the security forces. The different viewpoints of the two communities led to radically different perspectives on the IRA campaign. Republicans would say they deliberately killed only those involved with the security forces, but many Protestants pointed out that most of the victims, deliberate or accidental, were Protestants, and alleged that all or part of the motivation was sectarian. Many Catholics tended to accept the republican explanation, but very many Protestants did not.

1989 brought one of the numerous incidents which over the years raised human rights concerns, and produced republican allegations that the authorities were engaged in dirty tricks and underhand activity of various kinds. In this instance Pat Finucane, a Belfast solicitor who had represented republican clients in a series of high-profile cases, was shot dead in his home by loyalist gunmen.

The case, like many others throughout the troubles, led to long-running controversy, with allegations about the incident still being levelled by human rights groups more than a decade after his death. The accusation was that he had been such a thorn in the side of the authorities that they had urged loyalists to attack him, and had possibly helped them to do so.

The controversy surrounding his death arose from a number of sources, one of which was the statement by a junior government minister, three weeks before the shooting, that a number of solicitors were 'unduly sympathetic to the cause of the IRA'. Another aspect of the controversy arose from allegations that detectives interrogating loyalist prisoners in Castlereagh holding centre had urged loyalists to shoot the solicitor. The Finucane killing was the subject of several inquiries by international lawyers' groups, and in 1998 a United Nations report called for an independent inquiry.

Late in 1990 the IRA produced a new tactic which came to be known as the 'human bomb'. In the first instance of its use a Londonderry Catholic man, Patsy Gillespie, who worked in a local army canteen, was taken from his home by IRA members. While his wife and family were assured he would be returned safely, he was chained into a hijacked vehicle and ordered to drive to an army border checkpoint. When he arrived there the IRA detonated a large bomb which had been concealed in the vehicle. The checkpoint was heavily fortified but little defence was possible against such a powerful device, and five soldiers were killed. For many hours the security forces were unsure whether Gillespie himself had escaped or not, for no trace of his body could be found. Even after all the years of the troubles the incident, and several similar attacks, still managed to generate a fresh sense of horror.

1991

Some months later, in February 1991, the IRA staged one of its most audacious attacks in England. The target was originally Margaret Thatcher, but by the time the incident took place she had been replaced as prime minister by John Major. He was chairing a meeting of ministers during the Gulf War when a number of mortar bombs rained down in the vicinity of 10 Downing Street. Major described hearing 'a tremendous explosion' but no one was killed or injured even though damage was caused in the back garden of Number 10. The IRA had succeeded in exploding a substantial mortar bomb within yards of the prime minister, one of the most closely guarded people in Britain. The attack achieved major international publicity for the IRA and represented a serious embarrassment to the British security services. Major wrote later, 'If it had been ten feet closer half the cabinet could have been killed.'

The rest of 1991 brought more IRA attacks in Britain, more killings of IRA members by the SAS and an increase in loyalist activity. Much loyalist violence emanated from the County Armagh town of Portadown, where the local UVF was headed by a number of particularly violent leaders including Billy Wright, a local man who came to be known as King Rat. In March four Catholic men were killed in a UVF gun attack at a bar in the County Tyrone village of Cappagh. Although the UVF gunmen did not know it at the time, three of those killed were IRA members. In the same month the UVF killed two teenage girls and a man, all Catholics, in an attack on a mobile shop in a housing estate in Craigavon, County Armagh. In November two Catholics and a Protestant were killed as they left a factory near Lurgan in the same county.

The sluggish political scene had been enlivened a little in mid-1989 by the replacement of Tom King by Peter Brooke. King's years in Belfast had been dominated by the furious loyalist reaction to the Anglo-Irish Agreement, the frigid political atmosphere offering little hope of finding agreement among the parties. By the time Peter Brooke took his place something of a thaw had set in, with the political parties, in particular the Unionists, adopting a less confrontational stance.

The widespread early impression of Brooke was that he was a descendant of the old Anglo-Irish ascendancy, a quasi-aristocrat who would be out of his depth in the shark-infested waters he had been despatched to manage. His upbringing had been the picture of establishment orthodoxy: he was educated at Marlborough and Oxford, and his father had been a Tory Home Secretary. In fact, he would turn out to be one of the most thoughtful and imaginative, if not always the most deft, of the many politicians given the task of running Northern Ireland.

The first major stir of his tenure came in November 1989, when a journalist asked him whether he could ever imagine a British government talking to Sinn Féin. Instead of the standard ministerial response that there was no question of the government talking to terrorists, he gave a long and thoughtful answer. In the course of it he remarked:

> Let me remind you of the move towards independence in Cyprus, and a British Minister stood up in the House of Commons and used the word 'never' in a way which within two years there had been a retreat from that word. All I'm saying is that I would hope that the British government on a long-term basis would be sufficiently flexible, that if flexibility were required it could be used, but I am in no way predicating or predicting what those circumstances would be.

His mention of Cyprus also excited much republican interest in that it presented an example of an island which had been a British possession, but which in 1959 had achieved independence following a campaign which combined political agitation and violence.

A year later, in November 1990, Brooke delivered a speech which was to have far-reaching effects. In part of it he declared: 'The British government has no selfish strategic or economic interest in Northern

Ireland: our role is to help, enable and encourage. Britain's purpose, as I have sought to describe it, is not to occupy, oppress or exploit, but to ensure democratic debate and free democratic choice. That is our way.' His words, like his earlier reference to Cyprus, aroused intense interest within the republican movement.

When he took an initiative to try to get politics rolling again, however, Sinn Féin were excluded from it. He believed he saw a window of opportunity, and although none of the major parties was particularly keen to get round the table, he nonetheless embarked on a long process of nudging and persuading them towards talks. Many months of intricate political activity followed. He began the effort in January 1990, and it took more than a year to get agreement from all sides to sit down together.

The talks were conducted within parameters which would become a familiar formula in the years that followed. They were divided into three 'strands', originally formulated by John Hume, dealing with internal Northern Ireland matters, north–south relations and overall Anglo-Irish relations. The discussions were useful in exploring some political details, but they never looked like providing a solution to the troubles; indeed they never looked like producing even an agreement among the parties at the table. Despite the close attentions of London and Dublin the talks ran into the sands after a few months.

1992 violence

1992 was again marred by violence. Only seventeen days into the year an IRA bomb planted at the side of a County Tyrone road blew apart a van, killing eight Protestant workers travelling home after carrying out building work at an army base. The vehicle took the full force of the blast. The van's upper part was torn asunder, but instead of being blown into a field its momentum kept it tumbling along the road for thirty yards. Seven men were killed outright, an eighth dying shortly afterwards. The scene at that point was hellish, with dead, dying and injured bodies scattered on the road, in a field, and trapped under wreckage. Some passers-by who stopped to help were sent into shock by the sight of terrible mutilations. It took the emergency services a considerable time to work out how many had been killed. Yet another Northern Ireland place name, that of Teebane Crossroads, would forever afterwards be associated with violent death.

One of the survivors later described his ordeal: 'I looked and all I could see was fire. I was yelling, I was screeching and it was an experience I had never come through before. A flash came through my mind that overhead lines had fallen – the big overhead power lines. I thought we had been electrocuted because of the pain. I have experienced getting an electric shock, but fire was coming out of my eyes. I just squealed for breath and I seemed to be heading away. I seemed to be literally going to float away. I felt I was going backwards. I was lying on the broad of my back and I couldn't see down to see my legs and I couldn't feel them. I was trying to get up. I had plenty of power in my two arms but no power anywhere else. I saw a fella who had been sitting beside me on the bus staggering about and I yelled and shouted at him but he never heard me. I said to a man: "Are my legs on?" and he said, "You're all right" and he shook my legs but I couldn't feel them. I said: "Get me up", and part of my kneecap came off but I knew my leg was there and I thanked God that I was living.'

Just over two weeks later came another shocking and unprecedented attack. An off-duty RUC constable, Allen Moore, arrived in plain clothes at the Sinn Féin press office on the Falls Road in Belfast, posing as a journalist. Once admitted to the building he produced a pump-action shotgun and turned it on three men in a ground-floor office, killing them all. Constable Moore then drove out of Belfast to a secluded spot and shot himself dead.

The following day came yet more violence as loyalists exacted revenge for the Teebane attack. Two members of the UDA walked into a Catholic betting shop on the Ormeau Road in south Belfast and systematically shot as many men as they could. The attack only took a matter of minutes, leaving five dead.

An ambulance officer called to the scene described what he saw: 'I went in and had a quick look. The scene was horrific, with bodies everywhere. In that confined space there was a smell from the gunfire and all the bleeding and whatever that you couldn't describe. It has an effect on you as an individual. I get flashbacks to it, I get visions of what was going on – the smell, the smell, the feeling of being there. For other ambulancemen it was worse: they were knee deep in it, dealing with the dead and dying.'

Less than two weeks later the SAS was back in action, laying an ambush for IRA members who attacked an RUC station in the County Tyrone town of Coalisland. The authorities allowed the attack on the heavily fortified station to go ahead, the IRA men commandeering a lorry and firing a heavy machine gun from the back of it. The security forces took no action at that point, but when the IRA unit drove into the carpark of a church some distance away in order to abandon the lorry and disperse in getaway cars, the SAS opened fire. Locals said there was a call for the gang to surrender, followed by intense, prolonged gunfire. When it was all over, four IRA members lay dead with two others injured. The authorities celebrated the incident as a clean, clinical strike against the IRA.

Then in April came an IRA attack in London which had an extraordinary effect. Two bombs set off in the City of London, Britain's financial heartland, actually inflicted more financial damage than all the 10,000 bombs which had ever gone off in Northern Ireland. When the smoke and dust cleared it was found that the two bombs had caused more than £700 million of damage. The total paid out in compensation in Northern Ireland at that point was just over £600 million.

The device had been placed near the Baltic Exchange and the tall buildings around it created a canyon-like effect, preventing the blast from escaping and instead funnelling it into surrounding buildings. British newspapers carried full-page photographs of the devastation. The damage was so severe that the fact that the bomb had also killed three people, one of them a fifteen-year-old girl, was almost overlooked.

The spectacular destruction grabbed the attention of the world. Republican sources made no secret of the fact that they were both amazed and delighted at the extent of the damage and at the extraordinary bill for repairs. The idea of placing large bombs in the City, where so many expensive prestige buildings cluster in a tightly packed area, came late and largely by accident to them. Since 1988 they had carried out scores of attacks, but it took four years before they hit on the idea of bombing the City.

The scale of the Baltic Exchange damage opened a new avenue, the possibility of inflicting serious damage on the entire British economy. In the 1970s the IRA had naively held such a belief, but the idea faded as the government showed itself able to absorb, without great difficulty, the cost of dealing with terrorism and disorder. However, the fact that a single attack could cost Britain more than half a billion pounds lent a whole new dimension to the IRA campaign. The authorities were desperate to prevent any recurrence, and worried that if the IRA could strike again major financial institutions might relocate to other countries not subject to such dangers.

The Teebane attack claimed a political casualty in the form of Peter Brooke, in that he was judged to have made a *faux pas* on television on the night of the incident. Appearing on RTÉ's Friday night television programme *The Late Late Show*, he expressed his sympathy for the families of the dead but was later persuaded to sing one of his favourite songs, 'My Darling Clementine'. He later apologised in the Commons, saying his actions might have caused 'wholly justified offence' to the bereaved families. John Major turned down his resignation at the time but it was clear Brooke's days were numbered, and in April he moved on.

John Major's choice of successor was welcomed by Unionist politicians but caused dismay in Dublin. Sir Patrick Mayhew, as his name suggested, came from an Anglo-Irish background, but in his previous post as Attorney-General he had been involved in many acrimonious extradition disputes with Dublin. Within weeks of his arrival in Belfast Mayhew pushed ahead with a revival of the Brooke talks, with Sinn Féin again excluded because of its identification with the IRA. This session of talks would ultimately prove unsuccessful, but it did get beyond the procedural points which had defeated the Brooke discussions, and some serious debate took place.

In the talks the Unionist parties were primarily concerned to reduce the influence that Dublin had gained through the Anglo-Irish Agreement. They also wished to get rid of Articles 2 and 3 of the Irish constitution, which since 1937 had laid legal claim to Northern Ireland. Some Unionist politicians wanted a strong new devolved government re-established in Belfast, though others preferred to aim for closer links with Westminster, accompanied by a less powerful Belfast assembly. The first priority of the SDLP and the Irish government, on the other hand, was to protect the Anglo-Irish Agreement and if possible develop stronger north–south and Anglo-Irish links.

In pursuit of their conflicting goals the Unionist parties wanted to concentrate on discussing a new assembly while the SDLP and Dublin were more interested in dealing with north–south relations. A major stir was caused when Hume unveiled the SDLP's proposals, which advocated a direct role for both Dublin and Europe in running Northern Ireland. This controversial and innovative proposal dismayed Unionist politicians, some of whom had hoped the SDLP would settle for a Northern Ireland-centred arrangement with modest links to Dublin.

The talks sparked some interest when Molyneaux became the first Ulster Unionist leader to head a delegation to Dublin for talks with the Irish government, but in the end nothing emerged to bridge the gulf between the SDLP and the Unionist parties, and in November 1992 the exercise was wound up. The British government's approach continued to be that it would hope for an agreement among the constitutional parties with the purpose of isolating the republican and loyalist extremists. After the best efforts of Brooke and Mayhew, however, there seemed no real prospect of this coming about.

Political activity did not produce any significant progress and violence went remorselessly on. And, as always, there were innocent victims. One of the saddest incidents came in Warrington, near Liverpool, when two IRA bombs placed in litter bins in a shopping precinct killed 2 young children and injured 56 other people. Jonathan Ball was three years old, and an only child. Timothy Parry, aged twelve, had gone into the town to buy a pair of football shorts: in the explosion he suffered severe head injuries and died some days later. His father said, 'We produced a bloody good kid, he was a fine lad. He had his moments, he could be a cheeky, impudent pup, but a good kid. The IRA – I have no words for them at all.' The killings led to a wave of revulsion throughout Britain and especially in the Republic, where tens of thousands of people attended a Dublin peace rally.

The IRA, undeterred, within weeks staged another huge bombing in the City of London, repeating their Baltic Exchange attack of April 1992 by setting off a large bomb at Bishopsgate in the heart of the financial district. Again the damage was extraordinary, with estimates of the cost ranging as high as a billion pounds. Yet even as death and destruction continued at a high level, subterranean talks were going on. What became known as the peace process began to surface.

10

Peace process
1993–94

Most of the 1990s would be dominated by what came to be known as the peace process, which was to change the face of Northern Ireland politics and Anglo-Irish relations. It was a highly controversial enterprise regarded with the utmost suspicion by many as it threaded its way along a long and tortuous course. One of its starting points was the 1985 Anglo-Irish Agreement, which led to a gradual but important rethink in republican ranks. On one reading, the agreement had redefined the whole Irish question: the IRA had traditionally regarded itself as being engaged in an anti-colonial, anti-imperialist freedom struggle, but suddenly the supposed imperialist power had made an important move which was difficult to portray in an imperialist light.

At the same time it became clear that Sinn Féin's vote was going down, the party chalking up 102,000 votes in 1983 but only 76,000 two years later. Sinn Féin had established a solid foothold in electoral politics, but it was a far cry from the heady days when it aspired to eclipse the SDLP and become the main voice of northern nationalism.

Hume – Adams

Even as the IRA escalated its violence in the late 1980s, Sinn Féin was exploring the potential for talking, sending feelers out to church and state and seeking contact with a wide range of opinion. The result was a web of talks over the years, most of which were held in strict secrecy. It was not until April 1993 that the lid was lifted on at least part of the process when, entirely by accident, Gerry Adams was spotted entering John Hume's home in Londonderry. Within hours political figures of various persuasions were issuing statements condemning Hume for consorting with what they called the mouthpiece of terrorists. The media clamoured for an explanation: no one accused Hume of supporting republican violence but both critics and supporters demanded to know what he was doing talking to Adams. The heat on Hume was all the fiercer because IRA violence was at a high level, the two Warrington boys having died just weeks earlier.

On the surface Hume appeared to have breached the general rule that mainstream politicians should not speak to those associated with violence. Yet although few knew it at the time, the Hume–Adams channel was just the tip of an iceberg, since for years a concealed web of contacts had been in existence. It was not only Hume who had been in touch with the republicans but also the Catholic Church, the Irish government and, above all, the British government. London's line to the republicans stretched back not just for years but, intermittently, for decades. Almost all of this was however hidden from public view.

Sinn Féin had made approaches to many quarters over the years, often with the assistance of Father Alex Reid, a priest based in Clonard monastery off the Falls Road. As a result Adams had secretly met Catholic Cardinal Tomás Ó Fiaich and, on other occasions, representatives of the Irish government in talks authorised by Taoiseach Charles Haughey. To begin with, none of these produced visible results. 1988 had seen formal talks, whose existence were for once known to the public, between SDLP and Sinn Féin party delegations, with a series of meetings and exchanges of position papers. When the talks ended without agreement after some months most assumed this was the end of the matter. But Hume and Adams had privately agreed to keep in touch, a move which was the beginning of one of the most unusual relationships in Northern Ireland politics. During 1989 for instance they met four times, usually in rooms made available by Father Reid in the monastery.

The meetings did not inhibit Hume from publicly attacking the IRA. In one scathing denunciation he declared:

> They are more Irish than the rest of us, they believe. They are the pure master race of Irish. They are the keepers of the holy grail of the nation. That deep-seated attitude, married to their method, has all the hallmarks of undiluted fascism. They have all the other hallmarks of the fascist – the scapegoat – the Brits are to blame for everything, even their own atrocities! They know better than the rest of us.

Hume and Adams, the two dominant figures in northern nationalism, are individuals who have already, in very different ways, left their mark on Irish history. They were direct rivals for the nationalist vote and indeed for the leadership of northern nationalism, their parties fighting many bitter battles. Yet through all the bruising conflicts they forged a personal relationship of some trust and, in time, a sense of pursuing a common purpose. Although they differed fundamentally in their analysis of the problem, and above all disagreed on how to resolve it, they actually had much in common in their backgrounds. Hume, like Adams, came from a working-class Catholic background. He was born in Londonderry in 1937, one of a family of seven living in a two-bedroomed house. His father fought with the British army in France in World War One and was later unemployed for many years.

He attended grammar school in Londonderry and then Maynooth College in the Republic, where for several years he trained as a priest. He changed direction and became a teacher before becoming involved in self-help community projects such as the Credit Union. Coming to public prominence on civil rights issues, he took the moderate line in the many arguments within the movement.

In common with Garret FitzGerald, he challenged the traditional nationalist assertion that the root of the problem was the British presence. The historic mission of nationalism, he argued, was to convince Unionism that its concerns could be accommodated in a new agreed Ireland. He built up an international reputation, accumulating considerable influence especially in the Republic and, as a European MP, on the continent. In particular he wielded great influence in Washington, where powerful Irish-American figures such as Senator Edward Kennedy looked to him for advice. By the early 1990s he was, in sum, the most influential nationalist politician in Northern Ireland.

His behind-the-scenes contacts with Adams interacted with events in the public domain. When Brooke made his 1990 statement that Britain had no selfish strategic or economic interest in Northern Ireland he did so at the private prompting of Hume, who had been arguing this point in his talks with Adams. Brooke's statement, while by no means regarded by republicans as conclusive, was nonetheless strong evidence in support of Hume's contention that Britain was essentially neutral. This thought would play an important part in the embryonic peace process.

It would emerge at a later date that the British government itself had for years had its own line of contact to republicans. In 1990 Brooke had given his approval to a proposal from John Deverell, the head of MI5 in Northern Ireland, to reopen contacts with the republicans. Deverell said he believed there was potential for progress, and Brooke gave him permission to explore. Brooke would later recall: 'We had a substantial debate about it. It was not negotiation. I was not sanctioning a whole series of things – it was the opportunity to carry on conversation. It was essentially an intelligence process.' This was the start of a long sequence of contacts between the government and the republicans.

A highly significant moment came in October 1991 when Hume wrote a draft declaration which he hoped could form the basis of an agreed position between the British and Irish governments. The idea was to demonstrate, with a joint declaration, that Britain was not standing in the way of Irish unity, in the eventual hope of persuading republicans to halt their attempt to unite Ireland by violence. The intention was to find common ground in everyone's ideological positions, and to reconcile what had always appeared irreconcilable. It was to prove the first of many such drafts which would, in December 1993, culminate in what became known as the Downing Street Declaration.

Hume's first draft included statements on self-determination, an assurance from Britain that it had no selfish interest in remaining in Ireland, and a heavy emphasis on the need for agreement. The document set the Northern Ireland problem firmly in an Anglo-Irish context, drawing on the Anglo-Irish Agreement and envisaging the two governments working ever more closely together. It also stressed the European dimension. While it did not explicitly demand an IRA ceasefire, it was obvious that it was intended to produce one. It was also implicit that if violence ended, Sinn Féin would be admitted to mainstream Irish political life. The crucial part of Hume's draft lay in its attempt to address the republican demand for Irish self-determination. This could not be achieved, he wrote, without the agreement of the people of Northern Ireland. This was a subtle concept, for in effect it combined the principles of self-determination and consent. It thus combined, at least in theory, what republicans sought with the Unionist demand that the majority opinion should prevail within Northern Ireland.

Hume took the document to both Haughey and Adams. In the subsequent dozen or more drafts, Hume, Dublin and the republicans tested out each other's positions, seeking both common ground and a formula which might bring John Major into the exercise. Haughey was cautious but Albert Reynolds, who succeeded him as Taoiseach and leader of Fianna Fáil in January 1992, was much more interested and pursued the idea with enthusiasm. Reynolds, a canny Longford businessman, had little direct experience of Northern Ireland matters but respected Hume's opinion and had an instinct that a peace process might be productive. The years that followed saw the further development of many secret contacts. Hume, Reynolds and the republicans exchanged documents and kept London informed while the republicans separately, unknown to Hume and Reynolds, also dealt directly with London. The web survived both political turbulence and numerous acts of IRA violence such as the City of London bombings.

It was obvious that John Major was taking many risks in keeping open the channels of contact. He had only a slender majority at Westminster, with an awkward squad of right-wing Tories ready to rebel at any moment, principally on important votes concerning Europe. He also had in his government ministers such as Lord Cranborne who were strongly committed to the Unionist cause. The parliamentary arithmetic meant nine Ulster Unionist MPs led by James Molyneaux could be of great value to Major, and might be vital to the survival of his government. But on the other hand Major was very much of the opinion that Northern Ireland warranted serious and sustained attention. This attitude was in itself unusual in that so many senior British politicians had throughout their careers attempted to devote as little time and energy as possible to the issue. Major was different, taking a decision in his first months in office to pay attention to the problem. He and Reynolds, whom he found 'easy to get on with, naturally cheery and loquacious', got into the habit of writing to each other and speaking frequently on the telephone, often calling each other at home. Major recalled in his memoirs, 'I liked Albert a lot, and I thought we could move things forward together.'

The back-channel

The secret British–republican link in these years, which came to be known as the back-channel, had three distinct phases. In the first, which began in 1990 and lasted for three years, London actively courted the republicans, sending nineteen messages while Sinn Féin replied only once. Occasional meetings took place, sometimes in Northern Ireland and sometimes in London. In the second phase, between February and November 1993, the pace quickened with an average of a message a week passing back and forward as the possibility of a formal meeting between republicans and the government was explored. The third short phase followed before the contacts effectively came to an end in November 1993.

The back-channel opened with an approach from the British government representative who had been in touch with the republicans in earlier periods. He explained he was due for retirement and said he wanted to meet Martin McGuinness to prepare the way for a new representative. This overture opened a line of communication which went from the government to 'the government representative' who spoke to a person known as 'the contact', who in turn was in touch with Sinn Féin.

In 1992 messages were passed back and forth on the Hume–Adams talks. The British also appear to have kept Sinn Féin informed of the progress of Mayhew's talks with the political parties, passing on a detailed internal government report and assessment on the discussions. This was followed, in December 1992 and January 1993, by meetings between the contact and the British representative, together with a series of telephone calls, sometimes on a daily basis. Sinn Féin was pointedly unenthusiastic until the government representative indicated a face-to-face meeting was possible. Many messages followed, the republicans now taking the exercise seriously and establishing a committee chaired by Adams to oversee the enterprise. In the event, however, the go-ahead never came from London. Instead, the republicans were told that ministers had changed their minds.

In the end, after dozens of messages and exchanges of documents and a number of face-to-face meetings, the two sides never got together for serious talks. Both laid out their positions in formal documents, but much of the back-channel concerned the arrangements for talks, and no sub-stantive negotiations took place. The more meaningful negotiations throughout this period actually involved Adams, Hume and Dublin through the stream of draft declarations.

After all the years of moving at a snail's pace, the spring of 1993 ush-ered in a new phase of often frantic activity, with the public for the first time glimpsing a little of what had been going on. From then on, incident followed incident in a sometimes bewildering blur of events. Ahead lay moments of tremendous excitement, great controversy, much violence and on occasion near-despair.

The storm of protest which followed the disclosure of the April 1993 meeting between Hume and Adams did not deter the two men, and within weeks they issued the first of a series of statements saying they were involved in a search for agreement. However, the talks revelation put the still-secret joint declaration work under great strain. Reynolds would say later: 'When the news broke of the dialogue taking place be-tween Adams and Hume, it just brought more tensions and pressure on the situation. I would have preferred to have dealt with the whole lot nice and quietly behind the scenes – you make more progress that way. But it burst into the open and I had no control over it. It didn't help.'

It was clear from an early stage that London regarded the joint de-claration idea not so much as a potentially historic formula for peace but as an unwelcome hot potato. At the request of Reynolds, Major agreed that London would consider the declaration text but drew the distinction that his government would discuss it but would not negotiate on it. Mayhew as Northern Ireland Secretary was against the idea, wishing instead to persevere with his political talks. In a personal letter to Major, Reynolds wrote: 'There are risks, but peace is within our reach if we play our cards right. Peace, which could result from the present process, could transform the current climate and make that outcome not only possible but probable. I will therefore ask you in all sincerity to continue to give the process your full and enthusiastic backing.'

Eventually in the autumn of 1993 Hume, impatient at the pace of progress, went public, he and Adams announcing that they had made considerable progress and had agreed to forward a report to Dublin. They declared: 'We are convinced from our discussions that a process can be designed to lead to agreement among the divided people of this island which will provide a solid basis for peace.' This brought the already high level of public interest to an even more intense pitch, dominating news bulletins in Britain and Ireland. The statement produced acres of newsprint aimed at shedding light on how the north's two nationalist leaders, one identified with violence, the other with non-violence, could possibly be on the verge of agreement. The Hume–Adams statement gave the public another little glimpse of the secret world of talks and contacts. It was by then firmly established in the public mind that Hume and Adams had been in contact, but the bulk of the story remained hidden from view: the public, and the media, knew nothing of the years of talks between Adams and Hume, and of the British and Irish governmental contacts with Sinn Féin. They knew nothing of the succession of draft declarations, and were in complete ignorance of the fact that many of these had been passed to the British government.

Both London and Dublin were angry with Hume. They continued to work on the joint declaration process but both were anxious to keep it free from what they referred to as 'the fingerprints' of the Hume–Adams statement. Major despatched his cabinet secretary, Sir Robin Butler, to Dublin to tell Reynolds that the Hume–Adams initiative had become inextricably intertwined with the declaration work, and that this had effectively made the idea too hot to handle. The two governments should look to alternatives such as the Mayhew talks, Major suggested. The Reynolds–Butler meeting took place on 19 October, just four days before an act of violence in Belfast which started a cycle of killing that brought Northern Ireland to the brink of despair. October 1993 was one of the most awful, yet most crucial, months in the troubles. It began in confusion mixed with hope, then plunged into violence and near despair, almost as dark as any period of the troubles. The death toll was the highest of any month since 1976.

IRA bombs and loyalist retaliation

An IRA bomb went off on the Shankill Road around lunchtime on a Saturday, at a time when the road was thronged with hundreds of shoppers. It was aimed at leaders of the paramilitary Ulster Defence Association who the IRA thought were meeting in offices above a fish shop. IRA members attempted to place the bomb in the shop, in a very risky operation which carried a high chance of causing civilian casualties. In the event the bombing did not go as planned, for as IRA member

Thomas Begley was putting the device in place it detonated prematurely, killing him and nine Protestants. Four women and two children were among the dead but no UDA members were killed, for the upstairs office was empty at the time. The explosion demolished the old building. In the aftermath local men, police, firemen and ambulancemen tore at the rubble in a search for survivors, but the elderly building had collapsed like a house of cards, bringing heavy masonry crashing down on those inside.

A young police officer who arrived quickly at the scene said later: 'I was one of the first in. I remember an old man being recovered. His head was the first thing to appear from the rubble, and that was quite a frightening experience. I knew he was still alive because his eyes were blinking. An ambulanceman put an oxygen mask over his mouth but by the time he left the rubble he had died. After he was moved we continued to remove rubble from where we were standing, but unknown to anybody we were standing on other bodies. As the rubble was being removed – and it will stay with me until I die – I saw a young girl's foot. I knew it was a young girl's foot because her shoe size was about three or four. It poked through the rubble, and I wanted to stop digging then, because I knew I was going to see quite a horrendous sight; and in fact I did.' A paramedic later recounted: 'The scene was horrific. There was one lady lying in the road with head injuries and half her arm was blown off. She later died. But the worst part for me was when we unearthed the body of a young girl. I will never forget seeing that face staring up out of the rubble.'

The attack did not come out of the blue, for it was in effect the culmination of several months of increasingly desperate IRA attempts to assassinate leading loyalists. For months hardly a week passed without IRA gangs attempting to gun down or blow up those they believed to be associated with groups such as the UDA and UVF. Loyalist killings were running at a particularly high level and had developed a new feature. In addition to the standard pattern of loyalist attacks on random Catholic targets, loyalists had in addition begun to target members of Sinn Féin, together with members of their families and friends. In the five years leading up to the Shankill bombing, eighteen people with Sinn Féin connections were killed by Protestant extremists. Three of the dead were Sinn Féin councillors while another councillor lost a brother and a son in separate attacks. Republicans alleged collusion by the authorities in many of the killings, while the IRA retaliated by killing many alleged loyalist extremists. It was against this background of republican–loyalist violence that the Shankill attack took place.

The funeral of the dead bomber produced an electrifying moment when Adams was pictured carrying the coffin of Thomas Begley, an image reproduced on the front pages of most newspapers. The result was a huge outcry, with much questioning of how Adams could speak of peace while shouldering the coffin of a bomber who had caused so many deaths. From a republican point of view the bombing was one of the IRA's most disastrous mistakes since Enniskillen, in that at a stroke it killed nine civilians, lost one of its own members, and brought fierce international condemnation upon itself.

Reynolds later described a telephone call with Major who, he said, 'could hardly contain himself'. Reynolds recalled:

> He said, 'What's this about? How do you expect me to continue with any process when I take up the papers this morning and in every paper on the front page is Gerry Adams carrying a coffin?' I said, 'Look, John, you have to understand that if the guy didn't carry the coffin he wouldn't be able to maintain his credibility with that organisation and bring people with him.'

Reynolds said of the British prime minister: 'Here you had a guy with goodwill keeping it high on his agenda, giving it more time than any prime minister had ever given to the Irish problem since Gladstone, and this was blowing up in his face. He was put in an extremely difficult and delicate position. I was really annoyed with it – to be honest I thought for some time that it would probably blow the whole thing sky high.'

At this point Northern Ireland descended into something close to sheer dread, for loyalist gunmen went on the rampage, killing six people in a series of shootings. They then attempted to match the Shankill death toll with a Saturday night attack on a bar in the quiet mainly Catholic village of Greysteel near Londonderry, a week after the Shankill bombing. Two gunmen opened fire on around 200 people in the bar, killing or fatally injuring eight people, seven of them Catholics.

A young man charged with the murders was televised on his way into court, yelling defiantly and laughing almost maniacally at relatives of the victims in a display of naked sectarian hatred. After his subsequent conviction, the man would repent and become a born-again Christian, but his performance at the time added yet another nightmarish dimension to the atmosphere of poison and fear. Twenty-three people had died in the space of a week; the local television news seemed to consist of nothing except more and more violence, the grieving bereaved, and threats of more to come. There was a seemingly endless succession of multiple funerals as the victims were buried.

Social functions and other gatherings were cancelled as people stayed indoors and took extra security precautions. In the evenings many parts of Belfast, particularly Catholic districts, were virtually deserted. A senior trade unionist gave a flavour of the atmosphere at the time:

> I do think they are actually taking us back to the early 1970s. I really don't come across anyone now who doesn't talk about how dreadful it is. Everybody is frankly scared to talk to people of the other community or even talk to people of their own community, in case anything they say might be overheard and give offence. You can see the fear everywhere. When I went to mass on Sunday attendance was down by a third, and there were armed RUC officers on guard duty in the car park. The priest said at the end of mass that police advice was for us to leave quickly, not to congregate chatting, just to get into our cars and get going.

Although many at first assumed the peace process was over, it turned out that the killings had the opposite effect. When the first waves of shock and anger died down there was renewed determination in many quarters to keep the process going. Major was to suggest in his memoirs that the violence actually gave fresh impetus to a process which was about to expire: 'The process was on a knife-edge. I think it would have broken down had not the Shankill and Greysteel tragedies intervened.' A moving example of this at the human rather than political level came at the funeral of one of the victims of the Greysteel attack. Hume was approached by the daughter of one victim, who told him: 'Mr Hume, we've just buried my father. My family wants you to know that when we said the rosary around my daddy's coffin we prayed for you, for what you're trying to do to bring peace.' This caused Hume to break down in tears.

Overall, however, Hume was receiving more criticism than encouragement, to the point where it affected his health. He collapsed and spent several weeks in hospital. The violence was followed by more political shocks when Belfast journalist Eamonn Mallie revealed in November 1993 that, despite repeated public denials, the government had been in long-standing contact with republicans. The government admitted that there had been contact but said it had begun only in 1993, and that it had in essence been an investigation of a message from Martin McGuinness which had said: 'The conflict is over but we need your advice on how to bring it to a close.' It maintained that those meetings which had taken place had not been authorised by ministers.

London and Sinn Féin then each published their versions of their correspondence, which when examined were found to differ in important details. In particular McGuinness hotly denied that he had sent the 'conflict is over' message. Then came a development so embarrassing that it led to Mayhew offering his resignation to Major, since a comparison of the two versions showed that vital parts had been altered by one or other of the parties. Someone was engaged in a major deception exercise, forging, omitting and doctoring documents. Each accused the other of fabrication.

When points of detail were raised with the NIO, the government at first did not respond for a full day and then announced that a number of 'errors' had come to light. Mayhew detailed twenty-two of these which, he said, had been caused by typographical and transcription errors. The changes he announced removed some of the glaring inconsistencies in the British version, but the manner in which the correction had to be made was seen as a blow to the government's credibility. Mayhew's resignation offer was refused. Two years later the government version was undermined still further when Brooke, after leaving government office, readily confirmed that he had authorised the opening of contacts in 1990. In doing so he contradicted the official government assertion and confirmed the Sinn Féin version of events.

Major and Reynolds met at a summit in December 1993 which those present described as tense and bad-tempered. The various developments created much bad blood between London and Dublin. Major took exception to what he later described as 'a series of Irish leaks, threats and distorted press briefing' for which he suspected Reynolds was responsible. Dublin thought Major's undeclared contacts with republicans amounted to double-dealing. Reynolds considered that he had properly informed Major of his own contacts with the republicans, and felt Major should have reciprocated instead of denying they existed. Reynolds said later: 'With a revelation like this naturally one would feel betrayed. If you're going along in good faith you expect all the cards on the table and you expect to know what's going on on both sides. I felt that I was let down, that I should have been told.'

The two prime ministers spent an hour without officials in a private meeting during which they aired their differences, emerging 'very pale and very tense'. Major was to recall this as 'the frankest and fiercest exchanges I had with any fellow leader in my six and a half years as prime minister'. A Dublin aide has recorded for history the memorable reply given by Reynolds when he was asked how it went. Reynolds, he reported, half-grinned and replied: 'It went all right – I chewed his bollocks off and he took a few lumps outa me.' Despite all the bad temper and rancour and difficulties, it was a key meeting with crucial results. Reynolds and Major retained their working relationship and, against all the odds, the drafting work went on.

The Downing Street Declaration

It finally came to fruition in the Downing Street Declaration of December 1993, which Major and Reynolds unveiled together. The document contained nothing that could be interpreted as a British declaration of intent to leave. Rather, it had as its heart a serpentine sentence which intertwined the concepts of self-determination and consent on which Hume and Adams had spent so much time. It read: 'The British government agree that it is for the people of the island of Ireland alone, by agreement between the two parts respectively, to exercise their right of self-determination on the basis of consent, freely and concurrently given, North and South, to bring about a united Ireland, if that is their wish.' It was in effect an ambitious attempt to construct a finely balanced double helix in which self-determination and consent were inseparable.

Many republicans had assumed that Major's desire not to offend the Ulster Unionist party, with its nine Commons votes, would prevent him from going so far. But Major had handled Unionist leader James Molyneaux carefully, ensuring that he did not damn the declaration out of hand. Major had thus achieved the feat of producing a declaration which kept mainstream Unionism on board while putting maximum pressure on the republicans.

The joint declaration contained references to many of the elements contained in the drafts worked on by Hume and Adams, but most of the points the republicans had wished to see were very much diluted. The republicans had wanted the British to 'join the ranks of the persuaders' of the value of a united Ireland, and had wanted Northern Ireland's future status to be decided by a single act of self-determination by the people of Ireland as a whole. They had also sought a timetable for a British withdrawal, but none of these made it into the declaration's final form. Yet although the declaration fell far short of what republicans had sought, Sinn Féin reacted not by rejecting it but by calling for clarification. Major replied by announcing that no clarification was necessary and a stalemate developed, with much of the euphoria which accompanied the declaration draining away as weeks and months passed.

February 1994 brought a major propaganda coup for the republicans when the Clinton administration dropped the long-standing ban on Adams entering the US. This was a crushing defeat for the British government, which for weeks had fought an intense diplomatic battle to keep Adams out of America. The transatlantic drama, involving major figures in Britain, Ireland and the US, went right to the Oval Office of the White House, and was settled just days before the visit took place, Clinton himself taking the final decision.

Major was so furious that for some days afterwards he refused to accept telephone calls from Clinton. He wanted Adams, Sinn Féin and the IRA isolated and ostracised, but Clinton had responded to the argument of the Irish government and Hume for the use of the carrot rather than the stick. They believed an American visit would give the republicans a glimpse of the new vistas of support which could be available to them, though only if they moved away from violence. In the event the impact of the short visit exceeded all the hopes of Adams and the fears of Major. The republican leader was given a celebrity reception, being fêted like a movie star throughout New York, appearing on the most prestigious television shows and meeting many of the most influential people.

The following month however brought a bizarre incident which represented an attempt by republicans to use a finely orchestrated blend of violence, politics and propaganda. Mortars similar to those used to attack Downing Street in 1991 were fired over a period of days on to runways at Heathrow, causing major security alerts. One of them hit the ground only forty yards from a stationary Jumbo jet and another landed on the roof of Terminal Four, but none of the devices exploded. For a time this appeared to have put paid to hopes that the IRA was slowly moving towards a ceasefire. The IRA campaign in the wake of the declaration had been running at a relatively low level, and this was a dramatic escalation. Most baffling of all, the IRA seemed to have thrown all caution to the wind by firing mortars which could have hit an aircraft, causing multiple civilian casualties.

Many of those who believed in the peace process were dumbfounded. It seemed as if the IRA response to the declaration was an indiscriminate attack on a major international airport, used daily not only by the British public but by travellers from all over the world. The effect of a mortar bomb exploding inside a crowded terminal, or hitting an airliner, was almost too terrible to contemplate. Yet when the full facts began to emerge the attacks took on a different aspect. Although the mortars contained Semtex plastic explosive, it turned out that a key component had been doctored so that they would not explode: the purpose had been to terrify but not to kill. The whole thing had been an extraordinarily elaborate hoax, designed to pressurise the British government without actually killing anyone.

The month of May brought a change of heart from the British government, which dropped its objections to clarifying the Downing Street Declaration and published a lengthy 'amplification'. But there was still no final response from the republicans, as everyone watched anxiously to see whether a ceasefire might be forthcoming.

As they waited there was yet more violence, this time from loyalists. On a June night UVF gunmen burst into a Catholic bar in the quiet County Down hamlet of Loughinisland and fired repeatedly into the backs of customers watching a soccer match on television. Within seconds customers were dead, dying or injured, with bodies piled on top of each other and blood running freely on the floor. Six Catholics lay dead, one of them, at eighty-seven years of age, the oldest victim of the troubles. The owner of the bar and seven regulars escaped the slaughter because they had just flown out to Romania on a charity mission to help rebuild an orphanage.

The scale of the carnage, together with the fact that Loughinisland had previously been sheltered from the violence, increased the impact of the attack on the little community. Shock, incomprehension and disbelief mixed with grief, while to the rest of the world it seemed as if the peace process and the Downing Street Declaration had come to nothing. The Loughinisland attack was to be the last of the large-scale multiple murders before the IRA and loyalist ceasefires. Nobody knew that at the time, however, and even if they had, it was little consolation to the families and friends of the innocents who died. Pessimism became almost universal when a large-scale Sinn Féin conference in June sent out a message which was interpreted as ruling out a ceasefire. In fact the IRA was heading towards a ceasefire, but in the run-up to it there was a last-minute wave of violence, in which a number of prominent loyalist figures were shot dead.

IRA ceasefire

On 31 August came the ceasefire announcement. Just after 11 a.m. excited journalists and newsreaders read out an IRA statement proclaiming that, as of midnight that night 'there will be a complete cessation of military operations'. Few people in Ireland have forgotten where they were when they heard the news that after twenty-five years of conflict and more than 3,000 deaths the IRA, one of the world's most formidable terrorist organisations, had finally decided to call a halt. There was jubilation in the nationalist community but among Unionists the reaction was more uncertain. The IRA had not said the cessation was permanent, and there was apprehension that the move could be a cynical tactical manoeuvre aimed at having London drop its political and security guard.

In republican areas too it was a moment of great uncertainty. Many wondered whether Sinn Féin had reached some secret deal with the British government, but word was quickly circulated that no such deal had been done. It was a huge step, undertaken unilaterally, and no one was sure what would happen next. One thing was clear: Northern Ireland had entered a new phase.

11

Decommissioning, Docklands & Drumcree 1994–96

Though it was clearly a momentous development, the cessation statement was received in many quarters with suspicion rather than celebration. Unionist politicians warned that it was a delusion and a trick rather than a genuine move, though most nationalists and republicans instinctively believed the conflict had drawn to an end. These differing views of the peace process were to bedevil it in the years ahead. Reynolds moved quickly to demonstrate his faith in Adams, meeting him and Hume within a week of the ceasefire for a historic public handshake aimed at consolidating the cessation.

As the weeks passed and the ceasefire held, another major development came in October when the loyalist paramilitary groups followed the IRA's lead. They not only declared a ceasefire but set a new tone by including an unexpected note of apology, offering 'the loved ones of all innocent victims over the past 25 years abject and true remorse'. The announcement carried all the more weight because it was made by Augustus 'Gusty' Spence, who had been jailed for life for the 1966 Malvern Street killing and had since become an icon of loyalist paramilitarism.

This change in tone reflected the existence of a new phenomenon within militant loyalism with the emergence, from that violent underworld, of a political element. Groups such as the UVF and UDA remained in being, but now they too went on ceasefire and sprouted new political wings. There had been previous such attempts, but they had been short-lived and unsuccessful. In particular the UVF now produced the Progressive Unionist party, with articulate spokesmen such as David Ervine and Billy Hutchinson. They and most of the other new spokesmen were ex-prisoners who had learnt the hard way the cost of violence. Some like Hutchinson had served life sentences, spending a dozen years or more behind bars. A number had established discreet contacts with republicans whom they had met in jail, had come to know individual IRA members, and kept up contacts with them after their release, often through community groups. The sight of the previously violent loyalists embracing the peace process with such enthusiasm gave the process a huge boost, for many had assumed the loyalist groups would continue to pose an active threat. Instead they became at many points a force for moderation, eager for dialogue and presenting a very different approach from that of mainstream Unionist politicians.

Paisley, however, declared that Protestants faced 'the worst crisis in Ulster's history since the setting up of the state' and denounced the process. He asked his party faithful:

> Are we going to agree to a partnership with the IRA men of blood who have slain our loved ones, destroyed our country, burned our churches, tortured our people and now demand that we should become slaves in a country fit only for nuns' men and monks' women to live in? We cannot bow the knee to these traitors in Whitehall, nor to those offspring of the Vatican who walk the corrupted corridors of power.

Within the republican movement, meanwhile, it became clear that there was widespread though not universal approval of the IRA move. The initial reaction in the republican grassroots had been a mixture of competing feelings which included hope, fear, nervousness and uncertainty. It gradually became clear, however, that the predominant emotion was one of relief. Within the leadership of the IRA there were those who had doubts, but the generality of republicans welcomed the cessation.

Some of that sense of relief turned to irritation, and then by stages into a much more sour and dangerous anger, when it gradually became clear that the government had decided to play it long and resist the republican demand for early talks. Within weeks of the cessation, in fact, the British government had made a private assessment that the start of all-inclusive round-table negotiations was probably two years away. This approach was received with incredulity by nationalists who wished to move with all speed to enfold the republicans into the political system. The government, however, exuded scepticism and suspicion of republican motives, an attitude which was to prevail during the seventeen months which the ceasefire lasted.

Dublin pressed ahead with the approach of welcoming the republicans into politics, setting up a new body, the Forum for Peace and Reconciliation, in which they could publicly rub shoulders with mainstream nationalist politicians. Viewed from London, however, things looked very different. John Major had an undoubted personal commitment to working for peace but he had many reservations about republican motives. The Unionist community was uncertain and nervous about the future, and although many grassroots Protestants welcomed the ceasefire, most of their political representatives found it an unsettling experience. Unionist party leader James Molyneaux said of the cessation: 'It started destabilising the whole population in Northern Ireland. It was not an occasion for celebration, quite the opposite.' Major noted that Unionists were 'deeply troubled' by the ceasefire.

Within weeks of the announcement it became obvious that the 'cessation of military operations' did not mean that the IRA would be entirely inactive. The practice of carrying out 'punishments' of alleged wrongdoers in republican areas continued, and although the practice of shooting them in the legs was temporarily ended, scores of men and youths were savagely beaten. It also emerged in late 1994 that the IRA was still watching members of the security forces, and continued to size up potential targets for attack in both Northern Ireland and Britain. November 1994 brought a moment of crisis when a postal worker was shot dead during an IRA robbery in Newry, County Down. The ceasefire seemed in doubt, but the IRA leadership quickly issued a statement saying it had not sanctioned the robbery and had granted no one permission to use arms. Major noted in his memoirs that the killing 'turned out to be botched criminality rather than a deliberate ceasefire breach'.

Within weeks of the Newry killing came the sudden political fall of

Albert Reynolds. Hailed as a hero of the peace process, he became embroiled in an unconnected political crisis and his government collapsed: rarely can such a political triumph have been followed so quickly by political oblivion.

The departure of Reynolds did not seem to endanger the process. The general nationalist view was that peace had come to stay, and that the process was robust enough to survive such domestic political turbulence. The new Fine Gael Taoiseach, John Bruton, had however been a frequent critic of the peace process and was never in tune with events to the extent that Reynolds had been. The republicans had looked to Reynolds to fight their corner with the British, commending him for in some ways acting as one of the elements of a broad nationalist front. Bruton, who had a deep distaste for Sinn Féin and the IRA, did not see this as his role.

As the months passed, day-to-day life in Northern Ireland steadily improved, with army patrols becoming less frequent and the RUC visibly relaxing. Police officers went on the streets without flak jackets and rifles, while armoured Land Rovers were increasingly replaced by saloon cars and even motor-cycle patrols. Many cross-border roads which had been closed for decades were reopened, while peaceline barriers were unlocked in various parts of Belfast.

An important development came in February 1995 with publication of what was known as the 'framework document'. This was a booklet largely drafted by Dublin diplomat Seán Ó hUiginn, and published jointly by the British and Irish governments, in which they set out a joint vision of the future. The framework document envisaged Northern Ireland remaining part of the United Kingdom, stressing the importance of Unionist consent. But it stipulated that the Irishness of nationalists should be formally expressed through progressively increased Dublin input, most tangibly through new cross-border institutions. Unionist politicians took strong exception to the document, refusing to accept it even as a basis for negotiations, while by contrast it was welcomed by nationalists. It was to form much of the basis for negotiations in the years that followed.

The decommissioning problem

Negotiations were at first widely expected to start within months of the IRA ceasefire, but those who hoped for this were to be disappointed. Instead, the year that followed was dominated not by political negotiation but by protracted arguments about the IRA's weaponry. The issue of what should be done with illegal weaponry once violence had been halted was obviously one of the most important issues in conflict resolution. During 1995, however, the peace process virtually stalled on the question of when arms decommissioning should take place. The issue had cropped up briefly in 1993 but it had not been emphasised. Now, in the wake of the IRA cessation, Major and Mayhew repeatedly called on the organisation to give up its weapons, journalists regularly pressing Adams on this point. Adams delivered what was to become a familiar republican response: 'I think the whole issue of decommissioning of weapons obviously has to be part of finding a political settlement, and there couldn't be a political settlement without that. But I don't think there's any point in anyone trying to leap ahead on any of these issues. Let's get a political settlement and of course let's get all of the guns out of Irish politics.' In his memoirs Major would accuse Sinn Féin of 'posturing and filibustering and avoiding genuine discussion'.

In March 1995, important adjustments were made to the positions of both governments. Mayhew, during a visit to Washington, laid down three new stipulations before Sinn Féin could be admitted to all-party talks. Republicans would have to demonstrate a willingness in principle to disarm, and then come to an understanding on the practicalities of decommissioning. There would also, he insisted, have to be 'the actual decommissioning of some arms as a tangible confidence-building measure' in advance of talks. The republican position was that the IRA had disengaged from armed conflict but had not been beaten and had not surrendered, and therefore did not contemplate any arms handover, regarding this as an act of capitulation. There was also a great deal of historical baggage. Irish insurgents had never in the past handed over their weapons in the wake of conflicts. The modern IRA had sprung from the vicious ghetto fighting of 1969, when the previous republican leadership was bitterly accused of leaving Catholic areas unarmed and undefended against loyalist incursions.

Dublin's initial reaction to what was known as Mayhew's 'Washington Three' speech illustrated that Bruton's approach was very different from that of Reynolds. The Reynolds technique was whenever possible to ease the republicans into politics and maintain pressure on the British to facilitate this. But Bruton, in responding to Mayhew's speech, took a line closer to the British stance. Rather than opposing the new precondition, he called for a gesture on decommissioning, thus helping to establish Mayhew's stance as a position agreed by the two governments.

It was not until May 1995, more than eight months after the cessation, that Sinn Féin representatives met British ministers. First Martin McGuinness met a junior minister in Belfast, then later that month Adams met Mayhew at a conference in Washington. By that stage Adams had already shaken hands with Bill Clinton, Nelson Mandela, British ministers and almost every major political figure in the Republic. Major did not meet Sinn Féin, though he had seen representatives of the parties linked to the loyalist paramilitary groups. The new loyalist parties remained enthusiastic about politics, and there were no real signs of strain on the loyalist cessation. The ceasefires had not however been underwritten by an agreed political settlement and this, coupled with traditional suspicions, meant a large element of uncertainty was always in the air. By mid-1995 the IRA ceasefire was showing signs of increasing strain, with Adams and other Sinn Féin figures repeatedly warning that the peace process was in crisis.

Drumcree and the rise of David Trimble

Tensions increased palpably with the loyalist marching season. A major confrontation developed in July when the RUC attempted to reroute an Orange demonstration at Drumcree near Portadown in County Armagh away from a Catholic district. After days in which thousands of Orangemen congregated at Drumcree the march was eventually allowed through in what was seen as a triumph for militant loyalism. Paisley and the local Unionist MP, David Trimble, later celebrated the success by walking, hands joined aloft in triumph, through crowds of cheering supporters. Controversial marches were nothing new, but for the rest of the 1990s the Drumcree dispute was to recur on an annual basis, often leading to large-scale disturbances and violence.

September brought a highly significant development when James Molyneaux was ousted as leader of the Ulster Unionist party after sixteen years and replaced by Trimble, a former law lecturer who had been an MP for only five years. Most of the political spectrum was dismayed by his election in that he was regarded as the most hardline of the five candidates for the post. Trimble had come to the fore, following a long career in the junior ranks of politics, through his prominent support of the Orange Order at Drumcree. His election seemed to prove the point that the IRA ceasefire declared a year earlier had led to a hardening rather than a relaxation of Unionist attitudes. The Protestant show of determination at Drumcree, together with Trimble's election, showed that many Unionists viewed the peace process as a hazard rather than an opportunity.

Trimble's career had been mostly spent on the uncompromising wing of Unionism. His views seemed to mirror his temperament, in that while his manner was generally polite he had a reputation for occasional surges of temper. In his early days he had been a protégé of former Stormont minister William Craig, following him in his unexpected trajectory from militancy to moderation in the mid-1970s. Craig, it will be recalled, had staged Mosley-style rallies and had made speeches in which he spoke of the liquidation of Unionism's enemies. A few years later, however, he had unexpectedly advocated bringing the SDLP into the cabinet, an idea so radical and unacceptable to his colleagues that he lost the leadership of his Vanguard party and was expelled from mainstream Unionism. Trimble went with him.

In the years that followed, Trimble had reverted to a generally hardline position. In his memoirs Major described him as 'one of the mutineers' who thought Molyneaux's line was too soft. A government minister recalled his reaction to seeing Trimble described in a British newspaper as a moderate: 'I was having my breakfast when I read that,' he said. 'Nearly puked up my Frosties.' To the surprise of many, however, Trimble would turn out to be anything but a traditional hardliner.

Enter George Mitchell

In November 1995, following a lengthy and complex Anglo-Irish negotiation, the two governments finally reached agreement on a three-man international body to report on the decommissioning issue. Chaired by former US Senator George Mitchell, it included a Canadian general, John de Chastelain, and Harri Holkeri, a former prime minister of Finland. Mitchell was a major American political player, whose despatch to Belfast by Clinton was a signal of the sustained US interest in Northern Ireland. He had by turns been an army intelligence officer, a lawyer and a federal judge. A liberal Democrat, he spent fourteen years as a US senator. He was majority leader in the senate, where for six consecutive years his peers voted him the most respected member of that body, and he had turned down a nomination to the US Supreme Court. One journalist wrote of him: 'It was obvious from the word go that this was a mature and seasoned statesman, a major player with abilities far in excess of those normally seen in Northern Ireland. It was often embarrassing to watch the mismatch between his consummate skills and some of Belfast's political pygmies.'

November also brought the visit to Belfast of Bill Clinton, as the American president, proud of his contribution to the peace process, came to celebrate the absence of violence. In Belfast and Londonderry he was given a rapturous reception, his visit turning into a huge communal celebration of peace as he delivered the message that the violence must be over for good. Within weeks of the visit and the celebrations, however, came ominous signs that the IRA ceasefire was under increasing strain, as four alleged drug dealers and petty criminals were shot dead on the streets of Belfast. Responsibility for these and two earlier killings was claimed by a previously unknown group styling itself Direct Action Against Drugs, but few doubted the IRA was behind the shootings.

Overall however the death toll was the lowest for decades, with nine killings in 1995 compared to sixty-nine in the previous year. One of the nine deaths, that of former RUC Constable Jim Seymour, had a particular poignancy. He had been shot in 1973 and for twenty-two years lay in a hospital bed with a bullet in his head, apparently conscious but unable to move or speak. He was visited daily by his wife for those twenty-two years before he died at the age of fifty-five. This ordeal was a reminder of the lasting suffering inflicted during the troubles on a great many families.

1996: the IRA ceasefire ends

The next major development came in January 1996, when Senator Mitchell's international body delivered its report. It said that prior decommissioning would not happen and suggested that decommissioning should instead take place in parallel with political negotiations. Mitchell had become convinced that the demand for prior decommissioning was unworkable, not least because he had been briefed to that effect by both the RUC and the gardaí. In his memoirs he recorded asking the RUC whether Adams could persuade the IRA to accept prior decommissioning. He was told, 'No, he couldn't do it even if he wanted to. He doesn't have that much control over them.' Mitchell already knew that parallel decommissioning would not find favour with Major for, as he revealed in his memoirs, Major had privately told him so. The American reported on their meeting: 'Major spoke directly to us. His words had a steely candour. If we recommended parallel decommissioning he would have to reject the report. He didn't want to, but he would have to.'

Reacting to the Mitchell report in the Commons, Major thanked the senator and his colleagues for their efforts, but said the road to talks lay either through prior decommissioning or by the holding of an election in Northern Ireland. Trimble was delighted at this new tack, since he had called for elections, but republicans and nationalists responded angrily. Dublin, Hume and the republicans wanted to get into talks as soon as possible, but it would clearly take months to organise and stage an election.

This was the state of the peace process when, on a Friday evening in February, after a confused series of warnings, a huge bomb concealed in a lorry exploded in London, not far from the giant Canary Wharf building in London's Docklands. The blast claimed two lives, causing immense damage and apparently ending the process. Most participants in the process were sent into shock by the explosion. The British and the Irish, the Unionists and the nationalists, the Americans and the rest of the world wondered whether it meant another generation condemned to live through violence.

The bomb galvanised political activity. During Reynolds's period of office the cessation had gone reasonably well from a republican point of view, and Sinn Féin was pleased with the framework document of February 1995. But from then on they claimed Major's approach was intended to maintain pressure on Adams and Sinn Féin, and not to pressurise Unionist politicians. The decommissioning impasse, the absence of all-party talks, and the lack of movement on issues such as prisoner releases, all combined to increase republican disillusion.

The British authorities at some points believed that the IRA ceasefire was secure and at others thought it under strain, with some republican elements in favour and some against. Yet London continued to resist the Dublin argument that the peace could be shored up by creating greater momentum on issues such as talks and prisoners. Those who were always sceptical of the ceasefire argued that the IRA was never serious, and that the resumption of violence proved that the government and the Unionist parties were right to react to it with the utmost caution. Those who believed in the cessation by contrast contended that it was faulty intelligence and analysis, married to excessive caution and delay, which helped bring about its breakdown.

The Canary Wharf bomb delivered the message that the gun and the bomb had not yet been removed from Irish politics. There was shock, dismay and near-despair not just in Britain and Ireland but in many parts of the world. Lives had been taken and immense damage caused to property and no one could be confident that the process would be rebuilt. There were further bombings, though it gradually became clear that the IRA was opting not for a return to a full-scale campaign of terrorism but was rather establishing a pattern of sporadic attacks in Britain. Northern Ireland was left largely untouched.

The end of May brought the poll Unionist politicians wanted and nationalists did not in the form of elections to a debating forum whose members were to provide delegations for inter-party talks. Sinn Féin opposed the exercise and boycotted the forum, but contested the election, and when the ballot boxes were opened it turned out that they were the main beneficiaries. The party vote surged to an unprecedented 15.5 per cent. The regular republican vote had turned out, but so too had many people who had never voted before, or who had refrained from supporting the party while IRA violence was at its height. The SDLP's vote dropped by a fraction, but John Hume and Gerry Adams both received massive personal endorsements. This was interpreted as a message from the republican and nationalist grassroots of overwhelming support for the peace process.

Yet what they got was not peace but more violence and disturbance. 1996 was punctuated by occasional bombing attacks, civil disturbances on a large scale, and important political developments. Political talks convened in Belfast in June without Sinn Féin. Adams, surrounded by the largest media posse ever seen in Belfast, led a delegation to the gates of the talks where the cameras recorded an official informing the Sinn Féin representatives that they would not be allowed in until a new ceasefire was called.

June brought a wave of IRA violence. In that single month an Irish policeman was shot dead in the Republic, a large bomb devastated much of Manchester's city centre and injured more than 200 people, and a mortar attack was staged on a British army base in Germany. The killing of the Irish detective Jerry McCabe, who was shot dead during a robbery, sent shock waves through the south. He was buried at a state funeral attended by the Irish president and the Taoiseach. The IRA at first denied responsibility but later admitted that 'individual volunteers' had been involved. The episode raised many questions about the state of play within the republican movement, centring on the IRA's evident lack of control of its members and its commitment to a renewed peace process.

Drumcree 1996

Next came what was known as Drumcree 1996. The Orange Order had been so proud of its success in pushing the 1995 march through that it had struck 'Siege of Drumcree' medals to commemorate the occasion. Unionist party members had been so pleased with Trimble's part in the exercise that they had elected him leader. When the occasion came round again in July 1996 there was much apprehension that another clash was on the cards, yet no one foresaw how grave a confrontation it would become. The Protestant marchers were determined to get through; the Catholic residents were equally determined that they should not. Academics Neil Jarman and Dominic Bryan summarised the clash of perspectives: 'Each parade which is challenged is a symbolic threat to Protestant security and the Unionist position, while each parade which passes through a nationalist area is a re-statement of the dominance of the Protestant community and the inferiority of nationalist rights.'

RUC Chief Constable Sir Hugh Annesley, in one of his last major decisions before retirement, again banned the parade from going along the Catholic Garvaghy Road. When Orangemen sought to get through they were halted by armoured Land Rovers, barbed wire and RUC officers in full riot gear. Rather than dispersing they stayed put around the grounds of a Drumcree church, announcing they would remain 'for as long as it takes'. Thousands of supporters joined them, including Trimble, and some loyalist protesters engaged in vitriolic abuse of the police. The protests were not confined to Drumcree, developing into one of the most destabilising episodes of the troubles. Loyalists staged hundreds of roadblocks and erected barricades over much of Northern Ireland, bringing life in whole areas to a standstill. Some towns were completely cut off, and there was widespread intimidation of police officers and their families. There was burning and looting in some areas of Belfast, widespread destruction of property, and more than a hundred people were injured. Near Drumcree itself a Catholic man was shot dead by loyalists.

The crisis came to a head on the morning of the Twelfth of July when it became evident that no negotiated settlement of the dispute was in sight. A number of loyalists appeared with a bulldozer fitted with makeshift armour, threatening to drive it through the police lines. Tens of thousands of Orangemen were poised to march in processions all over Northern Ireland, and there were not enough RUC members and troops to police them all. Faced with the prospect of widespread and uncontrolled disorder Annesley backed down, reversed his original decision, and let the marchers through. The logic of allowing the Orangemen along the Garvaghy Road meant it had to be cleared of its Catholic residents, many of whom had gathered to protest. Riot police cleared the road, with some rough-handling of residents captured in graphic detail by the television cameras. Nationalists in a number of districts responded with rioting, and in Londonderry a man was killed. The Orangemen got through and the immediate threat of unrestrained civil commotion was eased.

The cost was high. As one commentator put it: 'The underlying instability of the state was exposed, the very fabric of society ripped and damaged, and the most fundamental questions posed about the reform-ability of Northern Ireland. The episode left community relations in tatters and left a vast new reservoir of bitterness in its wake.' Sir Ronnie Flanagan, who was to succeed Annesley as head of the RUC, said of Drumcree 1996: 'Northern Ireland cannot withstand another summer like this one. The intensity of the violence which our officers withstood was of a scale that I hadn't seen over 25 years. The country stared into the face of great difficulty and crept right to the edge of the abyss.' Another senior policing figure went even further, saying privately: 'We were on the brink of all-out civil war. Letting the march through was bad but the alternative was a thousand times worse. We kid ourselves that we live in a democracy. We have the potential in this community to have a Bosnia-style situation.' A senior Presbyterian minister summed it up as 'Northern Ireland's Chernobyl, with almost a melt-down in community relations'.

Yet despite the intensified bitterness and the deepening chasm between the two communities, paramilitary groups on both sides did not revert to full-scale violence. Although fringe elements on each side staged arson and other attacks, the mainstream groups did not go back to uninhibited conflict.

The talks continue

The political talks went on, with George Mitchell moving from his role in decommissioning to chair proceedings which proved to be long-drawn-out, tedious and initially unproductive. Trimble took his party into the talks with more enthusiasm than his predecessor Molyneaux had ever shown, though his position within Unionism was not a secure one. In the forum election Protestant votes had been scattered around various Unionist parties so that while Trimble won 46 per cent of the vote, Paisley together with other hardline parties took 43 per cent. This competition was too close for comfort for any Unionist leader and was clearly not conducive to any thought of making substantial concessions in negotiations. Against such a background, it was hardly surprising that Trimble resisted suggestions that he should soften his party line on issues such as decommissioning. By this stage Paisley was in his fourth decade of making life difficult for any Unionist leader who contemplated making an accommodation.

In early October the IRA carried out an ingenious and particularly cold-blooded attack on a prestige target, the army's Northern Ireland headquarters in Lisburn, County Antrim. The base was such an obvious target, and so heavily guarded, that it had long been assumed to be immune from republican assault. The IRA penetrated its defences, however, with three cars, two of them containing 800lb bombs. The bombs exploded, shattering the base's illusion of security and injuring thirty-one people. A soldier later died of his wounds. The devices were placed so as to inflict maximum casualties. The first went off without warning in a car park, while the second exploded fifteen minutes later a hundred yards away. It had been placed with singular callousness outside a nearby medical centre. The obvious intention was that the second device should blow up the injured and those bringing them for medical help.

The soldier killed was the first to die in Northern Ireland since August 1994. He died on the day John Major addressed the Conservative party's annual conference, and in his speech the prime minister attacked Adams in the most scathingly personal terms: 'For many months, Sinn Féin leaders have mouthed the word peace. Warrant Officer James Bradwell was 43, with a wife and with children, Mr Adams. He joined the army, prepared to lose his life defending the British nation. Soldiers do. But he was murdered in cold blood in the United Kingdom. I sent him there, Mr

Adams, so save me any crocodile tears. Don't tell me this has nothing to do with you. I don't believe you, Mr Adams, I don't believe you.'

The 1996 death toll was twenty-two, an increase on the 1995 figure of nine. The IRA killed eight people, the INLA six and loyalists five. In private meanwhile Hume presented Major with a document known as 'Hume–Adams Mark 2' which was said to be a formula for a renewed ceasefire. There was little surprise when Major rebuffed the initiative. In doing so he described the 1994–96 ceasefire as fake and said he did not want another phoney cessation. Clearly there was to be no more engagement between London and the republicans in advance of the next British general election.

12

Breakthrough
1997–2000

1997

This year was to bring a continuation of violence but also, eventually, a restoration of the IRA ceasefire. Both republicans and loyalists remained active, an IRA sniper in south Armagh killing the last soldier to die in the 1990s, Bombardier Stephen Restorick. In the run-up to the Westminster general election in May, the IRA used small bombs and hoaxes to cause major disruption which included a last-minute abandonment of the Grand National steeplechase.

A number of killings carried out by loyalists during 1997 were regarded as particularly brutal. In one incident a Portadown Catholic, Robert Hamill, was beaten and kicked to death by a mob in the town centre, a killing which brought much criticism of a nearby RUC patrol for allegedly failing to intervene to help him. Three weeks later it was the turn of an RUC officer, Gregory Taylor, to be killed in a similar manner by loyalists.

He had been in a County Antrim bar in a district where tensions were high because of a long-running Orange marching controversy in which police had halted a loyalist parade. Identified as a policeman, he was first jostled and abused in the bar and then, when he left in the early hours of the morning, attacked by loyalists who kicked and stamped on his head. In another widely condemned killing, Catholic teenager Bernadette Martin was shot in the head by a loyalist gunman as she slept at the home of her Protestant boyfriend in a loyalist area of County Antrim.

The May general election transformed the peace process, with the departure of John Major and the arrival in Downing Street of Tony Blair. The statistics of the election, together with those from council elections in the same month, provided unmistakable evidence of a significant shift in the power balance between Unionism and nationalism. Nationalists were clearly on the move, making dramatic political advances in tandem with their social, economic and numerical growth. The changing statistics meant that, since Northern Ireland's history and politics had from the very start been based on the numbers game, its very fabric changed too. After the election, five of Northern Ireland's eighteen seats in the Westminster parliament were held by nationalists, with Martin McGuinness joining Gerry Adams as an MP. The combined SDLP–Sinn Féin vote, which in 1983 had totalled 240,000, rose to almost 320,000.

The striking increase in the nationalist vote meant Unionists lost control of four councils including, for the first time ever, Belfast. While Northern Ireland still had a clear Protestant majority Protestants were increasingly concentrated in the east and particularly in the towns around Belfast. In the city itself the Ulster Unionists and Sinn Féin, with thirteen councillors each, were the joint largest parties. On the nationalist side Sinn Féin was seen as reaping a rich harvest of new nationalist voters, in particular those who were apparently jolted into voting for the first time by the 1996 Drumcree disturbances. Sinn Féin was also believed to have received many votes from nationalists wishing to encourage the IRA towards another ceasefire.

Like everyone else, Blair was unsure whether there would be a second ceasefire. In a key speech he had declared:

> When the IRA ceasefire was called originally, we all took this as firm evidence that there was a real desire on the part of Sinn Féin to put the past behind it. When it ended, renewed violence did not just cause dismay, it

caused fundamental doubts about the desire for peace. Is participation in the peace process a tactic in an otherwise unbroken armed conflict, or is it a genuine search for a new way forward? If it is the latter, then the door is open – but only if it is the latter.

His own election changed the political landscape, installing as it did a Labour leader whose large majority had given him great authority both inside and outside parliament. Within weeks he moved to break the deadlock, visiting Belfast to announce the reopening of direct contacts with Sinn Féin. While this pleased republicans, Unionists drew comfort from his statement that 'none of us in this hall today, even the youngest, is likely to see Northern Ireland as anything but a part of the United Kingdom'.

His Northern Ireland Secretary, Mo Mowlam, was the first woman to hold the post. Where Mayhew was often described as patrician and remote, she quickly established a reputation for the common touch. In his memoirs George Mitchell summed her up: 'She is blunt and outspoken and she swears a lot. She is also intelligent, decisive, daring and unpretentious. The combination is irresistible. The people love her, though many politicians in Northern Ireland do not.' Most of her detractors were Unionist politicians who did not care for her informality and would later charge that she was too 'green'.

The new contacts between the government and Sinn Féin went well, raising hopes for a renewed ceasefire. Such hopes received a setback, however, with the IRA killing of two policemen on foot patrol in the County Armagh town of Lurgan. The fact that this attack took place only a few miles from Drumcree, just weeks before the now annual marching confrontation, led many to conclude that the IRA was bent on generating confrontation rather than stopping their campaign. Blair, though clearly shaken by the killings, persevered with the process and attempted to maintain its momentum. Crucially, London and Dublin together laid down that IRA decommissioning was not a precondition for Sinn Féin entry to talks. In what was seen as a calculated gamble by Blair and Mowlam it was announced that political talks would begin in earnest in September, and that Sinn Féin would be allowed in six weeks after a new IRA ceasefire. Part of the gamble lay in the possibility that, if Sinn Féin were allowed in, Trimble might lead his Ulster Unionists out. Paisley and other hardliners had already made it clear that if republicans entered the talks they would immediately leave.

Blair's gamble worked. Much bad feeling was generated among republicans and nationalists when the authorities pushed the Drumcree march through the Garvaghy Road. But even so the IRA announced a second cessation later in July, doing so this time in a low-key fashion. The general reaction too was low-key, for the Canary Wharf bombing had demonstrated that ceasefires could be broken as easily as they were called. A newspaper summed it up:

> Nobody in Northern Ireland was indifferent to the IRA cessation of violence, but nearly everyone pretended to be. Most people simply stayed home, lounged in the garden or visited the pub or the supermarket: no cheers went up, no champagne popped, no church bells rang. It was a most understated ceasefire.
>
> If few emotions were expressed it was not because they did not exist: rather it was that there were too many of them, and that they went too deep. There is hope for the future, relief and a deep desire for peace; but there is also bitterness, suspicion, fear and even rejection. The IRA is putting the same deal on the table again: soldiers and police and town centres and Canary Wharf are no longer at risk, but the organisation will not disband or hand over guns and will never say that the cessation is permanent. London and Dublin have accepted these terms; the Protestant and Unionist community is wondering whether it should too.

The spotlight thus fell on Trimble, who spent many weeks consulting widely on whether he should remain in the talks with republicans. It was clearly an agonising decision, and a critical one, but in the end his Ulster Unionist party decided to remain. John Major, looking back in his memoirs, would describe Trimble as a more flexible and adept leader than had been expected, though he also recalled clashes between Trimble and Mayhew when 'voices were raised and papers thrown down as David proved his macho credentials'. When Trimble led the way into the Stormont talks he took some other macho credentials with him, walking into the building flanked not just by his own party but also by members of the parties associated with loyalist paramilitary groups. Those who accompanied him included a number of loyalist ex-prisoners who had served life sentences for murder. Paisley and his associates left the negotiations at that point and did not return.

The talks moved painfully slowly, with Blair arriving at Stormont in

October in an attempt to inject fresh impetus by meeting leaders of the parties, including Sinn Féin. His handshake with Adams was the first between a British prime minister and a republican leader since the 1920s.

At twenty-one, the death toll in 1997 was just one down from the previous year. The pattern of killings had reversed, with loyalists responsible for two-thirds of the deaths whereas republicans had killed roughly two-thirds of those who died in 1996. The end of the year brought turmoil, however, created once again by paramilitary violence.

Although the major republican and loyalist groups were on ceasefire a collection of minor paramilitary organisations were not, actively opposing the peace process and seeking to sabotage it. On the republican side such elements included the INLA, while on the loyalist side those still active included the Loyalist Volunteer Force (LVF), which was based mostly in Portadown and had broken away from the much larger UVF. The LVF's leader Billy Wright, King Rat, had become a larger-than-life public figure of considerable notoriety.

His prominence meant he was at great risk. As one paper had earlier put it: 'Figures like King Rat often remain active for a long time, but most in the end either wind up in jail or in an early grave. When their profile becomes so high, as King Rat's has, intense pressure goes on both the police and the IRA to deal with them. The question may be which one will get to him first.' As it turned out, the RUC got to him first and by the end of 1997 he was held in the Maze prison serving a sentence for intimidation. It was there that republicans caught up with him, and he was shot dead by an INLA prisoner using a smuggled weapon. The shooting, which took place two days after Christmas, ensured that 1998 would open not with peace but with a wave of retaliatory violence.

1998

A combination of violence and unprecedented political movement made 1998 one of the most remarkable years of the troubles. The shooting of Wright was followed by a stream of killings, particularly in Belfast, as loyalists took revenge by shooting Catholic civilians. When UDA prisoners in the Maze voted to withhold their support from the peace process, Mowlam took the unprecedented step of going into their H-block to meet them. Though controversial the move worked, and within hours of the meeting UDA prisoners renewed their support for the peace process. But on the outside the loyalist killings continued together with some republican attacks. Apart from the mainstream IRA, a group styling itself the Continuity IRA was also active. Consisting mainly of former IRA members who disapproved of the peace process, it was responsible for bombings which caused considerable damage to a number of towns.

As the killings continued one newspaper reported: 'People in Belfast now fall silent at television and radio news bulletins, waiting in dread to hear whether and where the gunmen have struck again, wondering how long the slaughter will go on at this appallingly metronomic rate. Hope remains alive for the peace process, but it takes a fresh pounding as news of each incident comes through.' The killings had immediate political implications for the talks, since the RUC said it believed that both the IRA and UDA had been involved in the killings. As a result the political representatives for each, Sinn Féin and the Ulster Democratic party, were for a time excluded from the negotiations. A particularly poignant incident took place in March in the quiet County Armagh village of Poyntzpass, which had until then largely escaped the worst effects of the troubles. When LVF gunmen machine-gunned a bar they killed a Protestant and a Catholic, Philip Allen and Damien Trainor, who had been best friends. But neither the violence nor the temporary expulsions, though disruptive, deflected the talks.

Unionists developed working relationships with the SDLP and Irish government, but no basis of trust was established between them and Sinn Féin. In fact the Unionists and Sinn Féin did not formally meet or speak during the negotiations, though they were often participants together in round-table talks. There were many uncertainties and difficult moments before, against the odds, it all seemed to come together. Tony Blair, Bertie Ahern, George Mitchell and the others gathered for a tense and often fraught all-night session which eventually produced, on 10 April, what came to be known as the Good Friday Agreement.

This historic agreement was a lengthy document, complex and subtle, which attempted nothing less than an ambitious rewriting of the 1920s settlement. The idea was to convince everyone that a level playing field was being provided as the new basis on which Northern Ireland politics and Anglo-Irish relations would be conducted in the future. The principles of powersharing and the Irish dimension, familiar from the 1973 Sunningdale Agreement, were very much in evidence. But this document went further, and was full of ingenious formulations which together provided a closely interlocking system designed to take account of all the political relationships within Northern Ireland, between north and south and between Britain and Ireland.

The accord addressed the republican preoccupation with self-determination but crucially it defined consent as requiring that the people of Northern Ireland would decide whether it stayed with Britain or joined a united Ireland. It provided for a rewriting of Articles 2 and 3 of the Irish constitution to remove what Unionists regarded as the objectionable claim to the territory of Northern Ireland. It provided for a new 108-member Belfast assembly, to which Westminster would devolve full power over areas such as education, health and agriculture, including the right to make new laws. London would retain responsibility for matters such as defence and law and order, though it promised to consider devolving security powers at a later stage.

The new devolved government was to consist of a First Minister, who it was clear would be a Unionist, and a Deputy First Minister who would be a nationalist. This was in effect a joint post requiring the two to agree on important decisions. Beneath them were to be up to ten departmental ministers. The ten ministries would be allocated in proportion to party strengths, on an agreed mathematical formula. A battery of safeguards was built into the assembly's rules to ensure that important decisions had to be taken on a cross-community basis, which meant they needed the support of both Unionist and nationalist members. A powerful committee system would shadow each government department, with committee chairs and membership again in proportion to party strengths.

The assembly was to be linked with London, Dublin, Scotland and Wales by a whole new constitutional architecture. A British–Irish council would be established, consisting of representatives of both governments and of the new devolved institutions in Northern Ireland, Scotland and Wales. There was to be a new British–Irish agreement and a north–south ministerial council, with associated implementation bodies, to develop co-operation on an all-Ireland basis. Major new commissions would review policing and emergency legislation. New bodies would safeguard human rights and equality while, most controversially, prisoners from subscribing paramilitary groups could expect release within two years. On the arms question the document said resolution of the decommissioning issue was an indispensable part of the process of negotiation, with all parties confirming their intention to use their influence to achieve the decommissioning of all paramilitary arms within two years.

There was a great deal more in the text and indeed between the lines of the 11,000-word document. Unionism and nationalism appeared to be given equal legitimacy and respect. Commentators such as Professor Brendan O'Leary argued that the subtlest part of the agreement was a 'tacit double protection' which meant that all the protections of rights afforded to nationalists would also be available to Unionists in a future united Ireland. There were very many loose ends, most ominously the fact that the decommissioning section was vague and open to different interpretations. But the deal was breathtaking both in its scope and in the fact that so many of the major political parties signed up to it. For many it seemed the stuff of history.

The republican community did not take long to give its general endorsement, but the agreement produced deep divisions within the Ulster Unionist party and, unsurprisingly, outright hostility from Paisley. Trimble secured his party's support, but some important party figures disapproved and did so vocally. Accepting the agreement was a huge step for Trimble, given that a large proportion of the Unionist community was clearly against making a deal with nationalists or republicans. Trimble kept many guessing as to whether he really wanted to head a government which included republicans, being at different times tough and conciliatory.

Mitchell, who saw him at close quarters, would write in his memoirs: 'Every day of the nearly two years of negotiations was for him a struggle to avoid being thrown off balance. Attacked daily by some Unionists for selling out the Union, criticised often by some nationalists for recalcitrance, he threaded his way through a minefield of problems, guided by his intelligence, his sure grasp of the political situation, and his determination to reach agreement.' At the same time, Trimble attracted criticism for not attempting to sell the accord to Unionists with sufficient enthusiasm. Blair, who spent much time in Northern Ireland in this period, was to prove a much more determined and effective salesman for the new deal.

The next step came with the holding of simultaneous referendums, north and south, on 22 May, to give approval to the Good Friday Agreement. Catholics were well over 90 per cent in favour, north and south, but there was much agonising within the Protestant community. In the end it split down the middle, with around half of Unionists voting Yes in the referendum and around half voting No. The final outcome was an overwhelming endorsement in the south and a 71 per cent Yes vote in the north. This was more than many of the agreement's supporters had dared hope for, and amounted to a solid vote for the accord. Yet at the same time the outcome contained an imbalance in that the 71 per cent was made up of virtually 100 per cent of nationalist voters but only half of Unionism. The stage was thus set for yet another chapter in the familiar running battle between Unionist moderates and hardliners. There was great continuity in this pattern. Edward Heath had years earlier said of Unionist opinion in the early 1970s that 'they split evenly between moderate reformers and hardline incorrigibles'. The story was almost exactly the same in 1998, a quarter of a century later.

Even with such divisions, however, the sense of a new era was in the air, many feeling that nothing would ever be the same again. The agreement and the referendum vote did not defeat traditional tribalism, but the 71 per cent vote represented, potentially at least, the emergence of a new majority in favour of making a deal. A newspaper summed up the possibilities of the agreement:

> It offers the chance to settle disagreements by argument instead of by force. It is not perfect; it will not simply dissolve away the ancient problems; it will face many hurdles and stiff challenges. But it has allowed all the main paramilitary groups, and nearly all the politicians, to subscribe to an agreement which is nobody's ideal but almost everyone's acceptable second choice. It doesn't mean the big paramilitary groupings disbanding and handing in their weaponry, for paramilitarism is a symptom of mistrust and that still abounds. But it does mean that the people of Ireland have spoken, and they have spoken of an end to violence. This is an enormous advance, for not too long ago the widely held assumption was that Northern Ireland was fated to be locked forever in endless war. That cheerless belief has now been replaced by the sense that the agreement amounts to the terms for an honourable peace.

Elections to the new Northern Ireland assembly in June produced a solid pro-agreement majority. There were strong showings for the SDLP and Sinn Féin, but the vote again revealed a divided Ulster Unionist party. The party won the largest number of seats but its lowest-ever share of the vote, with Paisley and other anti-agreement elements only 3 per cent behind Trimble. When the assembly met, Trimble was elected as First Minister designate in readiness for the devolution of power, with Séamus Mallon of the SDLP elected Deputy First Minister designate.

When July arrived attention once again switched to the streets as Drumcree 1998 brought yet more confrontation. When the authorities banned the Garvaghy Road march, Orangemen created disruption across Northern Ireland. Orange roadblocks and protests were augmented by rioting youths, to the extent that one twenty-four-hour period brought 384 outbreaks of disorder, 115 attacks on the security forces, 19 injuries to police, with petrol bombs thrown on 96 occasions, 403 petrol bombs seized, 57 homes and businesses damaged, 27 vehicles hijacked and another 89 damaged. A newspaper reported:

> Those manning the road-blocks are not polite men in suits: often they are belligerent teenagers spoiling for a fight. Sometimes they are drunk. At times like these many of society's normal rules go by the board, as youths with cudgels become temporary rulers of their districts and its roads. Thus people on a routine car journey can suddenly come face to face with the prospect of anarchy and mob rule, of beery threats, of the loss of their vehicle or worse.

One of the many petrol-bombing incidents led to terrible tragedy, when in the early hours of the Twelfth of July three small boys died in a fire caused by a loyalist petrol bomb thrown into their house in the County Antrim town of Ballymoney. The Quinn children had a Catholic mother and a Protestant father. The protesters were chastened and the Drumcree disturbances quickly petered out. In the wake of the Ballymoney deaths tensions ebbed away and the sense of confrontation was replaced by a lull.

It did not last long, for August was to bring the Omagh bombing, when republican dissidents set off a car bomb in the County Tyrone town which killed twenty-nine people in what was regarded as possibly the worst single incident of the troubles. Its impact was all the greater since it came so unexpectedly, at a time when most presumed that violence was tailing off. The bomb was placed by a group styling itself 'the Real IRA', which was largely made up of former IRA members opposed to the peace process. The 500lb car bomb, placed in a crowded street on a busy Saturday shopping afternoon, produced devastation. A misleading telephone warning had caused police to direct many shoppers towards the device rather than away from it. The dead, all civilians, consisted of Protestants, Catholics and two Spanish visitors, and included young, old and middle-aged, fathers, mothers, sons, daughters and grandmothers. Unborn twins also died.

An eye-witness described how a burst water pipe sent a strong stream of water down the street: 'There were people, or actually pieces of people, bodies being washed in, which is something that you never forget. They were just basically piling up at the corner where the gully was. Bits and pieces of legs, arms, whatever, were floating down that street.' A woman told of carrying her injured daughter to one of the buses being used to ferry the dead and injured to hospital. She said: 'There were limbs hanging off, bodies being carried on doors, everything was chaotic. Then just as the bus was ready to leave, the door opened and someone handed a severed arm in. I think that was just too much for the driver. I think he cried all the way to the hospital.' The bus driver later said: 'It was like a scene from hell. I wasn't able to drive fast because people were screaming in pain. As we went over the ramps at the hospital I could hear the roars of pain.'

A volunteer nurse who turned up to help described the scene in the local hospital: 'Nothing could have prepared me for what I saw. People were lying on the floor with limbs missing and there was blood all over the place. People were crying for help and looking for something to kill the pain. Other people were crying out looking for relatives. You could not really be trained for what you had seen unless you were trained in Vietnam or somewhere like that.'

The incident generated a shock wave which reverberated around the world. Although at first there was speculation that the attack might spell the end of the peace process, it became evident within days that it had made most politicians more rather than less determined to go on. In the aftermath, the British and Irish governments hurried through tough new security measures, with Westminster and the Dáil recalled from summer recess to pass the necessary legislation. A fortnight after the explosion Clinton and Blair visited Omagh, meeting around 700 of the injured and relatives of the dead and injured.

September brought renewed political activity, with Trimble agreeing to his first ever direct contact with Adams. They met behind closed doors, the fact that they spoke but did not shake hands pointedly indicating that while new relationships were emerging they were accompanied by neither friendship nor trust. The hopes of the international community that a lasting settlement was on the way were symbolised by the conferring of the Nobel peace prize jointly on Hume and Trimble. Nationalists welcomed the move while Unionists regarded it more suspiciously, Trimble commenting that it was perhaps premature.

The twenty-nine fatalities caused by the Omagh bomb meant that the death toll rose steeply, to a total of fifty-seven in 1998 compared to twenty-one in the previous year.

1999

In 1999 the peace process stayed on track, but everything moved much more slowly than most of its supporters had hoped. Decommissioning remained an unresolved issue, with Unionists insisting on its centrality, while nationalists and republicans argued it had been given too high a priority.

The killings continued, though at a much-reduced rate. In south Armagh republicans killed Eamon Collins, a one-time IRA member who later became one of the organisation's most vocal critics. Loyalists were also active, taking the life of solicitor Rosemary Nelson, who as a leading human rights lawyer had represented leading republicans and Catholic residents of Portadown's Garvaghy Road. In addition to the violence there were reminders that the effects of killings carried out in previous times lasted for years. After much pressure the IRA admitted it was responsible for the deaths of most of 'the disappeared', a number of people who had vanished without trace, mostly in the 1970s. Gardaí in the Republic undertook major excavation work at a number of sites, uncovering some but not all of the bodies.

Various parts of the Good Friday Agreement were implemented, including the setting up of cross-border bodies and a new Human Rights Commission. Yet the devolution of power from Westminster to the assembly did not take place, being held up throughout the year by the decommissioning issue. Several intensive negotiating sessions attended by Blair and Ahern failed to make a breakthrough.

There was general relief, however, when confrontation was avoided at Drumcree 1999, the Orange Order opting for peaceful localised protest rather than widespread disruption. The summer brought renewed questioning of whether republicans were genuine about peace when the IRA was blamed for the killing of a west Belfast man, and for an attempt to smuggle in guns from America. These incidents gave rise to a formal government judgement in August by Mowlam on the state of the IRA cessation. She said she had 'come very close to judging that the IRA's ceasefire is no longer for real' but had concluded that it was not disintegrating or breaking down. She made a distinction however between breaches of the ceasefire and a full breakdown, declaring: 'I do not believe that there is a sufficient basis to conclude that the IRA ceasefire has broken down. Nor do I believe that it is disintegrating, or that these recent events represent a decision by the organisation to return to violence. The peace we have now is imperfect, but better than none.'

September brought George Mitchell back to Belfast at the request of Clinton, Blair and Ahern in an attempt to break the decommissioning deadlock. While Mitchell, Trimble and Adams were closeted for many weeks of tough talks, Mowlam was recalled to London by Blair, evidently against her will and possibly partly because Trimble and other Unionists made public complaints that she leaned towards the nationalists. Her replacement was Peter Mandelson, who as a close friend of Blair was expected to wield greater authority.

The Mitchell review produced movement which was initially regarded as a breakthrough. After ten weeks the parties emerged with what was assumed to be an understanding and then proceeded, after all the months of delay, to form an executive. After years of stipulating that he would not go into government with Sinn Féin without prior or simultaneous decommissioning, Trimble agreed to go ahead without any element of disarmament, though he made it clear he expected it to follow soon afterwards.

For the formation of the multi-party executive the Good Friday Agreement laid down a mathematical formula, known as the D'Hondt rules, which meant that Sinn Féin would occupy two of the ten executive seats. The big shock of the day came when Martin McGuinness, a particular Unionist hate-figure, became education minister. The other seats were taken by the Ulster Unionists, the SDLP and Paisley's Democratic Unionists. The DUP representatives became ministers but would not attend meetings of the executive. Power was transferred to this new devolved government at the beginning of December. All of the executive parties gave every sign of enthusiasm as the new ministers, departments and assembly committees set to work.

The 1999 death toll was seven, the lowest figure since the outbreak of the troubles in the 1960s and a dramatic drop from the 1997 total of fifty-two. As the year closed, the drop in killings and the formation of the new cross-community government seemed to many to represent a double cause for celebration.

2000

As it turned out, the executive was to last only two and a half months before it was suspended in a welter of recrimination. In selling the idea of going into government to his party's ruling Ulster Unionist Council in November, Trimble had given his party an assurance that he would not stay in office as First Minister unless a decommissioning process began, giving a senior party official a postdated letter of resignation. It was an increasingly restless time for Unionism, since it was clear that Protestant support for the Good Friday Agreement was ebbing away. The revival of devolution had been a traditional Unionist aim, but when power was actually returned to Stormont many Unionists were transfixed and even shocked by the sight of Martin McGuinness taking responsibility for their children's education. As a result devolution was, initially at least, widely perceived by Unionists not as a triumph for themselves but as a victory for republicanism.

Unionists took further offence with the publication in January 2000 of the report into policing which had been commissioned as part of the Good Friday Agreement. The committee, chaired by former Hong Kong governor Chris Patten, produced a blueprint for a radically transformed police service with a new human rights ethos and many more Catholic members. Crucially, it recommended changing the name of Royal Ulster Constabulary to Police Service of Northern Ireland. The support of many Unionists for the RUC was so deep as to be proprietorial, and they and many police officers took this as an affront against the record of the RUC. The government nonetheless accepted most of the report's many recommendations.

It was against this background that a crisis developed during January as it became obvious that there was no immediate sign of IRA decommissioning. The organisation had appointed a representative to liaise with a Decommissioning Commission which had been set up under John de Chastelain, the Canadian general who had served as a member of George

Mitchell's original committee on the weapons problem. But this liaison was a far cry from actual disarmament, and Trimble made it clear that he would resign as First Minister in the absence of actual decommissioning. His party's council was scheduled to meet on 12 February and he clearly hoped Mandelson would suspend the Good Friday institutions in advance of this.

An intensive flurry of political activity followed, with the Irish government seeking to extract from the republicans a commitment on arms. Republicans came up with a new form of words but it was judged to be insufficient to get through the Ulster Unionist party and Mandelson suspended the institutions, restoring direct rule from Westminster. The executive had lasted for just seventy-two days.

Suspension was traumatic for many but in particular for nationalists and republicans, many of whom had not really believed that Mandelson would suspend institutions which had taken years to put in place. Weeks of bitter exchanges followed until early May brought a breakthrough, the IRA offering to put its arms beyond use if the peace process remained on course and delivered on issues such as policing reform.

The IRA assurance that its guns would be 'completely and verifiably put beyond use' was hailed in most quarters as a highly significant development. It was coupled with IRA agreement to take the unprecedented step of allowing some of its arms dumps to be inspected by two international figures. These were Cyril Ramaphosa, former Secretary-General of the African National Congress, and former Finnish president Martti Ahtisaari. Although both the IRA statement and a joint Blair–Ahern statement spoke of putting arms completely and verifiably beyond use, neither spelt out precisely how this might be done.

While this was rejected by Paisley and other anti-agreement Unionists, the move was described as a historic opportunity by almost all other elements. An uncertain few weeks followed as Trimble referred the statement to his Ulster Unionist Council. In the event he won the vote by 459 votes to 403, a clear but hardly comfortable majority. Nonetheless the way was cleared for the return of devolution, which duly took place at the end of May. An inspection of some dumps was subsequently made by Ramaphosa and Ahtisaari in June.

The following month brought a difficult Drumcree, as the Orange Order in Portadown called on supporters to take to the streets all over Northern Ireland. Days of disruption and roadblocks followed, bringing many districts to a standstill. By the Twelfth of July, however, it became apparent that the Portadown Orangemen had overreached themselves. A large section of Protestant opinion did not approve of the disruption, taking particular exception to the refusal of Portadown Orange leader Harold Gracey to condemn violence. This, together with the prominence in protests of the west Belfast UDA's particularly militant commander, Johnny 'Mad Dog' Adair, alienated most Protestants. As a result support ebbed away and the protests fizzled out.

Adair was to the fore again in August when violent feuding broke out between the UDA and the UVF centring on the Shankill district of Belfast, resulting in the following months in well over a dozen deaths. Loyalists were responsible for 22 of the 29 deaths between January 2000 and July 2001, while the IRA was held responsible for the killings of a number of alleged drug-dealers.

Other violence continued on the republican side with the Real IRA staging a series of bombing and mortar attacks. Although most of these were in Northern Ireland the incidents which generated most publicity took place in London. In one attack a missile fired from a rocket-launcher hit the headquarters of MI6 while in another a car bomb exploded outside BBC premises.

On the political front the Westminster general election of June 2001 was seen as a watershed. David Trimble suffered a major setback, losing three of his party's nine seats, while Ian Paisley's DUP made gains. Sinn Féin too fared well, winning two seats and dealing a serious blow to the SDLP. In September John Hume announced his decision to step down as party leader. The results were seen as a setback for the more centrist parties and an advance for those on the extremes.

In July 2001 David Trimble carried out his pre-election threat to resign as First Minister in the absence of significant IRA movement on weapons decommissioning. This led to intensive rounds of negotiation with an IRA offer Trimble said did not go far enough followed by two six-week extensions to allow further talks.

All this took place against the background of a troubled summer, with many street clashes centring on the north Belfast area.

The peace process appears destined to proceed not smoothly but by a series of crises: and since many of these hold the capacity to bring the whole exercise to a halt, Northern Ireland seems fated to perpetual uncertainty.

Perspectives

The very real sense is that the worst of the troubles is over and that Northern Ireland is moving slowly but inexorably towards a more peaceful time. The feeling in almost every quarter is that violence will never again approach the levels of the 1970s or even those of the 1990s. Yet the fact that so many sharp political divisions remain, and that while they persist the major paramilitary groups are unlikely to disband, means it will be many years before the troubles can be confidently declared to be over.

It is obvious enough that they had their roots centuries earlier, stretching back at least to the plantations and the patterns established then. The Protestants of Northern Ireland have long been pilloried for their siege mentality, their resistance to change and for what their critics characterise as an unsavoury mixture of reactionary instincts and religious bigotry. The British encouraged them to move to Ireland essentially as a garrison community for Britain's own defensive purposes. Those settlers were bound to develop a siege mentality given that they experienced actual sieges, most famously Londonderry in 1689. The settlers valued the British connection, and their differences with the Catholic Irish were continuously sharpened by the fact that the two sides competed for territory and power, setting patterns which endured through the generations.

It is easy enough to see how the Protestant mentality developed, as the new arrivals were given land and political power in a land where they were outnumbered by the Catholic Irish. Centuries later a second endowment came in the form of the new state of Northern Ireland, which was conceived, designed and set up as a Unionist-controlled entity. The unwanted part of this for Unionists, the fly in the political ointment, took the form of northern nationalists who considered themselves trapped in an unwelcoming and even hostile state.

The two new states in Ireland were given a very high degree of independence. For Unionists it was a generous endowment, in that their British link was both guaranteed and in due course accompanied by substantial subsidies. At the same time they were allowed the freedom to run Northern Ireland much as they chose.

Westminster discreetly and gratefully withdrew, certainly psychologically, leaving Northern Ireland pretty much to its own devices. It was entirely natural that Unionists should have elevated, over all other considerations, the task of strengthening the security and political defences of the fledgeling state. It was also hardly surprising, in the light of the lack of outside supervision, that they would utilise some questionable means. But the fact that the Union turned out to be safe brought little ease to many Protestants whose chronic insecurity scarcely diminished over the decades.

This constant nagging anxiety led them in the first instance to exclude Catholics from virtually every important office in the land. The Unionist administration in the 1920s tightened up the system, perfected it, and was able to rebuff with ease any attempts to cry foul. Civil rights were not in vogue in those times, and the overwhelming numerical and political superiority of Unionism easily carried the day. Partly this was because critics, principally southern governments, put forward as their solution a united Ireland. After the 1920s this had few attractions for any but northern nationalists, since it would mean inflicting major upheaval on a generally peaceful island.

Perhaps the extraordinary thing is that the system lasted for so long, with even the World War Two failing to overturn the familiar patterns. One reason for its durability was the degree of disadvantage suffered by Catholics, which was less severe than that experienced by minorities in other countries. The Unionist state did not organise massacres of Catholics or their expulsion from its frontiers: it cannot be said to have engaged in active persecution or savage repression. Yet it was, as David Trimble was to admit in 1999, a cold house for Catholics. If it was not tyranny, it was undoubtedly unfair. There was institutionalised inequality, with Protestants enjoying advantage in very many walks of life. The practice of treating Catholics differently from Protestants permeated all levels of politics and reached down to the necessities of life such as housing and jobs.

Throughout the decades most Catholics believed they were treated as second-class citizens. Resentment rarely boiled over into active violent revolution, however, instead tending to take the form of surly abstentionism and the often unspoken nursing of grudges. This was a demoralised community, undermined when their southern kith and kin in effect abandoned them at partition. Protests beyond the strictly rhetorical were uncommon: there simply seemed little or no point, so that, for example, attempted IRA campaigns ignominiously petered out.

When the 1960s arrived, bringing new times and new challenges, it became apparent that politically there were three types of Unionists. There were the moderates who agreed with Terence O'Neill that a new era had dawned and that modest reforms were in order. Then there were the hardliners, who in clinging to tradition believed that almost any concession would set them on a slippery slope leading them out of the UK. Some of these held this as a political maxim: others were simply straightforward bigots who were not just anti-accommodation but anti-Catholic. The third strand of Unionist opinion was made up of the sizeable number of waverers who oscillated between the two poles, sometimes steeling themselves to support reform, sometimes retreating to the safety of the laager. Although their relative strengths were to vary from time to time, these three strands were visible all the way through the troubles, from O'Neill in 1963 to Trimble in 2000.

They were evident in all the battles within Unionism. O'Neill battled against Paisley, Craig and Faulkner; Chichester-Clark struggled against the first two, and then Faulkner was opposed by West, Craig, Paisley, the UDA, UWC and the Orange Order. Molyneaux, who led the Unionist party for sixteen years, was not a reformer but he too had to contend with unruly elements including Trimble, then cast as a hardliner. Later Trimble found himself pitched against Paisley and others inside his party. When John Major described the Unionist party as 'riven into factions, with its leader's authority constantly under threat' he was referring to Molyneaux's later years, but the description is applicable to many other periods.

O'Neill had an instinct that modernisation was called for, but he did not foresee the consequences of his new approach. He probably envisaged a Northern Ireland which would remain under exclusively Unionist control, though with a relaxation of communal divisions, but in the end he proved incapable of managing the tide of change. His essential decency was accompanied by limited political skills and he went under, unable to balance civil rights agitation and the urgings of Wilson and Callaghan with the pressures from Unionist hardliners. At the same time the bright young civil righters were running intellectual rings around most Unionist politicians.

In the Wilson and Callaghan era the talk was of reform and concessions to nationalists. O'Neill, Chichester-Clark and Faulkner each produced a stream of reforms, including one man – one vote, but in the end none of these came close to satisfying nationalist opinion. With hindsight the reason is clear, since it is now evident that no amount of reform would have sufficed. Expectations within nationalism had risen so high and so fast that they would only ever have been satisfied not by safeguards but by a slice of executive power.

A majority of civil rights supporters went on to support the SDLP. Another section of nationalists switched from civil rights to supporting republicanism, putting its faith in violence and the pursuit of victory rather then accommodation. This division of northern nationalists into two distinct elements, one constitutional and one violent, followed a fault-line which went back for many decades. As the twentieth century closed that distinction was still operative, with the SDLP and republicans continuing to compete for the Catholic vote.

John Hume has been one of the three dominant figures of the troubles. Nationalists had previously tended to take the view that it was not worth putting their energies into interacting with the Stormont system, and that everything would some day be sorted out in a united Ireland. Hume pursued the theory, which came to seem obvious but at the time was a major departure, that it was honourable to engage in politics short of millenarian rescue. Later he with others made another major psychological shift to aiming for a place in government inside Northern Ireland.

Later still, as an architect of the 1985 Anglo-Irish Agreement, he helped set the Northern Ireland question in an international context, and particularly in a Belfast–London–Dublin triangle, with American and to some extent European influences thrown in. In the late 1980s he was first to spot the early stirrings of the peace process within militant republicanism. He was also the first to act on it, setting out on a hazardous path which would eventually bring him the Nobel peace prize.

It was always unlikely that Unionist opinion would approve of him, since they regarded everything he did as dangerous attacks on the Unionist position. Many Unionists clung to the idea of exclusion of nationalists, and all of Hume's steps were, in different ways, in the direction of inclusion and participation. All were opposed by Unionists. He evolved through the inclusion of nationalists in government to establishing Dublin as a key element, then drawing in the international community and, finally and most controversially of all, the inclusion of militant republicans in politics and indeed in government. Given all that, it is probable that his critics will in years to come be outnumbered by admirers who will see him as one of the key figures in fashioning an exit route from the troubles. This is especially likely to be true if the peace process does eventually bring a definitive end to the troubles.

While that can be said with a fair degree of confidence, the jury is still out on the second dominant figure of the troubles, Gerry Adams. Important in republicanism since the early 1970s, he is today central both to his movement and to the peace process. For the first half of the troubles he was closely identified with the IRA and its violence, but in the second half he came to be regarded as a figure who aimed to steer Sinn Féin and the IRA away from violent militarism and into a new brand of republican politics.

When he first began to use the word 'peace' regularly in the early 1990s, many regarded this as sheer hypocrisy, as the IRA continued to kill. It took years, but gradually more and more important figures came to believe he was genuine. If he does prevail it will be a unique achievement in directing the energies of a movement so steeped in violence into politics. He may also be well positioned to some day inherit Hume's mantle as the leading figure in northern nationalism.

The third dominant figure has been Ian Paisley, who has been to the fore all the way through from the early 1960s into the new millennium. During that time he has strongly opposed all attempts at accommodation and been the bane of British ministerial lives. James Callaghan accused him of 'using the language of war cast in a biblical mould'. Reginald Maudling wrote: 'He was one of the most difficult characters anyone could hope to deal with. I always found his influence dangerous.' William Whitelaw marvelled at his 'unrivalled skill at undermining the plans of others. He can effectively destroy and obstruct, but he has never seemed able to act constructively.' Roy Mason remembered him as 'an oafish bully, a wild rabblerouser, to many a poisonous bigot because of his No Popery rantings'. James Prior thought him 'basically a man who thrives on the violent scene. His aim is to stir the emotions of the Protestant people. His bigotry easily boils over into bombast.'

As these judgements illustrate, few at Westminster found anything to commend in the Paisley record. The same went for nationalists and indeed the wider world in general, which regarded him as a symbol of intolerance and division. Paisley of course has never defined politics as a process of winning friends and influencing people, and so has been unmoved by the mountains of criticism heaped upon him. What is incontestable is that during his long career he made no friends for the Unionist cause anywhere outside the bounds of Unionism, and caused much damage to Unionism's general image.

Although he has opposed all the major efforts to find accommodation he has nonetheless been a central figure down the decades. The outside world might recoil from both his style and his substance but he holds an undeniable appeal for a large proportion of Protestants. Although his Democratic Unionist party has finished second to the Ulster Unionists in almost every election, for the last two decades of the century his party never polled less than 12 per cent of the overall vote, and on occasion reached 30 per cent. He probably speaks for a third of Unionist voters, a fact which helped wreck many political initiatives. The fact is that Paisley, one of the brightest and most subtle minds of his generation, has opted at every key juncture for opposition rather than accommodation. There may have been a few points at which he privately wavered about making a deal but now, in his seventies, he never will.

Many other figures played an important part during the troubles, though none as substantial as Hume, Adams and Paisley. The fact that

Molyneaux headed the Unionist party for sixteen years might be thought to give him a claim as one of the central figures, yet his passive personality and even more passive policy meant he left no easily discernible legacy. A leader so low-key that many of his own supporters were unsure how to pronounce his name, he had none of Paisley's histrionics but an equal determination not to compromise.

His successor Trimble quickly abandoned the politics of immobility, replacing inertia with a belief that Unionism needed to venture outside and engage with the outside world. In doing so he led his party into a peace process which he himself had originally so fiercely opposed. Along the way he evolved from the defiant hero of Drumcree into the head of a government which encompassed Sinn Féin. Despite his Nobel peace prize, it is too early to judge his contribution, partly because he has led his party for a relatively short time, and partly because no one can say with assurance how long he will remain at its head.

The troubles saw many difficult relationships. Britain's relations with Irish nationalists, both those in the SDLP and those in Dublin, went through many difficult patches. In the early days London kept Dublin at arm's length, though by the time of Sunningdale Heath had come to think of the Irish government as a partner in a joint venture. This sense disappeared however under the Labour administrations of the second half of the 1970s, as Harold Wilson's grandiose notions of uniting Ireland were hurriedly abandoned in the face of loyalist opposition.

By contrast, Thatcher's reputation as a jealous guardian of British sovereignty was not borne out by her attempts to foster partnerships with first Haughey and later FitzGerald. It was her 1985 Anglo-Irish Agreement which set the pattern of closer London–Dublin relations in the years that followed. Dublin, after the initial panic of 1969 and the subsequent arms trial, quickly settled on the idea of forming an inter-governmental partnership with London, putting the principle of containment of the northern problem well ahead of all other considerations.

One of the most problematic relationships has been that between Britain and Unionism, since Unionist distrust of London has always been present to a greater or lesser degree. Wilson pressurised the Stormont government, eventually took to threatening it and finally pretty much lost his temper with it. Heath gave Faulkner a chance, then surgically removed Stormont when he concluded Faulkner and a solely Unionist government were not capable of delivering stability. Heath and Whitelaw achieved a great deal in a short time by putting the Sunningdale agreement and powersharing executive in place, but Wilson and Rees proved no match for the loyalist strike, with its potent mixture of industrial action and intimidation. After that Wilson, Callaghan and initially Thatcher took no steps which might result in open conflict between London and Unionists until, with the Anglo-Irish accord, she broke that mould.

What is striking, from a series of comments in various memoirs and elsewhere, is the nervousness and even fear displayed by British politicians when considering Unionism. The memory of the 1912 period, when the UVF imported guns and threatened the use of force, certainly lasted until 1949, when cabinet minutes noted: 'Unless the people of Northern Ireland felt reasonably assured of the support of the people of this country, there might be a revival of the Ulster Volunteers and of other bodies intending to meet any threat of force by force; and this would bring nearer the danger of an outbreak of violence in Ireland.'

One of the London civil servants despatched to Belfast in 1969 reported back that force might have to be used to dismantle Catholic barricades, but that such 'clobbering', as he called it, might be in the long-term interests of Catholics. He wrote: 'It would be better than the use of force against the Protestant extremists, however repulsive their attitudes and behaviour, since they are the majority community and confrontation with them would fulfil Lord Craigavon's prophecy that the eventual resolution of the Ulster problem would come when the Protestants fought the British Army. And that, I should think, HMG would wish to avoid at all costs.'

Maudling was to indicate that security moves against the IRA were motivated not by the republican threat alone but by the loyalist threat as well. He noted in his memoirs: 'I think if we hadn't introduced internment there was the danger of the Protestant backlash. What we were always worried about was if people did not think the British government were doing all they could to deal with violence, they might take the law into their own hands.' When loyalists did take the law into their own hands, as their paramilitary groups began their killing campaign in late 1971, the authorities at first attempted to turn a Nelsonian blind eye to their activities.

In 1974 London shied away from direct confrontation with loyalists, conceding control of the streets, industry and commerce to the UWC. More than two decades later John Major would write of a Drumcree confrontation in which the Orange march was allowed through after first being banned: 'This decision provoked a risk of even greater violence, and had to be reversed.' This seems another clear illustration of a recurring British nervousness about a Protestant capacity for disruption.

Part of the explanation for this was that London was aware of the reality of Protestant numerical power. Even after the abolition of Stormont in 1972 the institutions of the state, including its security apparatus, were predominantly Protestant. The security forces were manifestly geared to containing disorder from the republican side. Any British policy-maker had to recognise that if serious disorder came from the Unionist community there was, during the 1970s at least, no reliable instrument with which to contain it. This was most obviously demonstrated in the UWC strike, though it has to be said that by 1985 London did decide to put forward an initiative which it knew would stir strong loyalist opposition.

London's problems with both republicans and loyalists have tended to reinforce the standard British posture that they are dealing with two inherently unreasonable tribes and in effect holding the ring between them. This perspective allows the average Englishman to exonerate himself from any element of responsibility for the conflict. It is however too simplistic and too complacent a viewpoint. It is certainly true that the two traditions, Unionist and nationalist, were in conflict or at least competition with each other long before Britain brought the state of Northern Ireland into being. With hindsight however the settlement put in place in the 1920s lacked balance and was an almost guaranteed recipe for tensions and instability. While Unionists were throughout the troubles vilified for an unwillingness to share power, it is obvious that any community allowed to wield virtually complete power would have great difficulty in coming to terms with the notion of giving some of it up.

Part of any unreasonableness is clearly traceable back to the system which London first set up and then forgot. It took half a century for the troubles to erupt, but the lethal energy with which they did is testimony to the lack of outside supervision for so long. A critic of Britain would lay at London's door a chapter of political and security misjudgements and mistakes, in which internment and Bloody Sunday would figure prominently. The model of the troubles as a clash between two unreasonable warring tribes is thus a misleading or at least an incomplete picture.

The full story of the peace process during the 1990s doubtless remains to be told, with many important secrets still to be unearthed. The republican route from guerrilla warfare to participation in government is an extraordinary tale, with an underground army gradually moving from violence into politics. One theory has it that the republicans simply realised that their campaign of violence was not working, and held out no hope of defeating the will of the British and that of Unionism. Another is that republicans shrewdly moved with the times, realising that a more political approach would pay richer dividends. This has certainly proved to be the case in the short run at least, with Gerry Adams assuming hero status abroad, a rising republican vote in Northern Ireland, two Sinn Féin members taking office in a Belfast administration and the prospect of increasing support in the south.

Adams and his party have had considerable success in persuading the world, much of which was originally highly sceptical, that they were genuinely in the business of leading republicanism away from the centuries-old tradition of armed rebellion. In the republican psyche power was traditionally held to come out of the barrel of a gun; and they resorted to the gun because they believed they had no other source of empowerment. This mindset has now been altered in a dramatic way. Now the republican sense is that an alternative is available in the shape of Sinn Féin, the establishment of an inclusive peace process and the terms of the Good Friday Agreement. After all these years, an effective unarmed struggle is now a real possibility.

Only time will tell if these things prove to be stepping stones to the traditional republican goal of Irish unity, or whether they are tracing a path in an entirely different direction. Sinn Féin say they are in the business of 'hollowing out' the Union, while Trimble claims his approach has strengthened the bonds with Britain.

Whatever happens, another imbalance has emerged. The Good Friday Agreement enjoyed overwhelming support among all shades of nationalism, who viewed it as a historic departure based on the principle of inclusion. Yet it is plainly not an inclusive settlement, since something approaching half of Unionists opposed its introduction. The 2001 general election results demonstrated unmistakably that Unionist anti-Agreement sentiment had significantly grown, undermining the accord's credibility. The difference with this new imbalance is that the exclusion results from a voluntary opting-out, with a section of Unionism turning down the opportunity to participate fully. The new Northern Ireland administration, containing as it does ministers from four parties, two Unionist and two nationalist, has been designed to institutionalise inclusion.

There are a great many unresolved issues and uncertainties. Within Unionism the eternal battle goes on between the Ulster Unionists and the Democratic Unionists, with the latter often ahead on publicity points but never quite managing to overtake the UUP. Paisley has the biggest voice but not the biggest party. The fact is that the DUP's septuagenarian leader, having failed over the decades to edge out in front, is hardly likely to do it now. Some assume his lengthy career must be approaching its end, yet as the 2001 Westminster election demonstrated he remains the greatest vote-getter Northern Ireland has ever seen, and he shows no sign of wishing to retire and rest those formidable lungs. Whenever he does step aside the DUP will probably pass into the hands of Peter Robinson and Nigel Dodds, two lieutenants who are long on ability but short on charisma.

Similarly on the nationalist side, no one can know how long Hume will remain in active politics, or how his eventual departure will affect the SDLP in its perennial competition with Sinn Féin for the nationalist vote. Hume's decision to give up his Belfast assembly seat in autumn 2000 and to give up the party leadership in autumn 2001 confirmed speculation that his long career was drawing to a close.

For up to a decade there have been forecasts that Sinn Féin might overtake the SDLP as the primary voice of nationalism, but although the Sinn Féin vote during the 1990s showed greater growth than that of any other party, the SDLP remained out in front. In the event of Hume leaving politics it is a fair bet that Adams would take his place as the leading spokesman for nationalism; but while this is bound to give Sinn Féin a substantial boost it does not necessarily mean the republicans would assume the top slot. As Paisley's record shows, the party with the most prominent leader is not always number one.

The election of 2001, with its surge of support for Sinn Féin, led to forecasts that the republicans will eventually establish itself as the largest nationalist party. Republicanism is clearly run by a small caucus of leaders who decide things in secret, who never criticise each other in public, and whose party has an obvious association with the IRA. These are deeply ingrained characteristics which will continue to alienate many Catholic voters. None the less the old whiff of cordite is being gradually overcome by the whiff of success, while the SDLP will have difficulty finding a leader to fill John Hume's shoes.

There are opposing views on how the Good Friday Agreement's structures will develop. One prediction, which most Unionists would prefer to see coming about, is that the Belfast assembly will become the centrepiece of political activity, eclipsing all the rest of the constitutional architecture. Nationalists, by contrast, hope to keep the political arena as broad as possible, maintaining London, Dublin and Washington as major and active players. This mindset is visible in Hume's decision to leave the assembly but to remain active in those other capital cities, and evident too in Adams's decision not to take office in the Belfast executive. Both the SDLP and Sinn Féin have sought to internationalise the issue, and can be expected to resist any moves to once again compress it into Stormont: they will seek to ensure that the rest the world maintains a close interest in the problem.

Although the Union remains in place and Northern Ireland once again has a Unionist prime minister, the troubles close with a psychological victory for nationalism and republicanism. Nationalists, and in particular Sinn Féin, exude confidence and an eagerness for political activity. The SDLP's long-standing argument that the problem is complex and multi-faceted has finally been accepted and is reflected in the new institutions. Sinn Féin has moved into politics while convincing both its followers and the wider world that this represents not a climbdown but a path to a brighter future.

Unionists by contrast have by and large not confronted or even systematically analysed their past or mapped out their future, forever leaving the initiative with Britain or the nationalists. On the Unionist side there continues to be uncertainty and insecurity, together with a lack of vision. There is much dissatisfaction with the Agreement and the peace process. But there is also no sign that rejectionist Unionists will ever be able to formulate an alternative which stands any chance of being acceptable to any section of nationalism, or to London.

These very different psychological outlooks are partly due to the important demographic changes which have taken place under cover of the troubles. As the years went by the political map changed dramatically, to the extent that the balance of power between nationalist and Unionist shifted fundamentally.

Nationalism was unmistakably on the move, making dramatic advances politically, socially, economically and numerically. Unionism lost Westminster seats and control of some key local councils. The old ratio of two-thirds Protestant to one-third Catholic has gone, to be replaced by a new mathematical and political model, with Catholics amounting to up to 45 per cent of the population. The day when they might one day actually have a majority is still far off but the rise in the Catholic population, taken together with this new nationalist confidence, has already produced huge changes to the political landscape.

It is too early to say whether the Good Friday Agreement will take root and begin to provide a level playing field on which the business of politics will in future be conducted without resort to violent conflict. It seems clear however that Northern Ireland cannot realistically expect a completely happy ending to all its woes. Politics, and life, is not like that, and existing problems have become so overlaid with the bitterness produced by the troubles that it is never going to be a placid place.

Whether the new government system succeeds or fails, however, there is a widespread sense that a corner has been decisively turned. It is too much to expect a future of friendship and harmony, for all of those involved inflicted much damage on each other. Yet it is not too much to hope that the major campaigns of organised violence are in their last days, and that the death toll will continue to decline. Peace, if there is to be peace, will always be imperfect, and there will always be controversy: yet, for all that, it can be forecast with some confidence that the future will bring much improvement on the last three turbulent decades.

Chronology

1920

The Government of Ireland Act led to the creation of NI.

1921

The first NI parliament was elected with James Craig as the first prime minister.

A truce was agreed between the IRA and the British army. It was followed by negotiations leading to the Anglo-Irish treaty and the creation of the Irish Free State consisting of twenty-six counties of Ireland.

1949

The south became the Irish Republic.

The Ireland Act was passed by the British parliament: it regularised the new constitutional position and affirmed that the status of NI would only change with the agreement of the NI parliament.

1956

The IRA launched its 'border campaign'.

1962

February   The IRA border campaign officially ended.

1963

March   **Terence O'Neill became PM of NI.**

June   The Protestant *News Letter* praised Pope John XXIII.

September   Following reports of a Unionist party leadership crisis, Brian Faulkner denied trying to oust O'Neill.

1964

January   The Campaign for Social Justice was founded in Dungannon, County Tyrone.

August   Stormont recognised the Northern Committee of the Irish Congress of Trade Unions.

September   **The Divis Street riots broke out after police removed a tricolour from a republican office following protests by the Reverend Ian Paisley.**

October   **A British general election brought Labour to power.**

1965

January   **Taoiseach Seán Lemass met O'Neill at Stormont.**

February   **O'Neill visited Lemass in Dublin.**
The Nationalist party assumed the role of official opposition.
The Lockwood committee recommended Coleraine rather than Londonderry as the site for NI's second university.

Spring   The Campaign for Democracy in Ulster became active at Westminster.

1966

February   Paisley brought Edward Carson junior to Belfast.
Unionist party headquarters was petrol-bombed.
Three Catholic schools were attacked.

March   The Ulster Protestant Volunteers, a loyalist group which supported Paisley, was formed.
The UVF issued a threat to the IRA.

1966   **In the British general election, Gerry Fitt was elected MP for West Belfast.**

April   Easter Rising celebrations were held north and south. They were controversial and tense, but there were no serious disturbances. O'Neill later said the commemorations soured the whole situation and from that moment on life became very difficult. *The Protestant Telegraph* was launched by Paisley.

May   **77-year-old Protestant widow Matilda Gould was severely burned in a UVF fire-bomb attack on a Catholic-owned bar in Belfast. She died in June.**

June   Paisleyites and nationalists clashed in Cromac Square, Belfast, with prolonged rioting. Paisley and others were charged with unlawful assembly. **Catholic man John Patrick Scullion died two weeks after being shot by the UVF in the Falls district. Peter Ward was shot dead by the UVF, and two others injured, in the Malvern Street shootings. The UVF was banned.**

July   A nationalist workman threw a brick at the Queen's car during a royal visit to Belfast. Paisley was imprisoned for unlawful assembly, his third conviction but first prison term.

September   **O'Neill flew back from England, declaring a conspiracy had been mounted against him in his absence. He won a party vote of confidence.**

November   Jack Lynch replaced Seán Lemass as Taoiseach.

1967

January/   **The Northern Ireland Civil Rights Association was**
February   **formed.**

March   The Republican Clubs organisation was banned.

April   O'Neill dismissed agriculture minister Harry West over a Fermanagh land deal.

1968

April   All parades were banned for one month in Armagh to avoid clashes between republicans

1968   commemorating the Easter Rising and a threatened
                                  UPV counter-demonstration.
                                  O'Neill's car was attacked by loyalist demonstrators
                                  in Belfast.

June   **Nationalist MP Austin Currie raised the Caledon
                                  housing issue after the local council allocated a
                                  house to teenage Protestant single girl. He staged a
                                  protest squat in the house, and was evicted by
                                  police.**

August   **The first civil rights march took place, from
                                  Coalisland to Dungannon in Tyrone, in protest at
                                  housing allocation. Hundreds of UPV members
                                  assembled to confront them.**

October   **A Londonderry civil rights march resulted in
                                  seventy-seven injured civilians as police batoned
                                  marchers.**
                                  The People's Democracy group was founded.
                                  The Nationalist party withdrew as official
                                  opposition.
                                  Lynch met PM Harold Wilson, blaming partition for
                                  Northern Ireland's problems.

November   **O'Neill and ministers Brian Faulkner and William
                                  Craig met Wilson and Home Secretary James
                                  Callaghan at Downing Street.
                                  O'Neill subsequently announced a five-point
                                  reform package which included an ombudsman,
                                  the end of the company vote in local elections, a
                                  review of the Special Powers Act, a new
                                  Londonderry Development Commission, and a
                                  points system for housing allocation.**
                                  A civil rights march was held in Armagh. Paisley
                                  supporters blocked the city centre.

December   Paisley was summonsed for taking part in an illegal
                                  assembly.
                                  **O'Neill delivered his 'crossroads' speech.
                                  O'Neill dismissed Craig from his cabinet.**
                                  Paisley greeted the historic gunrunning ship the
                                  Clydevalley on its return to NI.

1969

January   **A PD march from Belfast to Londonderry was**

1969   attacked by loyalists at Burntollet Bridge.
RUC members broke doors and windows in the
Bogside, Londonderry.
**A PD march in Newry was followed by rioting and
substantial damage.**
O'Neill announced the Cameron commission,
headed by a Scottish judge, to investigate the causes
of the 1968 disturbances.
**Faulkner resigned from O'Neill's cabinet, citing the
decision to set up the Cameron commission.**
Minister William Morgan also resigned.
**Paisley was sentenced to three months'
imprisonment in relation to the Armagh
demonstration.**
**A Londonderry Commission was named to replace
the Corporation.**

February   Paisley led 5,000 people from the Shankill to a rally in
the Ulster Hall.
Twelve dissident MPs held a meeting in Portadown,
calling for O'Neill's resignation.
**O'Neill called a Stormont election which produced
a poor result for him.**

March   It was announced that the RUC would carry arms on
daytime duties in border areas.
Paisley and Ronald Bunting lost their appeals and
were sent to jail.
**Castlereagh electricity substation was wrecked by
loyalist bombs. The IRA was blamed.**
O'Neill announced the part-time mobilisation of
1,000 B Specials to guard public utilities.

April   **A loyalist bomb damaged a water installation at
Dunadry, County Antrim. The IRA was blamed.**
**Bernadette Devlin won the Mid-Ulster
Westminster by-election.**
Rioting broke out in Londonderry after a banned
demonstration.
More loyalist bombs damaged the Silent Valley
water supply. The bombs cut off two-thirds of the
water supply to Belfast.
**A nationalist crowd stoned Hasting Street RUC
station in Belfast. Civil rights demonstrators in
Newry attacked the police station.**

1969   John Hume asked the civil rights movement to stay
                           off the streets.
                           James Chichester-Clark resigned from O'Neill's
                           cabinet.
                           The main Lough Neagh to Belfast water pipe was
                           blown up by loyalists.
                           An explosion in Annalong, County Down, caused by
                           loyalists, again hit Belfast's water supply. Five
                           hundred British troops were sent to NI.
                           O'Neill resigned. Celebration bonfires were lit on
                           the Shankill Road.
                           A NI Boundary Commission was set up.

May   **Chichester-Clark defeated Faulkner to become
                           prime minister.**
                           An amnesty was announced for those convicted since
                           October 1968. It resulted in the release of Paisley and
                           the dropping of charges against a number of
                           nationalist MPs.
                           Chichester-Clark and colleagues met Wilson and
                           Callaghan.
                           **Wilson announced that the one man – one vote
                           system would be used for 1971 NI local
                           elections.**

July   A white paper on local government reorganisation
                           recommended greatly reducing the number of local
                           government bodies.
                           Clashes during the Twelfth of July period led to
                           serious rioting in various areas.

August   **Major clashes broke out between Bogside residents
                           and the RUC after the Apprentice Boys march was
                           stoned. Lynch sent 'field hospitals' to the border
                           area. RUC stations were attacked in nationalist
                           areas.**
                           **In Londonderry the RUC used CS gas for the first
                           time. There was rioting in Derry and later Belfast.
                           Wilson and Callaghan met in Cornwall, and
                           decided to provide troops if Chichester-Clark
                           requested them. Callaghan later agreed to a
                           request.**

14 August   **The army arrived on the streets of Londonderry at
                           5 p.m. The army negotiated with the Bogside
                           Defence Association and agreed to pull the RUC**

1969	and B Specials back behind the army outside the Bogside.
14/15 August	**Major clashes occurred in west and north Belfast. A number of people were killed; 150 Catholic homes were burned and on the 15th barricades were strengthened in many areas.**
15 August	**The army was deployed on the streets of Belfast.**
19 August	Chichester-Clark was summoned to London where, at a stormy meeting, he was pressed for action on reform. **The Hunt inquiry into policing was announced.** Two senior British civil servants were appointed to the NI PM's office and the Ministry of Home Affairs. Callaghan arrived in NI, and was given a warm welcome in the Bogside. Chichester-Clark announced that a senior English judge, Lord Scarman, would chair an inquiry into the 1969 disturbances.
September	The Cameron report on the 1968 disturbances was published. The army completed 'peacelines' in Belfast, barricades intended to separate some loyalist and nationalist areas. A Ministry for Community Relations was established.
October	**The Hunt report on policing was published. It proposed disarming the RUC and abolition of the B Specials. English policeman Sir Arthur Young was appointed head of the RUC.** **In a night of loyalist rioting on the Shankill Road, a policeman and two civilians were killed.** **A loyalist was fatally injured when his bomb exploded prematurely.**
November	A white paper recommended the creation of the Ulster Defence Regiment to replace the B Specials.
1970	
January	The UDR came into existence, becoming operational in April. **Sinn Féin split into Official and Provisional Sinn**

1970   Féin. **A corresponding IRA split had already taken place.**

March   Five Unionist MPs were expelled from the parliamentary party after refusing to support a motion of confidence in the government.

April   **Rioting in Ballymurphy, west Belfast, led to a major gun battle with the army.**
In a by-election Paisley won O'Neill's Bannside seat. O'Neill had resigned the seat to become Lord O'Neill.
The Alliance Party of Northern Ireland was formed.
The B Specials formally ceased to exist.

May   **Lynch sacked ministers Charles Haughey and Neil Blaney from his cabinet amid allegations of illegal arms importation.** Haughey and Blaney were arrested on arms conspiracy charges.

June   **Labour lost the Westminster general election.**
Reginald Maudling became Home Secretary in Edward Heath's Conservative government.
Bernadette Devlin was jailed for her part in the August 1969 Londonderry rioting.
Serious rioting and clashes occurred in Belfast and Londonderry with five shot dead.

July   A new act imposed mandatory six-month sentences for disorderly or riotous behaviour.
The army placed part of the Falls Road area of Belfast under curfew while it searched 5,000 homes for arms.
Irish foreign minister Patrick Hillery visited the Falls area unannounced, displeasing both Stormont and London.
All marches were banned for six months.
The army's shooting of an alleged petrol-bomber in Londonderry was followed by protests and five nights of rioting.

August   The army began to use rubber bullets.
The SDLP was formed, with Gerry Fitt as leader.

September The one-hundredth explosion in NI in 1970 took place.

October **In Dublin, Haughey and others were acquitted on arms charges.**

1971

January   An independent commissioner was appointed to review local council boundaries.

February   **The IRA shot soldier Robert Curtis in north Belfast, the first serving soldier to die in the troubles.** In a television address Chichester-Clark said: 'Northern Ireland is at war with the IRA Provisionals.'
Two RUC officers were shot dead in Belfast.
The RUC was issued with bulletproof vests.

March   Maudling addressed Stormont, saying violence could not be tolerated.
Three off-duty British soldiers were shot dead by the IRA at Ligoniel in north Belfast.
4,000 shipyard workers marched in Belfast demanding internment without trial.
Chichester-Clark flew to London to demand support for tougher security measures. He was promised 1,300 extra troops.
Chichester-Clark resigned. Faulkner defeated Craig to become Unionist party leader and prime minister.

April   In the Commons Wilson said a bill existed for the imposition of direct rule from Westminster.

May   **The new independent Housing Executive met for the first time.**

June   Faulkner proposed the creation of three new parliamentary committees, some to be chaired by members of the opposition.

July   **During prolonged rioting in Londonderry, a man and a youth were shot dead by the army in controversial circumstances.**
Sinn Féin's Maire Drumm told a Bogside meeting: 'The only way you can avenge these deaths is by being organised ... until you can chase that accursed army away. I would personally prefer to see all the British army going back dead. You should not just shout "Up the IRA", you should join the IRA.' She later received a six-month prison sentence for the speech.
The SDLP withdrew from Stormont citing the

1971

government's refusal to hold a public inquiry into the two Londonderry deaths.

August   Faulkner flew to London to press Heath for the introduction of internment.
Internment was introduced. Hundreds of people were arrested and there were major outbreaks of violence.
The SDLP announced a civil disobedience campaign, including a rent-and-rates strike.
Approximately 25 per cent of Catholic tenants took part in the strike.
Many Catholic representatives withdrew from councils and public bodies over internment.
The Compton inquiry was established into the treatment of detainees in custody.
Heath held prolonged talks with Lynch at Chequers.
Maudling in the Commons said 'a permanent, active and guaranteed place in the life and public affairs of NI shall be available both to the majority and minority community'.
Internees were moved to Long Kesh.
Heath met Lynch and Faulkner at Chequers.

October   Five nationalist MPs staged a 48-hour hungerstrike in Downing Street in protest at internment.
A Catholic, G.B. Newe, was brought into government as a junior minister in Faulkner's office to advise on minority matters.
A nationalist alternative gathering, the Assembly of the Northern Irish People, was organised by the SDLP.
Paisley's Democratic Unionist party was launched at an Ulster Hall rally.
The Compton report said there had been ill-treatment of detainees but not brutality.
Wilson called for Irish unification after a fifteen-year transitional stage.

November   The Irish government referred the alleged ill-treatment of detainees to the European Commission on Human Rights.

December   **A bomb left by the UVF at McGurk's Bar in north Belfast killed fifteen people.**
Unionist Senator Jack Barnhill was killed at his home

1971   by the Official IRA.
                           After a visit to NI, Home Secretary Maudling was
                           criticised for speaking of an 'acceptable level of
                           violence'.

1972

         January   **On what became known as Bloody Sunday,
                           thirteen men were shot dead in Londonderry by the
                           army; another died later of his wounds.**

         February   **The British embassy in Dublin was burned down
                           by a protesting crowd.**
                           Faulkner met Heath at Downing Street.
                           William Craig launched the Ulster Vanguard
                           movement.
                           **Seven people were killed by a bomb planted by the
                           Official IRA at Aldershot military barracks in
                           England.**
                           NI minister John Taylor was seriously injured in an
                           Official IRA gun attack.

         March   **The Abercorn Bar in Belfast city centre was
                           bombed by the IRA, killing two people and
                           injuring 130.**
                           A four-hour loyalist stoppage was called in protest at
                           security policy.
                           Wilson met the IRA in Dublin and at a press
                           conference said internment should end, security
                           should be transferred to London, and IRA terms
                           should be put on the agenda for talks.
                           Heath informed Faulkner he intended to remove
                           security powers from Stormont.
                           **Direct rule was introduced when Faulkner refused
                           to give up security powers.**
                           Craig's Vanguard movement held a large Belfast
                           protest rally.
                           **An IRA bomb in Belfast's Donegall Street killed
                           seven people.
                           William Whitelaw, in the new post of Northern
                           Ireland Secretary, arrived in Belfast.
                           The Stormont parliament was wound up, with a
                           huge loyalist protest rally.**

         April   The Widgery report into Bloody Sunday was
                           published, largely exonerating the army.

1972   May   There were widespread protests after the Official IRA
                      killed a local man who was in Londonderry on home
                      leave from the army.
                      The Official IRA called off its campaign.
                      The SDLP called on those who had withdrawn from
                      public life to return.

            June   **The IRA called a ceasefire to allow for talks with
                      the government.
                      Whitelaw granted special category status to
                      imprisoned republicans and loyalists.**

            July   **The IRA met Whitelaw in London for talks. These
                      were unproductive and the IRA ceasefire ended a
                      short time later.
                      22 IRA bombs in Belfast killed eleven and injured
                      scores on 21 July, Bloody Friday.
                      The army took control of no-go areas in
                      Londonderry in Operation Motorman.
                      An IRA bomb attack killed eight people in the
                      County Londonderry village of Claudy.**

      September   A conference of NI political parties was held in
                      Darlington.

        October   **A government green paper on the future
                      government of NI was published.**

      December   **Loyalist bombs exploded in Dublin while the Dáil
                      was debating anti-terrorist legislation, killing two
                      people.**
                      Special category prisoners were moved to Long Kesh
                      prison near Belfast where they joined internees.
                      **The Diplock report on judicial procedure
                      recommended an end to jury trial in troubles-
                      related cases.**

1973

        January   **The UK and the Irish Republic joined the European
                      Economic Community.**

       February   **Two loyalists were interned, the first since
                      internment began, sparking off a violent one-day
                      loyalist strike.**
                      A general election in the south resulted in a Fine
                      Gael–Labour coalition headed by Liam Cosgrave.

1973 March   **A border poll asked voters if they wanted NI to remain within the UK: 591,820 said yes, 6,463 said no.** Most nationalists boycotted the poll.

An IRA gun-running boat, the *Claudia*, was captured; it contained arms from Libya.

A white paper was published, laying the groundwork for the assembly and the Sunningdale initiative.

The Unionist party's ruling council approved the white paper by 381 votes to 231, giving Faulkner the authority to negotiate.

Craig announced the creation of the Vanguard Unionist Progressive party.

May   Faulkner said he would not share power with those 'whose primary object is to break the link with Britain'.

June   SDLP senator and Belfast councillor Paddy Wilson and a woman were stabbed to death by UDA members.

Assembly elections were held.

An IRA bomb attack killed six people in Coleraine, County Londonderry.

The first meeting of the assembly took place amid rowdy scenes.

August   Former NI prime minister Lord Brookeborough died. Faulkner and Heath were booed at the funeral.

October   **Interparty talks involving the UUP, SDLP and Alliance on the formation of an executive began at Stormont Castle.**

After a six-hour debate Faulkner won the support of the party's standing committee for sharing power with the SDLP by 132 votes to 105.

November   The UVF announced a ceasefire which lasted 43 days.

The UUP's ruling council agreed in principle to powersharing by 379 votes to 369.

Agreement was reached on the setting up of a powersharing executive to administer Northern Ireland.

December   Heath announced Whitelaw's replacement as NI Secretary by Francis Pym.

An assembly meeting degenerated into violence

1973   and was adjourned in 'grave disorder'.
                           The Sunningdale conference was held in England,
                           clearing the way for the powersharing executive to
                           be formed.

1974

          January   The powersharing executive took office.
                           Faulkner was defeated by 457 votes to 374 in a vote
                           by the UUP ruling council on the Council of
                           Ireland.
                           Faulkner resigned as UUP leader, to be replaced by
                           hardliner Harry West.
                           The Boland case, in which a former Irish government
                           minister challenged Sunningdale as conflicting with
                           the Irish constitution, was heard in a Dublin court.
                           Faulkner flew to meet Cosgrave near Dublin to try to
                           resolve differences.
                           The first meeting of the assembly since
                           Sunningdale resulted in violent scenes during
                           which five RUC men were injured.

          February   Irish ministers met the Northern Ireland executive to
                           discuss cross-border links and harmonisation.
                           The British general election saw Heath replaced by
                           a minority Labour government under Wilson. In
                           NI, anti-Sunningdale Unionist candidates won
                           eleven of the twelve seats with 51 per cent of the
                           vote.

          March   Merlyn Rees was named as new Northern Ireland
                           Secretary.
                           The Assembly began to debate a motion calling for
                           complete renegotiation of the Sunningdale
                           Agreement. The presiding officer allowed the debate
                           to run for almost two months.

          May   Faulkner supporters began to organise a new party
                           to be known as the Unionist Party of Northern
                           Ireland (UPNI).
                           The assembly voted by 44 votes to 28 in favour of
                           the powersharing executive. The vote triggered the
                           Ulster Workers Council strike.
                           During the strike more than thirty people were
                           killed by loyalist bombs in Dublin and Monaghan.
                           As the strike progressed Wilson made a broadcast

1974 condemning 'people who spend their lives
sponging on Westminster', causing widespread
Protestant resentment.
**Faulkner and his colleagues resigned on 28 May.
The strike was called off following the collapse of
the executive.**

September Faulkner officially launched the UPNI.

October In the British general election, ten of the twelve NI
seats were retained by anti-Sunningdale Unionists.
**Five people were killed and 54 were injured when
IRA bombs exploded without warning in a pub in
Guildford, Surrey.**
Protesting republican prisoners burned down much
of Long Kesh prison.

November A UDA delegation visited Libya.
Twenty-three republican prisoners escaped from
Long Kesh. One prisoner was killed during the
escape and the others were recaptured.
**Twenty-one were killed and 182 injured when IRA
bombs exploded in Birmingham bars.**

December At Feakle, in County Clare, a group of Protestant
churchmen met IRA leaders.
**The IRA called a ceasefire until 2 January, and Rees
permitted officials to meet with Sinn Féin.**

1975

January The IRA announced an extension of its ceasefire.

February **The IRA announced an indefinite ceasefire.**
Sinn Féin was allowed to set up 'incident centres' to
monitor the ceasefire.

March The assembly was formally dissolved to allow for
elections to a new constitutional convention.

May In the convention elections, combined anti-
Sunningdale Unionists had an overall majority.
Faulkner's UPNI won only a handful of seats.
The convention opened with the task of devising a
system of government with the 'most widespread
acceptance throughout the community'.

July Three members of the Miami Showband were killed

1975   in an incident in which two UVF attackers also died.

August   Unionist talks with the SDLP broke down.

September   Craig proposed the possibility of the SDLP entering government at the discretion of a Unionist prime minister, an idea known as 'voluntary coalition'.

October   The Vanguard party split over the voluntary coalition plan.
The convention voted by 42 votes to 31 in favour of a report advocating a return to Unionist majority rule.

November   **The UVF was again banned after a day in which there were eleven deaths as a result of UVF attacks.** The Sinn Féin incident centres were closed.

December   Internment was ended, and the remaining detainees were released.

1976

January   **Six members of two Catholic families were killed by the UVF in County Armagh.**
Ten Protestant workers were shot dead at Kingsmills in County Armagh by the IRA.
The SAS was deployed in south Armagh.

February   Republican prisoner Frank Stagg died in England after a 62-day hungerstrike.

March   Those convicted of paramilitary offences were no longer eligible for special category status.
The final convention meeting ended amid rowdy scenes, and the body was officially dissolved.

June–September   The UUP was strongly criticised by other Unionists for holding talks with the SDLP.

July   **The British ambassador to Ireland, Christopher Ewart-Biggs, was killed by the IRA** in Dublin.

August   The deaths of the three Maguire children led to the emergence of the 'Peace People'.
Faulkner, by now Lord Faulkner, announced his retirement from political life.

September   **Roy Mason replaced Rees as Northern Ireland Secretary.**

1976	**The first IRA man sent to the Maze (formerly Long Kesh) after the ending of special category status refused to wear prison uniform.**
October	Sinn Féin vice-president Maire Drumm was shot dead by loyalists while a patient in Belfast's Mater Hospital.
November	Peace People leaders Mairead Corrigan and Betty Williams were awarded the Nobel peace prize.
December	The Fair Employment Act was passed, making it an offence to discriminate in employment on religious or political grounds. It created the Fair Employment Agency.
1977	
March	Faulkner died in a horse-riding accident. In Dublin eight SAS men were fined after being detained on the southern side of the border. Twenty-six men were sentenced to a total of 700 years in prison following a major UVF trial.
April	**Paisley and the UDA announced plans for a second loyalist workers' strike. It was opposed by the UUP and others.**
May	**The strike began on 2 May but was called off on 13 May.**
June	A general election in the south resulted in a Fianna Fáil government led by Jack Lynch.
July	Several people were killed in Belfast as a result of a feud between the Provisional IRA and the Official IRA.
August	The Queen visited Belfast as part of her jubilee celebrations. US President Jimmy Carter expressed support for a NI government that would have widespread acceptance, offering economic aid in the event of such agreement.
September	The SDLP declared its support for 'an agreed Ireland'.

1977   October   The Irish Independence Party was launched in opposition to the SDLP.

November   The SDLP conference rejected calls for a British withdrawal.

December   Five hotels were damaged by IRA bombs.

1978

January   The Fair Employment Agency reported that unemployment was higher among Catholics than among Protestants.
The European Court of Human Rights ruled that interrogation methods used on internees in 1971 did not constitute torture but did amount to 'inhuman and degrading treatment'.

February   **The IRA firebombing of La Mon Hotel outside Belfast killed twelve people.**

March   The Maze prison dispute escalated when republican inmates began spreading excrement around their cells.

April   Conservative spokesman Airey Neave said that powersharing was no longer practical politics.
James Callaghan announced that the number of NI MPs would be increased.

May   Belfast elected its first non-Unionist mayor, David Cook of the Alliance party.

July   The head of the Irish Catholic Church, Archbishop Tomás Ó Fiaich, visited the Maze prison and said it reminded him of a Calcutta slum.

August   The De Lorean car company announced plans to build luxury sports cars in south Belfast, with a £56 million government subsidy.

November   Widespread IRA bomb attacks caused serious damage. The deputy governor of the Maze prison was killed by the IRA.

1979

January   IRA bombs exploded across NI on the first day of the year.

1979 February Members of the loyalist Shankill Butchers gang were convicted and given long sentences for nineteen killings and other offences.

March A leading police doctor said he had seen a large number of people who had been physically ill-treated in Castlereagh interrogation centre.
The IRA shot and killed the British ambassador to Holland, Sir Richard Sykes.
Twenty-four IRA bombs exploded at different locations.
The Callaghan government was defeated in a Commons confidence vote, precipitating a general election.
Conservative NI spokesman Airey Neave was killed by an INLA bomb while leaving the Commons.

April **Four RUC men were killed in an IRA bomb attack at Bessbrook, County Armagh.**

May **The Conservatives won the general election, bringing Margaret Thatcher to power with former chief whip Humphrey Atkins as NI Secretary.**

August **Two major IRA attacks on 27 August killed Lord Mountbatten and others in a boat off the Sligo coast, while 18 soldiers and a civilian died in an ambush near Warrenpoint in County Down.**

September **Pope John Paul II visited Ireland.** Addressing himself to the IRA he appealed: 'On my knees I beg you to turn away from the paths of violence and return to the paths of peace.'

October Atkins launched an initiative, inviting the parties to talks.

November **Fitt resigned as SDLP leader, to be succeeded by Hume.**

December Charles Haughey was elected leader of Fianna Fáil and became Taoiseach.
Four soldiers were killed by an IRA landmine in County Tyrone.

1980

January	The Atkins conference opened with new Ulster Unionist party leader James Molyneaux boycotting the proceedings.
March	The Atkins conference was wound up.
May	**A meeting between Thatcher and Haughey in Downing Street appeared to improve Anglo-Irish relations.**
June	The European Commission of Human Rights rejected a case taken by a protesting Maze prisoner, but criticised British 'inflexibility'. Dr Miriam Daly, a prominent republican activist, was shot dead at her home in west Belfast by loyalist gunmen.
August	Three people were killed and 18 injured in widespread violence on the anniversary of internment.
October	Seven H-block prisoners began a hungerstrike to demand the return of special category status.
December	**The H-block hungerstrike was called off with one IRA prisoner critically ill.** A second Thatcher–Haughey summit in Dublin launched joint studies on possible areas of co-operation including economics and security.

1981

January	Bernadette McAliskey, née Devlin, and her husband were shot and seriously wounded by UDA gunmen at their County Tyrone home. Two leading Unionists, Sir Norman Stronge and his son James, were killed by the IRA.
March	**A second H-block hungerstrike was begun in support of special category status for prisoners. IRA prison leader Bobby Sands was the first to refuse food.** Irish Foreign Minister Brian Lenihan said the Anglo-Irish talks could lead to Irish unity in ten years. The death occurred of Frank Maguire, independent nationalist MP for Fermanagh–South Tyrone.

1981   Paisley held major rallies in protest at Anglo-Irish
                    talks.

April   **Sands won the Fermanagh–South Tyrone by-
                    election.**

May   **Sands died on the sixty-sixth day of his
                    hungerstrike. His funeral in Belfast was attended
                    by tens of thousands.
                    Three further hungerstrikers died, and five soldiers
                    were killed by a bomb in Bessbrook, County
                    Armagh.**

June   **Two H-block prisoners were elected to the Dáil in a
                    general election which brought to power a Fine
                    Gael–Labour coalition headed by Garret
                    FitzGerald.**

July   Two more hungerstrikers died.

August   Four more hungerstrikers died. Sinn Féin member
                    Owen Carron won the Fermanagh–South Tyrone by-
                    election caused by the death of Sands.

September   Paisley called for a 'third force' to be established on
                    the lines of the B Specials.
                    James Prior replaced Atkins as NI Secretary.

October   **The hungerstrike was called off.** Prior announced
                    that all prisoners could wear their own clothes and
                    made concessions on other prisons issues.

November   **The Anglo-Irish Intergovernmental Council was set
                    up by the two governments.
                    Unionist MP the Reverend Robert Bradford was
                    killed by the IRA in south Belfast.**
                    A loyalist 'day of action' was staged to protest at
                    security policy, with rallies and work stoppages.

December   Paisley claimed a new third force had between 15,000
                    and 20,000 members.

1982

January   Prominent loyalist John McKeague was shot dead by
                    the INLA.

February   A general election in the south returned Fianna Fáil
                    and Charles Haughey to power.

1982   March   Three soldiers were killed in west Belfast.

April   Prior proposed elections to an assembly which could have power devolved to it in stages.
Two people were killed, twelve were injured and £1 million worth of damage was caused by IRA bomb attacks in Belfast, Londonderry, and five towns.

May   **The De Lorean plant closed with the loss of hundreds of jobs.**

July   **IRA bomb attacks on military bands in London parks killed eleven soldiers.**

August   The SDLP decided to contest Northern Ireland assembly elections but not to take their seats.

October   Sinn Féin contested assembly elections on an abstentionist ticket, securing 10 per cent of the vote.
Three RUC officers were killed by an IRA bomb at Lurgan, County Armagh.
Three IRA members were shot dead by the RUC at Lurgan, County Armagh.

November   **The assembly met for first time, with no nationalists attending.**
Lenny Murphy, leader of the UVF Shankill Butchers gang, was shot dead by the IRA.
The third southern general election to be held in fifteen months produced a Fine Gael–Labour coalition.

December   **Seventeen people, including eleven soldiers, died in an INLA bombing in Ballykelly, County Londonderry.**

1983

January   Judge William Doyle was shot dead by the IRA as he left a Catholic church in Belfast.

February   The European Parliament's political committee voted for an inquiry on whether Europe could assist in tackling NI's economic and political problems. This was opposed by the British government and by Unionists.

March   The Irish government announced the setting up of the New Ireland Forum.

1983	April	Fourteen defendants were jailed on the evidence of a UVF supergrass.
	May	A 1000lb IRA bomb exploded outside Andersonstown police station in Belfast.
	May	The New Ireland Forum held its first meeting in Dublin.
	June	**In the British general election, Unionists won fifteen of the seventeen NI seats. Hume and Adams, who defeated Fitt in West Belfast, were elected to Westminster.**
	July	**Four UDR members were killed by an IRA landmine in County Tyrone.**
	August	After a 120-day trial of thirty-eight people implicated by IRA supergrass Christopher Black, twenty-two were jailed. Their sentences totalled more than 4,000 years.
	September	Thirty-eight IRA prisoners escaped from the Maze in a mass breakout. Nineteen were recaptured within days. **Thatcher and FitzGerald met at Chequers for the first meeting of the Anglo-Irish Intergovernmental Council.** **Adams was elected president of Sinn Féin.** **Three members of the congregation of Darkley Pentecostal church in south Armagh were shot dead in an INLA attack.**
	December	**UUP assembly member Edgar Graham was shot dead by the IRA at Queen's University, Belfast.** An Irish soldier and a Garda cadet were killed by the IRA during the rescue of a kidnapped supermarket executive. **Five people were killed and eighty were injured by an IRA bomb at Harrods department store in London.**
1984		
	January	Cardinal Ó Fiaich said that it was not morally wrong to join Sinn Féin. The Irish government said it could not identify with the cardinal's comments.

1984 March   **Adams was shot and wounded in Belfast by the UDA.**
INLA leader Dominic McGlinchey was extradited to NI from the Republic.

April   The IRA shot dead the daughter of magistrate Tom Travers as she left mass with him in south Belfast.

May   **The New Ireland Forum report was published.**

June   DUP assembly member George Seawright lost the party whip after saying that Catholics and their priests should be 'incinerated'.
Three RUC members were acquitted of the murder of an unarmed IRA member.

July   In the Commons, Prior rejected the main recommendations of the New Ireland Forum report.

August   An Armagh coroner resigned after finding 'grave irregularities' in RUC files relating to the shooting of two INLA men by police in 1982.

September   Douglas Hurd replaced Prior as Northern Ireland Secretary.
Seven tons of arms and ammunition intended for the IRA were recovered from the *Marita Ann* off the Irish coast, in the biggest arms seizure since the 1973 capture of the *Claudia*.

October   **An IRA bomb at the Conservative party conference hotel in Brighton killed five people.**
The European Commission of Human Rights ruled that the use of plastic bullets in riot situations was justified.

November   At the end of a summit with the Irish government Thatcher ruled out the three main New Ireland Forum options in what became known as her 'Out, out, out' pronouncement.

December   **Private Ian Thain was convicted of the murder of a civilian while on duty.**
35 defendants charged on the word of a republican supergrass were acquitted.
The Court of Appeal quashed the convictions of fourteen men jailed on the evidence of UVF supergrass Joseph Bennett.

1985

February   The US government refused Adams a visa.
             **Hume met members of the IRA's army council but
             walked out within minutes when the IRA insisted
             on making a video recording of the occasion.**
             Three IRA members were shot dead by soldiers at
             Strabane, County Tyrone.
             **Nine RUC officers were killed in an IRA mortar
             attack in Newry, County Down.**

May   **In the local government elections Sinn Féin won 59
             council seats. This led to disruption of meetings by
             Unionists.
             Four RUC officers were killed by an IRA bomb at
             Killeen, County Armagh.**

July   **Loyalist rioting over the rerouting of parades,
             especially in Portadown, led to loyalist attacks on
             police homes across Northern Ireland, forcing
             scores of RUC families to move house.**

August   Molyneaux and Paisley met Thatcher in Downing
             Street.

September   Tom King replaced Hurd as NI Secretary.

November   **Prime ministers Thatcher and FitzGerald signed
             the Anglo-Irish Agreement on 15 November,
             systematising co-operation with a permanent
             intergovernmental conference machinery and
             giving the Irish government a consultative role in
             NI affairs with a joint secretariat at Maryfield,
             outside Belfast.
             The new NI Secretary, Tom King, was assaulted by
             angry loyalists at Belfast's City Hall.
             An estimated 100,000 Unionists gathered in Belfast
             city centre to voice their anger at the Anglo-Irish
             Agreement.**

December   **The first meeting was held of the Anglo-Irish
             Intergovernmental Conference.
             All fifteen Unionist MPs resigned in order to force
             by-elections.**

1986

January   By-elections caused by the resignation of Unionist

1986   MPs gave the SDLP a second Westminster seat when
                           Séamus Mallon was elected in Newry–Armagh.

February   The Irish government announced its intention to sign
                           the European Convention on the Suppression of
                           Terrorism.
                           Paisley and Molyneaux were invited to Downing
                           Street. Although receptive to Thatcher's offer of
                           further talks, they were heavily criticised by
                           colleagues when they returned to Belfast.

March   **A Unionist day of action disrupted public services
                           and halted most industry. There was rioting in
                           some loyalist areas.**
                           Unionist leaders offered to talk to the government
                           but only if the Anglo-Irish Agreement was
                           suspended. This was ruled out by King.
                           Clashes took place between the RUC and loyalists in
                           Portadown after a ban on an Apprentice Boys
                           parade. Eleven Catholic homes in Lisburn, County
                           Antrim, were petrol-bombed.

April   A loyalist was killed by a plastic bullet during
                           renewed rioting in Portadown. Loyalist attacks on
                           Catholic and RUC homes continued.
                           Unionist leaders announced a civil disobedience plan
                           including non-payment of rates.
                           The UUP announced that it was ending its last links
                           with the Conservative party.

May   The Chief Constable Sir John Hermon condemned
                           the loyalist attacks on Catholic and RUC homes and
                           accused politicians of consorting with paramilitary
                           elements.
                           Belfast city council ended its adjournment protest
                           against the Anglo-Irish Agreement.

May   King announced the dissolution of the NI assembly.

June   **In controversial circumstances John Stalker was
                           removed from the inquiry into RUC 'shoot-to-kill'
                           incidents. Suggestions of improprieties on his part
                           were later dismissed and he was reinstated as
                           Deputy Chief Constable of the Manchester police.
                           The NI assembly was wound up. Twenty-two
                           assembly members who refused to leave the
                           chamber were physically removed by the RUC.**

1986	July	Portadown Orangemen accepted a compromise route along Garvaghy Road. However, rioting and clashes with the RUC continued. Hermon suspended two senior officers after investigations into the alleged 'shoot-to-kill' policy in 1982.
	August	The IRA announced it was widening its list of 'legitimate targets'. DUP deputy leader Peter Robinson was arrested and charged after crossing the border into County Monaghan with scores of other loyalists during a late-night protest demonstration.
	September	UUP and DUP politicians attended the funeral of assassinated UVF member John Bingham.
	November	**Sinn Féin decided to permit successful Sinn Féin candidates to take their seats in the Dáil. Ruairí Ó Brádaigh led a walkout.** Thatcher rejected the Irish call for Diplock trials to be heard by three judges. The UDA planted four bombs in Dublin. Ulster Resistance was formed 'to take direct action as and when required' to defeat the Anglo-Irish Agreement. DUP leaders featured at early meetings. A huge Anglo-Irish Agreement protest rally at Belfast City Hall ended with serious damage to nearby shops.
	December	King announced the repeal of the Flags and Emblems Act. Paisley was expelled from the European Parliament after repeatedly interrupting a speech by Thatcher. Lisburn Road RUC station in south Belfast was destroyed by an IRA bomb. Hundreds of homes and businesses were also damaged.
1987		
	January	DUP politician David Calvert was shot and wounded by the INLA. Robinson pleaded guilty in a Dublin court to unlawful assembly and paid £17,500 in fines. The UDA published a political manifesto called

1987   *Common Sense*, proposing devolved government with
                  a form of powersharing. This was greeted by
                  Unionist condemnation but some nationalist praise.

February   The UDA planted incendiary bombs in the Republic.
                  Unionist MPs delivered a petition with 400,000
                  signatures to Buckingham Palace. It called for a
                  referendum in NI on the Anglo-Irish Agreement.
                  Paisley and Molyneaux set up an inter-party task
                  force to draft an alternative to the Anglo-Irish
                  Agreement.

March   Fianna Fáil led by Charles Haughey returned to
                  power after a general election on 19 February.
                  President Reagan gave the first $50 million grant to
                  an international economic regeneration fund set up
                  alongside the Anglo-Irish Agreement.

April   **Northern Ireland's second most senior judge, Lord
                  Gibson, and his wife were killed by an IRA car
                  bomb at Killeen, County Armagh.**

May   Sinn Féin published a document entitled *Scenario for
                  Peace*, demanding British withdrawal and an all-
                  Ireland constitutional conference.
                  Paisley said that the DUP would have no part in any
                  powersharing system, after rumours that the
                  Unionist task force might be preparing to suggest it.
                  **Eight IRA members were shot dead by the SAS as
                  they launched an attack on an RUC station at
                  Loughgall, County Armagh. A civilian was also
                  killed.**

June   The Conservatives won a third general election
                  victory. Eddie McGrady's defeat of Enoch Powell
                  gave the SDLP three seats, while Adams retained
                  West Belfast.

July   Short Brothers closed a section of its plant in a
                  dispute about removing loyalist flags and emblems.

September   **Unionists ended a nineteen-month ban on meeting
                  NIO ministers, meeting King for 'talks about talks'.**

November   **The French authorities intercepted a large
                  consignment of arms and explosives on its way
                  to the IRA from Libya on board the *Eksund*. It later
                  emerged that earlier large shipments had got**

1987   through.
                            An IRA bomb in Enniskillen killed eleven
                            Protestants during a Remembrance Day ceremony.
                            Loyalist politician George Seawright was fatally
                            injured by the IPLO.

   December   A new extradition bill was passed by the Dáil.
                            Senior UDA figure John McMichael, who had helped
                            draft the *Common Sense* document, was killed by the
                            IRA.

1988

   January   **UDA members were arrested with a large haul of**
                            guns, revealing that loyalists had made a South
                            African arms deal.
                            Hume and Adams met at the request of a third
                            person.
                            Attorney-General Sir Patrick Mayhew announced
                            that there would be no prosecutions over the
                            Stalker inquiry 'in the interests of national
                            security'.
                            Molyneaux and Paisley met King to suggest
                            administrative devolution with committees chaired
                            according to party strengths.
                            The Birmingham Six lost their appeal against
                            conviction.

   February A Sinn Féin conference approved further talks
                            between Adams and Hume.
                            Private Thain, convicted of murder while on duty,
                            was released from a life sentence after twenty-six
                            months and returned to his regiment.
                            The FEA reported an increased Catholic share of
                            public sector employment.

   March   **Three IRA volunteers were shot dead by the SAS in**
                            Gibraltar.
                            In Milltown cemetery, Belfast, UDA member
                            Michael Stone attacked the funerals of the IRA
                            members killed in Gibraltar. He killed three people
                            and injured dozens of others.
                            Two plain clothes soldiers were attacked by a
                            crowd and then shot dead at an IRA funeral in west
                            Belfast.
                            Hume denied reports of tension within the SDLP

1988   over his talks with Adams.

Andy Tyrie was replaced as UDA leader.

April   At a republican Easter commemoration, McGuinness denied that talks with SDLP included the possibility of an IRA ceasefire.

Robinson, re-elected as DUP deputy leader, said there should be no talks with Sinn Féin even if the IRA ended its campaign.

King criticised the SDLP–Sinn Féin talks.

Adams said that as long as there was the possibility of common ground with the SDLP they were morally bound to seek it.

May   Three members of the RAF were killed in IRA attacks in Europe.

The IRA bombed an army base in Bielefeld, Germany.

A UVF gun attack on a Belfast bar killed three people.

Sinn Féin's Mitchel McLaughlin, a participant in the talks with SDLP, said it was time for all nationalists to agree on 'the Irish people's right to national self-determination'.

Further meetings took place between Sinn Féin and the SDLP.

Bishop Cahal Daly said SDLP–Sinn Féin dialogue was 'better than killing'.

Unionists said a precondition for talks would be an end to the SDLP–Sinn Féin dialogue.

June   The SDLP announced it would hold at least one further meeting with Sinn Féin.

A Conservative Association was launched in north Down.

UUP members brothers Chris and Michael McGimpsey took a case in the Irish courts arguing that the Anglo-Irish Agreement conflicted with Articles 2 and 3 of the Irish constitution.

An IRA bomb killed six soldiers at a Lisburn 'fun run'.

Sinn Féin's Pat Doherty said SDLP–Sinn Féin talks did not concern the IRA. There would be no ceasefire while British occupation continued, he said.

July   SDLP MP Eddie McGrady said he hoped talks with

1988

Sinn Féin would either produce progress or be ended.

It was announced that twenty RUC officers would be disciplined as a result of the Stalker–Sampson investigations.

A Belfast city council meeting was abandoned after Unionist and Sinn Féin members came to blows.

Three members of the Hanna family were killed in an IRA border bombing intended for a judge.

Séamus Mallon said the future of the talks with Sinn Féin would depend on Sinn Féin's attitude to IRA violence.

August

A soldier was killed by an IRA bomb at Inglis barracks, London.

Following another meeting with Adams, Hume rejected criticism of talks with Sinn Féin and called on republicans to abandon violence in favour of political methods.

Eight soldiers on a bus were killed by an IRA bomb at Ballygawley, County Tyrone. Thatcher ordered a security review.

Adams said IRA violence would continue until the British withdrew.

Three IRA members were killed by the SAS in County Tyrone.

September

The end of the Sinn Féin–SDLP talks was announced. The SDLP said it regretted being unable to persuade the republicans to end their military campaign; Sinn Féin said it found the SDLP attitude 'perplexing'.

Sinn Féin said the SDLP had allowed the British to believe that an internal settlement was possible.

The SDLP said the Irish had the right to self-determination but this could not be achieved by violence.

Adams said talks with SDLP had been 'good for nationalist morale'.

October

Paisley was ejected from the European Parliament chamber after interrupting an address by the Pope.

Leading UDA figure Jim Craig was killed by members of his own organisation.

Home Secretary Douglas Hurd announced a

| 1988 | | **broadcasting ban on members and supporters of paramilitary organisations.** |

November — An arms find in County Armagh was linked to Ulster Resistance.
The DUP said it had severed all links with Ulster Resistance some time earlier.
The European Court of Human Rights ruled against detention without charge for more than four days.

December — King said he would not meet Sinn Féin even if its elected representatives signed a non-violence oath.

1989

January — Hume said Unionists should sit down with Dublin and northern nationalists to make an agreement which would transcend the Anglo-Irish Agreement.
At the Sinn Féin ard fheis Adams warned the IRA to be 'careful and careful again' to avoid civilian casualties.

February — Meetings in Duisburg, West Germany, involving four NI parties were publicised.
Solicitor Pat Finucane was shot dead at his Belfast home by loyalist gunmen.
Sinn Féin councillor John Davey was shot dead at his Magherafelt, County Londonderry, home by loyalists.
An IRA campaign in Britain started with the planting of a bomb at Tern Hill paratroop barracks.

March — Adams said there was an urgent need for a non-armed political movement to secure self-determination.
Home Secretary Douglas Hurd warned that Britain was facing the threat of high-level IRA activity, adding that the IRA must be 'extirpated'.

April — The Anglo-Irish Intergovernmental Conference agreed to 'deepen and widen' its work.
Three alleged Ulster Resistance members were detained in Paris with a South African figure and an alleged arms dealer.

May — Sir John Hermon retired as Chief Constable of the RUC.

1989   July   Fianna Fáil and Haughey were returned to power in a coalition with the Progressive Democrats.
Peter Brooke succeeded King as NI Secretary.

August   Adams praised 'the men and women of the IRA' at an internment rally in west Belfast.
A split was revealed in Noraid, the main republican support organisation in the USA, over Sinn Féin's political direction.
The UDA produced confidential security force files on alleged IRA suspects.

September   **An IRA bomb at Deal in Kent killed eleven military bandsmen.**

October   Adams told a Labour party fringe meeting that he supported the IRA's right to engage in armed struggle.
Twenty-eight UDR men were arrested in early morning swoops on the orders of the Stevens inquiry team.
The Guildford Four were released by the Court of Appeal.
Adams attacked Cahal Daly as an 'enthusiastic supporter of the RUC'.

November   **NI Secretary Peter Brooke said the IRA could not be militarily defeated and that the government would have to be imaginative and flexible in its response if there was a ceasefire, citing the example of Cyprus. Adams said Brooke had admitted the 'inevitability' of talks with Sinn Féin.**
Republican News said Sinn Féin would not consider talks with British as long as there was a precondition of an IRA ceasefire, dismissing Hume's claim of a debate within Sinn Féin as 'a figment of his imagination'.
The Conservative party accepted the affiliation of four NI Conservative Associations.
Cahal Daly said if the IRA ended its campaign 'a just settlement could be agreed much more quickly than the sceptics believe'.
Adams and McGuinness relaunched Sinn Féin's *Scenario for Peace* document, denying the existence of any debate in the republican movement about ceasefires. They called on Brooke to enter talks

1989   without demanding that the IRA campaign must end
                        first.
                        Séamus Mallon praised Brooke for his remarks about
                        the possibility of talks with Sinn Féin.
                        Cardinal Ó Fiaich urged the British to state that they
                        would not stay 'for all time'.
                        Mitchel McLaughlin backed Ó Fiaich's remarks,
                        saying they were a recognition that 'the question of
                        Irish self-determination must be resolved'. Brooke
                        called them 'wrong and unhelpful'.

December   Adams said the British should hold talks with Sinn
                        Féin 'sooner rather than later'.
                        An IRA statement said the 1980s had ended with the
                        British 'not only knowing in their hearts that they
                        cannot defeat the freedom fighters of the IRA but
                        being forced to admit it publicly'.

1990

January   **Brooke launched a major political talks initiative.**
                        Unionists demanded the suspension of the Anglo-
                        Irish Agreement and the Maryfield Secretariat as
                        preconditions for talks.
                        Adams accused the SDLP of 'consistent and
                        inexcusable failure on the national question over
                        the last twenty years'.
                        The Bishop of Derry, Dr Edward Daly, called the IRA
                        'an evil sinister influence'.

February   At the Sinn Féin ard fheis it was said that demands
                        for an IRA ceasefire in advance of talks with Sinn
                        Féin were unacceptable. Adams said that Brooke's
                        remarks that the IRA could not be beaten meant talks
                        with Sinn Féin were inevitable.
                        Brooke said there could be no talks while IRA
                        violence continued.
                        McGuinness said Brooke was the first NI Secretary
                        'with some understanding of Irish history'. He urged
                        him to spell out what he meant by 'imaginative steps'
                        in the event of an IRA ceasefire. McGuinness said it
                        made 'no sense whatsoever' for the British to
                        demand as a precondition the ending of the IRA
                        campaign.
                        Adams criticised Brooke for 'intransigence' in his

1990

response to McGuinness, saying republican
resistance was inevitable so long as Britain remained
in Ireland.

March   The Dublin Supreme Court handed down the
McGimpsey judgement on Articles 2 and 3. The most
significant aspect of the ruling was that the Articles'
claim to Northern Ireland was not merely an
aspiration but a claim of legal right and thus a
constitutional imperative.
**Sinn Féin dismissed speculation about an IRA
ceasefire.**

April   Adams said an unannounced IRA ceasefire was
possible if Britain entered into talks with Sinn
Féin about eventual disengagement from NI.
The NIO said: 'We do not negotiate with terrorists.'

June   **Following the IRA killing of an ex-RUC reservist
and his wife, Adams said Sinn Féin's relationship
with the IRA was one of 'critical support'.**
The IRA planted bombs at a Territorial Army base in
London, at the home of leading Tory Lord McAlpine,
at an RAF base, and at the Carlton Club in the
West End.

July   The IRA planted a bomb at the London Stock
Exchange.
Cahal Daly said Sinn Féin would have to be talked to
at some stage but would have to repudiate violence.
**Ian Gow MP was killed at his home in Sussex by
an IRA boobytrap bomb.**

August   An IRA bomb was found in the garden of the
Oxfordshire home of Sir Anthony Farrar-Hockley, a
former army commander in NI.
Adams said the British had the power to bring the
conflict to an end by entering into dialogue without
preconditions.
Hume appealed to the IRA to end its campaign.

September   An IRA bomb exploded at an army recruiting office
in Derby.
The Governor of Gibraltar at the time of the 1988 SAS
Gibraltar killings was seriously wounded by the IRA
at his home at Milford in Staffordshire.
An IRA bomb was found at an anti-terrorism

1990   conference in London. The IRA said Foreign Office
                            minister William Waldegrave had been the target.
                            In an interview with *The Independent* an IRA
                            spokesman said the only debate within the
                            republican movement was how to 'prosecute the
                            war' adding, 'There will be no ceasefire, no truce, no
                            cessation of violence short of British withdrawal.'

October   Brooke called the IRA 'a parasitic organisation'
                            which fed off racketeering.

November   Mary Robinson was elected President of the
                            Republic.
                            **Brooke, in what became known as his 'no selfish
                            interest speech', said Britain had 'no selfish
                            strategic or economic interest' in the Union with NI.**
                            Adams said that the onus was on those who believed
                            there was an alternative to the IRA's armed struggle
                            to prove it. He called for talks without preconditions
                            and said Unionist politicians had no right to veto
                            unification.
                            Hume said Brooke's speech showed that Britain was
                            now neutral on partition and it was up to those who
                            supported Irish unity to persuade those who were
                            opposed.
                            **Margaret Thatcher resigned as PM, to be replaced
                            by John Major.**

December   Cahal Daly, installed as the new Catholic primate,
                            told a congregation that the IRA had no 'moral,
                            rational or political' justification for its campaign.
                            For the first time in fifteen years the IRA declared a
                            three-day Christmas ceasefire.

1991

January   Sinn Féin chairman Tom Hartley said Sinn Féin
                            would no longer speak for the IRA, adding, 'the IRA
                            is capable of speaking for itself'.

February   Adams said speculation about an IRA ceasefire was
                            unfounded. Brooke said there would be no place for
                            Sinn Féin until it renounced violence.
                            Adams described as fictitious reports that he was
                            preparing proposals for a ceasefire but said Sinn Féin
                            was ready to take political risks and was prepared

1991   for give and take.

The IRA fired three mortars at Downing Street: one landed 15 feet from the back window of the prime minister's residence.

An IRA spokesman said: 'There is no talk or pressure from within the IRA to call a ceasefire, and no pressure from our comrades in Sinn Féin.'

One man was killed by an IRA bomb at Victoria rail station, London. Another bomb was planted at Paddington.

PM John Major said of the IRA: 'They really ought to know after all these years that we are not going to be pushed around by terrorist acts.'

An IRA bomb on a rail line into the City of London caused rush-hour disruption.

March   McGuinness said that he saw a window of opportunity in Dublin's opposition to an internal settlement and Brooke's 'no selfish interest' speech. **Brooke published his 'three strand' approach to talks and announced a suspension of Anglo-Irish Conference meetings.**

April   Loyalist groups announced a ceasefire during a ten-week gap in Anglo-Irish meetings for the start of Brooke talks on 30 April.

June   At an IRA funeral, Adams said the Brooke talks were 'a non-starter' in the absence of Sinn Féin; he called on US President Bush to 'show more concern for the Irish situation'.

Cahal Daly claimed that documents he had seen indicated there was a debate within the republican movement on the continuation of violence. Sinn Féin said there was no document calling for an end to the IRA campaign.

July   **The Brooke talks were wound up without agreement.**

August   **McGuinness said that Sinn Féin was ready to set aside criticism of Britain 'and risk everything' for 'a real peace agenda'.**

September   Adams said he was prepared to engage in 'open dialogue' and wanted to see an end to all acts of violence.

1991   October   Brooke said there were signs that the leaders of the
republican movement had begun to recognise that
they could not combine the bullet and the ballot box.

November   Pat Doherty of Sinn Féin said the party 'does not
support violence' but does 'support the IRA's right to
exist'.
Two IRA members were killed by their own bomb in
England.

December   IRA firebombs exploded at Blackpool and
Manchester.
An IRA bomb on a rail line in London created
widespread disruption.
The IRA announced a three-day Christmas ceasefire.
Adams called on the British and Irish governments to
develop 'a real peace process'.

1992

January   Cahal Daly said that if the IRA called off its
campaign there would be a responsibility on the
British and Irish governments to 'find some means
whereby the Sinn Féin tradition of republicanism can
be fully represented at a conference table'.
The IRA said it possessed 'the means and the will,
not only to continue the struggle but to intensify it'.
Subsequently an 800lb IRA bomb exploded in
Bedford Street and a 500lb IRA bomb exploded in
High Street, Belfast.
McGuinness said Sinn Féin would 'make it as easy as
possible' for the British government to get into talks
with the party. Brooke said Sinn Féin could only
become involved if there was a cessation of violence
and not temporary ceasefires.
A 5lb IRA bomb exploded in Whitehall Place,
London.
**Eight Protestant workers were killed by an IRA
bomb at Teebane, County Tyrone.**
Cahal Daly said Sinn Féin could expect no place in
Irish politics while it was associated with the IRA.
Adams said Teebane had been a 'horrific incident'
and he denied any 'organic links' between Sinn Féin
and the IRA.
Haughey resigned and was succeeded as Taoiseach

1992   **by Albert Reynolds.**

February   An IRA spokesman said its campaign would cease
              only when it had secured a British declaration of
              intent to withdraw from NI.
              **Loyalists killed five Catholics in a gun attack on a
              bookmaker's office on Belfast's Ormeau Road.**
              The new Presbyterian moderator John Dunlop said
              there would have to be a proven, long-term
              commitment to peace before Sinn Féin could be
              allowed into talks.
              A Semtex bomb was defused near Downing Street
              after an IRA warning. Later in the month twenty-
              eight people were injured by an IRA bomb at London
              Bridge rail station, and another bomb was planted at
              the London office of the Crown Prosecution Service.
              Sinn Féin published *Towards a Lasting Peace in Ireland*.
              McGuinness said withdrawal had to come 'in
              consultation and co-operation' with Unionists.
              The chairman of the Ulster Bank, Sir George Quigley,
              said Ireland should become a one-island economy.

March   It was disclosed that senior Presbyterian ministers
              had met UDA leaders. Cahal Daly said there was no
              question of Catholic Church leaders talking to the
              IRA.
              The IRA planted bombs at Tottenham, Wandsworth
              Common and Liverpool Street rail stations in
              London.
              A 1,000lb IRA bomb devastated the centre of Lurgan,
              County Armagh.
              A large bomb wrecked offices in Belfast city centre.
              At the Fianna Fáil ard fheis Reynolds said that if
              Articles 2 and 3 were on the agenda for forthcoming
              renewed political talks so should the Government of
              Ireland Act.
              Adams said a vote in the forthcoming British general
              election for Sinn Féin would be a vote for peace.
              The IRA warned of a campaign in Britain: 'They
              haven't seen the half of it yet.'
              Brooke confirmed that 'everything is on the table for
              talks'.
              Launching Sinn Féin's election campaign Adams said
              the slogan of a ballot box in one hand, an Armalite in
              the other was outdated.

1992   April   Presidential candidate Bill Clinton said he would lift
the ban on Adams obtaining a visa to enter the US,
and support the idea of a peace envoy if elected.
**An IRA bomb attack on the Baltic Exchange area of
the City of London killed three people and caused
hundreds of millions of pounds' worth of damage.
Another bomb damaged a flyover near Heathrow
airport.
The Tories won the general election with a reduced
majority. Adams lost his Westminster seat to the
SDLP's Joe Hendron.
Sir Patrick Mayhew was appointed NI Secretary.**
At an Easter commemoration Adams said if Major
was 'prepared to grasp the nettle of his government's
involvement in our country and sue for peace',
republicans would assist him.
It emerged that Protestant churchmen had met
Adams.
**Political talks restarted at Stormont. A three-month
gap in Anglo-Irish Conference meetings had been
agreed.**

May   More talks took place between Protestant churchmen
and Sinn Féin representatives.

June   It was disclosed that Bishop Edward Daly had held
two meetings in previous weeks with McGuinness
and Mitchel McLaughlin. McGuinness called them
'useful and constructive'.
A policeman was killed by an IRA gunman as he
carried out a routine vehicle check in Yorkshire, and
a bomb was planted at the Royal Festival Hall. Later
in the month, London Underground was briefly
closed down by bomb hoaxes, and an IRA bomb in a
hijacked taxi exploded in London's West End.
**Sinn Féin's Jim Gibney said republicans accepted
that British withdrawal would entail negotiations
with all shades of opinion and would have to be
preceded 'by a sustained period of peace'. In a later
clarifying statement Gibney said a British
declaration of a long-term intention to withdraw
would mean conditions for peace could be speedily
agreed.**

July   A third meeting took place between Bishop Edward

1992   Daly and Sinn Féin representatives.
                        Gibney said talks between Unionists and Dublin in
                        the three-strand talks could be seen as 'historic
                        landmarks'.

August   **Adams did not rule out a change in Sinn Féin's
                        abstentionist attitude to a NI assembly.**
                        The UDA was proscribed after an increase in
                        violence.
                        There were a number of arrests in London after the
                        seizure of three vans, one carrying explosives.

September   Mitchel McLaughlin said the republican movement
                        'cannot and should not ever try to coerce the
                        Protestant people into a united Ireland'.
                        The IRA mounted a firebomb attack on the Hyde
                        Park Hilton Hotel, London, and later in the month a
                        2,000lb IRA bomb wrecked the NI Forensic Science
                        centre in Belfast, damaging 1,000 homes.
                        The DUP walked out of the political talks.
                        Former IRA Chief of Staff Seán Mac Stiofáin urged an
                        IRA ceasefire.

October   Two IRA bombs exploded in central London. Further
                        disruption was caused by IRA bombs at London
                        Bridge and in the West End, at an underground
                        station, at Southgate and outside Paddington Green
                        police station, London. A man was killed by an IRA
                        bomb in a bar in Covent Garden.
                        IRA bombs exploded at a hotel in Hammersmith and
                        in the West End of London.
                        Five IRA bombs were found in London, one of them
                        outside James Prior's flat, and another outside the
                        Cabinet Office in Whitehall.

November   **The political talks collapsed.
                        A one-ton IRA van bomb outside Canary Wharf in
                        London was defused.**
                        A general election in the Republic led to a Fianna
                        Fáil–Labour coalition.

December   A 1,000lb IRA bomb in London's Tottenham Court
                        Road was defused. Further disruption was caused by
                        two IRA bombs in Manchester city centre, and by a
                        car bomb near a London tube station. Two bombs
                        exploded in bins outside a north London shopping

1992   complex, and two IRA bombs were also found in Oxford Street.

In a speech at Coleraine Mayhew said he believed there were welcome signs of fresh thinking in some republican circles.

Adams in response to Mayhew said Sinn Féin's exclusion from the political process was 'undemocratic' and an 'obstacle to peace', adding that Britain should adopt a policy of ending partition.

The IRA announced a 72-hour Christmas ceasefire. The UDA threatened the 'pan-nationalist front'.

1993

January   Mayhew called on the IRA to renounce violence and join in talks. Adams called Mayhew's speech propagandist and demanded immediate government talks with Sinn Féin.

Adams said there was now a new opportunity for peace in the wake of recent statements by Mayhew which he said might signal a change in the policy of not talking to Sinn Féin.

Cahal Daly predicted there could be peace 'by the end of the year'.

February   The UDA attacked the homes of two Belfast SDLP councillors.

A gasworks was bombed at Warrington, and eighteen people were injured in an IRA explosion near Camden market in north London. Explosives were found near the home of Kenneth Clarke, the Home Secretary.

March   **Two boys were killed in an IRA explosion in Warrington.**

A UDA attack killed four Catholics in Castlerock, County Londonderry.

Reynolds said he was ready to have peace talks with anyone. A spokesman later said he meant only constitutional parties.

Hume called for an all-Ireland referendum on a blueprint for peace over the heads of political leaders if necessary.

April   The IRA planted a bomb outside a Conservative club

1993

in central London.

After Adams was spotted entering Hume's home, it was revealed that talks between the two had been going on in secret.

In newspaper articles Hume wrote: 'The IRA armed struggle [could be] totally undermined by a simple declaration. The British government should underline that the Irish people have the right to self-determination.'

Reynolds said he was willing to talk to Sinn Féin if the IRA ended its violence.

Mayhew rejected joint sovereignty and stressed his desire to devolve wide powers.

In a joint statement Hume and Adams rejected any internal solution to the conflict in the north. They also said they accepted that the Irish people as a whole 'have the right to national self-determination' but added, 'We both recognise that such a new agreement is only achievable and viable if it can earn and enjoy the allegiance of the different traditions on this island, by accommodating diversity and providing for national reconciliation.' The statement was the trigger for a series of media and political attacks on Hume, particularly in the Republic.

An IRA lorry bomb at Bishopsgate caused many millions of pounds' worth of damage to the City of London financial district. A journalist was killed while trying to photograph the lorry.

May

Fine Gael leader John Bruton joined media and Unionist criticism of the Hume–Adams talks.

Adams was refused a US visa.

Adams said the IRA demand for a British withdrawal was not aimed at Protestants.

A 1,000lb IRA bomb exploded in central Belfast. The SDLP's Joe Hendron said the Hume–Adams talks could not continue indefinitely if Adams did not condemn IRA violence.

IRA bombs exploded in Portadown, County Armagh, in Magherafelt, County Londonderry, and outside the Plaza hotel, Belfast. Hume said he would have further talks with Adams despite IRA bombs.

1993   June   **IRA bombs exploded at a gasometer at Gateshead
in Tyneside, destroying it, and at a petrol store
depot in North Shields.**
**In a joint statement Hume and Adams said they
had made progress towards 'agreeing an overall
strategy for lasting peace'.**
**President Mary Robinson visited west Belfast and
shook hands with Adams.**
McGuinness said the initiation of a peace process
'requires a clear and unambiguous indication from
the British government that it accepts the right of the
Irish people to national self-determination'.

July   A security cordon was set up around the City of
London to prevent IRA attacks.
A 1,500lb bomb exploded in the centre of
Newtownards, County Down.
Republican News reported that the IRA had written to
fifty heads of financial institutions in the City of
London warning of further attacks.
**Hume said he believed the IRA wanted to end its
campaign and that more talks with Adams were
planned.**

August   The US ambassador to Dublin, Jean Kennedy-Smith,
said a US peace envoy was an 'option for the future'.
Garret FitzGerald urged Hume to end talks with
Adams 'in the very near future' unless they yielded
concrete results.
The IRA said that while it was ready for a
'meaningful peace process' it was 'equipped and
utterly determined' to resist British policies.
The IRA planted a small bomb in the City of London.
It was revealed that former Anglo-Irish diplomat
Michael Lillis had held two lengthy secret meetings
with Adams in March.

September   The IRA planted a 1,000lb bomb in the centre of
Armagh.
A four-man US delegation arrived in Ireland for
wide-ranging talks.
Hume said he didn't give 'two balls of roasted snow'
what advice he was given about talks with Adams.
Mallon said patience with continued IRA violence
was 'finite'.

1993   A meeting of the four SDLP MPs gave Hume their
support.
The homes of Hendron and five SDLP councillors
were firebombed by the UDA.
**Hume and Adams announced they had reached
agreement in their talks and would submit their
ideas in a report to Dublin for both governments to
consider.**
Unionist MP John Taylor said the Hume–Adams
agreement could lead to civil war.
Mayhew said it would be 'childish' for the British
government not to look at any report on Hume–
Adams submitted by Dublin. There would have to be
a total cessation of violence for Sinn Féin to win a
place at the conference table.
The UDA threatened to step up attacks on the SDLP.
McGuinness said, 'The end of the process for us
means a British withdrawal from Ireland at some
stage in the future.'
The IRA planted two 300lb and 500lb bombs in
Belfast.
Mayhew said the only unit for self-determination
was Northern Ireland.

October   Taylor called for a 'pan-Unionist front' to put
pressure on the British government.
Republican Sinn Féin President Ruairí Ó Brádaigh
described the Hume–Adams initiative as a 'proposed
surrender'.
Major said the only message the IRA could send was
that it had finished with violence for good.
Mayhew demanded an unconditional end to IRA
violence and ruled out the notion of Britain
'persuading' Unionists to accept Irish unity. He said
Sinn Féin could only be involved in talks after IRA
had ended violence and a 'sufficient period' had
shown this was 'for real'.
Orange Order leader the Reverend Martin Smyth
said that if there was 'convincing proof' the IRA had
ended its campaign Sinn Féin could be admitted to
political talks.
IRA prisoners expressed support for the Hume–
Adams talks.
UUP leader James Molyneaux said that Sinn Féin

1993

would have to be 'quarantined' for five years after the IRA ended its campaign before being allowed to join talks.

Molyneaux met Major to express opposition to the Hume–Adams talks.

An IRA attempt to bomb UDA HQ on Belfast's Shankill Road killed nine Protestant civilians and an IRA bomber.

Adams was condemned for carrying the coffin of Thomas Begley, the IRA member killed in the Shankill explosion.

The IRA planted a bomb on a railway line in Berkshire.

Adams said that he would be able to persuade the IRA to end its campaign if the British responded positively to the Hume–Adams initiative.

Tánaiste Dick Spring stated six principles for progress on the north.

In a joint communiqué the British and Irish governments rejected the Hume–Adams initiative and renewed their support for the three-strand inter-party talks.

The UDA killed seven people in the Greysteel pub massacre, bringing to thirteen the number killed by loyalists since the Shankill bomb.

November

Citing the views of the Taoiseach in support, Major ruled out the Hume–Adams initiative. Speaking in the Commons, he told Hume it was 'not the right way to proceed'.

Paisley and Molyneaux held separate talks with Major. Molyneaux later said he was convinced Major was not going to be involved in any sort of secret deal on Hume–Adams.

A DUP blueprint for the government of NI was criticised for failing to acknowledge nationalist interests.

Mayhew said there had been no negotiations with Sinn Féin.

Major pledged that it would be for the people of NI alone to determine their constitutional future. He also said, 'We are ready to respond to a cessation of violence.'

McGuinness said he had been involved in

1993   'protracted contact and dialogue' with the British government.

Hume and Adams issued a joint statement reaffirming their commitment to their peace initiative and saying they would explore ways of advancing it. Dublin government sources later described this as unhelpful.

A large haul of explosives and weaponry bound for the UVF was seized at Teeside docks.

The British government was presented with an Irish paper on the framework for peace.

Details were revealed of secret contacts between the British government and the IRA. These included a proposal for a two-week IRA ceasefire accompanied by delegate talks.

At a Stormont press conference Mayhew denied official contact and claimed that intermediaries 'in a chain of communication' had been activated because the IRA had sent a message that the 'conflict is over' and that they needed British advice on how to bring it to a close. Mayhew claimed there was a difference between talking to the IRA and sending them documents.

Adams denied that such an IRA message was sent and claimed Major authorised the contacts.

The DUP called for Mayhew's resignation.

Mayhew released the British government's version of the secret IRA–government contacts.

Paisley was suspended from the House of Commons after calling Mayhew a liar.

At a press conference in Belfast Sinn Féin released some of their own documents and again denied Mayhew's claim that the IRA had sent a message of surrender.

December   **Reynolds confirmed that 'the right to national self-determination based on consent freely given, north and south', was one element in the peace process being developed.**

Mayhew admitted to twenty-two errors in the version of the secret IRA–government talks which he had lodged in the Commons library.

Mayhew told the Commons that Britain 'would not join the ranks of the persuaders' for Irish unity.

1993

Sinn Féin released a sheaf of documents detailing republican talks with British officials.

An IRA sniper killed a soldier in Keady, County Armagh. Subsequently 1,000 people attended a memorial service. Later in the month the IRA planted a bomb on a rail line near Woking, Surrey.

Reynolds said he was not seeking self-determination 'in Ireland as a whole collected in a single entity. There will be no change in Northern Ireland without a change of opinions there.'

The Combined Loyalist Military Command stated six principles which it said had to underpin any settlement.

Adams said: 'The Six Counties cannot have a right to self-determination. That is a matter for the Irish people as a whole to be exercised without impediment. However the shape of a future Ireland is a matter to be determined by all groups in Ireland obviously including the Unionists.'

The Downing Street Declaration was signed in London by Major and Reynolds. It included a commitment that the people of NI would decide its future and a demand that the IRA permanently renounce violence. Reynolds received a standing ovation in the Dáil.

Mayhew said any post-ceasefire talks with Sinn Féin would have to discuss the surrender of IRA arms.

Adams called for 'clarification' by Dublin of the Downing Street Declaration.

The IRA planted two bombs on a Surrey rail line.

Major insisted that the Downing Street Declaration was not about undermining the Union or leading to joint authority.

Adams called for clarification via unconditional talks between the two governments and Sinn Féin.

US president Bill Clinton welcomed the Downing Street Declaration and said the question of an Adams visa was kept under review.

The IRA announced a three-day ceasefire.

McGuinness said: 'The political situation hasn't developed to a position where Sinn Féin can use its influence to end attacks on the British Crown forces'.

Douglas Hurd said the IRA could 'expect no quarter' if it rejected the Downing Street Declaration.

1994

| January | IRA firebombs damaged eleven Belfast stores. |

Mayhew said that troop withdrawals would happen after a ceasefire but the UK would not be a persuader for a particular constitutional outcome.

Adams wrote to Major seeking clarification of the Downing Street Declaration.

Mayhew turned down the demand for clarification saying it would amount to negotiation.

Reynolds said he would continue to clarify the declaration for Sinn Féin.

The Reynolds government lifted the broadcasting ban on Sinn Féin.

Adams said he could not move until the British clarified the declaration. Major told Hume the declaration spoke for itself.

Adams said he would not accept a ceasefire as a precondition for involvement in talks.

Clinton, against strong British advice, granted a visa to Adams.

Adams arrived in New York on a three-day visa to address a foreign relations conference.

February   US Vice-president Al Gore urged Adams to accept the Downing Street Declaration and reject violence.

Adams addressed 1,500 people at the New York Plaza.

Reynolds said he had given enough clarification.

Mayhew said if there was no IRA response in 'a very few weeks' the government would know what conclusions to draw.

Spring said there could be no minimalist internal solution and that everything must be on the table.

Mayhew ruled out a purely internal settlement. He said the British government would not be persuaders for Irish unity.

Major repeated Brooke's British neutrality formula on NI.

Former INLA leader Dominic McGlinchey was shot dead in a revenge killing.

March   **The IRA launched mortar attacks on Heathrow airport. None exploded.**

Adams said of the Heathrow mortars that every now

1994   and again there had to be something 'spectacular' to
remind people of the conflict. Spring said the IRA's
credit was running very low.
Adams said every side to the conflict had to accept
democratic compromise.
**The IRA called a three-day ceasefire. Adams said
the ceasefire 'did not come easily'.**

April   Cardinal Daly and Hume supported Sinn Féin's call
for clarification.
Mayhew said ending the conflict did not require
surrender.
**The IRA killed an alleged drug dealer and attacked
sixteen other people. In previous days a wave of
IRA attacks had left three dead.**
Reacting to the attacks Reynolds questioned the good
faith of republicans. Reynolds and Mayhew urged
Sinn Féin to spell out what they wanted to be
clarified.

May   Sinn Féin gave Reynolds a list of questions on the
Downing Street Declaration to pass on to the British.
The British government said Sinn Féin need not
accept the declaration in full to participate in talks.
The British government responded to Sinn Féin's
demand for clarification by issuing a lengthy document.

June   **Spring said there would have to be a handover of
IRA guns following a ceasefire.
The crash of a Chinook helicopter on the Mull of
Kintyre in Scotland killed twenty-five senior RUC
officers, members of army intelligence and MI5
officers.**
Hume finished just behind Paisley in the European
elections. Sinn Féin won 9.9 per cent of the vote.
The INLA attacked three loyalists on the Shankill
Road, killing one and fatally injuring the two others.
**Six Catholics were killed in a loyalist attack on a
Loughinisland, County Down, pub.**
Reynolds said that cross-border institutions with
executive powers would be a *quid pro quo* for changes
to Articles 2 and 3.
The government announced that forty IRA prisoners
would be transferred from Britain to NI prisons.

July   Two tons of IRA explosives were found on a lorry

1994   at Heysham.

The CLMC said it would respond positively to an
IRA ceasefire.

**Mayhew called for the 'clear abandonment' of
Articles 2 and 3.**

The Libyan Foreign Minister said Libya would not
supply the IRA with more weapons.

An IRA arms cache was found near Athboy, County
Meath. It included twenty-four AK-47 rifles, a
flamethrower, 30,000 rounds of ammunition,
300 magazines and detonators.

The IRA killed three loyalists and bombed three
loyalist pubs in Belfast.

August   Adams confirmed a report that he had met the IRA
leadership to discuss a ceasefire and was 'guardedly
optimistic'.

**A part-time soldier was shot dead by the IRA in his
butcher's shop in Crossgar, County Down. He was
the last security force fatality caused by the IRA
before their ceasefire.**

The Reverend Martin Smyth said a termination of
IRA violence and the handover of weapons would
mean that Unionists would have to 'learn to deal'
with Sinn Féin.

An American delegation arrived for talks with Sinn
Féin and other bodies.

Hume and Adams issued a joint statement affirming
'the right of the Irish people as a whole to national
self-determination' by agreement.

**The IRA called a 'complete cessation' of its
campaign. Major called for evidence that it was
permanent. Reynolds said the campaign was over
'for good' and that he would swiftly recognise Sinn
Féin's mandate.**

September   *Republican News* referred to the ceasefire as 'a
suspension' of operations.

**Reynolds, Hume and Adams met at Government
Buildings in Dublin and shook hands publicly,
afterwards saying they were 'totally and absolutely
committed to peaceful and democratic methods'.**

Major walked out of a Downing Street meeting
with Paisley after the DUP leader refused to accept
his word that there was no deal with Sinn Féin

1994   and the IRA.

Soldiers began to patrol without helmets.

The CLMC issued six conditions for a loyalist ceasefire including an assurance that the IRA ceasefire was permanent and that the constitutional position of NI was not in danger.

Taylor said he thought the IRA ceasefire was 'for real'.

A UVF bomb on the Belfast–Dublin train partially exploded in Connolly station, Dublin.

Major said the IRA had to say it had abandoned violence 'for good'.

The Clinton White House lifted its ban on contacts with Sinn Féin.

Major lifted the broadcasting ban on Sinn Féin and promised a referendum on the outcome of any negotiations. Ten border crossings were reopened.

Reynolds promised referendums north and south. Reynolds said achievement of Irish unity would take at least twenty years. McGuinness expressed 'surprise and disappointment'.

Major ruled out an amnesty for paramilitary prisoners.

Major said exploratory talks with Sinn Féin could begin around Christmas if republicans indicated that they intended to give up violence for good. Mayhew said IRA arms would feature in the discussion.

Adams was given a visa for a second trip to the US. McGuinness said the word 'permanent' was not in the republican vocabulary.

The European Socialist Group in the European Parliament nominated Hume for the Nobel peace prize.

October   McGuinness told ex-prisoners that Sinn Féin would 'settle for nothing less than the objectives for which so many republicans and others have died'.

Reynolds called for an early army withdrawal to barracks, phased prisoner releases and an acceptable policing system in NI.

Mitchel McLaughlin said the Irish people would have the right to continue the conflict if the present conditions persisted.

Spring said Sinn Féin should be allowed to enter

1994 talks before the IRA handed in weapons and explosives.

The RUC patrolled in west Belfast unaccompanied by soldiers. Reynolds urged the British to speed up their response to the ceasefire.

Declaring the Union to be safe, the CLMC declared a loyalist ceasefire. They offered 'the loved ones of all innocent victims over the past 25 years abject and true remorse'.

Speaking in Belfast, Major said it was now his government's 'working assumption' that the IRA intended the ceasefire to be permanent. He lifted orders excluding Adams and McGuinness from Britain and announced the reopening of border roads.

Troops were withdrawn from street patrolling in Londonderry and County Tyrone towns. In Belfast, the RUC patrolled without flak jackets.

The Forum for Peace and Reconciliation set up by Reynolds opened in Dublin Castle. Its members included both constitutional nationalists and Sinn Féin.

November The Clinton administration announced an aid package for NI.

Newry post office worker Frank Kerr was killed by the IRA during an armed robbery. The IRA said its 31 August ceasefire statement stood. Adams expressed 'shock and regret' while McGuinness described the incident as 'very wrong'. The release of nine IRA prisoners in the Republic was suspended.

Reynolds resigned as Taoiseach and leader of Fianna Fáil. Bertie Ahern was elected as new leader of Fianna Fáil.

December The British government announced that exploratory dialogue with Sinn Féin would begin on 7 December. Clinton appointed George Mitchell as his economic envoy to NI.

Adams said it was unlikely weapons would be decommissioned 'short of a political settlement'.

The first official meeting took place between British government officials and Sinn Féin. Decommissioning of arms was identified as a major stumbling block.

1994

Acting Taoiseach Albert Reynolds said it was not 'a sensible precondition' to require the IRA to hand in weapons before multilateral talks.

Major said 'huge progress' would have to be made towards the destruction of IRA arms before exploratory talks with Sinn Féin could become formal.

Fine Gael leader John Bruton was elected Taoiseach in a coalition involving Labour and Democratic Left.

Delegations from the PUP and UDP met Stormont officials.

Bruton and Adams met and shook hands.

In what was seen as a policy reversal, Bruton said it was important not to get into a standoff over IRA arms.

A second meeting took place at Stormont between Sinn Féin and the NIO. Sinn Féin said the question of IRA weapons was best addressed at all-party talks.

After meeting Bruton at Downing Street, Major said 'substantial progress' was required on IRA weapons. Bruton cautioned against a one-item agenda.

Forty-six mortars were discovered by gardaí outside Longford.

Nine postponed prison releases in the south went ahead.

Major said Sinn Féin promises on arms would not be enough: there had to be 'significant progress' before the British and other parties would join Sinn Féin at the talks table. McGuinness called this 'ludicrous'.

1995

January

It was announced that daytime army patrols in Belfast would end.

The NIO announced the end of the ban on ministers meeting Sinn Féin, the UDP and PUP.

The NIO announced that weapons decommissioning was not a precondition to Sinn Féin participation in talks.

February

The Irish government released another five IRA prisoners.

A meeting between NIO officials and Sinn Féin at Stormont was called off after the party claimed the

1995   room was bugged.
                            **The document *Frameworks for the Future* was
                            released by the two governments.**

        March   **Mayhew outlined conditions for Sinn Féin joining
                            all-party talks, including 'actual decommissioning
                            of some arms'.**
                            The British government criticised Clinton's invitation
                            to Adams to attend a St Patrick's Day reception.
                            The UUP rejected the framework document.
                            UDP representatives attended the Clinton St Patrick's
                            Day reception and met officials of the US
                            administration.
                            The UUP's ruling council re-elected Molyneaux, but
                            15 per cent of votes cast went to a largely unknown
                            'stalking horse' candidate.
                            Ancram met the UDP and PUP.

        April   SDLP, UUP and DUP leaders met in preparation for
                            a new round of inter-party talks.

        May   **Mayhew met Adams in Washington during
                            Clinton's economic conference.**
                            Prince Charles paid a two-day visit to the Republic.

        June   Sinn Féin pulled out of talks with the government.
                            The RUC again rerouted an Orange march away
                            from Belfast's lower Ormeau Road.

        July   Private Lee Clegg, imprisoned for shooting dead
                            a teenage girl travelling in a stolen car, was
                            released after serving four years of a life sentence.
                            Widespread rioting followed in many nationalist
                            areas.
                            A confrontation developed when the RUC prevented
                            Orangemen from marching along Portadown's
                            Garvaghy Road. Trouble followed in other loyalist
                            areas.
                            The RUC subsequently permitted the Orange march
                            to go down the Garvaghy Road despite the protests
                            of nationalist residents. Paisley and Trimble
                            celebrated the success by walking together through
                            crowds of cheering supporters.
                            A heavy RUC presence pushed an Orange march
                            through the Ormeau Road.
                            Hume said the IRA would 'get rid' of its weapons if

1995 Sinn Féin were included in talks.
Mayhew and Ancram met Adams and McGuinness.

August Reynolds said weapons decommissioning had not
been a major British demand in the talks which led to
the Downing Street Declaration.
Adams said republicans were ready to make 'critical
compromises' to achieve peace.
The CLMC said it would not initiate a return to
violence.
**Molyneaux announced his resignation as UUP
leader.**

September Adams and Mayhew met but the stalemate over talks
and weapons decommissioning remained
unresolved.
**Trimble was elected leader of the UUP, defeating
Taylor, Ken Maginnis and others.**
Mayhew met UDP and PUP representatives.

October Trimble met Bruton in Dublin.
Mayhew told the Conservative party conference that
the two governments were considering inviting an
international commission to help resolve the
decommissioning dispute.
At the UUP conference Trimble announced outline
plans to end the Orange Order's block of delegates to
the party council.

November Trimble met Clinton in Washington.
The NIO published a paper, *Building Blocks*. It
proposed all-party preparatory talks and an
international body to consider decommissioning.
New legislation came into effect restoring 50 per cent
remission on sentences other than life sentences.
A referendum in the south narrowly confirmed the
right to divorce.
The twin-track initiative launched preparatory talks
as well as an International Body to examine
decommissioning.
Clinton shook hands with Adams during a visit to
Belfast in which the US president was greeted by
large cheering crowds.

December The British and Irish governments sent separate talks
invitations to the NI parties.

1995   It was announced that Belfast's Crumlin Road prison
                            was to close.
                            Robinson said that Sinn Féin could not be admitted
                            to talks before the surrender of all weapons.
                            Direct Action Against Drugs, believed to be an IRA
                            cover name, claimed the killing of an alleged drugs
                            dealer in Belfast. It was one in a series of such
                            shootings.

1996

January   The IRA killed a man in Lurgan using the DAAD
               cover name.
               The NI Tourist Board reported that the number of
               tourist visitors in 1995 had been 68 per cent higher
               than in 1994.
               British and Irish ministers met Sinn Féin leaders at
               Stormont.
               **The Mitchell Commission recommended that talks
               and weapons decommissioning should occur in
               parallel. In response Major announced plans for
               elections in NI. This was strongly criticised by the
               Irish government and the SDLP.**

February   The Irish government proposed proximity talks in
               which the various delegations would meet ministers
               but not each other.
               **The IRA ceasefire ended after eighteen months
               with the bombing of London's Canary Wharf
               district, killing two men and causing enormous
               damage.
               The Irish government suspended ministerial
               meetings with Sinn Féin and halted the release of
               IRA prisoners.**
               An IRA member died when a bomb he was carrying
               exploded prematurely on a London bus. Eight people
               were injured.
               Hume and Adams met members of the IRA Army
               Council.
               **Major and Bruton announced that talks would start
               on 10 June to decide the format of the proposed
               elections. Sinn Féin would be excluded in the
               absence of a ceasefire.**

March   The UUP and DUP said they would not attend talks

1996   which included Dick Spring.
                            The SDLP, Alliance and UDP met Mayhew and
                            Spring for talks. Sinn Féin was barred from entering
                            them.
                            The Irish and British governments disagreed on the
                            election method for the proposed NI forum.
                            An IRA spokesman told *Republican News* there would
                            be no decommissioning before a final settlement.
                            The NI Police Authority published its
                            recommendations on changes to the RUC. There
                            should be no change to the name, uniform, oath or
                            centralised structure but the name 'RUC – Northern
                            Ireland's police service' could be printed on
                            letterheads, it suggested.
                            The Irish Forum for Peace and Reconciliation was
                            adjourned pending a future ceasefire.

April   Loyalists rioted after the RUC blocked another
                            Orange march on the Ormeau Road.
                            An IRA bomb failed to detonate under London's
                            Hammersmith Bridge.

May   **Elections took place to the new NI Forum.
                            An IRA statement said there would be no
                            decommissioning in advance of an overall political
                            settlement. The Irish and British governments
                            announced details of multi-party talks.**

June   **Major and Bruton opened preliminary all-party
                            talks at Stormont chaired by Mitchell but without
                            Sinn Féin. The DUP at first refused to accept
                            Mitchell as chairman.**
                            The NI Forum met for the first time in Belfast.
                            **200 people were injured when a large IRA bomb
                            exploded in Manchester.**
                            Irish police found an IRA bomb factory in County
                            Laois and arrested five men. The Irish government
                            ended all contacts with Sinn Féin.
                            Three mortar bombs were fired by the IRA at a
                            British army base in Germany.

July   **Orangemen were prevented from marching along
                            Garvaghy Road at Drumcree, Portadown. A
                            Catholic taxi driver was shot dead near Lurgan.
                            Four days of loyalist roadblocks and disturbances
                            ensued.**

1996

The UUP, DUP and others withdrew from the talks in protest at the ban on the Drumcree march. Loyalist rioting and disruption were widespread.

The RUC reversed the Drumcree ban and forced the march down Garvaghy Road. Rioting followed in nationalist areas.

The RUC sealed off the lower Ormeau Road to allow an Orange march. Rioting intensified in nationalist areas.

The SDLP announced its intention to withdraw from the NI Forum.

Mayhew announced a review of marches in NI as disputes over parade routes escalated in many places.

August
Ronnie Flanagan was named as the new RUC Chief Constable, succeeding Sir Hugh Annesley.

September
A sixth INLA member was killed in the internal feud which had broken out in January.

The NI Forum resumed in the absence of the SDLP and Sinn Féin. Members voted to fly the Union flag while the Forum was in session.

Loyalists began picketing Catholic church services, particularly in County Antrim, in retaliation for nationalist protests against Orange parades.

An IRA man was killed and five men were arrested in police raids in London. Arms and explosives were found.

October
An IRA bomb attack on army headquarters in Lisburn, County Antrim, fatally injured a soldier. It was the first IRA bomb in NI since 1994.

November
The congregation at a Catholic church at Harryville, Ballymena, was attacked by loyalists.

December
An RUC officer was shot and wounded by the IRA at the Royal Victoria Hospital, Belfast, as he protected DUP politician Nigel Dodds who was visiting his terminally ill son.

1997

January
There was disruption in Belfast as a result of twenty bomb alerts.

The DUP attempted to have the loyalist parties

1997   excluded from the talks.

The IRA fired mortar bombs at an RUC patrol in Downpatrick.

The committee reviewing the marching issue recommended the creation of an independent parades commission.

February   Ken Maginnis called on the government to apologise for the Bloody Sunday deaths.

Bombardier Stephen Restorick was killed by the IRA in south Armagh.

Mayhew ruled out either an apology for or inquiry into Bloody Sunday.

March   Orange halls were firebombed in several places.

April   Adams said a vote for Sinn Féin was a vote for peace.

May   **The general election put Labour and Tony Blair in 10 Downing Street. It also returned Adams as MP for West Belfast and McGuinness as MP for Mid Ulster.**

Blair named Mo Mowlam as NI Secretary.

Catholic Robert Hamill was beaten to death by loyalists in Portadown.

An RUC officer was shot dead in Belfast by the INLA.

Blair visited Northern Ireland and gave the go-ahead for exploratory contacts between government officials and Sinn Féin.

June   An RUC officer was beaten to death by a loyalist mob in Ballymoney, County Antrim.

Sinn Féin was barred from entering the resumed inter-party talks at Stormont. The Loyalist Volunteer Force and Continuity Army Council were banned.

A general election in the Republic led to the creation of a coalition between Fianna Fáil and the Progressive Democrats led by Bertie Ahern.

The Queen visited NI.

Two RUC officers were shot dead in Lurgan.

The governments tabled proposals for weapons decommissioning.

July   **Adams announced that he had asked the IRA for a new ceasefire. A few days later the IRA announced**

1997   another cessation.

Mowlam met Garvaghy Road residents and Orange leaders in advance of the annual confrontation over the Drumcree Orange parade.

The RUC decision to force the march down the Garvaghy Road led to days of rioting in nationalist areas across NI.

A teenage Catholic girl was shot dead at the home of her Protestant boyfriend in Aghalee, County Antrim.

The DUP withdrew from talks.

Ahern, Hume and Adams met in Dublin and reaffirmed a commitment to 'exclusively democratic and peaceful methods'.

A Northern Ireland select committee of the Commons was set up.

August   Mowlam met a Sinn Féin delegation.

Sinn Féin leaders were granted US visas for a fundraising trip.

Gardaí found an IRA bomb factory in County Cavan.

An Independent Commission on Decommissioning, headed by Canadian General John de Chastelain, was established to oversee the weapons issue.

Mowlam pronounced the IRA ceasefire sufficient to allow Sinn Féin to join talks.

September   **Sinn Féin signed up to the Mitchell Principles of non-violence and entered all-party talks. The IRA later said it had 'problems' with the principles.**

The UUP's ruling council left decisions on the talks to Trimble and his colleagues.

A bomb planted by the dissident republican Continuity IRA in Markethill, County Armagh, caused widespread damage.

The Ulster Unionists joined the talks, emphasising that they wanted to 'confront' Sinn Féin not negotiate with them. Party members walked into the talks accompanied by PUP and UDP delegations.

After some dispute the two governments agreed on the composition of the international decommissioning body to be chaired by de Chastelain.

The first in a series of DUP rallies was held in the Ulster Hall.

1997   October   McGuinness said Sinn Féin was 'going to the
negotiating table to smash the Union'.
Substantive negotiations began at Stormont with the
participation of eight parties and the two
governments. Irish Foreign Minister Ray Burke
resigned and was replaced by David Andrews.
Andrews said that he imagined a united Ireland in
his lifetime 'won't be achievable'.
The Police Authority invited Sinn Féin to talks.
**Adams and McGuinness met Blair for the first time
at Stormont's Castle Buildings. Hours later the
prime minister was mobbed by an angry crowd of
loyalists at a shopping centre in east Belfast.**
Mary McAleese was elected Irish president, the first
to have been born in NI.

November   Flanagan said the IRA ceasefire was 'holding firm'.
Security forces reduced patrolling, particularly
by the army. Troops were withdrawn from
west Belfast.

December   **Adams and McGuinness made their first visit to
Downing Street.**
The Stormont talks were adjourned for Christmas,
the parties having failed to reach agreement on an
agenda.
UUP MP Jeffrey Donaldson said he was advising
party leader Trimble to withdraw from the talks
because of the 'concessions train'. Four UUP MPs
wrote to Trimble expressing their concern over UUP
participation.
**LVF leader Billy 'King Rat' Wright was shot dead
in the Maze prison by the INLA. In the resulting
upsurge of violence seven Catholics and a
Protestant were shot dead. The LVF was blamed for
many of the killings, though there was suspicion of
mainstream loyalist and IRA involvement.**

1998

January   **Mowlam visited the Maze prison to persuade UDA
inmates not to turn against the peace process.**
Sinn Féin formally rejected the two governments'
new proposals for a settlement.
The IRA rejected the Anglo-Irish proposals, accusing

1998   the governments of giving in to Unionist demands.
Ulster Unionists warned that if the government
backtracked on the proposals they would withdraw
from the talks.
Flanagan said he believed the UDA had been
involved in recent killings, putting pressure on the
PM to review the place of the UDA's political allies,
the Ulster Democratic Party, in the Stormont talks.
A bomb planted by the Continuity IRA exploded
outside a nightclub in Enniskillen, County
Fermanagh.
The talks moved to London for a week. **The UDP
was temporarily excluded because of UDA
violence.**
**Blair announced a new inquiry under Lord Saville
into the Bloody Sunday deaths.**
The LVF announced that it would continue to target
'known republicans'.

February   An alleged drugs dealer was shot dead outside a
south Belfast restaurant. The IRA was believed
responsible.
A UDA member was shot dead in Dunmurry, south
Belfast, where another UDA man had been killed
weeks earlier. Republicans were blamed for the
shooting, and there were calls for Sinn Féin to be
thrown out of the talks.
Adams insisted the IRA ceasefire was intact. He
warned that peace process would fail if Sinn Féin
were expelled.
**Sinn Féin was suspended from the talks because of
Flanagan's assessment that the IRA had been
involved in recent killings.**
A car bomb which damaged the village of Moira,
County Down, was blamed on the Continuity IRA.
**A Sinn Féin challenge to this expulsion in the
Irish courts was unsuccessful.**
A large car bomb caused widespread damage in
Portadown.

March   Taylor said the 'general picture' of an agreement was
coming together. A settlement in weeks was possible,
Mowlam said.
A 600lb bomb was foundin County Louth.
European Commission President Jacques Santer

1998

visited NI and promised European aid for peace efforts.

Two men were shot dead by the LVF in a bar in Poyntzpass, County Armagh.

Irish minister Liz O'Donnell said Articles 2 and 3 would be 'amended not dropped'.

Mowlam said: 'Agreement is within reach.'

Ahern said there was nothing to fear from change in the Irish constitution.

An LVF statement warned of more violence and specifically threatened 'collaborators'.

Sinn Féin called for a meeting with Blair before deciding to return to talks.

Mortar bombs were fired in Armagh.

Two men were charged with the Poyntzpass killings. The SDLP met Blair in Downing Street. Hume said a deal must be done soon. Subsequently a joint government paper on British–Irish relations was released to the parties.

Blair met Adams at Downing Street in an attempt to get the peace process back on track. Blair said agreement was 'agonisingly close' and that he was 'stubbornly optimistic', but Paisley, speaking to the Chamber of Commerce, accused them of paying ransom to terrorism. He said the talks were 'dead in the water'. Clinton pledged a push for peace.

The UUP repeated its demand for the continued exclusion of Sinn Féin. Mowlam said NI was 'on the brink of an historic opportunity', and there were widespread reports that Blair would take charge of the final stage of talks.

One of four men awaiting trial for the Poyntzpass killings was killed in the Maze prison by LVF prisoners.

Trimble and Adams attended a British embassy lunch in Washington.

Mowlam told a US media breakfast that she was unsure if Sinn Féin would settle. 'Do it now,' said Clinton.

There was Unionist anger when Sinn Féin announced that it would return to the talks.

A 1200lb bomb was found in Dundalk. Gardaí said it was intended for an attack in NI, probably by dissident republicans.

1998   Adams said a deal was possible in three weeks and
said he wanted Sinn Féin to be part of it.
Mitchell released a paper on north–south relations.
Talks resumed and Sinn Féin returned, Paisley
demonstrating outside the gates.
**After the talks resumed Mitchell set a deadline of
9 April for agreement, saying: 'The time for
discussion is over. It is now time for decision.'**
Ahern reassured Fianna Fáil backbenchers that
constitutional change would only be as part of a
balanced deal, and said there would be no deal
without Sinn Féin.
Mitchell said talks could succeed by 9 May.
An intense round of bilateral party meetings took
place at Stormont.

April   Ahern said there were 'large disagreements' with
London over the powers of cross-border bodies,
adding, 'I don't think we can cloak that fact. I don't
know whether we can surmount this.' The two
governments and Trimble took part in intensive
negotiations.
Mowlam said there would have to be reform of the
RUC.
Gardaí found a huge fertiliser bomb in a car bound
for Britain from a port near Dublin.
Ahern said: 'The Irish government will not be
moving any further. David Trimble would need to
understand that my compromises are completed. The
Framework Document is what has to stand.'
Mitchell released a sixty-two-page draft document,
asking the parties to observe complete secrecy over
its contents.
An Adams newspaper article said history could be
made but the deal would be 'transitional'. Paisley
said the UUP was selling out, while Sinn Féin
admitted there had been twelve protest resignations
from its ranks.

7 April   The UUP rejected as 'too green' the draft from
Mitchell, creating an air of crisis. The party said the
Mitchell paper amounted to a 'Sinn Féin wish list'.
Adams said it was time for Trimble to 'grow up and
negotiate properly'.
Within hours Blair announced he was flying to

1998   Belfast. On his arrival he said, 'I feel the hand of
                            history upon our shoulders.'

8 April   Ahern arrived at Stormont for a series of meetings
                            before returning to Dublin for his mother's funeral
                            then flying back to Belfast. At Stormont he said: 'It
                            requires everybody to move a little bit and we are all
                            prepared to do that.' Meanwhile intense activity
                            continued between the governments and parties.
                            Mowlam ended the day on an optimistic note, saying
                            progress had been made 'on all fronts'.
                            The PUP's David Ervine described the Mitchell paper
                            as 'unacceptable, unreasonable, unworkable'. His
                            colleague Billy Hutchinson said, 'We are talking
                            about people going back to war.'
                            Paisley arrived at Stormont in mid-afternoon and
                            said: 'No matter what happens at these talks there is
                            not going to be peace, there is going to be war.'
                            Four UUP MPs congratulated the party for rejecting
                            the document, saying it 'cannot be amended to make
                            it acceptable to the Unionist electorate'.

9 April   Blair spoke of an 'irresistible force' which he believed
                            would overcome the 'immovable object' of conflict.
                            The midnight deadline passed with no deal.
                            Flanagan said: 'If there is a settlement it will
                            undoubtedly have a very significant and positive
                            effect' but added that it would not mean an
                            immediate end to violence.
                            At 6 p.m. Trimble went to party headquarters to brief
                            the party executive and received backing in a two-
                            hour meeting.
                            At 8 p.m. PUP representative William Smith went to
                            the Maze prison to brief loyalist prisoners.
                            Paisley repeated that Trimble would be 'finished' as
                            a Unionist leader. He gave a stormy midnight press
                            conference where he was heckled by PUP and UDP
                            members who shouted, 'Your days are over,
                            dinosaur.'
                            Clinton telephoned the participants at regular
                            intervals through the night.

10 April   There was an apparent breakthrough at about 2 a.m.
                            as the UUP and the SDLP resolved differences. At
                            2.30 a.m. Clinton spoke to Adams. At 3 a.m. Taylor

1998

put the chances of an agreement being reached at 75 per cent.

A Blair letter was provided to reassure UUP members on decommissioning. This had been requested by Trimble in the face of opposition from colleagues. Trimble reportedly told colleagues: 'I am doing it.' At 4.45 p.m. Trimble telephoned Blair and Mitchell to inform them.

Jeffrey Donaldson withdrew, leaving Stormont before the speeches.

Former UVF prisoner Gusty Spence said the parties were now 'exorcising the ghosts of history'.

Trimble said: 'The question now for Mr Adams is will he accept the consent principle and also to say whether his dirty, squalid little terrorist war is over.'

Mitchell announced the agreement to a plenary session of the party delegations and through television to the NI public: 'If you support this agreement, and if you also reject the merchants of death and the purveyors of hate, if you make it clear to your political leaders that you want them to make it work, then it will. The choice is yours. I am dying to leave, but I hate to go.'

Trimble said it was 'a great opportunity to start a healing process. I have risen from this table with the Union stronger than when I sat down.'

The Queen congratulated Blair by phone on the deal. A statement from Buckingham Palace on behalf of the Queen said: 'Naturally she shares everyone's delight at the outcome.' Paisley protested at the royal support for the agreement.

Robinson said it was 'a turbo-charged model of Sunningdale, the Anglo-Irish Agreement with a vengeance, a fully armed version of the Framework Document'.

11 April   Trimble received UUP executive backing by 55 votes to 23 after a four-hour meeting.

13 April   The Pope told an audience at his summer residence outside Rome: 'I wish to invite you to thank God for the positive results reached in recent days in Northern Ireland.'

16 April   Trimble said the Good Friday Agreement was 'as

1998   good as it gets'.

18 April   The UUP ruling council supported the agreement by 540 votes to 210.

24 April   The NI Forum met for the last time.

26 April   Ahern said the British government was 'effectively out of the equation' on the future of NI.

27 April   Former Hong Kong governor Chris Patten was named as chairman of the Independent Commission on Policing.

30 April   The IRA said it had no plans to decommission.

May   UUP MP William Thompson called on Trimble to resign.
A special Sinn Féin ard fheis voted overwhelmingly to support the agreement and allow members to take seats in the assembly. The presence of some members of the Balcombe Street gang, who had served long sentences for a 1970s bombing campaign in London, provoked a Unionist outcry.
The agreement was approved in referendums on both sides of the border. In NI 71.1 per cent voted in favour. In the Republic, 94.4 per cent backed the agreement, in addition voting to drop the state's constitutional claim to the north. An exit poll in NI suggested that 96 per cent of Catholics and 55 per cent of Protestants voted yes.

June   The IRA's leader in the Maze prison was quoted as saying that after arrangements outlined in the agreement came into effect, 'a voluntary decommissioning of weapons would be a natural development of the peace process'.
In elections to the new assembly, supporters of the deal won eighty seats and opponents won twenty-eight.
The Parades Commission announced that the Orange Order would not be allowed to march along Garvaghy Road, Portadown, in July.

July   **The assembly met for the first time. Trimble was elected First Minister designate and the SDLP's Séamus Mallon was elected Deputy First Minister designate.**

1998   Ten Catholic churches across NI were attacked.
                     Days of rioting, roadblocks and disturbances
                     followed the ban on the Orange march at Drumcree.
                     In a loyalist arson attack in Ballymoney, County
                     Antrim, three young Catholic children were killed.
                     The legislation allowing for the early release of
                     prisoners under the Good Friday Agreement came
                     into force.

August   A Real IRA bomb damaged the centre of Banbridge,
                     County Down.
                     The LVF announced a ceasefire. The organisation
                     had not been included in the early release scheme.
                     **A Real IRA car bomb in Omagh killed 29 people. It
                     was the single deadliest attack of the troubles.**
                     The Real IRA announced a ceasefire.
                     The INLA announced a ceasefire.

September   Sinn Féin said it considered violence to be a thing of
                     the past. McGuinness was nominated to talk to the
                     arms decommissioning body.
                     Blair and Clinton travelled to Omagh to view the
                     scene of the explosion and meet some of the relatives
                     of the dead.
                     Clinton and Blair also met assembly members at
                     Stormont.
                     Trimble promised to create a 'pluralist parliament for
                     a pluralist people'.
                     Ahern suggested that a timetable should be
                     established for the handover of weapons.

October   RUC officer Frank O'Reilly died as a result of injuries
                     caused by a loyalist blast bomb in Portadown.
                     Trimble told the UUP conference that Sinn Féin could
                     not join an executive without IRA decommissioning.
                     Hume told the SDLP conference that
                     decommissioning was not a precondition for
                     implementation of the Good Friday Agreement but
                     that it was the will of the people that it should take
                     place.
                     On RTÉ radio Ahern said there was irresistible
                     movement towards Irish unity and that it would
                     occur within twenty years.

December   **Hume and Trimble received the Nobel peace prize
                     in Oslo.**

1998   Agreement was reached on the structure of the
                            executive and of the cross-border bodies.
                            The LVF handed over some weapons for destruction.

1999

            January   The UUP warned that an IRA failure to
                            decommission would force a renegotiation of the
                            Good Friday Agreement.
                            Catholic applications to the RUC were reported to
                            have doubled since the 1994 ceasefires.
                            Plans were announced by the UUP for a committee
                            to review the Orange Order's link with the party.
                            A member of the UUP assembly party lost the whip
                            for opposing party policy in the assembly.
                            The RUC announced the closure of seven border
                            army bases.

            February   **The assembly voted to confirm the new
                            government departments and cross-border bodies.**

            March   The NI Human Rights Commission came into being.
                            Blair called for IRA decommissioning to begin in
                            order to clear the way for Sinn Féin to join the
                            executive.
                            **The Dublin and London governments signed
                            treaties establishing the new north–south, British–
                            Irish and intergovernmental arrangements. The
                            1985 Anglo-Irish Agreement was superseded by the
                            new treaties.**
                            Lurgan solicitor Rosemary Nelson was killed by a
                            loyalist boobytrap bomb placed under her car.
                            The Chief Constable of Kent and the FBI were asked
                            by the RUC to help in the investigation of the Nelson
                            killing.
                            John Stevens, Deputy Commissioner of the
                            Metropolitan Police, was asked by the RUC to
                            investigate the 1989 killing of solicitor Pat Finucane.
                            Hume donated his £286,000 Nobel prize money to
                            charitable organisations.
                            Prolonged talks took place at Hillsborough Castle on
                            decommissioning and the formation of an executive.

            April   The Hillsborough talks continued but remained at
                            stalemate. The London and Dublin governments
                            produced a declaration calling for a collective act of

1999

reconciliation and the putting beyond use of some weapons on a voluntary basis.

Trimble met the Pope in a ceremony with other Nobel prize winners.

It was reported that UUP party chairman Dennis Rogan faced expulsion from the Orange Order for attending the funeral mass of three Omagh victims.

May

An alleged drugs dealer was shot dead in a Newry bar. Suspicion fell on the IRA.

The Church of Ireland synod called on the Drumcree church vestry to withdraw the annual invitation to the Orange Order if it did not give assurance about their conduct.

The Drumcree rector made it clear that his church would not accept the synod recommendation.

The body of Eamon Molloy, one of the so-called 'disappeared', was found in County Louth. The body of the man, who had been missing since 1975, had been recovered by the IRA and left in a coffin in a cemetery.

June

A Protestant woman, Elizabeth O'Neill, was killed by a pipe bomb thrown into her house in Portadown by loyalists.

Another alleged drug dealer was shot dead by the IRA in County Down.

Trimble called on Blair to sack Mowlam for allegedly turning a blind eye to repeated IRA ceasefire violations.

A Blair plan to resolve the decommissioning stalemate was rejected by the UUP.

The Parades Commission again rerouted the July Orange march away from Garvaghy Road.

Blair's deadline passed without agreement on decommissioning.

Another two of the bodies of the 'disappeared' were recovered.

July

Blair and Ahern set out a plan entitled *The Way Forward* under which devolution would begin on 15 July. Within days decommissioning would begin, to be completed by May 2000. Clinton urged all sides to accept the arrangement.

The Parades Commission allowed the Orange Order

1999   to switch its main gathering to Belfast's Ormeau
                             Park.
                             **The UUP rejected Blair's urging that it should join
                             a devolved government before the IRA started to
                             give up guns. Mowlam called on the assembly to
                             meet on 15 July to nominate an executive.**
                             **UUP members boycotted Stormont as the executive
                             was nominated causing it to be declared invalid for
                             lacking sufficient cross-community membership.
                             Mallon resigned as Deputy First Minister.**
                             Adams said delays in setting up the executive made
                             it almost impossible to meet a decommissioning
                             deadline of May 2000.
                             Arrests were made in the US over alleged IRA
                             transatlantic gun-running.
                             The IRA was blamed for the killing of west Belfast
                             man Charles Bennett.

August   **In a formal judgement Mowlam said she did not
                             believe the IRA ceasefire was breaking down. She
                             added however that the position of the IRA was
                             deeply worrying, warning that she had 'come very
                             close to judging the IRA's ceasefire is no longer for
                             real'.**

September   **Recalled by Blair and Ahern as a facilitator,
                             Mitchell began a review of the peace process.
                             Unionists reacted angrily to publication of the
                             Patten report, which proposed far-reaching changes
                             to policing and the RUC, including changing its
                             name to the Police Service of Northern Ireland.**
                             Michelle Williamson, whose parents died in the
                             1993 Shankill Road bomb, was granted the right to
                             seek a judicial review of Mowlam's ceasefire
                             decision.

October   **Peter Mandelson replaced Mowlam as Northern
                             Ireland Secretary.**
                             Adams called for UUP flexibility on the arms issue.
                             UUP elements warned they would resist any move
                             away from the party's 'no guns, no government'
                             policy.
                             Former MI5 officer Michael Oatley described the
                             demands for decommissioning as an 'excuse to avoid
                             the pursuit of peace'.

1999 November   There were suggestions that Trimble was prepared to
take the risk of accepting a deal with Sinn Féin.
Mitchell insisted parties 'now understand each
other's concerns and requirements far better than
before'.
The UUP and Sinn Féin both expressed a desire to set
up an inclusive executive. Pressure mounted on
Trimble from anti-Agreement Unionists.
The IRA said it was ready to discuss
decommissioning and would appoint a
representative to the de Chastelain decommissioning
body.
Mitchell concluded his review saying that the basis
existed for decommissioning and coalition
government.
Mandelson told the Commons that he would freeze
the workings of the Good Friday Agreement if the
IRA did not deliver on arms decommissioning.
It was announced that the RUC would be awarded
the George Cross.
**The UUP ruling council voted to accept a
leadership compromise paving the way for the
executive to operate. Trimble promised he would
return to seek the support of the party council in
February 2000. He revealed he had given a senior
party official a post-dated letter of resignation as
First Minister to come into effect in the event of
inadequate movement on arms.
The executive was formed, with Trimble at its head
and Mallon as his deputy. Ten other ministers were
appointed, two of them from Sinn Féin and two
from the DUP. The DUP said they would function
as ministers but would not attend executive
meetings.**

1 December   **Devolution was restored at midnight.**

2 December   **The Irish government formally amended Articles 2
and 3 of the Irish constitution laying claim to NI.
The IRA appointed an interlocutor to the
decommissioning body.**
Adams displayed a security forces electronic bugging
device which had been discovered attached to a car
used by Sinn Féin leaders.
De Chastelain issued an upbeat report saying that

1999
recent events and meetings 'provide the basis for an assessment that decommissioning will occur'.
The RUC announced the planned closure of Castlereagh holding centre.
The Irish cabinet met members of the NI executive in the first meeting of the north–south ministerial council.

2000

January
Loyalist Richard Jameson was shot dead in Portadown, apparently as part of a UVF–LVF feud.
De Chastelain met the two governments to deliver a report on progress on decommissioning. It was not immediately published, Blair reporting to the Commons that insufficient progress had been made.
Trimble made clear his intention to resign in the absence of progess on decommissioning in advance of his party council's meeting in February.
The governments continued to press Sinn Féin on decommissioning.

February
Mandelson announced the suspension of devolution and a return to direct rule. This led to major controversy and recrimination from nationalists and republicans. Sinn Féin said a major advance on decommissioning had been outlined in a new IRA statement.
The government welcomed the new IRA statement as a significant development.
The Ulster Unionist Council endorsed Trimble's handling of the issue.
The IRA announced its withdrawal from arms talks, saying proposals on arms were now off the table.
Talks began on ways to resolve the crisis.
The bodies of two young men from the Portadown area were found at the nearby village of Tandragee. The killings were thought to be part of the loyalist feud in the area.

March
In Washington for St Patrick's Day, Trimble told a press conference that the executive might be formed again without prior IRA decommissioning if there were firm guarantees that decommissioning would take place. There was widespread condemnation of his move from critics in the

2000   **Unionist party.**
Martin Smyth announced his intention to challenge
Trimble for the party leadership at the next party
council meeting.
**Trimble defeated Smyth by 57 per cent to 43 per
cent. The council also committed the party to refuse
to re-enter the executive unless the government
abandoned its plan to drop the name of the RUC.**

April   Trimble again announced that a review would
reconsider the question of the Orange Order's seats
on the party council.
Blair visited Belfast and Dublin.

May   Blair and Ahern spent two days at Hillsborough
Castle meeting local parties. The two governments
then announced the target date of 22 May for a return
to devolution. They called on armed groups to make
a commitment to put weapons beyond use.
The IRA issued a statement saying that if the Good
Friday Agreement were fully implemented they
would 'completely and verifiably put IRA weapons
beyond use'. They also agreed to a number of arms
dumps being monitored by international figures as a
confidence-building measure.
Trimble said the IRA statement 'does appear to break
new ground'.
Cyril Ramaphosa, former secretary-general of the
African National Congress of South Africa, and
former Finnish president Martti Ahtisaari, were
named as monitors of IRA arms dumps.
The closure of selected security bases around
Northern Ireland continued.
A man was shot dead in Belfast, apparently a victim
of the continuing UVF–LVF loyalist feud.
**On 27 May the Ulster Unionist Council approved
rejoining the executive on the basis of the IRA arms
offer. The voting was 459 to 403, a 53–47 per cent
split.**
At midnight on 29 May devolution was restored.
The two DUP ministers resumed office but the party
announced that if an assembly vote did not bring
down the executive they would resign their executive
offices, allowing other DUP members to take their
places in rotation.

2000   An alleged drugs dealer was shot dead in south
                      Belfast, apparently by the IRA.
                      Tom Constantine, former head of the US Drug
                      Enforcement Agency, was appointed as oversight
                      commissioner as part of the implementation of the
                      Patten report on policing.

June   Blair wrote to the wife of one of the Guildford Four
                      personally apologising for the imprisonment of the
                      four for the Guildford and Woolwich pub bombings.
                      Flanagan said the RUC appeared to be involved in
                      the May killing of an alleged drugs dealer.
                      **A number of IRA arms dumps were inspected and
                      secured by the international monitors. Sinn Féin
                      president Gerry Adams said of the development:
                      'In 200 years there has not been an initiative like
                      this.' Blair described the move as a 'very substantial
                      further step' towards a permanent peace.**
                      Hooded and armed UDA members threatened
                      an end to their ceasefire, accusing nationalists
                      of attacking Protestant homes in north and
                      west Belfast.
                      Around 2,000 troops were drafted into NI in
                      preparation for possible loyalist disturbances during
                      the Orange marching season.
                      A South African human rights lawyer, Brian Currin,
                      was involved in efforts to mediate between
                      Portadown's Catholic residents and the Orange
                      Order.

July   The Northern Ireland Parades Commission banned
                      the Drumcree march. The commission said a limited
                      parade could take place within three to eight months,
                      but only if the Order complied with a number of
                      conditions. These included the opening of dialogue
                      with Catholic residents and the avoidance of
                      anything which might raise tensions.
                      The Order called for thousands of loyalists to take to
                      the streets in protest against the ban. Nights of
                      widespread loyalist violence followed. Dozens of
                      roads were blocked by protests and barricades in
                      many areas, with clashes between rioters and police.
                      Harold Gracey, head of the Order in Portadown,
                      refused to condemn the violence. He declared: 'I am
                      not going to condemn violence because Gerry Adams

2000

never condemns it.' The Order's senior leaders refrained from endorsing his call and condemned the violence. Its Grand Master, Robert Saulters, said rioters were damaging the Order and should cease immediately.

In the days leading up to the Twelfth of July processions Portadown Orangemen announced plans to bring NI to a complete halt as part of the Drumcree protest.

Released UDA prisoner Johnny Adair appeared at Drumcree with supporters.

Archbishop Robin Eames, head of the Church of Ireland, said paramilitary involvement had 'removed any integrity which the Drumcree protest might have had'. He called on Portadown Orangemen to issue an immediate and unequivocal call for all violence to cease.

The Order succeeded in bringing much of NI to a standstill, paralysing economic life for short periods. Scores of roads were blocked and in some places there were violent clashes with the security forces.

The Orange Order's main Twelfth of July processions passed off peacefully, though they were preceded by a night which brought a killing, stabbings, and injuries to more than a score of RUC members. In the most serious incident a loyalist was shot dead by other loyalists in Larne, County Antrim.

It was announced that the Maze prison would be closed by the end of the year.

An arms consignment bound for dissident republicans was seized at the Croatian city of Split. A number of arrests were made.

The two DUP ministers on the executive resigned as part of the party's continued opposition to Sinn Féin involvement. Two other DUP members took up their executive posts.

The final prisoner releases were made under the Good Friday Agreement.

August

Sir Josias Cunningham, president of the Ulster Unionist party and an ally of its leader David Trimble, died in a road accident. He had been an important advocate of unity in the party.

In Londonderry an attempt by dissident republicans

2000

to stage a bombing in the run-up to a major loyalist parade in the city was foiled following a high-speed pursuit by police.

The RUC staged its last recruits passing-out parade before the force's planned transformation. The thirty-six new recruits were the last to join the RUC before it was overhauled by the recommendations of the Patten report.

A violent feud broke out between rival loyalist paramilitary groups, the UVF and UDA, centring on the Shankill area of Belfast. Following disturbances during a march on the Shankill Road two men were shot dead by the UVF and another was killed by the UDA.

In the weeks that followed houses and other premises were attacked in the Shankill and elsewhere. More than 160 families asked to be rehoused. Troops were drafted into the Shankill district, the first time in two years that they had appeared on Belfast streets.

Mandelson ordered the rearrest and jailing of UDA leader Johnny Adair, who had been released early under the terms of the Good Friday Agreement. The NI Secretary commented: 'My priority is public safety and I cannot give freedom to an individual intent on abusing it. I am satisfied that this particular individual has breached the terms of his licence.'

Hume announced that he would give up his assembly seat in the near future.

September

Former NI Secretary Mowlam announced she would stand down from parliament at the next general election.

The inquests opened into the deaths of the twenty-nine people killed in the 1998 Omagh bombing.

Dissident republicans launched a rocket attack on the London headquarters of MI6.

DUP candidate, the Reverend William McCrea, won the previously safe UUP South Antrim Westminster seat in a by-election.

October

Real IRA member Joseph O'Connor was shot dead in Belfast. The IRA was believed to have been responsible.

Trimble's UUP critics forced another meeting of the party council to reconsider involvement in the NI executive

2000   **There was a second inspection of IRA arms dumps by the international monitors.**

The UUP's ruling council narrowly supported Trimble after he announced a plan to exclude Sinn Féin ministers from north–south ministerial meetings unless significant progress was made on decommissioning IRA arms.

Three more people were killed in the continuing loyalist feud.

November   A loyalist feud killing took place on November 1st, the fourth in four days.

December   Two sectarian killings took place in the first days of the month.

President Clinton, in the last weeks of his presidency, visited both parts of Ireland for the third time.

The loyalist feud was declared to be at an end by the UDA and UVF.

The two Sinn Féin ministers initiated a legal challenge to their exclusion from north–south meetings.

A Protestant civilian was killed, apparently by the UDA. The killing was not believed to have been as part of the feud.

General de Chastelain issued a pessimistic report on the decommissioning process.

Ronnie Hill, who had been in a coma since the IRA bombing of a Remembrance Day ceremony in Enniskillen in 1987, died.

2001

January   Blair visited Belfast in an attempt to make progress on disputed issues such as decommissioning, demilitarisation and policing.

John Reid became Northern Ireland Secretary after the surprise resignation of Peter Mandelson.

A court ruled that Trimble had acted unlawfully in excluding the Sinn Féin ministers from north–south meetings. He lodged an appeal.

February   Bishop Edward Daly gave evidence to the Saville inquiry into Bloody Sunday, now moving into its third year.

2001   March   A Real IRA carbomb exploded outside a BBC building in London.
Blair and Ahern met local party leaders at Hillsborough.

April   A loyalist killing brought the feud death toll to sixteen in seventeen months.
Martin McGuinness confirmed he had been a leading member of the Derry IRA at the time of Bloody Sunday in 1972.

May   **For the second time Trimble wrote a letter of resignation, to take effect on 1 July in the absence of progress on decommissioning. The IRA announced that it had established regular contacts with General de Chastelain.**

June   **The UUP lost three of its nine Westminster seats in the Westminster general election while both the DUP and Sinn Féin made significant gains.**

July   **Trimble's resignation as First Minister came into effect, triggering rounds of negotiation, in particular at Weston Park in Shropshire.**
Repeated rioting broke out in a number of areas, in particular Ardoyne and elsewhere in north Belfast. Two youths were shot dead by loyalists.

August   **A method of decommissioning suggested by the IRA was accepted by General de Chastelain. The move was rejected by Trimble, who said actual decommissioning was required. Reid suspended the Good Friday Agreement for a day to allow a six-week period for talks.**
Three Irish republicans were arrested in Colombia, leading to a major clamour for an explanation of their association with FARC guerrillas.

September   Worldwide publicity was given to a loyalist protest in the Ardoyne area aimed at preventing Catholic schoolgirls from attending school.
John Hume announced his decision to stand down as SDLP leader on health grounds.
A second one-day suspension was announced to allow another six-week extension for talks. Trimble threatened to withdraw the UUP ministers from the executive.

TABLES

TABLES 1–4 are updated versions of material first published in *Lost Lives* (Mainstream Publishing, Edinburgh, 1999).

TABLE 5 totals the votes cast for Unionist and nationalist candidates in selected elections. It illustrates the narrowing of the gap between Unionist and nationalist votes over the years.

TABLE 1 DEATHS BY YEAR

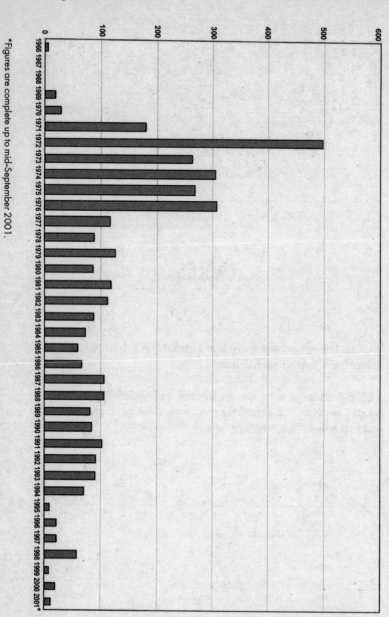

*Figures are complete up to mid-September 2001.

TABLE 2 DEATHS BY YEAR AND STATUS

	All Civilians	Protestant Civilians	Catholic Civilians	RUC	RUCR	UDR/RIR	ARMY	Paramilitaries Republican	Paramilitaries Loyalist	OTHER	TOTAL
1966	3	1	2	0	0	0	0	0	0	0	3
1967	0	0	0	0	0	0	0	0	0	0	0
1968	0	0	0	0	0	0	0	0	0	0	0
1969	15	6	9	1	0	0	0	2	0	0	19
1970	19	8	10	2	0	0	0	2	0	2	29
1971	94	27	65	11	0	5	44	23	0	2	180
1972	259	77	174	15	0	26	108	74	11	10	497
1973	132	48	80	9	0	8	59	38	13	4	263
1974	206	51	123	12	0	7	45	24	6	33	304
1975	173	62	100	7	1	7	15	31	28	13	267
1976	220	90	125	13	11	14	13	17	13	9	307
1977	55	21	32	8	6	16	15	8	7	5	116
1978	46	25	21	4	6	7	16	7	2	2	88
1979	44	15	22	9	5	10	37	9	2	16	125
1980	45	18	23	3	6	9	11	5	2	9	86
1981	54	18	34	13	8	13	32	16	0	2	118
1982	47	21	25	8	4	7	11	7	2	16	112
1983	28	7	18	9	4	10	9	12	0	9	87
1984	38	17	16	7	2	4	5	8	2	7	71
1985	23	6	16	14	9	8	2	6	1	3	59
1986	34	13	21	10	2	12	4	6	2	2	66
1987	45	29	16	9	7	2	3	26	0	9	106
1988	40	14	26	4	2	8	22	16	2	7	105
1989	38	14	22	7	5	8	24	6	1	3	81
1990	47	18	26	7	1	2	10	14	4	2	84
1991	63	19	42	5	1	8	5	13	6	5	102
1992	64	17	43	3	3	2	6	4	4	4	90
1993	68	20	45	3	0	2	4	7	3	3	91
1994	52	12	40	3	0	2	1	3	8	1	69
1995	8	1	7	0	0	0	0	0	1	0	9
1996	10	1	7	0	0	0	1	3	5	3	22
1997	13	4	8	3	1	0	0	0	1	0	22
1998	52	18	32	0	0	0	1	3	3	2	57
1999	7	1	5	0	0	0	0	0	1	0	7
2000	7	1	5	1	0	0	0	4	11	2	19
2001*	9	4	5	0	0	0	0	0	3	0	12
TOTAL	2058	707	1243	200	103	206	503	394	158	159	3673

TABLE 3   RESPONSIBILITY FOR DEATHS

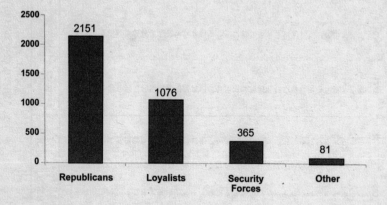

TABLE 4 RESPONSIBILITY FOR DEATHS

Year	IRA	INLA/ IPLO	OIRA	Other Reps.	UVF/ Red Hand	UDA/UFF	Other Loys.	ARMY	RUC/ RUCR	UDR/ RIR	OTHER	TOTAL
1966	0	0	0	0	3	0	0	0	0	0	0	3
1967	0	0	0	0	0	0	0	0	0	0	0	0
1968	0	0	0	0	0	0	0	0	0	0	0	0
1969	2	0	0	0	2	1	0	2	0	0	0	19
1970	18	0	9	3	17	4	0	5	0	0	1	29
1971	86	0	9	0	35	1	1	45	8	0	5	180
1972	235	0	20	0	34	71	0	79	0	0	4	497
1973	125	0	2	2	79	44	1	29	3	0	9	263
1974	130	12	0	10	100	41	1	15	0	0	6	304
1975	94	0	0	26	71	20	1	14	2	2	10	267
1976	138	5	0	12	14	50	2	6	0	0	2	307
1977	68	0	0	0	8	12	6	12	2	1	7	116
1978	60	8	1	0	7	9	11	7	2	0	4	88
1979	91	8	0	2	4	5	1	14	0	1	10	125
1980	45	11	0	2	7	10	3	4	2	0	6	86
1981	70	32	4	1	14	12	1	4	3	0	2	118
1982	52	10	1	1	7	2	2	8	6	0	5	112
1983	50	4	0	1	11	2	0	13	7	1	4	105
1984	44	3	0	4	2	6	0	7	3	1	7	106
1985	45	2	9	5	6	2	1	2	2	0	2	66
1986	37	14	1	4	8	12	3	3	0	1	6	59
1987	58	3	0	1	7	12	2	9	0	0	10	71
1988	66	2	0	1	2	6	1	11	2	1	4	87
1989	53	2	0	0	11	8	1	10	0	0	9	105
1990	50	7	0	2	13	17	5	2	3	1	2	81
1991	45	6	0	1	24	21	0	3	0	1	2	84
1992	34	2	0	1	15	31	1	0	2	0	1	102
1993	36	6	0	2	16	12	0	1	3	0	3	91
1994	19	7	0	0	25	12	5	0	0	0	3	90
1995	7	6	0	0	0	0	1	0	0	0	2	69
1996	8	2	0	0	0	0	0	0	0	0	0	9
1997	4	4	0	0	3	1	7	0	0	0	3	22
1998	3	6	0	0	4	6	0	1	0	0	2	22
1999	4	0	1	29	0	2	1	0	0	0	3	57
2000	4	0	0	1	6	4	15	0	0	0	0	7
2001*	2	0	1	1	1	1	3	0	0	0	0	19
												12
TOTAL	1780	150	54	167	555	415	106	301	50	8	87	3673

TABLE 5 UNIONIST – NATIONALIST VOTING

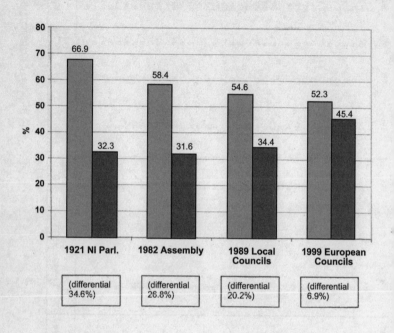

Unionist
Nationalist

Glossary

Alliance party – Founded in 1970, it was alone among the major parties in attracting significant support from both communities. Based mainly in the greater Belfast area, it attracted up to 14 per cent of the vote in the 1970s but its support fell to around 7 per cent in the late 1990s.

An Phoblacht/Republican News – Often known as *APRN*, the weekly newspaper is the official organ of the Provisional republican movement.

Apprentice Boys of Derry – One of the Protestant 'loyal orders', its main activity is organising various annual demonstrations commemorating the events surrounding the Siege of Derry in 1688. It has around 10,000 members. Some of its parades have been the subject of controversy, its major demonstration in Londonderry each August regularly being the occasion of increased tension. Many of the Apprentice Boys are also members of two other bodies, the Royal Black Preceptory and Orange Order.

Ard fheis – Irish term for an annual party conference.

Armalite – An American-made rifle favoured by the IRA, especially in the 1970s, because of its light weight and rapid rate of fire.

Army Council – The seven-member ruling body of the IRA which determines the organisation's strategy.

B Specials – See Ulster Special Constabulary.

Campaign for Democracy in Ulster – A pressure group set up by Labour members at Westminster in 1965 to press for reforms in Northern Ireland.

Campaign for Social Justice – An early civil rights pressure group established in Dungannon in 1964.

Combined Loyalist Military Command – An umbrella group established in 1991 comprising the UDA, UVF and Red Hand Commando. The CLMC declared the loyalist ceasefire in October 1994.

Dáil – The lower house of the Irish parliament in Dublin.

Democratic Unionist party – Founded in 1971 in succession to the Protestant Unionist Party, its leader is the Reverend Ian Paisley.

Diplock report – Produced in December 1972 by English judge Lord Diplock, it recommended that juries should be abolished in troubles-related trials. This gave rise to the term 'Diplock courts'.

E4A – The RUC's covert surveillance unit.

Fianna Fáil – Its name meaning 'Soldiers of Destiny', it is the largest of the Republic's political parties. During the troubles it was led by Jack Lynch, Charles Haughey, Albert Reynolds and Bertie Ahern, all of whom served as Taoiseach.

Fine Gael – Literally 'Tribe of the Gael', it is the second-largest political party in the Irish Republic. In 1985 its leader and then Taoiseach Garret FitzGerald signed the Anglo-Irish Agreement with Margaret Thatcher.

Free Presbyterian Church – The Church headed by the Reverend Ian Paisley.

Garda Síochána – The police force of the Republic. Most of its officers, known as gardaí, are routinely unarmed.

H-blocks – Cell blocks within the Maze prison, so named because of their shape. The H-blocks were the focus of major republican protest campaigns, most notably the 1981 hunger strike.

Irish National Liberation Army – An extreme republican paramilitary group, it was established in 1974 as a breakaway from the Official IRA. INLA members engaged in a number of republican feuds, and three of its number died in the 1981 hungerstrike.

Irish Republican Socialist party – The small political wing of the INLA.

Long Kesh – The original name of the Maze prison until it was changed by the authorities in the mid-1970s. Republicans continued to use the term 'Long Kesh'.

Loyal Orange Lodge – This is the basic unit of the Orange Order. The leader of a lodge has the title Worshipful Master. Lodges combine with others to form a District which in turn form a County Grand Lodge. The ruling body is the Grand Lodge of Ireland.

Loyalist Association of Workers – Set up in 1971 with close links to the UDA, it played a prominent role in harnessing loyalist industrial power for a short period in the 1970s. It was superseded by the Ulster Workers Council.

Loyalist Volunteer Force – A dissident faction of the UVF formed in the late 1990s, it was mainly made up of former mid-Ulster UVF members opposed to the organisation's ceasefire in the late 1990s. It carried out a number of sectarian killings, especially following the death of its leader, Billy Wright.

M-60 – A US army belt-fed general-purpose machine gun, several of which were acquired by the IRA in the 1980s and used in a number of attacks in which security force members were killed.

Northern Ireland Civil Rights Association – Established in 1967 and modelled on the tactics of the American black civil rights movement, it launched a campaign centring on marches and demonstrations.

Northern Ireland Labour party – A socialist party founded in 1924 and with links to the British Labour party, it had its greatest success in the NI elections of 1958 and 1962, winning four seats in each. It later ceased to be a political force.

Northern Ireland Office – The department of the British government established in 1972 to administer Northern Ireland under direct rule from Westminster, through a Northern Ireland Secretary who has a seat in the British cabinet.

Official IRA – A republican paramilitary group, it has remained largely dormant, or at least discreet, since declaring a ceasefire in 1972.

Orange Order – The largest of the 'loyal orders', it was founded in County Armagh in 1795, and by the time of the Home Rule controversies in the late nineteenth century it expanded into an important Protestant umbrella group. Throughout its existence its tradition of marching has led to recurring controversy. Its extensive programme of marches culminates annually on 12 July in a commemoration of the victory of King William III at the Battle of the Boyne in 1690.

Peaceline – Originally large fences made from corrugated metal, these were erected in the early 1970s to provide a physical barrier between some Catholic and Protestant districts. Many of the peacelines in north and west Belfast have been replaced by permanent structures.

Plastic bullet – Officially described as a plastic baton round (PBR), it is a controversial riot-control weapon used extensively from 1973 on. Use of the weapon in Northern Ireland resulted in sixteen deaths.

Progressive Unionist party – The political wing of the UVF, it is a small political party which is strongest in working-class areas of Belfast. Its most prominent spokesmen are David Ervine and Billy Hutchinson.

Proportional representation – An electoral system designed to ensure that representation is closely related to votes cast in an election. In use for elections in the first years of Northern Ireland's history, it was abolished during the 1920s. It was reintroduced in the early years of the troubles and is now in use for all elections other than for Westminster.

Provisional Irish Republican Army – Generally known simply as the IRA and by the security forces as PIRA, it is the largest of the republican paramilitary groups. Following a split with the Official IRA in 1969, its violent campaign proceeded virtually unbroken for almost three decades. Known in Irish by republicans as Óglaigh na hÉireann, in August 1994 it declared a ceasefire which was later broken and then restored.

Royal Irish Regiment – A regiment of the British army established in 1992 when the UDR and Royal Irish Rangers were merged. The RIR is made up of the Home Service battalion of full-time and part-time soldiers, which is effectively the former UDR, and the regular General Service battalions which mainly comprise members of the former Royal Irish Rangers.

Royal Ulster Constabulary – The police force for Northern Ireland established in 1921.

Royal Ulster Constabulary Reserve – Made up of both full-time and part-time members, it has an identical uniform to the RUC and functions alongside regular officers.

Rubber bullet – A riot-control weapon, it was used extensively until its replacement by plastic bullets. According to official figures, 55,688 were fired between 1970 and 1974.

Sinn Féin – Regarded as the political wing of the IRA, it claims descent from a party established in the early years of the twentieth century. An all-Ireland political organisation, it has representation in the Dáil, the House of Commons and the Northern Ireland assembly. Headed by Gerry Adams, its MPs do not take their seats at Westminster.

Social Democratic and Labour party – The main nationalist party in Northern Ireland, it was established in 1970 with the aim of promoting a united Ireland by peaceful means. Its leader is John Hume.

Special Air Services – A special forces unit of the British army officially known as 22 SAS Regiment, it was formally deployed in Northern Ireland in 1976.

Stormont – The building, completed in 1932, which housed the Northern Ireland parliament until it was prorogued in 1972. It became the seat of the assembly established after the 1998 Good Friday Agreement. The term 'Stormont' is often used to refer to the Unionist government of the period 1921–72.

Supergrass – A person formerly active in a republican or loyalist group who agreed to give evidence against alleged former associates. The emergence of more than two dozen such figures in the early 1980s led to a series of large-scale trials in Belfast.

Taoiseach – The term, literally meaning 'chief', for the Irish prime minister.

TD – A member of the Dáil, the Irish parliament.

Third Force – This was a loyalist militia, more often threatened than sighted, which was said to exist at various times during the troubles.

Ulster Defence Association – The largest loyalist paramilitary organisation, the UDA was established in Belfast in 1971 and proscribed in 1992.

Ulster Defence Regiment – A regiment of the British army made up of full-time and part-time members recruited exclusively in Northern Ireland, it was raised in 1970 after the disbandment of the B Specials. In 1992 the UDR was amalgamated with the Royal Irish Rangers to form the Royal Irish Regiment.

Ulster Democratic party – The political wing of the UDA, its most prominent representatives have been Gary McMichael, David Adams and released prisoner John White.

Ulster Freedom Fighters – An alternative name for the UDA, first used in 1973.

Ulster Protestant Volunteers – A loyalist group which supported Ian Paisley; its members often appeared at counter-demonstrations against the civil rights movement.

Ulster Special Constabulary – Established in 1920, it was an armed auxiliary force under the command of the RUC. An exclusively Protestant force which attracted much nationalist criticism, it was abolished and replaced by the UDR. In later years it was more commonly referred to as the B Specials.

Ulster Unionist Council – The 800-strong ruling body of the Ulster Unionist party.

Ulster Unionist party – The main Unionist party in Northern Ireland, it provided the government from 1921 until 1972, securing an overall majority in every election. From 1974 until the early 1990s it was sometimes referred to as the Official Unionist Party. In 1995 David Trimble MP became its leader.

Ulster Volunteer Force – A loyalist paramilitary group which emerged in the mid-1960s, it carried out the first three killings of the troubles. Banned in June 1966, it was legalised in April 1974 before again being declared illegal in October 1975.

Ulster Workers Council – A loyalist grouping which helped organise the loyalist strike that brought down the powersharing executive in May 1974.

Unionist Party of Northern Ireland – A short-lived political party
established by Brian Faulkner in 1974 to promote the aims of the
powersharing tendency within Unionism.

United Ulster Unionist Council – An umbrella group of Unionist parties
opposed to powersharing, it existed from April 1974 until 1977.

United Unionist Action Council (UUAC) – An umbrella group of loyalist
parties and other groups which staged the 1977 loyalist strike.

Vanguard Unionist Progressive party – A political party established in
1973 by William Craig, the former minister of home affairs in the
Stormont government. The party developed from the earlier Ulster
Vanguard movement which emerged in early 1972.

Bibliographical notes

Our bookshelves contain more than 500 books concerned with the troubles and Irish history generally, most of which contain bibliographies. Since this work is intended as a straightforward and accessible account of the troubles, we have opted for an informal note rather than a more formal bibliography.

We are indebted to Belfast's three most important reference sources, Belfast Central Library, in particular its newspaper archive, the Linen Hall Library and the Public Record Office of Northern Ireland, each of which is both invaluable and staffed by invaluable people. We also made use of material released by the National Archives in Dublin. The thirty-year rule means government papers after the late 1960s were not available, a minor exception being material released in the course of the Bloody Sunday inquiry. While there are official government reports by the dozen, the most valuable for our purposes were the Cameron and Scarman reports.

The history books we found most useful were those of Jonathan Bardon, Alvin Jackson and Patrick Buckland. John Whyte's work is a model of how to write with scrupulous fairness on the most controversial of subjects.

In terms of the troubles the most useful reference books were the

Flackes & Elliott *Political Directory* and *Lost Lives*, to which both of us contributed, which records the circumstances of every death of the troubles. We drew too on the extensive files, documents, notes and records accumulated by David McKittrick in three decades of reporting on the troubles as a journalist. During this time he has had access to sources on all points of the political compass. David McVea also has records accumulated during three decades as a teacher of history and politics.

On specific aspects of the troubles, the most useful books were by Fionnuala O Connor, Brendan O'Leary & John McGarry, Robert Fisk, and Eamonn Mallie & Patrick Bishop. We also drew on work by Ed Moloney & Andy Pollak, Padraig O'Malley, Richard Rose, Bob Purdie, David Beresford, Peter Taylor, Paul Bew *et al.*, Henry Kelly, Steve Bruce, Eamonn McCann, and Arthur Aughey. We would particularly like to thank Eamonn Mallie for agreeing to our extensive use of the Mallie & McKittrick book *The Fight for Peace*.

A substantial amount of autobiographical material is available and was of great use to us. On the British side this includes books by Harold Wilson, Wilson's aides Joe Haines and Bernard Donoughue, James Callaghan, Edward Heath, former ambassador to Dublin Sir John Peck, Reginald Maudling, William Whitelaw, Merlyn Rees, Roy Mason, James Prior, Margaret Thatcher, Geoffrey Howe and John Major.

There are also autobiographies by Terence O'Neill, Brian Faulkner, Paddy Devlin, Gerry Adams, Seán Mac Stiofáin, Basil McIvor, Garret FitzGerald and Senator George Mitchell. In addition there are works on O'Neill, Faulkner, Adams, Wilson, Callaghan, John Hume, James Molyneaux, Thatcher, David Trimble, Peter Mandelson, Seán Lemass, FitzGerald and Charles Haughey.

We also drew on books by Albert Reynolds's aide Sean Duignan and Dick Spring's aide Fergus Finlay. The memoirs of civil servants such as Patrick Shea, Ken Bloomfield and Maurice Hayes were highly informative. Maurice Hayes in particular provided many pen portraits and descriptions which proved irresistible to us: our text is strewn and we hope enlivened with his wit and insights.

Index

Page numbers in italics refer to chronology entries.

Abercorn Bar, 78, *253*
abstention, 19, 74, 168, *264*, *283*
Adair, Johnny, 229, *319*, *320*
Adams, Gerry, 61, 77, 111, 129, 239, 240.
    see also Hume–Adams talks
    abstention ends, 168
    arrested, 130
    assessment of, 234
    Begley funeral, 193
    and Brooke talks, *275–9*
    bugged, *315*
    ceasefire hopes, *278–9*, *293*
    on civilian casualties, 175–6, *274*
    Clinton meeting, *298*
    and decommissioning, 204, 207, *314*
    and Downing Street Declaration, *291*
    exclusion order lifted, *295*
    forum elections, 209
    Hume–Adams talks, 185–9, 190–1, 196–7,
        271–3
    and hungerstrikes, 141, 143–5, 147, 148
    and IRA, 127, *275*, *280*, *299*, *318*
    loses seat, *282*
    MP, 215, *265*, *270*, *302*
    peace process, 212–13, *290*
        Mayhew meeting, *298*
        Mayhew talks, 205, *284*
        meets Reynolds, 200
        Trimble meeting, 224–5
        US visa, 197, *282*, *291*, *294*, *297*, *306*
    political involvement, 158–9
    Sinn Féin president, *265*
    US visa refused, *267*, *285*
    Whitelaw talks, 85–6
    wounded, *266*
African National Congress, 228, *317*
Aghalee, Co. Antrim, shooting, 215, *303*
Ahern, Bertie, 225, 228, *295*, *302*, *303*, *306*,
    307, *321*
    decommissioning timetable, *311*
    Good Friday Agreement, 219, *310*
    Stormont talks, *308*
    The Way Forward, *313*
Ahtisaari, Martti, 228, *317*
Aldershot bomb, 78, *253*
Allen, Philip, 219
Alliance party, 93, 94, *250*, *260*
    NI executive, 95, 98, *255*
    Stormont talks, *300*
Amnesty International, 131

Ancram, Michael, *298*
Andersonstown bomb, *265*
Andrews, David, *304*
Andrews, J.M., 15, 22
Anglo-Irish Agreement, 158, 163–70, 178,
        182, 184, 187, 234, *267*, *274*, *276*
    by-elections, *267–8*
    effects of, 236
    and Irish constitution, *272*
    negotiations, 160–2
    security, 167–8
    superseded, *312*
    Unionist resistance to, 168–9, *269*, *270*
Anglo-Irish Intergovernmental Conference,
    267, *274*
    suspended, *279*, *282*
Anglo-Irish Intergovernmental Council, *263*,
    265
Anglo-Irish treaty (1921), *243*
Annalong, Co. Down, *248*
Annesley, Sir Hugh, 210, 211, *301*
Antrim, County, 22, 32, 214–15, *301*
Apprentice Boys of Derry, 54, *248*, *268*
Arbuckle, Constable Victor, 57, 60
Archdale, Sir Edward, 15
Ardoyne, *322*
Armagh, County, 13, 21, 110, 111, 114–15,
    214
    arms find, *274*
    coroner resigns, *266*
    deaths, 63, 153–4, 215, *258*
Armagh city, 49, *286*, *306*
    civil rights march, *246*
    parades banned, *245*
arms crisis, *250*
Armstrong, Sir Robert, 160–1
Assembly of the Northern Irish People,
    252
Atkins, Humphrey, 132, 144, 156, *261*, *263*
    devolution conference, 134–6, *262*
Attlee, Clement, 23, 37
Australia, 16

B Specials, 11, 14, 32, 38, 48, 49, 55, 72, *247*,
    248–9
    disbandment, 56, 57, *250*
Baird, Ernest, 114, 120, 125
Balcombe Street gang, 115, *310*
Ball, Jonathan, 183
Ballygawley, Co. Tyrone, bomb, 175, *273*

Ballykelly, Co. Londonderry, bomb, 151–2, 264
Ballylumford power station, 121
Ballymoney, Co. Antrim, 302
  arson attack, 223, 311
Baltic Exchange bomb, 181, 282
Banbridge, Co. Down, bomb, 311
Barnhill, Jack, 252
Battle of the Bogside, 54
Battle of the Diamond, 13
BBC car bomb, 229, 321
Begley, Thomas, 192, 193, 288
Belfast, 28, 39, 46, 61, 86, 194, 280
  army deployed, 249
  bomb alerts, 301
  bombs, 78–9, 110–11, 191–3, 264, 281, 285, 287, 288, 291
  capital of NI, 5
  Clinton visit, 207
  deaths, 57, 60–2, 64–5, 69, 144–5, 149, 245, 263, 264, 293
    betting shop, 180, 281
    Bloody Friday, 87, 254
    Dunmurry, 305
    La Mon House, 129–30
    loyalist feuds, 320
    McGurk's, 75
    paramilitary feuds, 229, 259, 317
    Shankill Road, 110–11, 191–3, 249, 288
  displacements, 59, 69
  economy, 3
  Falls Road curfew, 61–2, 250
  first non-Unionist mayor, 260
  internment riots, 65, 68–9
  IRA ceasefire, 295, 304
  loyalist violence, 35–6
  nationalist politics, 19
  1970s, 64–5
  Orange parades, 297, 300, 301, 313–14
  People's Democracy march, 48–9
  'peacelines', 56, 249
  Queen's visit, 245, 259
  riots, 34, 54–5, 244, 245, 247, 248, 250, 322
  sectarian violence, 4, 218–19
Belfast Chamber of Trade, 47
Belfast city council, 215, 268, 273
Belfast Telegraph, 30, 35–6, 37, 50, 78–9
Bennett, Charles, 314
Bennett, Joseph, 266
Bessbrook, Co. Armagh, 261, 263
Bingham, John, 269
Birmingham bombs, 109, 257
Birmingham Six, 169, 271
Bishopsgate bomb, 183, 285
Black, Christopher, 265
Blackpool firebomb, 280
Blair, Tony, 77, 215–16, 225, 228, 302, 306, 313, 316, 321

  on decommissioning, 312
  in Dublin, 317
  Good Friday Agreement, 221, 307–9
  Guildford Four apology, 318
  in NI, 217–18, 304
  in Omagh, 224, 311
  The Way Forward, 313
Blaney, Neil, 64, 250
Bloody Friday (1972), 87, 254
Bloody Sunday (1972), 76–8, 79, 82, 238, 253, 321, 322
  apology sought, 302
  inquiry, 74, 75, 77, 305
Bloomfield, Ken, 33, 46, 57
Bogside Defence Association, 248–9
Boland constitutional case, 256
border crossings, 294, 295
border poll (1973), 91, 255
Boundary Commission, 5, 248
Boyne, Battle of the, 13
Bradford, Reverend Robert, 146–7, 263
Bradwell, Warrant Officer James, 212–13
Brighton hotel bomb, 162, 266
Britain, 273, 274, 277–8, 280, 282–4, 286, 288, 290, 292–3. see also Anglo-Irish Agreement; peace process
  acceptance of future unity, 88
  arrests, 283, 300, 301
  attitude to NI, 2, 5–6, 10, 23–4
  Canary Wharf, 208–9
  City of London, 181–2, 285
  and civil rights movement, 37
  Deal, 175, 275
  Downing Street, 177, 279, 281
  EEC entry, 90
  Harrods, 265
  Heathrow, 197–8, 291–2
  Hyde Park, 150, 264
  IRA campaign, 91, 115, 171, 183, 188
  IRA ceasefire, 202
    official Sinn Féin talks, 295
  IRA contacts, 109–10, 185, 187, 189–90, 194–5, 290
  'no selfish interest', 178–9, 187, 278
  pressure on O'Neill, 41–8
  relations with Unionists, 57, 236–9
  Sinn Féin contacts, 216, 286, 288–9
  Sunningdale agreement, 95–7
  withdrawal declaration sought, 282
  withdrawal sought, 109, 111, 113, 128, 159–60
British army, 65, 86, 203, 249, 250
  arrives, 55–6, 248
  assessment of IRA, 131–2
  Belfast searches, 250
  Bloody Sunday, 76–8
  casualties, 110, 114, 128, 175, 251, 254, 264, 273, 275, 301, 302

Andersonstown funeral, 174, 271
Bessbrook, 263
continental, 171
Crossgar, 293
'fun run', Lisburn, 272
three Scottish soldiers shot, 64–5
Warrenpoint, 132–3, 261
casualties of, 60, 62, 65, 71–2, 114, 144, 251–2, 266, 267
on direct rule, 74–5
distrust of, 70–2
Falls Road curfew, 61–2
gradual replacement, 123
internment, 67–70
IRA ceasefires, 294, 295, 296, 304
bases closed, 317
Lisburn HQ bombed, 212–13
in Londonderry, 87, 248–9
numbers of, 83
Operation Motorman, 254
role of, 63
UUAC strike, 120–1
UWC strike, 103–4, 106
British intelligence, 104, 170
British-Irish agreement, 220
broadcasting ban, 274, 291, 294
Brooke, Peter, 178–9, 182, 183, 187, 280, 281, 291
'no selfish interest', 278
Sinn Féin talks, 275–7
'three strand' talks, 279
Brooke, Sir Basil (Lord Brookeborough), 15, 16, 22, 24, 26, 27, 31, 32, 33
death of, 255
Bruton, John, 203, 204–5, 285, 296, 299
Stormont talks, 300
Trimble meeting, 298
Bryan, Dominic, 210
Bunting, Ronald, 48, 247
Bunting, Ronnie, 137
Burke, Ray, 304
Burntollet Bridge, 48–9, 246–7
Bush, George, 279
Butler, Sir Robin, 191

Cahill, Joe, 141
Caledon, Co. Tyrone, 40
Callaghan, James, 33, 62, 125, 233, 235, 237, 246, 248, 261
in NI, 57, 249
pressure on Unionists, 44, 45, 61
and Republic, 58–9
sends in troops, 55–6
Unionists in Commons, 126, 260
Calvert, David, 269
Cameron commission, 49, 247, 249
Campaign for Democracy in Ulster, 37, 244
Campaign for Social Justice, 37, 244

Canary Wharf bomb, 208–9, 217, 299
Cappagh, Co. Tyrone, 177
car bombs, 83, 87, 305
Carlton Club, 277
Carron, Owen, 263
Carson, Edward Jnr, 244
Carter, President Jimmy, 259
Castlereagh electricity substation, 247
Castlereagh interrogation centre, 124, 127, 130–1, 133, 176, 261
to close, 316
Castlerock, Co. Londonderry, shootings, 284
Catholic Church, 16, 145
education, 17
IRA contacts, 185
Catholics. see also civil rights movement
army searches, 61–2
boycotting, 5
discrimination against, 11–12, 24, 231–2
'enemies of the state', 31
history in NI, 2–3
minority in NI, 4–5
O'Neill on, 51
participation of, 73–4
refugees, 59–60
status in NI state, 17–21
support for IRA, 70–1
support for violence, 19
Cavan, County, 303
ceasefires
1972, 254
1974, 257
1993, 290
1994–5, 201–2, 292–5
drugs killings, 207
ends, 207–10, 299
punishment beatings, 202
under strain, 205
1997, 217, 219, 225–6, 302–3, 305
violations claimed, 313, 314
Christmas 1990, 278
Christmas 1991, 280
Christmas 1992, 284
Charles, Prince, 297
Chichester-Clark, Captain James Lenox-Conyngham, 22
Chichester-Clark, Major James, 22, 50, 53–5, 65, 73, 232, 233, 248
London meeting, 249
PM, 248
in power, 53–5, 57, 61, 63–5
reforms, 63
resigns, 251
Chinook helicopter crash, 292
Church of Ireland, 313, 319
Churchill, Winston, 23, 24–5
civil rights movement, 7, 12–13, 24, 34, 36–40, 64, 233

Craig on, 46–7
  marches, 40–4, 246, 247
  riots, 54–5, 247–8
civil service, British, 160–1
civil service, Irish, 161
civil service, NI, 11, 16, 17, 83
  British appointments, 237, 249
Civil Service Commission, 11
civil war, 20
Clarke, Kenneth, 284
Claudia, 255
Claudy, Co. Londonderry, car bomb, 87,
  254
Clegg, Private Lee, 297
Clinton, President Bill, 197, 205, 206, 282,
  290, 306, 313, 321
  Adams invitation, 297
  Adams visa, 291
  aid for NI, 295
  Good Friday Agreement, 308–9
  NI visit, 207, 298
  in Omagh, 224, 311
  and Sinn Féin, 294
  Trimble meeting, 298
Clonard monastery, Belfast, 185
Clydevalley, 246
Coalisland, Co. Tyrone, 180–1
  march, 41, 246
Coleraine, Co. Londonderry, 39, 94, 244
  bomb, 255
Collins, Eamon, 225
Colombia, 322
Combined Loyalist Military Command
  (CLMC), 290, 293, 294, 298
  ceasefire, 295
community groups, 201
Community Relations, Ministry for, 249
Compton inquiry, 252
Conservative Associations, 272, 275
Conservative party, 83, 84, 132, 136, 175,
  212, 282, 298
  Brighton bomb, 162, 266
  in power, 250, 261, 270
Constantine, Tom, 318
Constitution of Ireland, 107
  Anglo-Irish Agreement, 272
  Articles 2 and 3, 96, 100, 182, 272, 277, 281,
    293, 307
  amendment, 220, 306, 315
  Boland case, 256
constitutional convention, 109, 111–14, 119,
  125, 257–8
Continuity Army Council, 302
Continuity IRA, 219, 305
Cook, David, 260
Cooper, Sir Frank, 109
Corrigan, Mairead, 117, 259
Cosgrave, Liam, 99–100, 254, 256

Council of Ireland, 107
  advocated, 91, 92
  condemned by Ulster Unionist Council,
    99
  postponed, 105
  proposed, 94
  renegotiation, 101
  Sunningdale agreement, 95–6, 97
Craig, Jim (UDA), 273
Craig, Sir James, 7–8, 9, 13, 27, 29, 49–50, 91,
  237, 243
  length of career, 22
  on nationalists, 15, 16, 31
  and proportional representation, 7–8, 9,
    10
  siege warfare, 9–10
Craig, William, 41, 43, 44, 46, 49, 65, 90, 101,
  114, 206, 232
  on civil rights, 46–7
  leaves Unionist party, 91–2
  London meeting, 246
  sacked, 47, 246
  UUUC, 112
  Vanguard, 80, 81, 89, 253
  'voluntary coalition', 113
Craigavon, Co. Armagh, 39, 178
Cranborne, Lord, 188
'criminalisation', 123, 137, 147
Croatia, 319
cross-border co-operation, 96, 97
cross-border institutions, 203, 225, 292,
  312
Crossgar, Co. Down, shooting, 293
Crumlin Road prison, 299
CS gas, 248
Cummings, Hugh, 153
Cunningham, Sir Josias, 319
Currie, Austin, 40–1, 43, 98, 102, 246
Currin, Brian, 318
Curtis, Robert, 251
Cyprus, 178

Dáil Éireann, 21, 173, 290
  extradition bill, 271
  hungerstrikers elected, 158–9, 263
  security legislation, 224, 254
  Sinn Féin ends abstention, 269
Daly, Dr Cahal (later Cardinal), 272, 275,
  277, 279, 280, 292
  and IRA talks, 281
  prediction, 284
  primate, 278
Daly, Dr Edward, Bishop of Derry, 77, 276,
  282–3, 321
Daly, Dr Miriam, 137, 262
Darkley, Co. Armagh, shootings, 152, 265
Darlington conference, 254
Davey, John, 274

de Chastelain, General John, 206, *303*, *315*, *321*, *322*
  report, 227–8, *315–16*
De Lorean, John, 127, 133, *260*, *264*
de Valera, Eamon, 23, 29
Deal music school bomb, 175, *275*
decommissioning, 225, 229, *290*, *297–8*, *300*, *310*, *321*, *322*
  calls for, *312*
  de Chastelain commission, 227–8, *303*, *315*, *316*
  and devolution, *313–14*
  in Good Friday Agreement, 220–1
  Hillsborough talks, *312*
  international body, 206–7, *298*, *299*
  McGuinness to talk, *311*
  Mitchell report, 207–8
  in negotiations, 203–5
  problem of, *295*, *296*
  proposals, 216, *296*, *302*
  voluntary, *313*
Defence, Ministry of, 171
demilitarisation, *294*, *321*
Democratic Left, *296*
Democratic Unionist party (DUP), 34, 229, 235, *266*, *269*, *270*, *272*, *289*, *301*, *322*.
  see also peace process
  blueprint, *288*
  in executive, 226, *315*, *317*
  executive resignations, *319*
  launched, *252*
  leaves talks, *283*
  rallies, *303*
  and Ulster Resistance, *274*
  and UUP, 239–40
  wins by-election (2000), *320*
Derby bomb, *277*
Derry, *322*
detention without charge, *274*
Deverell, John, 187
Devlin, Bernadette (later McAliskey), 40, 50, 77, 93, 137, *247*
  jailed, *250*
  shot, *262*
Devlin, Paddy, 135
devolution, 159, 182, 220, *313–14*
  conference, 134–6
  delayed, 225
  restored, 228, *315*, *317*
  suspended, *316*
  Unionist attitudes to, 227
D'Hondt rules, 226
Diplock courts, 123–4, *254*, *269*
Direct Action Against Drugs (DAAD), 207, *299*
direct rule, 126–7, 236–7
  established, 80–1, 83–4, *253*
  proposed, 74–5

  reinstated, 228, *316*
  threat of, 63–4, 65, 79–80, *251*
  Unionist resistance, 89–90
'disappeared', bodies of, 225, *313*
divorce referendum, *298*
Dodds, Nigel, 240, *301*
Doherty, Pat, *272*, *280*
Donaldson, Jeffrey, *304*, *309*
Donegal, County, 59
Donegall Street bomb, 78–9, *253*
Donlon, Seán, 161
'doomsday' groups, 112
Down, County, 50–1, 105, 132, *313*
Downing Street attacks, 177, *279*, *281*
Downing Street Declaration, 187, 196–9, *290*, *291*, *298*
  clarification sought, *291*, *292*
Downpatrick, Co. Down, attack, *302*
Doyle, Judge William, *264*
drug dealers, 229, *292*, *299*, *305*, *313*, *318*
Drug Enforcement Agency, USA, *318*
Drumcree, 237–8
  1995, 205, *297*
  1996, 210–11, 215, *300–1*
  1997, 216, 217, *303*
  1998, 223, *310*, *311*
  1999, 225, *313*
  2000, 228–9, *318–19*
  Mowlam meeting, *303*
Drumm, Jimmy, 127
Drumm, Maire, *251*, *259*
Dublin
  bombs, 104, 108, *254*, *256*, *269*
  British embassy burned, *253*
  train bomb, *294*
Duisburg talks, *274*
Dunadry, Co. Antrim, bomb, *247*
Dundalk, Co. Louth, *306*
Dungannon, Co. Tyrone, protest, 40–1, *244*
Dunlop, Dr John, *281*

Eames, Archbishop Robin, *319*
Easter Rising (1916), 3–4, 35, 60, *245*, *246*
economy, 3, 39, 119, 133
  pressures, 28–9
education, 17, 36, 45
Eksund, *270–1*
elections
  1965, 30
  1966, *245*
  1969, 49–50, *247*
  1970, 34
  1974, 100–1, 112, *256*, *257*
  1979, *261*
  1983, *265*
  1987, *270*
  1992, *281–2*
  1997, 214, 215, *302*

2001, 229, 239, 240, *322*
Anglo-Irish Agreement by-elections, *267–8*
assembly, 92–3
by-election (1969), *247*
by-election (1981), *262, 263*
by-election (2000), *320*
convention, 112
forum, 209, *300*
local, 121–2
Elizabeth II, Queen, *245, 309*
visits NI, *259, 302*
emergency legislation, 45, 46
emigration, 17
Enniskillen, Co. Fermanagh, 13, 193, *305, 321*
Remembrance Day bomb, 171–2, *271*
Erskine, Lord, 34
Ervine, David, 201, *308*
European Commission, *305–6*
European Commission of Human Rights, 262
internees, *252*
plastic bullets, *266*
European Convention on the Suppression of Terrorism, *268*
European Court of Human Rights, 68, 145
detention, *274*
internees, *260*
European Economic Community (EEC), 90, *254*
European Parliament, *264, 294*
elections (1994), *292*
Paisley ejected, *269, 273*
Ewart-Biggs, Christopher, 116, *258*
extradition, 96, 101, 169, *266, 271*

Fair Employment Act, *259*
Fair Employment Agency, *259, 260, 271*
Falklands war, 157
FARC guerrillas, *322*
Farrar-Hockley, Sir Anthony, *277*
Farrell, Michael, 50
Faul, Father Denis, 145
Faulkner, Brian, 28, 32, 44, 89, 90, 121–2, 232, 233, 236, *244, 248*
assembly elections, 92–3
convention, 112
Cosgrave meeting, *256*
death of, 125, *259*
direct rule threat, 79–80
Heath–Lynch meeting, 73–4, *252*
Heath meetings, 74–5, *252, 253*
internment, 67, 69–70, 82
leads UUP, 65–6, *251*
Lynch broadcast, 58
memoirs, 57, 87
new proposals, 87–8
NI assembly, 100–2

NI executive, 94–5, 98, *255*
resigns as chief minister, 105–6, 107, *257*
resigns as UUP leader, 99, *256*
resigns from O'Neill cabinet, 49, *247*
retires, *258*
vigilantes, 86
and white paper, 91–2
Wilson meeting, *246*
Feakle, Co. Clare, 110, *257*
federation, 92
Ferguson, Richard, 43
Fermanagh, County, 7, 36, 38
Fianna Fáil, 58–9, 159, *259, 261, 281*
Ahern leads, *295*
coalition (1989), *275*
coalition (1992), *283*
coalition (1997), *302*
and constitutional change, *307*
in power, *263, 270*
field hospitals, 58, *248*
Fine Gael, 85, 159
coalition (1973), *254*
coalition (1981), *263*
coalition (1982), *264*
coalition (1994), *296*
Finucane, Pat, 176, *274, 312*
Fisk, Robert, 106
Fitt, Gerry, 19, 37, 40, 41–2, 43, 64, 101, 102, *245, 250*
deputy minister, 98
loses seat to Adams, *265*
resigns, 134–5, *261*
FitzGerald, Garret, 85, 97, 113, 116, 124, 186, *263, 286*
Anglo-Irish Agreement, 163–6, *267–8*
New Ireland Forum, 159–60
Thatcher meetings, 161–2, *265*
Flags and Emblems Act, *269*
Flanagan, Sir Ronnie, 211, *301, 304, 305, 308, 318*
Foot, Michael, 24
Forensic Science Centre, NI, *283*
Forum for Peace and Reconciliation, 202, *295, 300*
Framework Document (*Frameworks for the Future*), 203, 208, 297, *307*
France, 172–3
franchise, 43, 45, 50
local elections, *248*
reform, 54, 63, *246*
reforms, 233
Free Presbyterian Church, 34
Future of Northern Ireland, The, 88

Gaddafi, Colonel, 170–1
Garda Síochána, 207, 225, *307*
Garvaghy Road. *see* Drumcree
George Cross, *315*

Germany, 171, 175, 209, 272, *300*
gerrymandering, 8–9, 12–13, 38
Gibney, Jim, *282, 283*
Gibraltar SAS shootings, 173–4, *271, 277*
Gibson, Lord, *270*
Gillespie, Patsy, *177*
Good Friday Agreement, 51, 219–21, 239, 241–2, *308–10, 322*
Goodyear, 28
Gore, Al, *291*
Gould, Matilda, *245*
Government of Ireland Act (1920), 4, 6, 10, *243, 281*
Gow, Ian, 175, *277*
Gracey, Harold, 229, *318–19*
Graham, Edgar, *265*
Grand National, 214
Greysteel, Co. Londonderry, shootings, 193, *288*
Grundig, 28
Guildford bombs, 109, *257*
Guildford Four, 169, *275*
   Blair apology, *318*
Guiney, Eric and Desmond, 145
Gulf War, 177
gun-running, 3, *255, 266, 270–1, 274, 314*
   from Croatia, *319*
   from Libya, 170–1, 172–3
   from USA, *314*

Haines, Joe, 118
Hamill, Robert, 214, *302*
Hanna family, *273*
Harrods bomb, 150, *265*
Harryville, Ballymena, church pickets, *301*
Hartley, Tom, *278*
Haughey, Charles, 64, 185, 188, *261, 263, 270*
   arms crisis, *250*
   resignation, *280*
   and Thatcher, 156–7, *262*
Hayes, Maurice, 50, 107
H-blocks. *see* hungerstrikes
Heath, Edward, 62, 65, 69, 86, 95, 125, 132, 169, 222, 236–7, *250, 255*
   aims of, 81–2
   direct rule, 79–80, *253*
   election, 100
   Faulkner meeting, 74–5, *252*
   'Irish dimension', 88
   loses election, 101
   and Lynch, 72
Heathrow airport attacks, 197–8, *291–2*
Hendron, Joe, *282, 285, 287*
Hermon, Sir John, *268, 274*
Hill, Ronnie, *321*
Hillery, Patrick, *250*
Hillsborough talks, *317*
Holkeri, Harri, 206

Holland, *261*
Home Affairs, Ministry of, NI, *249*
Home Rule, 3, 4
House of Commons, 154, 157
   Anglo-Irish Agreement, 165, 166
   decommissioning report, *316*
   direct rule possible, 63–4
   forum report rejected, *266*
   Neave killing, *261*
   NI seats, 4, 113, 215, *260*
      Unionist balance of power, 119, 126, 188, 196
   NI select committee, *303*
   Paisley elected, 61
   Paisley suspended, *289*
   security legislation, 224
housing, 12–13, 28, 38, 44, 45
   Currie squat, 40–1, *246*
   reform, 63
Housing Executive, *251*
Howe, Sir Geoffrey, 161, 162, 163
human bombs, 177
Human Rights Commission, NI, 225, *312*
Hume, John, 36–7, 71–2, 145, 159, 200, *275, 278, 306. see also* Hume–Adams talks; peace process
   appeals for calm, *247–8*
   assessment of, 233–4, 240
   Brooke talks, 179
   career of, 186
   civil rights movement, 40
   commerce minister, 98
   on decommissioning, *297–8, 311*
   Downing Street Declaration, *292*
   forum elections, 209
   ill-health, 194
   IRA appeal, *277*
   IRA meeting, *267, 299*
   Irish dimension, 182–3
   leads SDLP, *261*
   MEP, *292*
   MP, *265*
   nationalism redefined, 164–5
   New Ireland Forum, 160
   Nobel prize, 225, *294*
   to resign from Assembly, *320*
   SDLP established, 64
   seeks referendum, *284*
   Stormont MP, 49
   Sunningdale, 96–7
   US contacts, 125–6
Hume–Adams talks, 185–9, 190–1, 196–7, *271–3, 285–7, 288*
   joint statement, *289, 293*
   Mark 2, 213
hungerstrikes, 157, *262*
   in Maze, 141–6, *262, 263*
      aftermath, 146–8

elections, 158–9
nationalist MPs, 252
special category status, 85
Stagg, Frank, 258
Hunt inquiry, 57, 249
Hurd, Douglas, 165, 266, 267, 273–4, 290
Hutchinson, Billy, 201, 308
Hyde Park bomb, 150

incident centres, 110, 111, 257, 258
Independent, 278
Independent Commission on Policing. see
    Patten report
Independent Unionists, 9
industry, 12, 28, 65
integration, 89–90, 92, 126, 136, 159, 164
internment, 16, 19, 65, 67–74, 79–82, 86, 92,
    94, 117, 123, 237, 238
  anniversary violence, 262
  demanded, 251
  ends, 258
  interrogation methods, 260
  introduced, 252
  loyalists, 90, 254
  releases, 85, 110, 111
interrogation centres, 124, 130–1
interrogation techniques, 68, 260, 261
Ireland Act (1949), 23, 24, 243
Irish army, 58–9
Irish Congress of Trade Unions (ICTU)
  Northern Committee, 244
Irish Free State, 5, 23, 243
Irish Independence Party, 259–60
Irish National Liberation Army (INLA), 132,
    137, 141, 153, 173, 218, 291
  Ballykelly bomb, 151–2
  casualties, 266
  casualties of, 213, 261, 263, 264, 265, 292,
    302, 304
  ceasefire, 311
  feuds, 150–1, 301
  hungerstrikes, 142, 145
    leader extradited, 266
    supergrasses, 154–5
Irish News, 16, 50
Irish People's Liberation Organisation
    (IPLO), 271
Irish Republic, 23, 113, 243. see also peace
    process
  Anglo-Irish Agreement, 163–6
  arms crisis, 64
  arms/bomb finds, 293, 296, 300, 303, 306,
    307
  attitudes to NI, 2, 19–21
  bombs, 60, 270
  British ambassador assassinated, 116
  British embassy burned, 77–8
  and British–IRA contacts, 110

divorce referendum, 298
EEC entry, 90
elections, 254, 302
extradition, 101
garda shot, 209–10
Good Friday Agreement, 310
and hungerstrikes, 145, 158–9
involvement in NI, 57–9, 79, 82, 87–9, 125
  ruled out by Atkins, 136
IRA contacts, 185
north–south relations, 29–30, 91, 182–3
O'Hare kidnapping, 173
Peter Robinson in, 269
Prince Charles visits, 297
prisoner releases, 295, 296
relations with Britain, 72–3, 236
republicanism in, 148
SAS in, 259
Sunningdale agreement, 95–7
Terrorism Convention signed, 268
Unionist attitude to, 107, 108
Irish Republican Army (IRA), 4, 19, 35, 49,
    65, 67, 75, 80, 81, 93, 160, 164, 232, 234,
    244, 247, 318, 321, 322. see also
    ceasefires; hungerstrikes
  and Anglo-Irish Agreement, 167–8, 184
  'arms beyond use', 228
  arms caches, 293, 296, 300, 303
    to be monitored, 317
  Bloody Sunday, 76–7
  bombs, 78–9, 82–3, 87, 94
  border campaign, 243, 244
  British campaign (see under Britain)
  British contacts, 83, 84–5, 109–10, 142, 253,
    289, 290
  casualties, 60–1, 109–10, 175, 177–8, 264,
    267
    Gibraltar, 173–4, 271
    SAS ambushes, 124, 171, 180–1, 270, 273
    self-inflicted, 280, 299
    shoot-to-kill policy, 153
  casualties of, 61, 63, 64–5, 109, 116–17,
    146–7, 150, 153, 162, 170, 199, 209, 213,
    251, 253, 255, 257, 261, 263, 265, 270,
    272, 277, 283, 290, 292, 293, 301
    Ballygawley, 175, 273
    Bloody Friday, 87, 254
    Brighton bomb, 266
    civilian casualties, 175–7
    Enniskillen, 171–2, 271
    Kingsmills, 114–15, 258
    La Mon, 129–30, 260
    last soldier, 214, 302
    RUC, 216
    Shankill Road, 191–3
    'spectaculars', 171–2
    Stronges, 262
    Teebane, 179–80

Warrenpoint, 132–3
and civil rights movement, 39, 43, 44
criminalisation, 122–3, 137, 147
dirty protest, 139–40
and drug dealers, 229, 299, 313
Europe campaign, 272
feuds, 259
growth of, 82
gun-running, 170–1, 172–3, 255, 266, 270–1, 314
'human bombs', 177
Hume meeting, 267
'I Ran Away', 59–60
internment, 68, 69, 70–1
kidnappings, 265
leadership changes, 127–30
'legitimate targets', 269
Mason policy, 119
and new nationalism, 36
and NI assembly, 99
peace process, 197, 276, 285
arms dumps inspected, 318
arms dumps monitoring, 317
bodies of 'disappeared', 225, 313
decommissioning statement, 316
Good Friday Agreement, 310
Mitchell Principles, 303
in Republic, 73, 101
and Sinn Féin, 240
split, 250
supergrasses, 155–6
US support, 126
Whitelaw proposals, 89

Jackson, Alvin, 166
Jameson, Richard, 316
Jarman, Neil, 210
Jenkins, Roy, 38
John Paul II, Pope, 261, 273, 309, 313
John XXIII, Pope, 34, 244
joint authority, 161
judiciary, 11, 16, 24

Keady, Co. Armagh, 290
Kennedy, Senator Edward, 125, 186
Kennedy, President John F., 27
Kennedy-Smith, Jean, 286
Kerr, Frank, 295
Killeen, Co. Armagh, bombs, 267, 270
King, General Sir Frank, 103–5, 106
King, Martin Luther, 40
King, Tom, 165–6, 169, 178, 267, 268, 270, 272, 274, 275
Kingsmills, Co. Armagh, shootings, 114–15, 258
Kissinger, Henry, 113

La Mon House bomb, 129–30, 260

Labour party, Irish
coalition (1973), 254
coalition (1981), 263
coalition (1982), 264
coalition (1992), 283
coalition (1994), 296
Labour party, UK, 23, 27, 29, 41, 42, 52, 54, 62, 137, 275
and assembly, 101
and civil rights movement, 37–8
out of power (1970), 250
in power (1964), 244
in power (1974), 256
in power (1997), 215, 302
Laneside talks, 109, 119
Laois, County, 300
Larne, Co. Antrim, 319
Late Late Show, 182
Lemass, Seán, 20–1, 58, 245
O'Neill meetings, 29–30, 244
Lenihan, Brian, 262
Libya, 170–1, 172–3, 255, 257, 270–1, 293
Lillis, Michael, 286
Lisburn, Co. Antrim, 175, 268
army HQ bombed, 212–13, 301
'fun run', 272
Livingstone, Julie, 144, 145
Livingstone, Ken, 158
local government, 7–8
boundary review, 251
elections (1977), 121–2
elections (1985), 267
franchise reform, 248
reform, 45
Lockwood committee, 244
London
bombs, 91, 229, 264, 265, 277–86, 321
Canary Wharf, 208–9, 299
Hammersmith, 300
police raids, 301
Stock Exchange, 277
MI6 attacked, 229, 320
Londonderry, County, 21–2, 87
Burntollet Bridge, 48–9
Londonderry city, 7, 28, 38, 143, 211, 244, 264, 295, 319–20. see also Bloody Sunday
army in, 65, 254
Battle of the Bogside, 54, 247, 248–9
Callaghan visit, 57
civil rights march, 41–2, 246
Clinton visit, 207
commission, 46, 49, 246, 247
deaths, 71–2, 250, 251–2, 254
marches, 45–6, 51
'no-go areas' removed, 87
riots, 247, 248, 250
siege of, 13, 231

troops arrive, 56
Unionist control, 8
university decision, 39
Londonderry Development Commission,
    246, 247
Long Kesh. see Maze prison
Longford, County, 296
Longford, Lord, 23, 24
Longh Neagh, 28, 52
Loughgall, Co. Armagh, ambush, 171,
    270
Loughinisland, Co. Down, shootings, 198,
    292
Louth, County, 305, 313
loyalist paramilitaries, 57, 67, 70, 93, 99, 105,
    129, 149–50, 217, 237–8, 247, 248,
    319–20
  and Anglo-Irish Agreement, 166
  arms deals, 274
  assassinations, 110–11, 214, 218–19
    politicians targeted, 137
    Sinn Féin targeted, 192–4
  attacks on RUC, 214–15, 267, 268
  casualties, 199, 249
  casualties of, 60, 61, 114, 121, 122, 152–3,
    174–5, 177–8, 210, 213, 274
    Loughinisland, 198, 292
    Shankill Butchers, 115–16
  ceasefire (1991), 279
  ceasefire (1994), 200–1, 295
    sectarian killings, 304, 305
  development of, 35–6, 60–1, 75, 82, 83
  feuds, 229, 316, 317, 321
  internment, 90
  security force collusion alleged, 192
  torture killings, 94, 115–16
  and Unionist politicians, 89, 108, 112
  Ulster Protestant Volunteers, 244
  UUAC strike, 121
  violence of, 85–6
Loyalist Volunteer Force, 218, 302, 304, 305,
    306
  ceasefire, 311
  UVF feud, 316, 317
  weapons handover, 312
Lurgan, Co. Armagh, 178, 264, 281
  deaths, 216, 300, 302, 312
    DAAD, 299
Lynch, Jack, 58, 78, 156, 169, 245, 248, 259
  arms crisis, 64, 250
  Faulkner meeting, 73–4
  Heath talks, 252
  and internment, 72–3
  Wilson meeting, 246
Lyons, Dame Enid, 16
Lyons, Joseph, 16

M60 gang, 128

Mac Stiofáin, Seán, 283
McAleese, Mary, 304
McAlpine, Lord, 277
McAteer, Eddie, 18, 20, 21
McCabe, Detective Garda Jerry, 209–10
McCluskey, Francis, 152–3
McCrea, Reverend William, 320
McCusker, Harold, 165
McFarlane, Brendan, 145
McGimpsey, Chris and Michael, 272, 277
McGlinchey, Dominic, 151, 152, 266, 291
McGrady, Eddie, 270, 272–3
McGuinness, Martin, 111, 322
  on abstention, 168
  Bishop Daly talks, 282
  British talks, 288–9
  on Brooke, 276–7
  and decommissioning body, 311
  education minister, 226, 227
  exclusion order lifted, 295
  and IRA, 127
  MP, 215, 302
  peace process, 189, 195, 205, 272, 279, 280,
    286, 304
    ceasefire, 294
    decommissioning, 296
    Mayhew meeting, 298
    Scenario for Peace, 275–6
  Whitelaw talks, 85–6
  on withdrawal, 281, 287
McGurk's Bar shootings, 75, 82, 86, 252
McKeague, John, 263
McKee, Billy, 61
McLaughlin, Mitchel, 272, 276, 283, 294
  Bishop Daly talks, 282
McMichael, John, 271
Magherafelt, Co. Londonderry, 274, 285
Maginnis, Ken, 298, 302
Maguire, Anne, 116–17, 258
Maguire, Frank, 143, 262
Maguire family, 169
Major, John, 182, 193, 194, 206, 217, 233, 278
  Downing Street attack, 177, 279
  Downing Street Declaration, 196–9, 290,
    291
  on Drumcree, 237–8
  and Hume–Adams talks, 190, 191, 288
  IRA ceasefire, 202, 205, 293, 295
    decommissioning, 204, 207–8, 296
  Lisburn bomb, 212–13
  loses power, 215
  NI elections, 299
  Reynolds summit, 195–6
  Stormont talks, 300
Mallie, Eamonn, 194
Mallon, Seamus, 268, 273, 276, 286, 315
  Deputy First Minister, 223, 310
  resignation, 314

Malvern Street shootings, 35, 200–1, 245
Manchester, 209, 283
  bombs, 280, 300
Mandela, Nelson, 205
Mandelson, Peter, 226, 228, 314, 315, 316,
    320, 321
marches. see Orange Order
Marita Ann, 266
Martin, Bernadette, 215
Marxism, 44, 60, 132, 159
Maryfield Secretariat, 163, 267, 276
Mason, Roy, 114, 118–19, 120, 125, 132, 137,
    235, 258
  blanket protest, 139
  De Lorean project, 127
  dirty protest, 140
  security policy, 130, 131–2, 133
  UUAC strike, 121
Maudling, Reginald, 62–3, 77, 79, 235, 237,
    250, 252
  'acceptable level of violence', 62, 253
  on internment, 67, 70
  Stormont address, 251
Mayhew, Sir Patrick, 182, 216, 271, 282, 287,
    302
  Articles 2 and 3, 293
  decommissioning, 297
  Downing Street Declaration, 290, 291
  IRA contacts, 289
  marches review, 301
  role of Britain, 291
  Sinn Féin contacts, 195, 288, 298
  surrender not required, 292
  talks, 189, 190, 217, 284, 300
  'Washington Three', 204–5
Maze prison, 69–70, 252, 262, 306, 310. see
    also hungerstrikes
  blanket protest, 258–9
  burned, 257
  to close, 319
  dirty protest, 260
  escapes, 257, 265
  Mowlam visit, 304
  protest campaigns, 137–41
  special category prisoners, 254
  Wright killing, 218, 304
Meath, County, 293
media
  influence of, 45–6
  Paisley's use of, 34–5
Methodism, 14
MI5, 170, 187, 314
MI6, 142, 145, 170, 229, 320
Miami Showband, 257
Michelin, 28
Milltown cemetery, 174, 271
Mitchell, George, 206–8, 216, 295
  chairs talks, 212, 300

  draft proposals, 307–8
  Good Friday Agreement, 309
  review of process, 226, 314–15
  on Trimble, 221
Mitchell Commission, 299
Mitchell Principles, 303
Moira, Co. Down, bomb, 305
Molloy, Eamon, 313
Molyneaux, James, 126, 136, 159, 183, 188,
    202, 205, 206, 212, 232–3
  and Anglo-Irish Agreement, 163–4, 165,
    270
  assessment of, 236
  boycotts conference, 262
  and Downing Street Declaration,
    196
  and Hume–Adams talks, 287–8
  leadership challenged, 297
  Major talks, 288
  Mayhew talks, 271
  resignation, 298
  Thatcher talks, 267, 268
Monaghan, County, 166, 269
Monaghan bombs, 104, 108, 256
Monday Club, 89
Moore, Allen, 180
Morgan, William, 247
Morrison, Danny, 148
Morrison, Herbert, 23
Mountbatten, Lord, 132, 133, 141, 261
Mowlam, Mo, 216, 302, 303, 305, 306, 314,
    320
  on ceasefire, 225, 314
  Good Friday Agreement, 308–9
  on RUC reform, 307
  sacking sought, 313
  visits Maze, 218–19, 304
Mull of Kintyre crash, 292
Murphy, Lenny, 115–16, 149, 264

Nally, Dermot, 161
nationalism, 72, 113, 221–2, 236. see also civil
    rights movement
  and Anglo-Irish Agreement, 169–70
  border poll boycott, 91
  changes within, 64
  demographic changes, 241–2
  divisions within, 233
  effects of gerrymandering, 8–9
  election results (1997), 215
  and hungerstrikes, 143
  and IRA ceasefire, 202
  and O'Neill, 27
  parades, 14
  political sidelines, 22
  redefinition, 159–60, 164–5, 186–7
  SDLP support, 93
  shift to right, 135

Nationalist party, 18–19, 30, 36, 39, 49, 244, 246
Neave, Airey, 132, 141, 260, 261
Nelson, Rosemary, 225, 312
New Ireland Forum, 264, 265, 266
New York Times, 19
Newe, G.B., 74, 252
Newman, Kenneth, 123
Newry, Co. Down, 162, 171, 267, 313
  Frank Kerr, shot, 202, 295
  People's Democracy march, 247
  riots, 247
News Letter, 244
Newtownards, Co. Down, 286
Nobel peace prize, 117, 234, 236, 294, 313
  Hume and Trimble, 225, 311, 312
  Peace People, 259
non-jury trials, 123–4, 254, 269
Noraid, 275
Normanbrook, Lord, 24
Northern Ireland assembly (1973), 91–2, 113, 255
  collapse, 98–109, 256–7
  devolution, 264
  dissolved, 268
  elections, 92–3, 255
  violence in, 100
  workings of, 93–4
Northern Ireland assembly (1998), 220, 311
  departments confirmed, 312
  elections, 222–3, 310
  executive, 226, 314, 315
  future of, 241
  imbalance, 239–40
  reinstated, 228
  restored, 317
  suspended, 227–8, 316
Northern Ireland Civil Rights Association (NICRA), 38, 93, 245
Northern Ireland Constitutional Proposals (white paper), 91–2
Northern Ireland executive (1973), 91–2, 94–5, 102, 237, 255
  collapse, 98–109, 256–7
  Sunningdale agreement, 95–7
Northern Ireland Executive (1999), 237
  talks, 312
Northern Ireland Forum, 300, 301, 310
  elections, 300
Northern Ireland Labour Party (NILP), 28–9, 65
Northern Ireland (NI)
  1921–63
    established, 4–7
    government of, 5–6
    political stagnation, 21–5
    Unionist control, 7–13
  1972–73, 76–97

  1977–79, 118–33
  1980–81, 134–48
  1982–85, 149–66
  1986–93, 167–83
  1993–94, 184–99
  1994–96, 199–213
  British responsibility for, 238
  British subsidies, 45
  EEC entry, 90
  green paper on, 254
  independence of, 231
  reforms, 73–4, 233
Northern Ireland Office (NIO), 83–4, 106, 109, 110, 119, 270, 277
  Building Blocks, 298
  ends Sinn Féin ban, 296–7
  hungerstrikes, 141–2
  Sinn Féin contacts, 195, 296
north–south ministerial council, 220, 316

Ó Brádaigh, Ruairí, 111, 127, 168, 269, 287
Ó Conaill, Dáithí, 111, 127
Ó Fiaich, Cardinal Tomás, 140, 185, 260, 265, 276
Ó hUiginn, Seán, 203
oath of allegiance, 113–14
Oatley, Michael, 314
Observer, 33
O'Donnell, Liz, 306
Official IRA, 60, 76–7, 78, 93, 250
  casualties of, 252, 253, 254
  ends campaign, 254
  PIRA feud, 111, 259
Official Sinn Féin, 249–50
O'Hare, Dessie, 151, 173
O'Leary, Professor Brendan, 221
Omagh bomb, 223–4, 225, 311, 313
  inquests, 229, 320
ombudsman, 246
O'Neill, Captain Terence, 54, 58, 63, 92, 232, 233, 244, 245, 247
  assessments of, 50–2
  career of, 27–8
  civil rights movement, 36–44
  'crossroads' speech, 47, 246
  economic pressures, 28–9
  and Faulkner, 65–6
  Lemass meetings, 29–30, 244
  London meetings, 246
  Lord O'Neill, 250
  loyalist violence, 35–6
  and Paisley, 33–5
  personality, 32–3, 50–1
  in power, 26–52
  resignation of, 48–50, 248
  Unionist opposition, 31–3
O'Neill, Elizabeth, 313
O'Neill, Tip, 125

Operation Demetrius, 67–8
Operation Motorman, 87, *254*
Orange Order, 3, 34, 54, 61, 99, 120, 215, 232, *318. see also* Drumcree
  Belfast parades, *300, 313–14*
  block vote in UUP, *298*
  denounces white paper, 92
  effects of Drumcree protests, *318–19*
  expulsion threat, *313*
  halls firebombed, *302*
  history of, 13–17
  meeting attacked, 110
  and O'Neill, 36
  parades rerouted, *297*
  UUP links, *312, 317*
Orange Volunteers, 122
O'Reilly, Frank, *311*
Ormeau Road shootings, *281*

'PAG', 73
Paisley, Reverend Ian, 30, 36, 41, 47, 48, 125, 228, 232, 233, 244
  and Anglo-Irish Agreement, 165, *270*
  Assembly election (1998), 222–3
  assessment of, 31–2, 235, 240
  and ceasefire, 201
  denounces white paper, 92
  at Drumcree, 205–6, *297*
  election wins, 61, 63, 101, *250*
  European Parliament expulsions, *269, 273*
  forum elections, 212
  Good Friday Agreement, 221, *308, 309*
  imprisoned, 49, *245, 247, 248*
  integrationist, 89–90, 126
  launches DUP, *252*
  Major talks, *288, 293–4*
  and Mayhew, *271, 289*
  MEP, 136, *292*
  and O'Neill, 33–5, 51–2
  and peace process, 216–17, *306, 307*
  protest rallies, *263*
  strike (1977), *259*
  summonsed, *246*
  Thatcher meeting, *267, 268*
  'third force', 147, *263*
  UUAC strike, 120, 121
  UUUC, 99, 112
Parachute Regiment, 76, 78, 132–3
Parades Commission, NI, *302, 310, 313–14, 318*
Parker, Dehra, 21–2
Parry, Timothy, 183
Patten, Chris, 227, *310*
Patten report, 227, *314, 317, 320*
  oversight commissioner, *318*
Peace People, 117, *258, 259*
peace process, 183, 215, 234, 238–9, *289. see also* ceasefire, 1993; ceasefire, 1997

  1993–94, 184–99
  1994–96, 199–213
  agreement approved, *310*
  Ahern meets Hume and Adams, *303*
  Blair meets Sinn Féin, *304*
  bodies set up, 225
  ceasefires, 207–10, 217, *293–4*
    Canary Wharf bomb, *299*
  conditions for, *290*
  deal possible, *306–7*
  decommissioning body, 206–7
  decommissioning problem, 203–5
  devolution plan, *313–14*
  Downing Street Declaration, 196–9
  Drumcree, 205, 210–11, *301*
  DUP and talks, *300, 303*
  DUP role, *301–2*
  first north–south meeting, *316*
  forum, 209, 212–13
  framework document, 203, *297, 307*
  Good Friday Agreement, 219–21, 239, *308–10*
    future developments, 241–2
  Hillsborough talks, *312*
  Hume–Adams talks, 185–9
  Mitchell draft, *307–8*
  Mitchell Principles, *303*
  Mitchell review, 226, *314–15*
  prisoner releases, *311, 319*
  referendums, 221–2
  Sinn Féin–Mayhew meetings, *298*
  Stormont talks, 217–18, 219, *298, 299, 300*
    barred by UUP and DUP, *299–300*
    Sinn Féin and IRA reject proposals, *304*
    Sinn Féin excluded, 219, *300, 302*
    Sinn Féin returns to talks, *306, 307*
    Sinn Féin suspended, *305*
    treaties signed, *312*
    UDP excluded, 219, *305*
    UUP concerns, *304, 305*
    UUP joins, *303*
  Unionist dissatisfaction, 229
Peck, Sir John, 70, 72–3, 77–8
People's Democracy, 48–9, *246–7*
plastic bullets, 144, 166, *266, 268*
Police Authority, NI, *300, 304*
policing, 57, *321. see also* Patten report
  Hunt inquiry, *249*
  north–south zone, 161
  Patten Commission, *310*
  Sunningdale agreement, 96–7
Portadown, Co. Armagh, 166, 177, *247, 285. see also* Drumcree
  car bomb, *305*
  compromise route, *269*
  deaths, 214, *311, 313, 316*
  riots, *267, 268*
Powell, Enoch, 126, *270*

powersharing, 73–4, 82, 108, 111–12, 119, 125, 219, *260, 270. see also* Northern Ireland executive (1973)
  Faulkner opposition, 79–80
  proposals, 87–9
  SDLP move away, 135
  UDA scheme, *269–70*
  Unionist resistance, 107
  white paper, 91–2
Poyntzpass, Co. Down, shootings, 219, *306*
Presbyterian Church, 34, 124
Prior, James, 144, 147, 153, 156, 165, *266, 283*
  Ballykelly, 152
  hungerstrikes, 145, 146, *263*
  on Paisley, 235
  rolling devolution, 157, 159, *264*
prison officers, 139
prison ships, 69
prisoners, 111, 201. *see also* hungerstrikes
  and Hume–Adams talks, *287*
  loss of remission, 175
  numbers of, 150
  protest campaigns, 137–41
  releases, 208, 220, *295, 296, 311, 319*
  remission, *298*
  special category status, 85, *254, 258–9*
  transfers to NI, *292*
Progressive Democrats (PDs), *275, 302*
Progressive Unionist party (PUP), 201, *296, 297, 298, 303, 308*
proportional representation, 7–8, 9, 10, 91
Protestant Telegraph, 34, 245
Protestant Unionist party, 34
Protestants
  history in NI, 1–3
  middle classes, 105, 106
  support for violence, 19
Provisional IRA, 60. *see* Irish Republican Army (IRA)
Provisional Sinn Féin, *249–50*
public sector, 11, 16, 17–18
punishment beatings, 202
Pym, Francis, 95, *255*

Queen's University Belfast, 265
Quigley, Sir George, *281*
Quinn family, 223

Ramaphosa, Cyril, 228, *317*
Reagan, President Ronald, *270*
Real IRA, 223–4, 229, *311, 321*
reconciliation, act of, *312–13*
Red Cross, 145
Rees, Merlyn, 101, 105, 116, 118–19, 120, *256, 258*
  constitutional convention, 109, 111–14
  criminalisation, 137–8
  IRA ceasefire, 110

security policy, 122
  Sinn Féin talks, 119, *257*
  UWC strike, 103–4, 106, 108, 237
Regent's Park bomb, 150
Reid, Father Alex, 185
Reid, John, *321, 322*
Remembrance Day bomb, 171–2
rent and rates strike, 72, 82, 94, *252*
Republican Clubs, *245*
Republican Labour party, 37
Republican News, *275, 286, 293, 300*
Republican Sinn Féin, *287*
republicanism, changes within, 59–60, 127–30, 238–9
Restorick, Bombardier Stephen, 214, *302*
Reynolds, Albert, 190, 191, 204, *281, 284, 289*
  on decommissioning, *296*
  Downing Street Declaration, 196–9, *290, 291, 292, 298*
  IRA ceasefire, 208, *293, 295*
  and Major, 188–9
  Major summit, 195–6
  meets Adams, 200
  resignation, 202–3, *295*
Reynolds, Father Gerry, 193
right to silence, 175
Robinson, President Mary, *278, 286*
Robinson, Peter, 240, *272, 299*
  Anglo-Irish Agreement, 165, 166
  border crossing, *269*
  Good Friday Agreement, *309*
Rogan, Dennis, *313*
rolling devolution, 157, *264*
Rose, Paul, 37
Royal Air Force (RAF), *272, 277*
Royal Ulster Constabulary (RUC), 34, 35, 45, 81, 83, 180, 218, *256, 275, 316. see also* Drumcree
  acquittals, *266*
  and Anglo-Irish Agreement, 166
  armed, 11, *247*
  Battle of the Bogside, 54, *247*
  casualties, 64, 129, *261, 277, 302, 311*
    first, 63, *251*
    helicopter crash, *292*
    Killeen, *267*
    Lurgan, 216, *264*
    Newry, 162, 171
    Seymour, 207
  casualties of, 55, 56, *264, 266*
  Catholic applications, *312*
  civil rights marches, 41–2, 45–6, 48–9, 54–5
  CS gas, *248*
  on decommissioning, 207
  E4A, 153–4, 156
  George Cross, *315*
  Hunt report, *249*
  interrogation techniques, 130–1

and IRA ceasefire, 203, 219, *295*
loyalist attacks on, 214–15, 267, *268*, *311*
NI assembly violence, 100
Orange lodge, 14
Orange parades, 268, *269*, *297*, *300*, *301*
Patten report, 227, *314*, *317*
police primacy, 123
reforms, 57, 63, *300*, *307*, *320*
relations with Catholics, 56
'shoot-to-kill' inquiry, *268*, *269*
Special Branch, 67–8, 69
Stalker inquiry, *273*
stations attacked, 162, 171, 247, *248*, *269*
Sunningdale agreement, 96–7
use of supergrasses, 154–6
UUAC strike, 120–1
UWC strike, 103–4, 106
Royal Victoria Hospital, Belfast, 78, *301*
RTÉ, 182
rubber bullets, *250*

Sampson inquiry, 273
Sands, Bobby, 142–4, 147, 158, 262, 263
Santer, Jacques, *305–6*
SAS, 124, 171, 177, 180–1, *258*, *273*
  Gibraltar shootings, 173–4, *271*, *277*
  Loughgall ambush, *270*
  in Republic, *259*
Saulters, Robert, *319*
Saville inquiry, *305*, *321*
Sayers, Jack, 30
Scarman inquiry, 55, *249*
Scotland, 64, 65, 220
Scullion, John Patrick, *245*
Seawright, George, *266*, *271*
sectarian assassinations, 60–1, 86–7, 110–11,
  115–16, 152–3, 175–8, 192–4, 225, *304*,
  305
security policy, 169–70, 237–8
  clampdown, 175
  control of, 79–80, 104, 220
  co-operation, 96, 97
  Mason policy, 119, 122–4, 125
Sefton (horse), 150
Seymour, Constable Jim, 207
Shankill Butchers, 115–16, 149, *260–1*, *264*
Shankill Road
  bomb, 191–3, *288*, *314*
  pub bomb, 110–11
'shoot-to-kill' policy, 153–4, *268*, *269*
Short Brothers, *270*
Silent Valley reservoir, 247
Sinn Féin, 8, 19, 36, 110, 157, 160, 164, 178,
  179, 203, 234, *251*, *263*, *274*, *321*. *322*.
  see also peace process
  abstention policy, *269*, *283*
  Adams president, *265*
  and Anglo-Irish Agreement, 167–8, 184
  assembly election (1998), 222–3, *264*
  banned, 175
  British contacts, 189–90, 216, *257*, *275*, *286*,
    288–9, *290*
    official, *295*
  and Brooke talks, *276–7*, *280*
  bugged, *315*
  casualties, 175, 180, 192, *259*, 274
  and ceasefire, *293–5*
    decommissioning, *296*
  ceasefire rumours, *278–9*
  and decommissioning, *316*
  election gains, 215, *267*, *281–2*
  and executive (1998), 226, 239, *315*
  growth of, 128, 158–62
  Hume–Adams talks, 185–9, 190–1, 196–7,
    271–3
  and hungerstrikes, 142, 143, 147–8
  incident centres, 257, *258*
  and IRA, *280*
  legalised, 109
  and Mayhew talks, *284*
  office attacked, 180
  political direction, *275*
  Protestant clergy meet, *282*
  in Republic, 173
  Scenario for Peace, 270, *275*
  SDLP rivalry, 240
  split, 60, *249–50*
  Towards a Lasting Peace in Ireland, *281*
  US visas, *303*
Sligo, County, 132
Smith, William, *308*
Smyth, Reverend Martin, *287*, *293*, *317*
Social Democratic and Labour Party (SDLP),
  73, 89, 94, 157, 206, 229, 233, 236, *254*,
  299. *see also* peace process
  'agreed Ireland', *259*
  Anglo-Irish Agreement, 166
  assembly election (1973), *264*
  assembly election (1998), 222–3
  attacks on, *284*, *287*
  and British–IRA contacts, 110
  casualties, *255*
  constitutional convention, *258*
  doomsday scenario, 113
  election (1997), 215
  forum elections, 209
  founded, 64, *250*
  Hume leads, 134–5, *261*
  Hume–Adams talks, 185–9, 190–1, 196–7,
    271–3
  and internment, *252*
  joint sovereignty, 87
  MPs, *268*, 270, *282*
  NI assembly (1973), 92–4, 108
  NI executive, (1973), 95, 98, *255*
  NI executive (1998), 226

north–south relations, 182–3
rejects withdrawal, 260
Sinn Féin rivalry, 159, 184, 240, 276
Stormont withdrawal, 65, 72, 74, 82, 251–2
Sunningdale conference, 96–7
US contacts, 125–6
and Whitelaw, 85
South Africa, 271, 317
special category status, 137, 140, 147, 258–9
Special Powers Act, 11, 38, 246
Spence, Gusty, 200–1, 309
Spring, Dick, 288, 291, 292, 294–5, 300
Stagg, Frank, 258
Stalker, John, 154, 169, 268
Stalker inquiry, 271, 273
statistics of violence, 322–5
    1972, 83
    1973, 94
    1976–77, 117, 122, 123
    1981, 144
    1993, 191
    1995, 207
    1996, 213
    1997, 218
    1998, 225
    1999, 226
Steenson, Gerard, 155–6
Stevens, John, 312
Stevens inquiry, 275
Stone, Michael, 174, 271
Stormont, 10, 11, 22, 23, 244
    discrimination alleged, 24
    first Catholic minister, 74
    first non-Unionist minister, 65
    first parliament, 243
    housing protest, 40–1
    Labour challenge, 28–9
    nationalist involvement, 17, 18–19, 30, 49,
        73, 244, 246
    Orange Order influence, 15
    Paisley elected, 34, 61
    parliamentary committees, 251
    political talks, 282, 299, 304
    proportional representation dropped, 9
    prorogued, 76–97, 253
    relations with Britain, 57
    SDLP withdraws, 65, 72, 74, 251–2
Strabane, Co. Tyrone, 153, 267
strikes
    1977–78, 120
    loyalists (1973), 90
    UWC (1974), 102–7
    Vanguard, 81
Stronge family, 262
Sunningdale agreement, 95–7, 99–100,
    120, 125, 136, 163, 219, 236, 237,
    256
    collapse, 98–109

renegotiation sought, 256
white paper, 255
supergrasses, 154–6, 265, 266
Sykes, Sir Richard, 261

Tandragee, Co. Armagh, 316
Taylor, Gregory, 214–15
Taylor, John, 90, 94, 287, 298, 305
    on ceasefire, 294
    Good Friday Agreement, 308–9
    shot, 253
Teebane, Co. Tyrone, shootings, 179–80,
    182, 280
Tern Hill barracks, 274
Thain, Private Ian, 266, 271
Thatcher, Margaret, 132, 169, 177, 236, 237,
    261, 263, 269, 273
    Anglo-Irish Agreement, 158, 161–2, 163–6,
        267–8
    Brighton bomb, 162
    clampdown, 175
    Diplock courts, 269
    FitzGerald meeting, 265
    Haughey meetings, 262
    hungerstrikes, 141, 143, 144, 145, 146
    and Irish government, 156–7
    New Ireland Forum, 160, 266
    Paisley–Molyneaux meetings, 267, 268
    resignation, 278
'third force', 147, 263
Thompson, William, 310
'tit-for-tat' murders, 110–11, 129
Trainor, Damien, 219
Travers, Tom, 266
Trimble, David, 5, 208, 232, 239, 303, 307,
    315, 319, 321, 322
    Adams meeting, 224–5
    assessment of, 236
    and decommissioning, 216, 316–17
    Drumcree, 210, 297
    executive formed, 315
    First Minister, 223, 310, 311
    forum talks, 212
    Good Friday Agreement, 221, 308–9
    leads UUP, 205–6, 298
    meets Pope, 313
    Mitchell review, 226
    on Mowlam, 313
    Nobel prize, 225
    resignation threat, 227, 228, 229, 316
    Unionist dissension, 233
    in US, 306
    UUUC, 113
Turnly, John, 137
Tyrie, Andy, 103, 104, 272
Tyrone, County, 7, 38, 40–1, 64, 179–80,
    295
    deaths, 261, 265, 273

Ulster Constitutional Defence Committee, 34
Ulster Defence Association (UDA), 75, 80, 86, 94, 112, 114, 120, 229, 232, 272, 319, 321
  Adams attacked by, 266
  arms deals, 271
  bombs in Republic, 270
  casualties of, 137, 175, 180, 255, 262, 284
  ceasefire, 305, 318
  Common Sense, 269–70, 271
  confidential files, 275
  Dublin bombs, 269
  HQ bombed, 288
  leader killed, 273
  Libya visit, 257
  membership drops, 122
  and peace process, 218–19, 304
  political wing, 201
  Presbyterian ministers meet, 281
  proscribed, 283
  SDLP attacked by, 287
  Shankill Road bomb, 191–2
  threat to 'pan-nationalist front', 284
  UVF feud, 229, 320
  UWC strike, 102–3, 104
Ulster Defence Regiment (UDR), 72, 123, 151
  arrests, 275
  casualties, 129, 153, 171, 265
  established, 249
Ulster Democratic party (UDP), 296, 297, 298, 303, 308
  Stormont talks, 219, 300, 305
Ulster Freedom Fighters (UFF), 305
Ulster Protestant Volunteers (UPV), 34, 41, 244, 246
Ulster Resistance, 269, 274
Ulster Special Constabulary (USC). see B Specials
Ulster Unionist Council, 3, 14, 99, 227, 316, 317
Ulster Unionist party (UUP), 3, 5, 107, 259, 321, 322. see also peace process
  and Anglo-Irish Agreement, 267–8, 270
  assembly elections (1973), 92–3
  British pressure on, 41–8
  and Brooke talks, 276
  cabinet resigns, 80–1
  casualties, 265
  devolution conference, 136
  direct rule threat, 63–4, 80–1
  and Downing Street Declaration, 196
  and DUP, 240
  election (1983), 265
  executive (1973), 94–5, 98, 255
  executive (1998), 226
  Faulkner leads, 65, 251

  forum elections, 212
  HQ bombed, 244
  and Hume–Adams talks, 272
  internal dissension, 31–2, 34, 232–3
  Molyneaux leads, 262
  MPs expelled, 250
  Orange Order links, 312, 317
  party president killed, 319
  peace process
    assembly election (1998), 222–3
    by-election (2000), 320
    and decommissioning, 216, 225, 228, 311–17
    framework document, 297
    reform package, 46–7
    and SDLP, 257–8
    Trimble leads, 205–6, 298
  UUAC strike, 120
  wary of British government, 74
  West leads, 256
  and Whitelaw proposals, 89
  William Craig leaves, 91–2
Ulster Vanguard movement. see Vanguard movement
Ulster Volunteer Force (UVF), 3, 49, 60, 104, 112, 218, 264, 294, 309, 321
  banned, 245, 258
  casualties, 192, 257, 269
  casualties of, 35, 114–15, 175, 177–8, 198, 245, 252, 257, 258, 272
    McGurk's, 75
  ceasefire (1973), 255
  gun-running, 289
  legalised, 109
  LVF feud, 316, 317
  Orange lodges, 14
  political wing, 201
  revival feared, 23–4, 237
  supergrass, 265, 266
  trial (1977), 259
  UDA feud, 229, 320
Ulster Workers Council (UWC), 120, 232
  strike (1974), 102–8, 111, 112, 114, 119, 125, 237, 238, 256–7
'Ulsterisation', 123, 171
unemployment, 12, 28, 39
Unionist Party of Northern Ireland (UPNI), 99, 112, 256, 257
Unionists, 2, 20
  and Anglo-Irish Agreement, 163–9
  attitudes to Britain, 83, 85, 156, 236–9
  attitudes to nationalists, 15–16
  attitudes to O'Neill, 31–3
  attitudes to Republic, 58, 107, 108
  attitudes to Sinn Féin representatives, 158
  border poll, 91
  and civil rights movement, 37–9, 41, 49–50, 51